Designing the Exterior Wall

An Architectural Guide to the Vertical Envelope

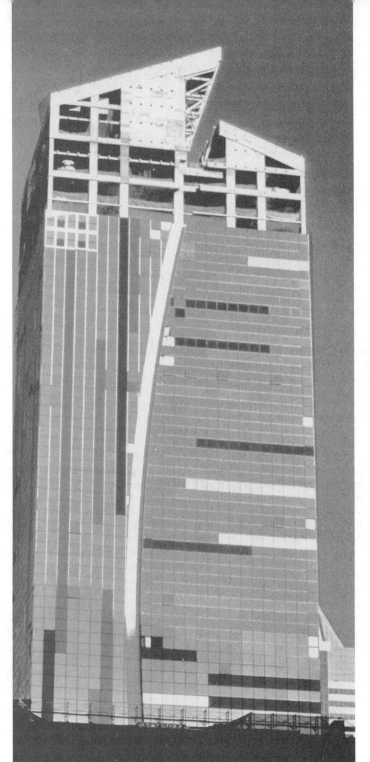

Designing the Exterior Wall

An Architectural Guide to the Vertical Envelope

Linda Brock

WILEY

John Wiley & Sons, Inc.

This book is printed on acid-free paper. ∞

Copyright © 2005 by John Wiley & Sons, Inc. All rights reserved.

Published by John Wiley & Sons, Inc., Hoboken, New Jersey.
Published simultaneously in Canada.

The drawings, tables, descriptions, and photographs in this book have been obtained from many sources, including trade associations, suppliers and manufacturers of building materials, government organizations, and architectural and engineering firms. They are presented in good faith, but the author and publisher do not warrant, and assume no liability for, their accuracy, completeness, or fitness for any particular purpose. It is the responsibility of users to apply their professional knowledge in the use of information contained in this book, to consult the original sources for additional information when appropriate, and to seek expert advice when appropriate. The fact that an organization or Web site is referred to in this work as a citation or a potential source of further information does not mean that the author or the publisher endorses the information the organization or Web site may provide or recommendations it may make. Further, readers should be aware that the Internet Web sites listed in this work may have changed or disappeared between the writing and the publishing of this book.

For general information on our other products and services or for technical support, please contact our Customer Care Department within the United States at 800-762-2974, outside the United States at (317) 572-3993 or fax (317) 572-4002.

Wiley also publishes its books in a variety of electronic formats. Some content that appears in print may not be available in electronic books.

Library of Congress Cataloging-in-Publications Data:

Brock, Linda, 1948–
 Designing the exterior wall : an architectural guide to the vertical
envelope / by Linda Brock.
    p. cm.
 Includes bibliographical references and index.
 ISBN 0-471-45191-6 (cloth)
 1. Exterior walls--Design and construction. 2. Curtain walls—Design and
construction. I. Title.
 TH2235.B76 2005
 721'.2--dc22
 2004014939

Printed in the United States of America

10 9 8 7 6 5 4 3 2 1

Contents

CHAPTER **7** Exterior Insulation Finish System (EIFS) and Concrete Masonry Walls 169

CHAPTER **8** Wood-Frame Construction, Stucco, and Fiber-Cement Siding 203

Preface

During the 1980s, I was teaching design at a school of architecture while investigating anchored brick veneer failures, with my partner Russell Heliker, on buildings usually no more than 20 years old. Wondering if my students would provide work for our masonry consulting firm when they graduated, I started to look closely at failure mechanisms of the exterior wall and the role architects played in them. Accepting a position to teach building technology at the University of British Columbia in 1991 allowed me access to the extensive Canadian research on exterior wall design as related to climate. It became clear that failures of the exterior wall were widespread, and architects were losing on two accounts. First, the liability issues surrounding these failures had serious consequences for the profession; second, these pervasive failures were undermining the aesthetic design.

The rash of building envelope failures in the United States and Canada has focused public attention on the need for effective envelope design, particularly of the facade or exterior wall. Examples include problems on residential projects clad with Exterior Insulation and Finish Systems (EIFS) in North Carolina; moisture problems in hotels in the southeastern United States, where impermeable vinyl wall coverings function as a vapor barrier on the wrong side; the failure of anchored brick veneer after the building codes changed in the 1970s and steel-stud backup walls became popular; and the "leaky condo" problems of the West Coast. Some of these building envelope failures have been catastrophic—for example, the recladding of the Amoco Building in Chicago, which cost close to $80 million. Other failures are more pervasive, like the over $1 billion in repairs to wood frame condominiums constructed after 1984 in Vancouver, British Columbia. Unfortunately, the failures are neither bound by geography nor unique to a particular building type or cladding system.

These failures—costly to the architectural profession and to society—have caused the public to question the expertise of architects at times. Liability insurance is expensive and sometimes difficult to obtain. Building envelope consultants are becoming common and are required in some jurisdictions for certain types of construction. Often these specialists come from the engineering, not the architectural profession. This book is written in response to these problems and in the hope that the architectural profession will reclaim design of the building enclosure. It is written for those architects who want to marry their aesthetic intentions with a cost-effective, functional, and long-lasting wall, which is usually their clients' desire as well.

Although the exterior wall performs a myriad of functions, this book—in the context of durability, function, economics, and aesthetics—focuses on the control of water, water vapor, air, and thermal transfer, as well as the differential movement and lateral loading imposed on the exterior wall. Part I, "Choosing the Components," delineates, as simply as possible, how to select and place the components that will effectively control these elements. Part II, "Detailing for Durability," provides details for designing the most common of wall types. My intention is not to provide a set of details that can be copied but to help the designer understand how a particular wall assembly in a specific location can be detailed to assure a good, effective envelope design that meets the budget. Understanding one assemblage can offer direction for designing another with different constraints. The claddings described are those that are most frequently used. Brick, concrete masonry, and EIFS represented almost half of the square footage of cladding material used on new, nonresidential buildings in 2002, according to the *Ducker Report.*[1] Adding in residential buildings, which account for the majority of new construction, stucco and sidings of wood, wood products, and vinyl represented 72 percent of the square footage of all cladding.

Advances in the design of the exterior wall occur by examining failures and by testing new ideas. Part III, "Advancing the Envelope," discusses "pushing" the envelope and provides examples of the extraordinary and the commonplace, the successful and the unsuccessful in the design of the building envelope.

This book also addresses sustainability through durability. Long-lasting exterior walls play a vital role in decreasing the construction materials used over a specific period of time as well as reducing ongoing energy expenditures. A wall designed to last 50 years, rather than a wall that needs considerable repair at 20 years, makes a significant contribution to sustainability. We, as architects, have control over the durability of the exterior wall. Design of the building enclosure is fundamental to the architecture of the building. Forfeiting this expertise means losing control of design in general.

Finally, I hope you enjoy reading this book. In particular, Part III, "Advancing the Envelope," is included for those of us who are fascinated with how and why particular materials are chosen and the consequences of those decisions for the exterior wall.

Acknowledgments

Many people helped with the preparation of this book. I would like to acknowledge the following individuals, organizations, and firms.

Claude Patrick Louvouezo, Alexander Lik Mo Chang, and Patrick O'Sullivan produced the illustrations for the book. Their dedicated effort and good humor were greatly appreciated. Louvouezo oversaw the detail drawings in Part II and served as a valuable information checker.

Individuals from several forensic engineering firms gave willingly of their time and expertise. They include: Tom Schwartz, Ken Klein, Mathew Bronski, and Dean Rutila of Simpson Gumpertz & Heger; Ian Chin, Kimball Beasley, and Timothy Allanbrook of Wiss, Janey, Elstner Associates; Mark Brook of Brook Van Dalen & Associates; Pierre Gallant of Morrison-Hershfield; Paul Kernan and Michael Aoki-Kramer of RDH Building Engineering; and Doug Watts of Read Jones Christoffersen.

The resources provided by the Canada Mortgage and Housing Corporation (CMHC) were invaluable, and the help of the following individuals, in particular, was appreciated: Sandra Marshall, Luis de Miguel, and Jacques Rousseau.

A special thanks to Phil Green for all of his work on Chapter 6 and Richard Keleher for his initial review, continued advice, and general enthusiasm about the building enclosure.

The firms and companies whose work is included in this book are credited but not necessarily the individuals who helped put together the entries. My thanks to Steve Parry of Brand + Allen Architects; Ash Botros of Centura/Lakeview/Optima Building Systems; Keith Mendenhall of Gehry Partners; Roger A. Reed of A. Zahner Company; Richard Kielar and David Horowitz of Tishman Construction Corporation; Jennifer Briley and Dennis Wilhelm of Arquitectonica; Christine Shaffer and Pam Ellis of Viracon; Carlo Ferrieisner, Isidro Gonzalez, and Charles Ersando of Permasteelisa; John Fulton of Walters and Wolf; Greg Johnson and Craig Burns of Marceau Evans Architects; Kerry Hegedus of NBBJ; Scott Wolf of Miller/Hull Partnership; Mark Otsea of HOK; and Dana Scott of Scott Systems.

Reviewers of this work include Theresa Weston of DuPont, Bruce Sychuk of SMACNA-BC, Mike Ennis of Dow, Dave Olson of Fortifiber Building Systems Group, Golnar Riahi of Hal Industries, Brian LeVoguer of Bakor, Lester Hensley of Emseal Joint Systems, Mason Knowles of the Spray Polyethylene Foam Alliance, Jenny Lovell of the University of Virginia, Ron Brock of Highlander Construction, Wagdy Anis of Shepley Bulfinch Richardson and Abbott, Paul Fisette of the University of Massachusetts, Randy Straight of CertainTeed Insulation, Robert Taylor of the American Wood Council, J. Gregg Borchelt of the Brick Industry Association, Bill McEwen of the Masonry Institute of British Columbia, Sidney Freedman of the Precast Concrete Institute, Ehab Nain Ibrahim of Fulton Windows, Doug Hindes of Walters and Wolf Glass Company, Wally Momsen of Kawneer, John Edgar of Sto Corporation, Peter Cuyler of Dryvit, Gregg Lowes of British Columbia Wall and Ceiling Association, Mark Fowler of Northwest Wall and Ceiling Bureau, Daryl Wilson of Starline Windows, John Fernandez of the Massachusetts Institute of Technology, Brian Palmquist of ECO Design.ca, Hugh Rawlings of H. H. Roberston Asia/Pacific, Kathleen Conway of the Vinyl Siding Institute, Roxanne Navrides of the City of Seattle, John Dybsky of James Hardie, Pete Pederson of Gladding McBean, and Björn Schouenborg and Paola Blasi of TEAM.

My thanks also go to John Czarnecki, Lauren LaFrance, and David Sassian at John Wiley and Sons for their exceptional perseverance in creatively turning a mountain of text and images into a book.

In addition, this book would not have been possible without the help and support of the following individuals. Amanda Miller of John Wiley and Sons endorsed and supported the idea of this book. Akiro Yamaguchi of KST and Fuyusoken, the Winter Research Institute, provided financial support and, more importantly, a philosophy of sustainable construction. A special thanks goes to Edward Allen. His numerous publications set a high standard and were a source of frequent reference. His continuing support for this book is appreciated. Christopher Macdonald, director of the School of Architecture at the University of British Columbia, understood, better than I did, the time required to write a book and granted that time. Finally, there is a hidden voice behind this book, that of my partner and husband, Russell Heliker. In addition to writing much of Chapter 6 and section 9.4, his persistence in designing walls that work, sometimes over the protest of our clients, has served as a model for my work as an architect. This book is dedicated to Russell, to my mother, Dorothy Brock, and in memory of my father, Robert Brock.

Using this Book

Architectural design merges function with durability, aesthetics with affordability. This book defines the parameters for designing the exterior wall of the building envelope so that it is functional and durable while meeting aesthetic intentions and budget constraints. It is organized into thee parts—"Choosing the Components," "Detailing for Durability," and "Advancing the Envelope"—and appendices. What is covered in these is briefly outlined here. Addressed as well are: the areas not covered by this book; how to use this book at the beginning of a project; how to detail a specific cladding; and how to use this book over the long term. Terms used, disclaimers, and a list of sources for further information are also provided.

PART I: CHOOSING THE COMPONENTS

This section includes:

- Discussion of the decisions made at the beginning of a project and during the preliminary design phase (Chapter 1)
- Basic information for understanding building science to make informed choices about envelope design (Chapters 2 through 4)
- Specific information about the selection and placement of barriers and retarders to:
  - Stop water (Chapter 2)
  - Stop air movement, retard vapor diffusion, and control thermal transfer through the wall. (Chapter 3)
- Specific information about designing joints to accommodate differential movement (Chapter 4)

Checklists at the end of chapters 1 and 4 guide architects to the right choices when designing the exterior wall for a given climate, construction type, aesthetic, budget, and expected performance. "Quick notes" summarize the chapter or section information. After reading Part I, architects should be able to determine the components of the exterior wall and their placement.

PART II: DETAILING FOR DURABILITY

Four types of cladding are detailed, each showing a specific construction type and using a particular method for managing water in a specific climate:

- Wall Type A: Brick veneer anchored to steel-stud backup walls (ABV/SS) on a concrete frame for a mid-rise building of 4 to 20 stories in a heating climate with a drainage cavity wall (Chapter 6)
- Wall Type B: Exterior Insulation and Finish Systems (EIFS) on a concrete masonry wall in a cooling climate with an internal drainage plane wall (Chapter 7)
- Wall Type C: Three-coat stucco on a wood-frame wall in a mixed climate with an internal drainage plane wall (Chapter 8)
- Wall Type D: Fiber-cement board siding on a wood-frame wall in a mixed climate with a drainage cavity wall (Chapter 8)

General information is given on aluminum glass curtain walls, stone- and metal-panel curtain walls, and precast concrete panels (Chapter 5) and also concrete masonry (Chapter 7) and sidings (Chapter 8).

Case studies include look at an anchored brick veneer (ABV) recladding project, the use of prefabricated EIFS panels on a high-rise building, open-joint calcium silicate panels on a school, and medium-density overlay (MDO) plywood panels and cedar siding on a college building.

PART III: ADVANCING THE ENVELOPE

These three chapters discuss durability and cladding, the architect's design kit, and sustainability through long-lasting walls. Specific information is included on:

- Terra-cotta cladding (Chapter 9)
- Marble cladding and its problems (Chapter 9)
- Brick veneer and its problems (Chapter 9)
- Glass curtain walls (Chapter 10)
- Digital metal skins (Chapter 10)
- Thin brick cast in concrete (Chapter 10)
- Double-skin facades (Chapter 10)
- Wood framing adapted for different climates and cultures (Chapter 11)

APPENDICES

Included in the appendices are discussions of climate and hygrothermal maps and how the building form affects durability of the exterior wall. Trade and industry association Web site URLs are provided as well as more general references on the exterior wall.

SUBJECTS THIS BOOK DOES NOT COVER

Not covered in this book are the less visible parts of the building enclosure, such as roofs and below-grade foundations. Aesthetic decisions are usually not part of the design process for the less visible building assemblies. The problematic areas, such as where the wall connects with the roof and the ground, are included as part of the detailing of the wall. Acoustics, fire ratings, sustainability issues other than durability, passive environmental controls, health issues, light control, and security functions are not covered. There are ample resources in these areas, and the basics of enclosure design for durability and function remain the same.

USING THIS BOOK FROM THE BEGINNING OF A PROJECT

Design of the exterior wall begins by understanding the decisions that affect the exterior wall, as discussed in Chapter 1. At the end of the predesign and conceptual phase, the cladding and structural frame is known, along with the specific climate, and the overall form of the building. With this information, the various barriers and retarders of the wall can be selected and positioned as discussed in Chapters 2, 3, and 4. Design begins in Part II, where the different wall types are detailed. Some of these steps will become intuitive, if they are not already.

Check your design by reviewing each barrier and retarder to see if it is doing its job. Draw two lines through every section and every detail—one for the water barrier system and the other for the air barrier system. Then check to make sure that there are no unintended vapor retarders. Think about differential movement and structural forces. Redline every transition on the plans and elevations; then, make sure the wall is detailed and the water and air seal systems are continuous. Every transition in the wall is an invitation for a leak, of water or air or both. Select good products with a proven track record. Finally, do everything possible to make sure the wall is constructed as detailed and specified. But be open to the inevitable changes that occur during construction. It is best if you and the contractor have established a good relationship and have the same goal—producing a durable wall that meets your clients' expectations as well as your own concerning the aesthetic design.

USING THIS BOOK TO DETAIL A SPECIFIC CLADDING

The cladding type may have been decided and the budget set before you first open this book. In this case, you may be tempted to turn directly to the chapter that covers the selected cladding. But before doing this, some of the basics from Part I should be reviewed. It is critical to understand the expected interior climate and the actual exterior climate and how the building form will respond. A review of the Preliminary Design Information and Decisions checklist (p. 23) will indicate where there might be problems. If a less than optimal cladding has been selected and you are concerned about the quality of the construction, it may be possible to argue for a good water barrier as damage control. It will also be necessary to return to the Selecting and Positioning Barriers and Retarders checklist (p. 85) to be sure the correct components have been selected and properly placed for the wall type and the climate.

LONG-TERM USE OF THIS BOOK

Developing standard details and specifications can reduce the time spent on each project as well as reduce the risk of a failure. This book can be used as a starting point for these standards. There is no need to reinvent the wheel with each project. If you have figured out that a certain sealant works well and you know how to design a coping that works, why not repeat these successes? Each project will be different, but good details can be modified to suit a variety of conditions and intentions. Equally important is the development of minimum quality standards that foster good envelope design and minimize liability. This may include measures such as refusing contracts that do not include contract administration or not using particular wall assemblies that have been problematic in a given climate.

DISCLAIMER

Because specific products are noted and their use discussed, the following warning is important.

- These references were current at the time this book was written. All information should be verified with the manufacturer. A manufacturer may have changed the product or the installation methods.
- Specific products were chosen because they were good, frequently used products at the time this book was written. There may be better products and certainly many more that are not listed. Inclusion of a product in no way signifies that it is superior to others.

Every effort has been made to produce an error-free book. The information is based on a variety of sources, including books; magazines; discussions with building envelope specialists, architects, engineers, and industry representatives; and the author's own experience. This information is referenced in the notes at the end of the book. However, each project presents unique challenges, new research changes conventional thinking, and errors do occur. Therefore, the information should not be used without understanding the intent and without challenging its applicability to your project.

TERMINOLOGY

Terms often differ from one region to another or between the United States and Canada. When there is more than one term for the same function, the difference is noted. Imperial notation is generally used, with metric in parentheses. You may find some terms confusing. The literature and product promotions often use different terms for the same thing. The following explanations of a few terms might help in understanding some of the vocabulary in this book.

The outside face of the cladding—whether brick or wood siding—stops the majority of the water and is called the first layer of defense. The layer or membrane beneath the cladding, which acts as a secondary defense, is called the *water barrier*. Common water barriers include building paper or felt; building wrap (also called "housewrap" and termed SBPO when it is a nonperforated spun-bonded polyolefin); and "peel-and-stick," or self-adhesive membrane (SAM). The *water barrier system* comprises the flashings, sills, copings, tapes, gaskets, and sealants that ensure that the entire wall—including, for example, openings for windows and hose bibs—has a watertight, second line of defense.

An *air barrier,* placed anywhere within the wall, is the membrane or layer that stops ingress or egress of air. The air barrier can be building wrap, polyethylene, peel-and-stick membrane, or gypsum board, to name a few options. The *air barrier system* makes the entire wall airtight (or tries to) and includes the tapes, gaskets, sealant, and structural support necessary for this task. A common system, which uses the interior gypsum board as the air barrier, is called the airtight drywall approach (or ADA). A similar system is called simple caulk and seal (SCS).

Vapor retarders are for stopping vapor movement by diffusion and are measured by the degree of permeability. They should be continuous; but you do not have to worry about sealing all of the interfaces and laps. Common vapor retarders include vapor resistant paints and wall coverings, polyethylene, peel-and-stick, and some board insulation. Most important is understanding the permeability of *all* materials in the wall, as an unintended vapor retarder in the wrong place can create havoc.

Insulation and *radiant barriers* are two terms with agreed upon definitions.

Terms used to describe rainwater management systems can be confusing. When there is no water barrier—in other words, the face of the cladding stops all water—this is called a face-sealed barrier wall. If the distance between the water barrier and the back of the cladding is no more than ⅜ inch (10 mm), the water management system is called an internal drainage plane wall. If it is greater than ⅜ inch (10 mm), it is called a drainage cavity wall. The most confusing is the use of the term *rain screen.* For more information on this, see the sidebar, "What is a Rain Screen?" in Section 2.2. While architects and the public want to think they have a rain screen, depending on which definition is used, most likely what they have is a drainage cavity wall. To some, the term *rain screen* means simply that there is a screen for the rain. By this definition, vinyl siding over a water barrier is a rain screen. Use the term that makes you or your clients happy. Just be sure that you understand how the wall functions and have made sure it works.

Climates are discussed in three broad categories: heating climates (in which providing adequate heating is the focus), mixed climates, and cooling climates (in which adequate cooling is the focus). See Appendix A for more information.

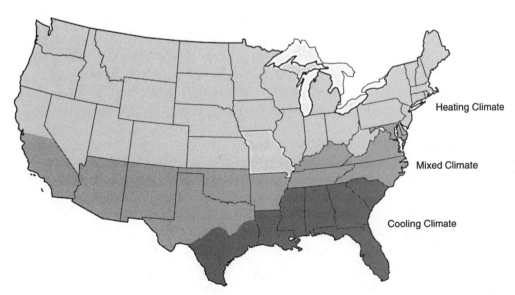

Heating Climate

Mixed Climate

Cooling Climate

Climatic zones used in this book. All of Canada falls under the heating climate zone. Reproduced by permission of the publisher from Joseph W. Lstiburek and John Carmody, *Moisture Control Handbook: Principles and Practices for Residential and Small Commercial Buildings* (New York: John Wiley & Sons, Inc., 1994). © 1994 by John Wiley & Sons, Inc.

ADDITIONAL INFORMATION

This single book will not tell you everything you need to know. Additional information should be sought from manufacturers, tradespeople, consultants, and (possibly) a building envelope specialist. These individuals should be part of your design team. Further research can be done through the references provided here. These have been carefully chosen for relevancy and annotated when necessary. References for more information on particular cladding types are listed after each chapter in Part II. General references are listed in "Bibliography and Resources," page 357.

Many organizations provide a wealth of information on durable exterior walls. The organizations listed below are referenced throughout the book by their complete name and by acronym.

BSC:	Building Science Corporation, http://www.buildingscience.com
CMHC:	Canada Mortgage and Housing Corporation, http://www.cmhc.ca
DOE:	Department of Energy, specifically the Office of Energy Efficiency and Renewable Energy, http://www.energycodes.gov
NAHB:	National Association of Home Builders Research Center, http://www.nahbrc.org
NIBS:	National Institute of Building Sciences, http://www.nibs.org
NRCC/IRC:	National Research Council of Canada, Institute for Research in Construction, http://www.nrc.ca/irc
ORNL:	Oak Ridge National Laboratory, http://www.ornl.gov

Designing the Exterior Wall

An Architectural Guide to the Vertical Envelope

CHOOSING THE COMPONENTS

PART I OF THIS BOOK DISCUSSES THE DECISIONS MADE prior to choosing the components of the wall; these decisions are based on the exterior environment, interior environment, construction type, facade aesthetics, form of the building, expected performance of the enclosure, and other envelope requirements. Part I discusses as well selecting and positioning the wall's components.

The exterior wall is a complex system that includes the cladding and structure, windows and doors, and a series of barriers and retarders that mediate the environment. These must be evaluated in terms of function, durability, appearance, and cost. Selecting and positioning the components is the next step in designing the exterior wall. The components can be grouped based on their primary function, but they often do double duty—a paint may be chosen for both its color and as a vapor-diffusion retarder. On the other hand, vinyl wallpaper, selected solely for its aesthetic value, may inadvertently act as a vapor retarder, making its placement on an interior surface problematic in some climates. Every material has some resistance to air movement, water vapor diffusion, heat transfer, and water ingress. Understanding the resistance of each component and how it is affected by the other components helps to select and position properly the barriers and retarders within a wall, given a specific climate. Long-term performance or durability of these components and the ease of maintenance or repair of the system are also considerations. Although detailing the wall (covered in Part II, "Detailing for Durability") may modify some of the choices, it is important that the wall must first function as a system.

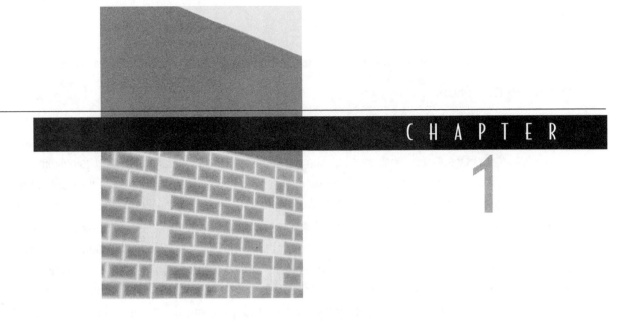

Decisions That Affect the Exterior Wall

1.1 INTRODUCTION TO THE BUILDING ENVELOPE

The building envelope—the skin supported by the skeleton of the structure, or the monolithic load-bearing wall—mediates the environment and provides security. The structure determines form while the envelope protects. It keeps rain and snow out while controlling the relative humidity of the interior. It stops wind and sun when deemed uncomfortable, allowing passage when desired. Warmth and coolness are regulated by the envelope, as are fire and sound.

The need for shelter is as basic as the need for food and water. Clothes made of animal skins and tree bark, along with the shelter of caves and overhangs of rock or trees, were perhaps our earliest attempt at protecting ourselves from the environment. Protection was needed from excessive cold and heat, rain and snow, as well as from the threat of other humans and animals. Fires, earthquakes, floods, and other natural occurrences presented further challenges. These basic shelters were sometimes decorated—the need for aesthetic expression closely followed the need for protection. As humans moved from a nomadic to an agrarian society, it was necessary to protect foodstuffs from the elements.

Today our needs are similar, and while we are less likely to fear the wild animal at our door, we do emphasize security. Creating an enclosure to mediate the environment is a basic human instinct. It is only our level of expectation, combined with the availability of sophisticated materials and complex systems, that has changed.

The Igloo Enclosure

The simple dome of the igloo belies the complexity of this enclosure. The domed form is strong enough to resist the wind and carry any additional snow loads; it also presents the least amount of surface area for the volume enclosed. In the Arctic, blocks are cut from wind-packed snow and laid in an increasingly smaller spiral. The snow contains air voids that serve as insulation. On completion of the dome, a fire is lit—or in recent years a gas cooking stove—to melt the interior surface. The fire is then dampened, and a vent hole is opened at the top of the igloo. The heat from the fire softens the snow, fills in the gaps, and forms a skin of ice that serves as an air barrier. Animal skins might be hung on the interior to increase the insulation and to stop excessive melting from fires. In the Arctic, the size was typically limited by how high the builder could reach, as there was no suitable scaffolding material, although domes as large as twenty feet in diameter have been constructed.[1] The entry to the igloo is located perpendicular to the wind and below the sleeping platforms. Today, tools such as the ICEBOX, manufactured by Grand Shelters, make building snow structures even easier. Positioned on the wall, the box is packed with snow, a shovel at a time. Acting as a slip form, it is then moved to the next position. Eight adjustments allow for the correct catenary shape. This modern igloo has a ¾ inch (19 mm) vent at the top and can maintain an indoor temperature above freezing with little more than a lantern and body heat.

---

1. Fred Anderes and Ann Agranoff, *Ice Palaces* (Toronto: Macmillan of Canada, 1983), 16–17.

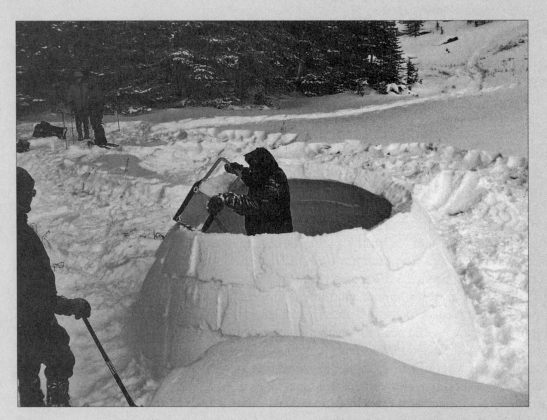

FIGURE 1.1 A modern igloo under construction. Photo courtesy of Grand Shelters, Inc.

1.1.1 MODERN BUILDINGS AND THEIR ENVELOPES

Modern buildings can be divided into four parts: the form-giving structure; the equipment and systems that help control the interior environment and deliver services; the partitions and finishes defining interior function; and the building envelope. The envelope, also called the enclosure, includes the exterior wall, the roof, openings within the envelope such as windows and doors, and the foundation wall below grade. Today the engineering professions design a building's structure and the environmental control systems and services. Interiors are often laid out and specified by interior designers. It is only the building envelope that was, until recently, solely the purview of the architect.

It is critical that architects design the building envelope for a number of reasons. As the facade, the enclosure presents the public face of the building. The aggregate of facades, in context, creates our urban landscape. If the facade fails, this public face is compromised. As a matter of liability, the envelope must function properly. Insurance claims against architects involve the building envelope more often than any other building component. As a measure of responsibility on the part of architects to their clients and as a contribution toward more sustainable practices, the envelope needs to be well designed. This responsibility is no better defined than by the following comment from Edward Ford:

> The traditional role of the architect as advocate of the concerns of permanence against the concerns of expediency is one from which he or she is often excluded by modern construction practices. Many have been glad to forsake this role. There is a tendency, perhaps growing, for architects to migrate into related, nontraditional fields, leaving behind what they consider the minutiae of the profession—those issues dealing with construction—to specialists, to consultants, to engineers, to contractors. It is a practice that is probably in many cases necessary, but if the architectural profession cannot accomplish so simple a task as the correct building of a wall, a window, a roof, or a door, it can hardly expect society to entrust it with a city.[1]

The design of the enclosure has become much more complicated with the advent of modern synthetic and composite materials, sophisticated new fabrication systems, new methods of construction, trends toward lighter and more economical skins, stress on energy efficiency, and the requirements for a highly controlled interior environment. This is all coupled with a desire for long-lasting buildings and an emphasis on "green" architecture. If architects are to control the appearance of the facade, both in the initial design and as the building ages, they must understand the function of the exterior wall. Building envelope specialists are sometimes responsible for this work, often working only indirectly with the designer. The conflict between function and form is often the beginning of envelope problems. If the function of the enclosure is not resolved, problems are guaranteed. Furthermore, when the contractor or the owner, rather than the designer, determines the solution, the building's aesthetic may be compromised.

1.1.2 CONUNDRUM OF ENVELOPE DESIGN

Durability has been described as "the quality of maintaining satisfactory aesthetic, economic, and functional performance for the useful life of a system."[2] These three elements are the basis of architectural design and form the three-part conundrum of enclosure (or envelope) design. Eliminate one and the other two are relatively simple to solve. It is much easier to design a functioning enclosure, based on aesthetics, with an unlimited budget. If appearance is no concern, function and affordability are more readily achieved. However, it is a rare project where the budget or the building's appearance are not critical factors. This book is about not compromising the third part, function, no matter what the budget constraints or the aesthetic intentions.

1.2 DECISIONS AFFECTING AESTHETICS, FUNCTION, DURABILITY, AND THE BUDGET

Many decisions concerning the exterior wall are made prior to "detailing" the envelope, some before considering the preliminary design of a building. These decisions set in motion a number of envelope design parameters. Although there may not be a contract between the owner and the architect when some of these determinations are made, it is important that the designer recognize the implications. Other design decisions are made during the preparation of documents, bidding phase, and construction and maintenance of the building. They are noted in this chapter, as they should be considered before signing a contract for architectural services. For example, producing a "maintenance manual for the exterior wall" will require fees to cover this additional service. Testing requires that the owner have an adequate construction budget. As many projects today are fast-tracked, it is even more critical to lay the groundwork for the entire design and construction process so that all parties understand their obligations and the consequences of their decisions.

The following decisions are meant to be made sequentially, although some may be made simultaneously.

Floor-Space-Ratio

The calculation of the floor-space-ratio (FSR) can affect the durability of the exterior wall. In many jurisdictions, the FSR is measured to the exterior face of the cladding. This discourages using thicker and possibly more durable claddings such as brick veneer. It also discourages the use of rigid insulation on the outside of the structure where it does the most good. A study in Vancouver, British Columbia, showed that the square footage lost by using brick veneer instead of a thin cladding on an urban, high-rise condominium project could cost the developer up to $3,500 (CA$) per unit in lost salable space.[1] This reasoning caused the City of Vancouver to exclude the area of the exterior wall that exceeds 6 inches (152 mm) —to a maximum of 6 inches—if recommended by a building envelope professional for the purpose of increasing durability.

1. "Position of the Masonry Industry on the F.S.R. Study Consultation," Masonry Institute of British Columbia for Brook Development and Planning, Inc. (November 9, 1995).

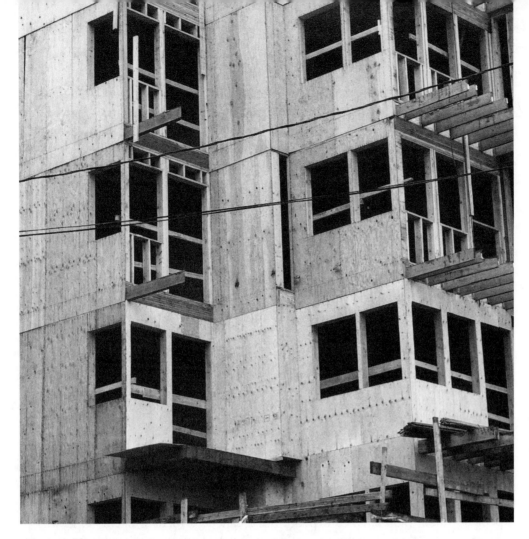

FIGURE 1.2 Zoning codes dictate the construction types permitted in different jurisdictions. Some regions on the West Coast allow five-story wood-frame buildings on noncombustible lower floors to a maximum height of 75 feet. Photo by G. Russell Heliker.

1.2.1 PRE-DESIGN

The *location of a building* determines the microclimate and macroclimate. Air temperature, prevailing winds, precipitation, relative humidity, as well as likelihood of natural disasters such as flooding, earthquakes, and hurricanes are all established by the selection of a site. It is unlikely that a different site would be chosen based on the general climatic conditions, but the microclimate might influence the building form or its placement on the site.

Building use dictates the interior climate and the mechanical systems required to maintain that climate. A museum, a swimming pool, an office building, and a residential building each have different requirements for optimal conditions, and their use produces different levels of heat and water vapor.

Codes further limit the options available for enclosure design. Building, zoning, and energy codes regulate the location on the lot, the occupancy type, construction type, material selection, energy requirements, and the size and height of the building. Energy codes are becoming more prevalent. Some codes are prescriptive, others performance-based. Canada is moving toward an "objective"-based code that combines the two. This book may reference a particular code for emphasis, but local jurisdictions should be contacted to verify the exact requirements. The two model codes referenced are the International Building Code (IBC) and the National Building Code (NBC) of Canada. The designer should remember that codes are minimums and often have not caught up with recent research, especially concerning envelope design.

The *team of consultants* should be identified along with the responsibilities of each. Mechanical and structural engineers have a part in the design of the exterior wall. Complex assemblages such as metal-and-glass curtain walls may require working directly with the manufacturer and specialized consultants. A building envelope consultant is beneficial if expertise on this subject is not available in-house, the wall design is complicated, or the building or energy code is under challenge. An integrated approach to design requires that all parties work together from the beginning of the project.

1.2.2 BUDGET

Architectural fees need to be sufficient to design an exterior wall that meets the client's aesthetics, life expectancy, and maintenance requirements. Inadequate fees will affect the long-term durability and aesthetics of the exterior wall—the client should be made aware of this fact.

Value engineering may be advantageous and required on public buildings. This can be a good opportunity to reassess decisions concerning the envelope. Unfortunately, it is also a point at which decisions can be made to use lower-cost substitutions that detrimentally affect the function of the wall. It is critical that compensation be allocated for the architect to respond fully to all proposed changes of the exterior wall.

The *construction budget* must be adequate to ensure that the exterior wall functions as designed. If the budget is at odds with the type and size of the building or the aesthetic intentions of the project, the problems will only worsen as the envelope is detailed. A discussion of the desired life of the building, along with the expected annual maintenance expenditures, can help focus a client. One way to help ensure an adequate exterior wall budget is to have a good enclosure strategy ready to present to the client during the preliminary design stage. For example, clients of public buildings often want a life expectancy of 100 years, but then they select a cladding with a 15–20 year life. A clear strategy that covers what is required to achieve the desired function, aesthetic, and enclosure life can guide later decisions. Good enclosures cost money, and the client should be made aware of the costs while there is still flexibility within the budget.

Budget decisions can affect exterior wall design in obvious ways (having to select a stucco cladding over a precast concrete cladding) and less obvious ways (money spent on interiors instead of stainless steel, brick veneer anchors)—the less obvious being more insidious. The money saved by deleting or changing an item, which results in increased potential for failure, may be spent many times over in the long term.

The budget should include an adequate *construction contingency* to ensure that durability and function are not compromised during construction. Delays, mistakes, and unforeseen conditions cost money. While parties may argue about who is responsible for correcting the problem, the cost ultimately comes out of the project. Too often the items deleted or changed to keep a project on budget are those that cannot be seen. When the enclosure is involved, more likely than not, the changes adversely affect the function. A larger contingency is necessary with a more experimental enclosure design or when control over construction quality is questionable. The contingency should not be used to compensate for a project that comes in over the budget. To meet the budget, the design can include a number of alternatives that do not affect the function of the exterior wall.

Architectural fees and the construction budget are also dependent on the *construction strategy* and the *contractor selection process.* Fast-tracking, negotiated contracts, and design-build stragegies all have potential advantages and disadvantages in terms of schedule, budget, and function.

The *cost to the environment* is the final budget concern that needs to be addressed. Essential to the budget is factoring in the cost of the embodied energy in construction materials; the disposal, recycling, or reuse of demolished building materials; and the energy required for the building's operation. Also of concern is the indoor air quality of the finished construction. These issues are well covered in other publications and will not be an emphasis in this book with one exception. A sometimes overlooked component of "green building" is durability. The longer a system or component functions as intended, the less embodied energy consumed per year of use. Even a material with a slightly higher, first-time "energy cost" may wreak less havoc on the environment if it performs twice as long. A simple flashing detail may prolong the life of a component. Durability is not a major criterion within the LEED 2.1 Green Building Rating System. The United States Green Building Council produces this rating system to "provide a national standard for what constitutes a 'green building.' Through its use as a design guideline and third-party certification tool, it aims to improve occupant well-being, environmental performance and economic returns of buildings using established and innovative practices, standards, and technologies."[3]

While acknowledging the efficacy of the program, in 2002 the National Institute of Standards and Technology (NIST) undertook a "critical analysis of the LEED program" and examined "individual credits within the LEED program utilizing a life cycle approach based on a case study building." The study noted that "architects have a central role in the development of environmental building practice [as they] are in the unique position of integrating many competing elements of a building into a cohesive and successful form." However, they further noted that "because LEED is presented as a standard, architects have limited incentive to evaluate the environmental benefits of individual credit options."[4]

Durability was added to the LEED Canada-NC Version 1.0. One point is given for developing and implementing a "Building Durability Plan, In accordance with the principles in *CSA S478-95 (R2001)—Guideline on Durability in Buildings.*" Design strategies include minimizing premature deterioration of the walls and roof with regionally appropriate devices such as "shading screens, eaves, overhangs, scuppers" and using "surface materials appropriate to exterior conditions...[and] drained walls and continuous air-barrier systems of appropriate strength."[5] This is a step in the right direction. I hope architects will introduce durability as part of their green strategies even without the incentive of LEED points.

Although durability may be difficult to promote, many designers and developers are doing just that. This often happens after a number of failures. In Vancouver, British Columbia, when the "leaky condo" crisis was front-page news, prospective buyers were asking about "rain-screen construction" while pondering the manufacturer of the kitchen appliances. Durability is a major, and marketable, component of the "green" architecture package. As such, durability can help convince the client to adopt a budget in line with their expectations. Presently there is much concern about mold growth in walls. Again, the problems of indoor air quality are not covered in this book; but one thing is certain—without moisture there is no mold.

1.2.3 DESIGN

The *structure* of the building determines the building's form and the range of enclosure options. Three structural (or construction) types typify modern buildings. Steel or concrete frames used for high-rise construction are common for buildings of any height. A backup wall of steel studs or concrete masonry completes the structural enclosure. A curtain wall attached to the exterior protects the structure from climatic changes. With a load-bearing masonry or a cast-in-place concrete wall, usually reserved for low- to mid-rise buildings, the structure and the enclosure elements are often the same, although additional layers may be added to fulfill some requirements of the enclosure. Cast-in-place walls have the advantage of a distinct aesthetic but the disadvantage of high cost. Both have the advantages of noncombustible construction, high-impact resistance, and thermal mass to delay exterior temperature changes. Light-frame wood or steel construction is a very versatile and economical system. It is constrained by codes in terms of size and height of building and fire protection. Its flexibility, when coupled with certain architectural styles, can create an overly complicated form, making envelope design more difficult. If the project is also low-budget, the problems are exacerbated.

There are no right or wrong decisions concerning construction type, just consequences for the design. It is important to coordinate closely all decisions about the exterior wall with the engineer designing the structure.

Form has a significant effect on envelope performance. Simple forms that readily shed water help the building enclosure perform its function. But program or aesthetics may dictate a less efficient form. The designer should be aware of the potential problems created by the geometry of the building. The more complex—that is, the more corners and stepped back walls—and the higher the building, the more emphasis the envelope design should be given. A simple low-rise building with a roof overhang on all four walls does not require the same attention as a multistory building with no overhangs. Drainage of water is critical; the greater the slope on nonvertical surfaces and the broader the overhangs at roofs and elsewhere, the better the natural protection. The fewer the number of penetrations in the exterior wall, the more functional the envelope design.

Facade aesthetics, other than form, generally refer to the selection of cladding. Often a cladding type is selected during the early planning stages to obtain a certain look. The cladding type should be a proven system that is appropriate for the height and exposure of the building, as the selection will have consequences for the durability, cost, and function of the enclosure.

Construction variables can shift with geographical location and construction type. Methods of installation or preference for materials may vary widely from one region to another. Culture dictates construction type in many instances. The overwhelming majority of single-family housing is wood-framed and constructed on site even though there are persuasive arguments for prefabrication or the use of light-frame steel construction. These variables need to be understood and challenged if they are not producing the best building enclosure design. Availability of materials and labor is another consideration. For example, some open-screen cladding systems, popular in Europe, may be too costly or too slow in delivery to be considered for many projects. Or an area may not have the experienced tradespeople required for a finely articulated cladding system. Knowing these limitations ahead of time will save headaches down the road. With the prevailing global economy, it is critical to understand these regional differences, as often the architect and consultants have little or no experience in the geographic area where the project is located.

Quality standards for the enclosure design should be determined. Envelope problems are often blamed on the contractor or on a lack of maintenance on the part of the owner. However, architects need to share this responsibility. An article in the *Magazine of Masonry Construction* noted, in a study of masonry problems in 33 states and two Canadian provinces, that 50 percent of the problems were due to errors during the design phase; problems of poor construction, material failure, or lack of maintenance made up the remaining percentage.[6] Often the design "error" is merely insufficient or incomplete drawings and specifications. The legal profession, in writing insurance policies for architects, appropriately selected the term "errors and omissions." Fundamental to the success of a project are good detailing of the most complex and not only the most commonplace transitions, and specifications carefully written for the particular project. Care should be taken to coordinate the drawings with the specifications. A mix of prescriptive and performance specifications usually ensures the best compliance. Those familiar with local construction practices should carefully review the constructability of the enclosure during the design process.

Specification writers can require that only qualified contractors bid on the project and only qualified subcontractors work on the project. Even public clients will usually allow for precertification of contractors and subcontractors. Materials and systems that the architect has confidence in should be selected. Substitutions should not be allowed unless they are performance equals.

Fire ratings, acoustics, and *security* and *environmental controls* are among the envelope requirements that are not covered in this book; however, they are critical to a properly designed exterior wall and must be considered.

1.2.4 CONSTRUCTION

A *preconstruction meeting* with the general contractor, subcontractors, consultants, architect, and owner assures that everyone understands the construction of the "whole wall." Problems with sequencing and constructability can be identified and solved. This is especially critical with fast-tracked projects.

A *shop drawing and sample review* by competent staff during construction is essential. The project architect should check the drawings to be sure the function, aesthetics, and durability of the enclosure are maintained. Samples should be verified and retained and should include methods of joining components where critical. The architect will have little recourse without a sample, should the installed material appear different than what was selected. Sample cladding panels should be erected on-site as part of the mock-up wall and left on-site until construction is completed.

Testing is critical both prior to and during construction. A testing program, including *mock-up walls,* should be delineated in the specifications. Mock-ups of the exterior wall serve two purposes. First, the mock-up can be tested and used to set the standard of quality. But equally important is bringing together all trades so that constructability problems can be discovered prior to beginning construction. Testing should also continue during construction—often a false sense of security is derived from preconstruction testing.

Construction "observation" is the term used in most architect-owner contracts to describe the architect's site visits. Wary of liability, some architects have taken a more hands-off approach during construction with insurers sometimes promoting the trend. But if the architect is not aware of what is happening during construction, there is a greater likelihood of problems occurring. And if the bidding and construction phases are not included in the contract between the owner and the architect, control of the exterior wall is lost. It is the foolhardy designer who would accept such a commission. The liability may be substantially increased as many of the problems that show up during the construction phase have their roots in the design. To abdicate the opportunity to correct these problems is not good architectural practice.

Record drawings and *specifications* should carefully record all changes that occur during the construction phase. They will become part of the "maintenance manual" for the building and will be invaluable when the inevitable replacement or restoration of the components of the wall occurs.

1.2.5 MAINTENANCE

The ability to clean and maintain the facade, particularly important with vision lites, is a requirement that is sometimes overlooked. The maintenance requirements for the exterior wall should be in accordance with the owner's expectations.

A *maintenance manual for the exterior wall* should be given to the owner at the completion of the project. The owner is often given a book of instructions for the operation of mechanical and electrical equipment, but rarely a reference manual for maintenance of the exterior wall. Some of the envelope components, such as sealants, will need surveying and possible replacement within the first five years. Other components, such as precast concrete panels, may not have problems for 30 years or more. The client must understand that all exterior wall components have a predictable service life, and many lower cost enclosure components may fail prematurely and need to be replaced. The compromise that ensues when function and durability is balanced with aesthetics and cost is the beginning of such a "mainte-

FIGURE 1.3 Window washing is an integral component of all buildings but particularly the glass-clad high-rise. Sophisticated equipment such as this example from Japan is one way of accomplishing the task. Whatever the size of the building, thought must be given as to how the exteriors will be cleaned and maintained. Photo by G. Russell Heliker.

nance manual." Once a firm has established a format for such a manual, it should be relatively easy to work up one for a particular project. (Maintenance of other parts of the building envelope, such as the roof, should also be included in the manual.)

1.3 CLIMATE AND THE EXTERIOR WALL

The exterior wall must be designed for a wide range of climatic conditions, even before considering anomalies such as hurricanes and other natural disasters. The cold blustery winters and heavy snows of Buffalo, New York, are often matched with very hot and humid days in the summer. Computer programs can model the exterior wall's performance over the climatic fluctuations seen in a 24-hour period and over a calendar year. While a sophisticated program can model the dynamic nature of the local climate, the dynamic wall is still in its infancy. Automated venting, selective coatings, and "smart" retarders all point to a future when the exterior wall might better respond to the changing climate. Until this occurs, the challenge is designing a single wall for a multitude of conditions.

"Finishing ends construction, weathering constructs finishes" is the opening statement of Mohsen Mostafavi and David Leatherbarrow's *On Weathering: The Life of Buildings in Time*.[7] The quality of those finishes is dependent on a firm understanding of what happens as the exterior wall weathers. Moisture decays and corrodes components. Thermal and moisture changes create internal forces as materials expand and contract, sometimes permanently. Heat transfer, air movement, and water vapor diffusion through the wall complete the list of environmental forces that the exterior wall manages. Lateral loads from wind, in combination with gravity loads, complicate the design of the vertical envelope. To this add challenges such as flying debris from a Florida hurricane or the story drift of a building frame from an earthquake in California.

Hygrothermal maps define zones by heating degree days (HDD), coupled with annual precipitation. The maps provide only general guidelines—microclimates exist within these regions. Hawaii is a good example: tourists flock to the beaches of the island of Hawaii for sun during the winter, while at the same time the nearby slopes of the Mauna Loa volcano may be experiencing below-freezing temperatures and snow. Using the actual data for the area where the project is located provides better information than relying on a geographical map.

As previously discussed, many decisions are made prior to selecting the cladding and other components of the wall. Summarizing this information can help the designer, with the help of consultants and manufacturers, select components and systems that will be economical and functional, and provide the intended aesthetic for the life of the exterior wall. Additional attention can be given to any problematic areas identified.

1.4 FUNCTION OF THE EXTERIOR WALL

The components of the exterior wall include the *structure, cladding, interior finishes, doors* and *windows,* and the *barriers* and *retarders* that mediate the environment. With the exception of the cladding and interior finishes, doors and windows and sometimes the structure, these components are not visible, making aesthetics less important than durability and function. The barriers and retarders between the interior finish and the exterior cladding usually constitute a small fraction of the overall cost of a building; however, failures can be very expensive. For example, a more effective air barrier system will affect the project's budget only marginally but may substantially influence the durability of the wall and reduce annual heating, ventilation, and air-conditioning (HVAC) operating costs. To repair or upgrade an air barrier system is very costly and often not feasible.

1.4.1 DESIGN OF THE EXTERIOR WALL

WHEN DESIGNING THE EXTERIOR WALL, THE FOCUS SHOULD BE ON:

1. **Stopping**
   - *water ingress from rain and melted snow and ice:* to minimize degradation of wall components
   - *air flow:* to minimize water entry, passage of conditioned air (heated or cooled), and migration of water vapor

   Stopping the incursion of these elements completely may not be possible but should be the goal.

2. **Controlling**
   - *heat transfer by radiation and conduction:* to minimize heat loss and gain
   - *water vapor diffusion:* to minimize diffusion of water vapor to areas in the wall where condensation might occur

3. **Transferring structural loads,** including
   - *lateral loads* from wind and seismic events
   - *gravity loads*

4. **Accommodating differential movement**
   - between the different *components* within an *assembly*
   - between the *assemblies* of the exterior wall and the *structure*

5. **Providing the aesthetic face of the building**

1.5 CLADDING SYSTEMS

The term "cladding" denotes the visible materials on the exterior of the wall. Claddings act as the primary weather barrier, and as such, they are sometimes called a rain screen. Some claddings—such as insulated glass units—perform all of the wall's functions. Often the selection of cladding has more to do with appearance than function. The aesthetic decisions are relatively straightforward, constrained primarily by cost. Selecting a cladding that maintains its function and appearance long-term is more difficult. Listed below are general considerations for cladding systems.

- All claddings leak, some just more than others.
- Claddings installed on-site with materials that must cure, such as brick veneer, stucco, and exterior insulation and finish systems (EIFS), are more dependent on good installation by skilled tradespeople than other systems.

FIGURES 1.4, 1.5, 1.6 Claddings are not always what they seem to be at first glance. This is an example of in-situ concrete wall, painted to resemble brick, on an apartment block in Gifu Prefecture, Japan. (Hasagana General Contractors). First, a black waterproofing layer is sprayed on. Next, a self-adhesive template of mortar joints is affixed to the black surface, which is then sprayed with a white paint. When the templates are removed, the "mortar joints" are black and the "brick face" is white. The templates come in a variety of bond patterns. Photos by Thomas Allan Palmer.

- Reputable manufacturers are critical for systems such as EIFS, curtain walls, window walls, glass-fiber reinforced concrete (GFRC), and precast concrete panels.
- Claddings need a secondary system to remove water. At a minimum, there should be a drainage plane with a weep system to ensure that water gets to the exterior. The one exception may be mass walls of concrete or concrete masonry.
- Impact resistance for the first floor should be considered.
- The heavier the cladding, the greater the life safety problems if it fails.
- Freeze-thaw cycles will affect porous materials, such as stucco and brick.
- Trying to seal a wall so that no water enters from the outside is unrealistic.
- Water vapor permeability is a critical consideration, particularly with coatings.
- Claddings must be able to transfer their own weight and all lateral loads to the structure. This includes wind suction.
- Claddings must be capable of accommodating all differential movement, including story drift from seismic events.
- Cladding attachments must support positive and negative (pull-out) loads.
- The transfer of lateral and gravity loads of heavy cladding is often not adequately considered by the structural engineer or the designer.
- Replacing sealant joints is a high-maintenance item. The more joints, the more costly the inevitable replacement.
- Periodic cleaning of all claddings is another maintenance item. The smoother and denser the surface, the less frequently cleaning is necessary. Porous materials such as stucco, concrete, brick, and unpainted wood will support organic growth if repeatedly wet.

1.6 "WHOLE-WALL" DESIGN

The performance of the "whole wall" depends on more than just the capacity of each component to act as a barrier or retarder to water, water vapor, heat, and air. Equally important are:

- How each component affects the performance of other components
- How the wall reacts to changing climatic conditions during a 24-hour period and across seasons
- How the wall functions in the long term

Hygrothermal performance—defined by heat, air, and moisture (water and vapor) transfer, sometimes called HAM—is the final measure in determining how well a wall "works." Water vapor diffusion and heat transfer can be graphed for given conditions. However, these conditions are always in a state of flux, making even these transfers dynamic. Water ingress and air movement through the wall— the more potentially damaging of the functions—are system problems. Only testing the completed building can determine the actual amount of water and air passing through the exterior wall.

Selecting and positioning the components is simple in comparison to detailing the transitions. The exterior wall would have few problems if it were covered with a monolithic material from the ground through the roof, void of any penetrations

Computer Models of Wall Performance

Computer models are a good tool for approximating "whole wall" performance. There are a number of hygrothermal programs that model heat, air, and moisture conditions in a wall over time. The Canada Mortgage and Housing Corporation (CMHC) recently reviewed forty-five programs and found three that met their criteria of availability (in the public domain or available at cost) and suitability for evaluating a series of specific walls— MATCH from Denmark, WUFI from Germany, and MOIST from the United States. All three are one-dimensional models that graph heat and moisture transport through a wall.[1]

WUFI and MOIST are user-friendly and include North American data. Both are available at no cost and can be downloaded from the Internet. The Web sites give detailed information about the programs.

- MOIST 3: Building and Fire Research Laboratory of the National Institute of Standards and Technology (NIST), http://www.bfrl.nist.gov/info/software.html

- WUFI-ORNL/IBP: Oak Ridge National Laboratory, http://www.ornl.gov/bct/apps/moisture/ibpe_sof1.html

1. Canada Mortgage and Housing Corporation, "Review of Hygrothermal Models for Building Envelope Retrofit Analysis," Technical Series 03-128 (Ottawa, Ont.: Canada Mortgage and Housing Corporation, 2003).

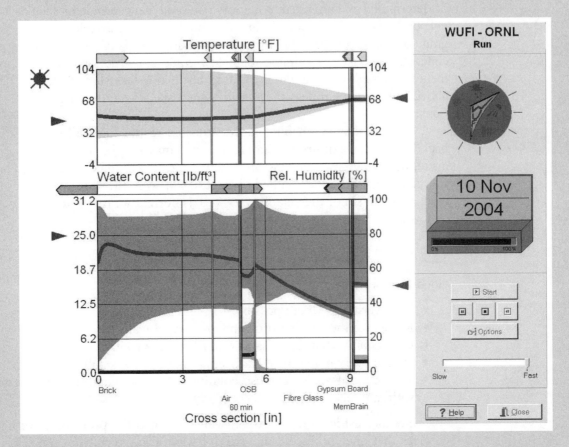

FIGURE 1.7 The WUFI program calculates and graphs temperature, water content, and relative humidity for a specific time and date. The lowest line indicates the buildup of moisture in each component. Illustration courtesy of Oak Ridge National Laboratories.

or joints. Water ingress is at the top of the list of potential problems. A study of failures of the exterior walls of condominiums on the West Coast pointed out that water from the exterior caused the majority of the problems. Ninety percent of the problems were related to transitions in the wall. Only 10 percent were directly related to the actual assemblage of components.[8] These figures will change based on climate and construction type, but it is safe to say that the majority of problems with the exterior wall are because of water entry, and the majority of this water is entering at transitions. Although each cladding type requires unique detailing for each climate and each component within the wall may change that detailing, some concerns can be generalized.

1.6.1 WALLS AT GRADE

Keep water away from the wall.

- Slope grade away from the exterior wall
- Do not bury cladding materials in the ground
- Consider moisture uptake from the ground due to hydrostatic pressure

The ground should slope away from the exterior wall with a minimum of 10 percent slope for at least 10 feet (3 meters) for drainage. Use of the unbuilt site should be determined and analyzed to identify potential water problems such as large non-porous surfaces that slope toward the building. Most exterior walls begin above grade on a concrete foundation. Only foundation walls of well-drained concrete or concrete masonry are suitable for below-grade construction. All other materials, including claddings, should preferably begin not less than 8 inches (200 mm) above finish grade, unless they are designed specifically for below-grade applications.

A drainage mat, with filter fabric attached to the foundation wall and gravel backfill, promotes drainage. Subgrade drains may also be needed. Maintenance of a site, including lawn mowing and snow removal, can mechanically damage exterior claddings. Sprinklers aimed at the exterior wall introduce water. Also of concern is vandalism of the cladding, as well as normal wear and tear at the pedestrian level.

1.6.2 WALLS AT THE ROOF

Good roof design protects the exterior wall.

- Use overhangs where possible
- Recognize the specific problems of parapet walls
- Understand what happens to water from the roof
- Design *every* nonvertical surface, no matter how small, as a roof
- Determine if soffits enclose conditioned or nonconditioned spaces; design soffit and enclosing wall accordingly

The modernist ideal of "roofless" walls banished the projecting overhangs and cornices that once protected the exterior wall. The typical roof now slopes minimally to internal drains, with a parapet wall at the perimeter. This extension of the exterior wall is exposed to the elements on both sides and top. The transition between the parapet wall and roof can be a major source of problems. Steeply sloped roofs are also not without problems. Ice damming, resulting in water ingress at the top of the wall, can occur in cold climates on roofs with overhangs.

The manufacturer of a low-slope roofing system may not be named until the contract has been let. However, the systems and the detailing for each type of membrane are similar. With well-detailed drawings, showing the continuation of the membrane as the water barrier, and careful review of shop drawings, a change in the manufacturer of the roof membrane should not adversely affect the enclosure's function. Some single-ply roofing manufacturers require that the membrane extend up and over the parapet wall. When designing the wall and roof transition, understand the requirements of the roofing system's warranty and the consequences if the plan is to deviate. If the roofing manufacturer changes during the bidding or construction phase, these items have to be rechecked. There are a number of good references covering roofing design, published by organizations such as the National Roofing Contractors' Association (NRCA) and the Canadian Roofing Contractors' Association (CRCA).

The designer should also be aware of what happens to the water from the roof. Gutter systems should be durable and capable of handling the calculated volume of water. Maintenance of gutter systems and roof drains should be an integral part of the "maintenance manual." Water should be diverted away from parapet walls. Overflow scuppers are a potential source for water leakage and require careful detailing.

Perhaps the most important point regarding roof design and the exterior wall is to remember that every surface that is not vertical should be treated as a roof. Detailing the exterior wall often includes designing a multitude of small roof coverings for cantilevered elements or recessed sills.

1.6.3 JOINTS AT OPENINGS IN WALLS AND TRANSITIONS

The joints around openings, large or small, and at transitions are a major source of water ingress.

- Accommodate differential movement and the continuation of barriers and retarders at openings and through transitions.
- Specify the best windows available and then assume they will leak.
- Specify the best doors, another major source of leakage.

Openings fall into two categories: larger openings, such as those created by doors and windows; and smaller openings, for electrical, plumbing, HVAC, and signage penetrations. Whether large or small, the joint between the opening and the wall must fulfill all of the functions of the envelope while under stress from differential movement—this is not an easy task. The joints that surround an opening may need to be carried through claddings such as brick veneer or stucco. For example, a brick expansion joint might continue from the side of a window (or door) to the top of the veneer panel, to avoid cracking of the veneer. The placement of openings has an aesthetic effect—they are formal elements in the wall. The aesthetic design must consider the rhythm of the exterior, including the subtleties of the lines created by expansion and control joints.

Expansion and control joints will be required at a number of locations in addition to those around openings. Corners and parapets see heavy wind loads and may require different treatment. Intersecting balcony walls are a problematic interface.

Every time materials or components are joined, or change planes, the transition is made at a joint. Large cladding components, such as precast concrete panels, have few joints, whereas brick veneer has a joint surrounding each individual brick. Others, such as EIFS and stucco, which are applied in a plastic state, need joints to accommodate the differential movement as the material cures. Cladding materials, such as metal, overlap in complex joints that are sometimes mechanically fabricated in place. Each of these joints is part of the building envelope.

Design of the multitude of joints is one of the more important tasks a designer faces. Unfortunately, it is often a task overlooked, left to the last minute, or left to the contractor. Perhaps designers would pay more attention to these details if they understood the aesthetic disasters that can occur when detailing of joints is poor. Remembering

TABLE 1.1 Barriers and Retarders

Wall Components	**Primary Function**	**Possible Secondary Functions** (*Review sections for information*)
Interior Finishes, Aesthetics		
Paint		may inadvertently act as a vapor retarder (VR)
Wall coverings		may inadvertently act as a VR
Interior Sheathing, Structural		
Gypsum board		may have reflective surface
Thermal Insulation		
Batts, blanket	INS	may have reflective surface
Blown-in, loose-fill	INS	ABS
Blown-in with binder	INS	ABS
Rigid boards	INS	ABS, VR, WB, may have reflective surface
Spray polyurethane foam	INS	ABS, VR
Air cavities, including inert gases	INS	
Reflective and Low-Emission Surfaces		
Foil	RB	VR
Paint	RB	VR
Coatings on glass	RB	
Water Vapor Retarders		
Vapor retarder paint	VR	RB
Polyethylene	VR	ABS
Wall coverings, nonpermeable	VR	

that the majority of water enters the exterior wall through poorly designed joints should put the emphasis back where it belongs.

1.7 SELECTING AND POSITIONING THE BARRIERS AND RETARDERS

"Before I built a wall I'd ask to know / what I was walling in or walling out." We understand that Robert Frost, in his poem "The Mending Wall," was not referring to controlling the climate—in fact, the wall was a rock fence, not an environmental separator. But this warning is as appropriate for the designer of the exterior wall as it is for neighbors. Every component of a wall may be walling in or walling out something, with the potential to cause damage later.

Wall Components	Primary Function	Possible Secondary Functions (Review sections for information)
Air Barrier Systems		
Sealed/taped polyethylene	ABS	VR
Taped, nonperforated building wrap	ABS	WB
Airtight drywall approach (ADA)	ABS	
Simple caulk and seal (SCS)	ABS	
Sheet- and fluid-applied membranes	WB	ABS
Exterior Sheathing, Structural*		
Oriented strand board (OSB)		may inadvertently act as a VR
Plywood		may inadvertently act as a VR
Nonpaper faced gypsum sheathing		
Water Barriers		
Building paper and felts	WB	
Nonperforated building wrap	WB	ABS
Sheet membranes, including "peel-and-stick"	WB	ABS, VR
Fluid-applied, reinforced membranes	WB	ABS, VR
Exterior Finishes, Aesthetics, and Primary Weather Barrier		
Cladding systems		WB, VR
Paint, sealers, and coatings		WB, VR

Abbreviation	Function	Discussed In
WB	Water Barriers	Chapter 2
ABS	Air Barrier Systems	Chapter 3
VR	Vapor Retarders	Chapter 3
INS	Thermal Insulation	Chapter 3
RB	Radiant Barriers	Chapter 3

*Bracing must be used for lateral stability if metal or wood stud walls are not sheathed

The following chapters contain the information necessary to select and position exterior wall components that resist water ingress, air movement, vapor transmission by diffusion, and heat transfer by conduction and radiation. Components are discussed separately to point out the importance of fully understanding the capabilities of each; selecting a particular air barrier may also mean inadvertently selecting a vapor retarder. The primary and secondary functions of each component are listed in Table 1, "Barriers and Retarders." For example, information about "peel-and-stick" self-adhesive sheet membrane is under water barriers, as this is the primary function. This component is also mentioned under air barriers and vapor retarders. All sections should be consulted, as the "peel-and-stick" membrane may perform all three functions, whether intended or not.

1.7.1 RESOURCES

There are several ways to obtain specific data about cladding systems and other components of the wall. Trade associations provide information for systems that are not product-driven, such as stucco and precast concrete cladding. Information should also be available directly from the manufacturer, whether it is a system or an individual component. Carefully weigh what manufacturers and trade organizations state about their products and components. It may be a very good system or component, but the designer must balance cost with durability and function with aesthetics. The designer must also understand how this system or component will interface with others in the building. A list of trade and manufacturers associations for different cladding types and wall components is included in Bibliography and Resources. These associations offer publications, general information, and links to other relevant material.

1.7.2 PRODUCTS

One problem with writing any book that involves the selection of components is that these components are products. While there may be some generic similarities and quality control enforced by codes and standards, each product is potentially different. For this reason, references to specific products are made with the following caveats:

- These references were current at the time this book was written. All information should be verified with the manufacturer.
- There are many other products available. The products chosen are good, frequently used products. There may be better products and certainly there are many more that are not listed. Inclusion of a product in no way signifies that it is superior to others.

As research into specific products is time consuming, an architectural firm can limit liability while increasing productivity by choosing a group of components and systems that they know how to detail and the properties of which they fully understand. They should be reliable and easily obtained products that are backed by warranties. As well, installation of the product should be well understood by local tradespeople. It is best to let someone else do the empirical testing for new products. The more often a product is specified, the better the firm's understanding of its weaknesses and strengths. Warranties of each product should be carefully reviewed. As it is often the application that fails, not the product, the

CHECKLIST
PRELIMINARY DESIGN INFORMATION AND DECISIONS

Location of a Building Determines	Exterior design temperatures
	Exterior relative humidity
	Precipitation
	Wind-driven rain indices
	Seismic zone
	Flood data
	Wind and hurricane loads
	Snow loads
Building Use Determines	Interior design temperatures
	Interior relative humidity
	Heating, ventilating, and air-conditioning (HVAC) requirements
Relevant Codes	Zoning codes
	Building codes
	Energy codes
	Fire codes
Form and Structure Design Decisions	Type of structure and backup wall, if required
	Height of building
	Geometry of the facade
	Complexity of form
	Preliminary cladding choice
Construction and Bidding Strategies	Design-build
	Fast-tracked
	Negotiated construction contract
	Competitive bid
Budget	Architectural fee considerations:
	Consultant selection, including building envelope specialists
	Role of architect and consultants during construction
	Inclusion of "maintenance manual" for the exterior wall
	Construction budget considerations:
	Quality standards defined
	Construction variables determined
	Mock-up walls
	Testing program
	Construction contingency
Environmental Costs— Durability	Expected service life of exterior wall
	Expected maintenance
Exterior Wall Requirements Not Covered in this Book	Fire ratings
	Acoustics
	Passive environmental controls
	Additional sustainable practices
	Security

installers' warranties are equally important. Tight specifications must be written to ensure the products actually will be used. Substitutions can wreak havoc with the building envelope. Use of generic terms, such as air barrier, and leaving the selection of a product to a consulting specification writer or the contractor can create headaches. This is something a designer would never do when aesthetics are involved.

Ideally, architects should keep up to date with new products and new concepts. Waiting for building codes to mandate changes puts the architect well behind current research and is not in the best interest of clients. But having a standard list of products will keep down the day-to-day frustration and simplify the selection process.

Water Barriers and Flashings

2.1 MANAGING WATER

Water deteriorates materials—it rots wood, oxidizes metals, and provides a growth medium for mold and mildew. Wet components such as fiberglass batt insulation do not function as well. Water causes swelling or expansion of some materials and can transport pollutants and dissolved substances such as the salts that cause efflorescence. Continual freezing and thawing of wet materials adds additional forces—water increases 4 percent in volume when it freezes. Corrosion of steel also produces forces, as the iron oxide takes up more volume than the steel it replaced. In the worst case, water ingress may threaten life safety, as when the steel anchoring system of a cladding begins to corrode.

Water can enter a wall from rain or snow or ice melt. Improperly adjusted sprinkler heads that direct water to the exterior wall and poorly functioning or designed gutter systems and scuppers are other sources of water entry. The form or articulation of the vertical envelope can help or hinder the control of the water flow down the face of the exterior wall. Air pressure differentials and capillary suction across the wall can draw water through the wall. Condensation of vapor from interior or exterior sources produces water. Wet construction applications—such as pouring concrete floor toppings, dry-walling, and some sprayed-on insulation such as cellulose—add moisture to a wall. Water may enter wall components dur-

Water Definitions

Terms used to describe water, in its various phases, and water management systems vary from region to region and between the United States and Canada. The discussion below explains these differences and sets the vocabulary for this book.

- The term *moisture* is often used to denote either liquid water or water vapor. To avoid confusion, in its liquid form water will be termed *water,* and water vapor will be differentiated by the use of the term *water vapor* or simply *vapor.* Only when discussing a combination of water and water vapor will the term *moisture* be used.

- *Moisture* is also useful to describe water or vapor that has been absorbed or bound by a material, for example, the "moisture content of wood."

- There are a number of products designed, as a second layer of defense, to stop water from entering a wall. The term *water barrier* will be used for all of these. Building paper, felts, and building wraps have been called sheathing membranes in Canada and weather- or water-resistive barriers and drainage planes in the United States. Building wraps are commonly called house wraps. (*SBPO* will be used only for nonperforated, nonwoven, spun-bonded building wraps such as Tyvek.) Below grade, the terms *waterproofing* and *damp-proofing* are often used.

- When the face of the exterior wall stops all water, it is called a barrier wall in the United States and a face-sealed wall in Canada. When the wall relies on an exterior "seal" to stop all water, it will be termed a *face-sealed barrier wall.*

- An *internal drainage plane wall* has a drainage plane or narrow cavity and a water barrier behind the cladding. This is also called a concealed barrier wall or a concealed weather barrier wall.

- The term *drainage cavity wall* will be used when the cavity is greater than ⅜ inch (10 mm) in width and drainage is provided. Other terms used are *drain screen* and *rain screen.*

- *Pressure-equalized rain screens (PER)* are perhaps the most misunderstood of wall types. The term *PER* or *rain screen* will only be used if the wall is a drainage cavity wall with a vented, compartmentalized cavity and a continuous, supported air barrier system.

- Pressure-equalized joints between face-sealed cladding units are another method of water management. They are called *pressure-equalized joints* or *PE joints.*

- *Drained, two-stage joints* are sealant joints between face-sealed panels that are drained. The standard, single sealant joint is a *face-sealed joint.* See Chapter 4 for more information on joint design.

ing manufacturing, transporting, or storing of the materials. Using gas heaters during construction adds moisture to the interior. Stopping water is critical. As noted in "ASTM Practices for Increased Durability of Building Constructions Against Water-Induced Damage" (E241), "except for structural errors, about 90% of all building construction problems are associated with water in some way."[1]

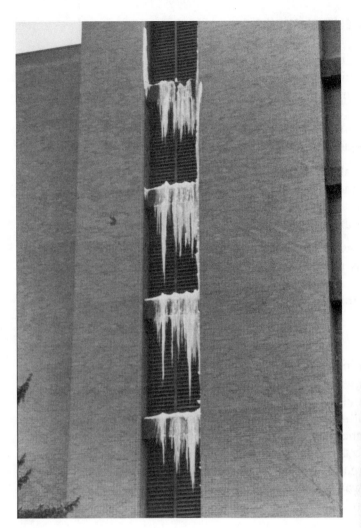

FIGURE 2.1 There are occasions when water comes from the interior—pipes break or HVAC equipment malfunctions. The failure of mechanical equipment flooded the interior of this university building. The water flowed to an exterior vent, where it froze on reaching the outside. Photo by G. Russell Heliker.

FIGURE 2.2 It is easy to see where the downspout is discontinuous from the deterioration of the brick on this exterior wall. Drainage systems should be maintained to ensure that they are directing water away from the wall, not toward it. Neglecting this problem made for a more costly rehabilitation. Photo by Linda Brock.

2.2 WATER MANAGEMENT SYSTEMS

Moisture trapped in the wall during construction can be limited with the active on-site involvement of the architect, especially when backed by carefully written specifications and detailed drawings. Air barrier systems, thermal insulation, and vapor retarders all play a role in controlling condensation of water vapor in a wall. Water management systems prevent the entry of water from the exterior.

The four basic systems used to manage water are:

- face-sealed barrier walls
- internal drainage plane walls
- drainage cavity walls
- pressure-equalized rain-screen walls

They are described below in order of their relative cost and effectiveness. With cladding materials such as metal, which is watertight, the management of water ingress occurs at the joints between the cladding units. These joints can be face-sealed, two-stage drained joints, pressure-equalized joints, or open joints.

2.2.1 FACE-SEALED BARRIER WALLS

A face-sealed barrier wall implies that a cladding or exterior finish stops *all* water at the outside face of the wall. The cladding or coating is the water management system—there is no redundancy. Traditionally, the term *barrier wall* referred to a solid masonry or mass wall that formed a weather barrier because of its thickness. It leaked. It was just a much slower process, and one hoped that the wall dried before the moisture got to the interior. Today, poured-in-place concrete walls and concrete masonry walls are the most common true barrier walls. Concrete can take on a certain amount of water without detrimental effects, making these barrier walls an option that depends also on climate and exposure.

2.2.2 INTERNAL DRAINAGE PLANE WALLS

Most claddings allow for some passage of water, either through the material itself or at the joints. A secondary line of defense is required to stop any water that passes through the cladding and drain any condensed vapor. An internal drainage plane wall has a drainage plane up to ⅜ inch (10 mm) in depth as well as a water barrier and weep holes. The redundancy offered by the water barrier provides much more protection than the face-sealed barrier wall.

2.2.3 DRAINAGE CAVITY WALLS

The drainage cavity wall—consisting of a cavity and a water barrier—has openings or weep holes at the base for drainage of any water that passes through the cladding and vapor that condenses in the cavity. It may or may not have additional openings to promote drying through air circulation. The cavity must be of sufficient width to stop water from bridging the gap—⅜ inch (10 mm) is the dividing line used in this book. A larger dimension may be necessary to compensate for construction tolerances and workmanship.

Face-Sealed Barrier Wall

The standard product for Exterior Insulation Finish Systems (EIFS) relies on a complete seal at the exterior face, including the joints. (Newer systems have introduced redundancy, with a water barrier and a drainage plane or small drainage cavities.)

Other examples include face-sealed concrete block, concrete, or stucco. Curtain walls, window walls, and claddings that rely on a single sealant bead to stop water from entering the wall between the units or panels are face-sealed barrier walls. A wall clad with siding of any material but no cavity and no water barrier, or one where the siding is in full contact with the water barrier, is also considered a face-sealed barrier wall.

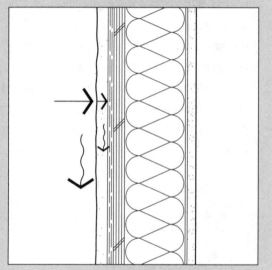

FIGURE 2.3

Internal Drainage Plane Wall

An internal drainage plane is common with stucco applications. Using building paper or one of the new, corrugated nonperforated building wraps as the water barrier, with a drainage screed at the base, increases the possibility for water drainage and, consequently, of the stucco drying. An internal drainage plane also describes walls with a drainage plane and a water barrier under wood, fiber-cement, metal, or vinyl sidings and proprietary, drained EIFS systems.

FIGURE 2.4

Drainage Cavity Wall

Although brick veneer in the past was part of a composite masonry wall, today the backup wall is as likely to be made of steel studs. Brick veneer requires a minimum cavity depth of 2 inches (50 mm) to ensure the cavity is kept free of mortar droppings during construction.

A drainage cavity wall is standard with many cladding systems such as stone veneer and panel systems of metal. It is also commonly used for wood cladding in many western European countries and is required in some jurisdictions, with excessive rain, in Canada.

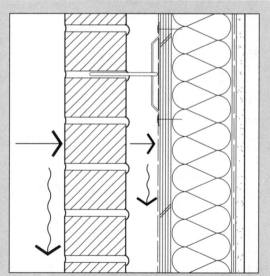

FIGURE 2.5

Pressure-Equalized Rain-Screen Wall

A pressure-equalized rain screen (PER) is a drainage cavity wall designed so that the air pressure of the cavity behind the cladding is similar to the exterior air pressure. *Pressure-moderating rain screen* is a more descriptive term for a PER, as designing a wall that will equalize the pressure instantly and under all conditions is not practical. The following must be in place for this system to work:

- Compartmentalized cavity to limit airflow from one area of the cavity to another
- Vents in compartments to allow for pressure equalization between the exterior environment and the compartment and to drain any water
- Air barrier system that is continuous and structurally supported

The size of vents required for a PER depends on the static and dynamic pressure equalization across the rain screen. Under dynamic-pressure conditions, the size is dependent on the volume of air in the compartment, the resistance to airflow at the vent holes, and the rigidity of the wall assembly. Static pressure is primarily dependent on leakage in the air barrier system.[1] *Construction Technology Update No. 17,* "Pressure Equalization in Rainscreen Wall Systems," published by the Institute for Research in Construction, provides an excellent primer in addition to the formulas for determining vent size.[2]

The use of vertical 1x spacers, or furring, at stud spacing for drainage and through-wall flashing at each floor, in wood-framed walls, comes close to creating the required compartment size for a PER. Combining this with a good air barrier system and vents can turn a light-frame wall with a drainage cavity into something approaching a PER at little additional cost (see Figure 2.7).

---

1. M. Z. Rousseau, G. F. Poirier, and W. C. Brown, "Pressure Equalization in Rainscreen Wall Systems," *Construction Technology Update No. 17* (Ottawa, Ont.: Institute for Research in Construction, 1998), pp. 4–5.
2. Ibid., 4–5.

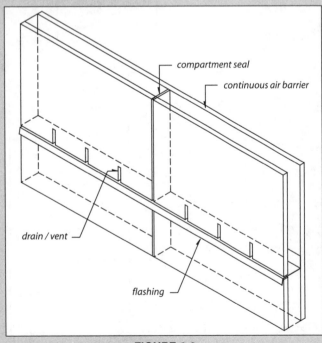

compartment seal

continuous air barrier

drain / vent

flashing

FIGURE 2.6

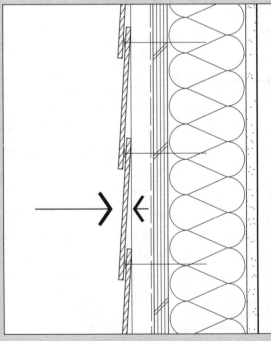

FIGURE 2.7

2.2.4 Pressure-Equalized Rain-Screen Walls

True pressure-equalized rain-screen walls are rare. A metal and glass curtain wall is an example of such a wall; but even this shows only moderate success. A report by Rick Quirouette, written for Canada Mortgage and Housing Corporation (CMHC) noted that "the most advanced rainscreen system design is the metal and glass curtain wall." But measurements in the field would appear to indicate substantially less than 25 percent pressure equalization in a spandrel even during low-pressure winds. However, Quirouette comments that even with these pressure differences, there did not appear to be any leakage during a "moderately severe storm." [2]

What Is a Rain Screen?

A rain screen means different things to different people. The word itself seems to suggest a panacea for all water entry problems. Often the term is used whenever there is a drainage cavity or even just a drainage plane with vents. As M. Z. Rousseau noted in "Facts and Fictions of Rain-Screen Walls," there is a "myth spread in the industry which claims that simply venting a cavity (no matter how big the cavity behind the exterior cladding…no matter how leaky the inner wall) does the trick of applying the rain-screen principle."[1] In Europe the term often refers to an open-jointed "screen."

Considered the Cadillac of water management, rain screens have sparked much discussion. The idea of a screen for the rain has been around for centuries. The principles of a "rain barrier" were explained in a small booklet produced by the Norwegian Building Research Institute in the early 1960s. G. K. Garden, of the National Research Council of Canada, introduced the concept to North America in 1963. In *Construction Building Digest: 40,* Garden named and detailed the requirements of our modern pressure-equalized rain screen—a compartmentalized and vented drainage cavity with a continuous air barrier.[2]

In its initial use, *rain screen* meant the outer leaf or cladding that "screened" the rain. An inner leaf acted as a drainage plane and stopped the movement of air. Originally called *two-stage weather tightening* (a term still used in Europe), this is sometimes called an *open* or *simple* rain screen in North America.

Used frequently for marketing purposes, there is no consensus on what the word means. To avoid confusion, this book only uses the term *rain screen* if there is pressure equalization. A better approach is to specify the components and their function. A PER is a recommended water management system for metal and glass curtain walls; but realistically, most wall types fall somewhere between a PER and a drainage cavity wall even when specified as a PER. Again the focus should be on function, not semantics.

The best advice is to concentrate on designing a well-functioning drainage cavity with a continuous air barrier system and detailing and specifying these functions such that they are affordable and constructable. Tom Schwartz, of Simpson Gumpertz and Heger, comments on the practicality of the drained cavity wall versus the PER: "Pressure equalization is a sound concept, but this complication of the time tested drained cavity wall approach may be unnecessary given the fact that properly designed and constructed cavity walls (i.e., without pressure equalization) are simple, cost effective, and reliable. Pressure equalization holds the promise of extending wall durability by reducing cavity moisture. But this advantage comes along with the risk of introducing performance problems due to the increased complexity of the system compared to traditional drained cavity walls."[3]

1. M. Z. Rousseau, "Facts and Fictions of Rain-Screen Walls," *Construction Practice* (Ottawa, Ont.: IRC-National Research Council of Canada).
2. G. K. Garden, *Rain Penetration and Its Control: CBD-40* (Ottawa, Ont.: Division of Building Research, NRCC, 1963).
3. Tom Schwarz (Simpson Gumpertz and Heger), in correspondence with the author, October 2003. Quoted by permission.

TABLE 2.1 Water Management Systems

Components and Function	Face-Sealed Barrier Wall	Internal Drainage Plane Wall	Drainage Cavity Wall	Pressure-Equalized Rain-Screen
Drainage plane or cavity less than ³⁄₈" (10 mm) in width		required		
Drainage cavity greater than ³⁄₈" (10 mm) in width			required	required
Compartmentalized cavity				required
Water barrier in addition to cladding		required	required	required
Openings for drainage		required	required	required
Openings for venting		optional	optional	required
Openings for ventilation		optional	optional	not recommended
Structurally supported air barrier system	recommended	recommended	recommended	required

2.3 SELECTING THE RIGHT WATER MANAGEMENT SYSTEM

On low-rise buildings, particularly those with overhangs and in protected areas, a less efficient water management system may be acceptable. The Partnership for Advancing Technology in Housing (PATH), a collaboration of U.S. Housing and Urban Development (HUD) and the Federal Housing Administration (FHA), states that face-sealed barrier walls are effective in climates with less than 30 inches (762 mm) of annual precipitation whereas internal drainage plane walls are effective in areas with annual precipitation, from 30 to 50 inches (762–1270 mm). Drainage cavity walls are suggested for climates with less than 60 inches (1524 mm) of rain a year. Over this amount, a pressure-equalized rain screen (PER) is recommended.[3] It should be noted that, for the most part, the recommendations are for small, one to two story residences that are more likely to have overhangs and be protected from winds. (According to the U.S. Census Bureau, only about 7 percent of the housing units in the United States were higher than three stories and less than 16 percent were in buildings with five or more attached units in 2001.)[4] The Builder's Guides, published by the Building Science Corporation, recommend only using face-sealed walls in climates with less than 20 inches (508 mm) of annual precipitation—a more conservative and safe recommendation.[5] Again, these are recommendations for homes and smaller buildings.

This book recommends the following minimums in areas where water penetration is of concern and a long exterior wall life is desired:

- A secondary line of defense in the form of a water barrier
- A flashed cavity of a constructable dimension to drain interstitial water to the exterior and break capillary action between the cladding and the backup wall, taking construction tolerances into consideration
- As complete an air barrier system as constructable and affordable

2.3.1 Deflect, Drain, or Dry? Vent or Ventilate?

An important part of managing water is ensuring that wet components dry before any damage occurs. Ventilating a drainage cavity accelerates the drying of components within the wall through evaporation. The amount of ventilation must be balanced between the drying potential and the increased potential for water entering the wall through the additional openings. In areas with high indices of wind-driven rain and long cool-wet periods, which slow drying, such as in the Pacific Northwest, it may be prudent to reduce the number of openings to only those required for drainage.

The surest way to stop water ingress is not to let the materials get wet in the first place. Deflection of water, by using overhangs and drips on flashings, will reduce the amount of water that flows down the wall. Drainage of water is equally important, be it from a cavity, the roof, the adjacent hard or soft landscaping, or any other potential "catch basin," however small or large. Venting, as opposed to ventilating, helps stop water from entering the wall by minimizing air pressure differences across the cladding. A pressure-equalized rain screen does not promote ventilation of the cavity—in fact, it does the opposite. The National Research Council of Canada (NRCC) recommends that vent holes be located at the same height, to reduce airflow through the compartment.[6]

FIGURES 2.8, 2.9 These photographs show conditions on a building when it was approximately 14 years old. It is located in an area that receives about 19 inches (480 mm) of precipitation a year. The bench (Figure 2.8), located on a bridge that connects two wings of the building and the parapet (Figure 2.9), were waterproofed with an elastomeric coating. When water entered the walls through the inevitable cracks and pinholes, it could not get back out. Freeze-thaw action exacerbated the damage. Photos by G. Russell Heliker.

2.3.2 FORCES THAT MOVE WATER

If water cannot be diverted, the only option left is to eliminate the forces that move water through a wall. The force of gravity can be a problem with any components that are not vertical. (However, wind on the exterior wall can cause water to flow uphill on vertical surfaces, particularly at building corners and parapets.) Any non-vertical surface exposed to water should be treated as a roof. This simple reasoning would do much to alleviate leakage in buildings. A sloping sill is *not* a wall; it is a roof and should be clad with materials appropriate for a roof. Surface tension, capillary suction, and momentum can be stopped through simple geometry. Minimizing air pressure differences across the cladding, with a PER, eliminates the final force.

FIGURES 2.10, 2.11 While we often see windowsills constructed of brick (Figure 2.10), few would consider using brick as a roofing material on a similar slope. The brick sills on this load-bearing masonry building from the eighteenth century (Figure 2.11) are protected with overlapping slate shingles. Photos by G. Russell Heliker and Linda Brock.

TABLE 2.2 Forces That Move Water Through The Wall

Force	To Stop the Force
Surface tension causes water to cling to the underside of horizontal surfaces.	• Incorporate a drip under all projecting horizontal surfaces. • Use only metal flashings with a drip edge.
Capillary suction draws water into permeable materials and small openings.	• Lap, or shingle, joints. • Ensure openings to the cavity are a minimum of ³⁄₈ inch (10 mm). • Use materials with minimum absorption capacity or use a thickness that delays water transport through the material: "For example, ⁷⁄₈ inch (22 mm) thick stucco that is subject to continuous wetting will saturate in two days. Therefore, if the building location often experiences rain for this long, change the material or shield the wall with an overhang." • Back (and end) prime wood siding with a water sealer.
Momentum or *kinetic energy* propels raindrops into unprotected openings.	• Shield openings from direct rain entry. • Splash water can be a problem at all horizontal planes, such as at the base of the wall.
Gravity draws water downward and into sloped openings.	• Use overhangs at the roof and over any openings. • Slope *all* nonvertical surfaces to the exterior a minimum of 5 percent, preferably 15 percent. • Slope parapet caps to the roof a minimum of 15 percent. • Avoid butt joints; use laps. • Lap horizontal joints. • Provide drainage holes or paths for all horizontal surfaces that act as troughs. • Recess windows and doors.
Air pressure differences draw water in the direction of lower air pressure.	• Minimize air pressure differences with a vented, compartmentalized drainage cavity and a structurally supported continuous air barrier system. • Detail a *complete* air barrier system for the entire enclosure.

Source: Adapted from W .C. Brown, G. A. Chown, G. F. Poirier, and M. Z. Rousseau, *Designing Exterior Walls According to the Rainscreen Principle,* Construction Technology Update No. 34 (Ottawa, Ont.: IRC, NRCC, 1999).

2.4 WATER BARRIERS AND THEIR PLACEMENT

2.4.1 BUILDING WRAPS

Microporous plastic water barriers that stop water and air but are permeable to vapor are called building wraps or "housewraps." Dupont developed the first in the late 1970s—a nonperforated, nonwoven, spun-bonded polyethylene called Tyvek HouseWrap—and a generic term was born. Today Tyvek water barriers are made of spun-bonded polyolefin and include HomeWrap, CommercialWrap, and also StuccoWrap. Another nonperforated building wrap is Typar HouseWrap, which is a coated spun-bonded polypropylene. The permeability of these products comes from the manufacturing process. Some plastic building wraps are mechanically punched or perforated for permeability. The term SBPO (spun-bonded polyolefin) is reserved for materials such as Tyvek that are made of nonperforated, nonwoven, spun-bonded polyolefin.

The perforated building wraps generally allow more water to pass than the nonperforated. Also many perforated building wraps are not classified as air barriers. Nonperforated building wraps are commonly used as an air barrier, the function for which they were originally marketed. Nonperforated building wraps generally have good vapor permeability. Tear resistance varies from product to product. Available in story-high widths, building wraps can be used to "weatherproof" a wall quickly. There is much research in this area, with new products continually coming on the market, some nonperforated. Dow has introduced Styrofoam Weathermate and Owens Corning has PinkWrap, both building wraps with some transparency. Self-draining building wraps, such as the nonperforated StuccoWrap, have a textured surface with small rivulets or channels for water drainage. More discussion on building wraps can be found in Chapter 3 under "Air Barrier Systems."

2.4.2 BUILDING PAPER AND FELT

The conventional water barrier is building paper, an asphalt saturated Kraft paper, or felt. The common product is #15 or #30 felt, or Grade D building paper, with 20-, 30-, or 60-minute ratings. While sharing some similarities, building paper and felt also have different characteristics. Felt today is made from recycled paper fiber from corrugated boxes and newspapers. These cellulose fibers result in a material that is thicker and less dense than the Kraft paper used for building paper. The more open pore structure of the felt allows a high percentage of asphalt impregnation. The result is a thick, stiff material that has high water resistance but tends to crack when folded around corners. Building papers use cellulose fiber made from wood pulp, resulting in a dense, strong fiber mat. The tighter pore structure reduces the percentage of asphalt that can be impregnated. The result is a less saturated paper that is still water resistant but more vapor permeable and pliable around corners. Because building paper is substantially thinner than felt, two layers are often recommended to obtain a double drainage plane—for example, using two layers of 30-minute paper in place of one layer of 60-minute paper.

Both building paper and felt come in widths of 36 to 40 inches. Although air movement is decreased, they are not considered air barriers even with the seams taped. Both building paper and felt will absorb some moisture. Their vapor permeability increases when saturated, helping wet materials dry to the exterior. If any water leakage occurs to the inside of the building paper or felt, they can absorb the water, allowing it to pass to the exterior through evaporation.

As with all components, building paper and felt have evolved over the years. The new generations include a 30-minute double-ply building paper with 2-inch (50 mm) wide asphalt mastic strips at 16-inch (400 mm) intervals to increase water protection at nail and staple holes, a proprietary product of Hal Industries. Fortafiber has a two-ply paper with a 150-minute water holdout rating. Hal Industries also produces a corrugated two-ply building paper with a 150-minute water holdout rating.

2.4.3 BUILDING WRAP OR FELT?

A reputed problem with some building wraps, primarily the perforated ones, is that surfactants (surface-active contaminants) can reduce the surface tension of the water, making it easier for the water to pass through a smaller opening. Surfactants can be found in lignin from wood, such as cedar and redwood, and in substances such as soap, which is sometimes used though not recommended as a plasticizer with stucco. Other stucco additives can work as surfactants, leading some building envelope specialists to advise against using building wraps with stucco. These same surfactants have caused less severe problems with paper and felt. A good recommendation is to ensure that any material in direct contact with the water barrier will not create problems by asking the manufacturer to address the issue in writing.

Paul Fisette (of the University of Massachusetts), in an article titled, "Housewrap vs. Felt," discussed the problems with surfactants. He concluded that soaps and extractives from cedar do have an effect on the water resistance of building wrap. Testing by Fisette further suggested that nonperforated building wrap displayed better water resistance. Felt may seal better around nails and staples, depending on the thickness and asphalt content. However, in the end, Fisette decided that it does not matter "a whole lot" whether you choose a building wrap or felt if you get the flashing details right and are careful with installation.[7] In general, felt costs less than building wrap, but the installation cost is higher. Felt, and to some extent building paper, is manufactured by a large number of companies and rarely identified as a product. Felts are governed by a host of codes, from which the manufacturers can pick and choose, making it difficult to compare one to another. Building wraps are identified as products. However, comparisons are also difficult with building wraps, as different manufacturers may use different testing methods.

2.4.4 SHEET MEMBRANES

Adhered sheet membranes can be hot- or cold-applied. In general, any roofing material suitable for a vertical application can be used as a water barrier if the substrate, attachment, and method of installation is acceptable—some are torched-in-place, creating a potential fire hazard during installation.

2.4.5 SELF-ADHESIVE MEMBRANES, OR "PEEL-AND-STICK"

The newest water barriers are self-adhesive sheet membranes, descriptively called peel-and-stick. They are manufactured by laminating a rubberized asphalt compound to a polyethylene film. Though the membrane is self-adhesive, many substrates require careful priming. Proper installation is critical, including lapping at edges and ends. It may be prudent to also attach the membrane mechanically—this can often occur in tandem with the fastening of another component such as rigid insulation to the exterior of the peel-and-stick. A popular combination is using products such as Grace Perm-a-Barrier or Bakor Blueskin over nonpaper faced gypsum sheathing. This combination requires a specific primer to bond with the moisture-resistant fibers of the sheathing. Peel-and-stick comes in widths from 4 to 36 inches (100–910 mm); the narrower widths are used to seal joints and for flashing.

In addition to stopping water, peel-and-stick is an air barrier and usually a vapor retarder, making placement potentially problematic, depending on the location of the thermal insulation and the climate. Bakor has introduced a peel-and-stick called Blueskin Breather that is vapor permeable.

2.4.6 FLUID APPLIED MEMBRANES

A similar type of barrier can be sprayed, brushed, or troweled in place. A peel-and-stick membrane or an embedded reinforcing mat is used to bridge transitions. Waterproofing coatings that do not include reinforcement to bridge cracks are not durable enough for exterior wall applications. There is concern that even some of the reinforced systems may not be able to withstand the differential movement of the substrate. Some of the fluid applied systems, such as Bakor's Air-Bloc and Sto Guard by Sto Corporation, are vapor permeable.

2.4.7 SHEATHING MATERIALS

Several sheathing materials are relatively impervious to water, including plywood and oriented strand board (OSB), although their moisture resistance changes as they take on water. OSB, in general, takes on more water than plywood. The non-paper-faced gypsum sheathings are more impervious to water than the paper-faced sheathings. Fiber-faced Dens-Glass Gold was developed by Georgia-Pacific to give a stronger, more waterproof, reinforced face on which to apply EIFS. Fiberock by CGC and Weatherock by USGC are gypsum fiber composites. Although superior to exterior gypsum sheathing, nonpaper-faced gypsum sheathings are a marginal water barrier. With all sheathing materials, water entry is most likely to occur at the joints. Many tapes are available. While these may be adequate to stop air, stopping water running down the face of the sheathing is more difficult. The cost of adding a water barrier over sheathing is inexpensive insurance against water penetration.

2.4.8 RIGID AND FOAMED-IN-PLACE INSULATION

Insulation boards of impervious plastics or those faced with foil act as water barriers. Again the problem is at the joints. Some board insulations shrink with aging, exacerbating the problem. Shiplapped, extruded polystyrene, with all butt edges taped, will stop water better than insulation with untaped square edges. Dow Styrofoam manufactures boards with tongue-and-groove joints on all four edges. Some foamed-in-place insulations stop the majority of water, although trimming off the cured surface may allow more water to enter. Two-pound, and denser, spray polyurethane foam will resist water absorbtion even when trimmed. See the section on insulation in Chapter 3.

2.4.9 PAINTS AND SEALERS

New paints and sealers that stop water frequently come on the market. Many are very good water barriers, provided the substrate never moves, or they never have to bridge transitions. Applied in liquid form, they are meant to adhere fully to the surface. Movement at a crack in the substrate creates extreme stress within the bonded paint or sealer. An unbonded elastomeric coating sample may stretch many times its width, as frequently demonstrated in advertisements for these products. But 300 percent elongation may not be enough when fully bonded. These are good products with specific applications—they are just not suitable for stopping water in the long term on a substrate that moves. Any coating designed to keep out water will eventually fail, or water will enter the wall from another location such as a window. If the coating is not vapor-permeable, the moisture behind the coating will be trapped (see Figures 2.8 and 2.9). Some sealers, such as silanes and siloxanes, are highly permeable.

2.4.10 DRAINAGE MATS

Drainage can be greatly enhanced by the addition of a drainage mat, a three-dimensional, tangled net of filament, which is attached to the water barrier. Most drainage mats are ¼ inch (6 mm) thick and 39 inches (1 meter) wide. The mats are stapled or nailed to the substrate with butt joints. Some mats come bonded to building paper. The mat is generally 3 inches (75 mm) narrower than the building paper, to allow for lapping of the paper. Senergy's Drainage Wrap is a plastic three-dimensional drainage mat bonded to 60-minute building paper. Drainage Wrap by Finestone is a similar product.

2.5 INSTALLATION

Water barriers should be lapped, or "shingled," with each other and with flashings to ensure that all interstitial water drains to the exterior of the wall. This is true for adhesive as well as nonadhesive products. Vertical laps of nonadhesive barriers should be sealed with a tape recommended by the manufacturer. There is more information on tapes in Chapter 3, "Air Barrier Systems."

The water barrier will be penetrated by fasteners attaching the barrier and other components. Additional sealing may be required around the penetrations. This is dependent on the barrier (some thicker asphaltic barriers claim to self-seal), the size of the penetration (staples versus large anchors), and the exposure. Water droplets can find a circuitous route into the smallest of openings. Water tightness at openings in this barrier, such as windows, is particularly critical.

The flashings and sealants that keep buildings watertight are part of water management systems. While it is impossible to eliminate sealants, reliance on these materials should be minimized. Chapter 4 covers sealants in more detail.

As with all components, be aware of what else the water barrier is stopping. It is critical to understand its ability to retard vapor and determine if this will cause a problem. If the water barrier is also a vapor retarder, it must be on the "warm side" of the thermal insulation to minimize condensation. All materials to the exterior of the water barrier must be able to withstand continual wetting, including claddings, insulation in the drainage cavity, and the metal fasteners attaching the cladding.

2.6 FLASHINGS

Designers often try to conceal flashings. If they understood the havoc that ensues when a wall flashing is terminated before it reaches the outside or a cap flashing extends down the face of the wall only a short distance or is omitted entirely, this practice would end. Better to spend time designing an aesthetically acceptable flashing profile than worry about replacing the cladding and perhaps other components down the road. Good design and durability of the flashing is important, as it is often costly and sometimes not possible to retrofit. Concealed flashing must last as long as the exterior wall. When the flashing is omitted, such as at the top of a parapet wall, an owner may retrofit the wall with a cap flashing after the building is complete, without the designer's consideration of aesthetics (see Figures 2.12 and 2.13).

Flashing is required at:

- Changes in the vertical plane of the cladding
- Penetrations or openings in the exterior wall, such as windows, doors, vents, hose bibs, light fixtures, and signage
- All horizontal interruptions through the cladding, such as a shelf angle for brick veneer

- The roof edge
- The top of a parapet wall
- Any termination of the water barrier

Checking each wall section for nonvertical surfaces, discontinuity in the water barrier, and terminations of cladding panels will point out many of the areas that require flashing. A second check of the exterior wall in plan will point out where the flashing extends around corners or will have to be lapped onto itself in long runs.

The *Architectural Sheet Metal Manual* (Sheet Metal and Air Conditioning Contractor's National Association, SMACNA) is an excellent reference for all types of metal flashing.[8] Flashings that terminate on the exterior of the building should be corrosive-resistant metal and should end in a drip. Some flashings require an adjustable depth to accommodate construction tolerances while maintaining a consistent edge at the outside. An example is the two-part shelf-angle flashing detailed in Figure 6.13. Others, used primarily on roofs, have a removable component so that the embedded flashing does not have to be replaced when the roof is replaced. Peel-and-stick or reinforced plastics can be used for flashings that are not exposed to the exterior or subject to wear and tear during construction and the life of the wall. Water barrier manufacturers, such as Dupont, have proprietary flashings; Dupont's FlexWrap and StraightFlash work as a system with Tyvek.

If surface attachment of the flashing is absolutely necessary, the surface mounted reglet, or termination bar, should be designed for easy installion of the sealant. Flashing attachments should be designed to withstand wind loads—wind uplift can tear the metal coping off a building. Continuous cleats eliminate exposed fasteners, a potential leakage site. Another difficulty, and an often overlooked area, is designing the corners, joints, and terminations of the flashing. All such transitions should be welded, soldered, or sealed, including lapped joints. Flashing should always slope to the exterior. Preformed or fabricated corners and end dams should be used when possible.

Horizontal and vertical joints of metal flashing can be sealed in several ways. SMACNA's *Architectural Sheet Metal Manual* details a variety of metal locks and seams for lapped and butt joints. Another method of joining two pieces of metal flashing is to position a 1-inch (25 mm) strip of bond-breaker tape at both ends of the metal flashing. A peel-and-stick splice is then adhered for 3 to 4 inches (75–100 mm) on each side of the flashing. Leaving a ¼-inch (6 mm) gap between the two pieces of metal flashing, in combination with the bond-breaker tape, will allow expansion and contraction of the metal flashing while the peel-and-stick keeps the water out. If the joint is exposed, it can be covered with a metal plate. Lapped horizontal joints should be fully adhered with mastic sealant. Horizontal flashings should never be penetrated—an obvious but often disregarded caution. Metals should be designed in a gauge thick enough to prevent "oil canning" when visible. Flashings must be compatible with each other, their fasteners, and with the substrate.

2.6.1 FLASHING PROBLEMS

Flashings frequently fail to keep water out of the wall. This is another area where design time, insistence on an adequate construction budget, and careful construction observation will pay off in the long run. Some of the more common problems are:

 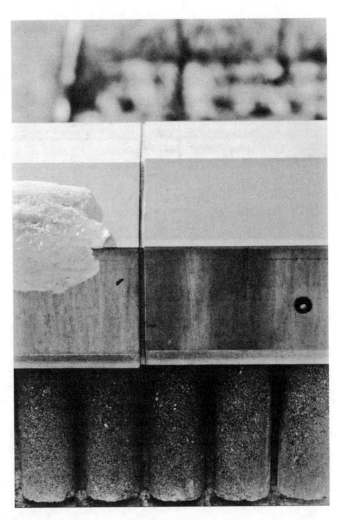

FIGURES 2.12, 2.13 The top of this parapet wall (Figure 2.12) was detailed by the architect with a decorative concrete block course. Aesthetically interesting, it leaked considerably. The owners retrofitted the metal flashing (Figure 2.13), which did a good job of keeping out the water, but the aesthetic was changed. Photos by G. Russell Heliker.

- *Discontinuous flashings:* Continuity should be detailed, specified, and carefully checked during construction. Horizontal and vertical joints and all other transitions should be detailed on the drawings. Specify a maximum length (to accommodate expansions and contraction) and a minimum length (to minimize the number of joints). Flashings frequently stop at either side of corners. A three-dimensional drawing can delineate how the flashing, and any counter-flashing, turns the corner (see Figure 2.16).

- *Lack of end dams at flashing terminations:* End dams are required with sill flashing, when one cladding system joins another, and at vertical expansion joints. Flexible flashings can be continuous through vertical expansion joints if there is enough slack in the flashing to accommodate the movement of the joint.

- *Punctured flashing:* Metal flashings can be easily punctured and flexible flashings more so. The flashing installation on a window shelf-angle lintel may be very good, but if the window installer shoots a powder-driven fastener through it when installing the head can, watertightness is compromised. Flexible flashings should be protected from bolt heads and other protruding objects.

- *Poor drainage:* In the best of worlds, all flashings would slope. This minimizes the chance that water will travel horizontally, inevitably finding the less watertight, horizontal lap.
- *Inadequate attachment:* Flashings high on a building are subjected to excessive wind loads. The fastening must consider these loads, along with the problems created by fastening directly through the face of the flashing. Continuous cleats can better resist wind uplift.

Constructability and the importance of good installation are sometimes overlooked in flashing design. Complicated areas requiring flashing should be detailed in a three-dimensional drawing. If it cannot be drawn, the contractor will have problems fabricating it. SMACNA's *Architectural Sheet Metal Manual* should be consulted for all metal flashing concerns. Installation should not be left to the cladding trades. A flashing contractor who understands the importance of continuity and good installation will do a better job.

FIGURES 2.14, 2.15 These two buildings in Krakow, Poland, show careful flashing of sills. While both may be remedial, they complement the appearance. The sills, even at the ocular window, of this stuccoed masonry building (Figure 2.14) are flashed in metal. In Figure 2.15, the layers of the wood windowsill have been carefully flashed, with small up-stands or dams at the ends. Photos by Linda Brock.

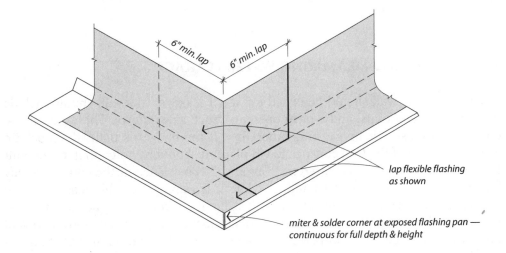

FIGURE 2.16 Three-dimensional drawings are necessary to show how flashings and other barriers turn corners. This drawing shows flexible flashing lapping a metal flashing pan to be installed on a brick-veneer shelf angle. Not shown is how the water barrier would turn the corner.

6" min. lap   6" min. lap

lap flexible flashing as shown

miter & solder corner at exposed flashing pan — continuous for full depth & height

TABLE 2.3 Flashing Materials

Metal Flashing Materials	Comments	Expansion Coefficient
Aluminum	• Textured and prepainted finishes are available • Anodized finishes are not always uniform • Avoid contact with other metals and concrete or mortar unless separated with a bituminous layer • Corrosion resistant • Does not stain adjacent surfaces • Cannot be soldered • Factory weld	.0000129
Copper	• Color changes from reddish brown to brown to green patina, depending on atmosphere; in dry climates green may not be achieved • Corrosion resistant • Easy to work in the field • Can stain adjacent surfaces • Use lead-coated copper to avoid staining • Avoid contact with noncompatible metals • May be used in contact with cementitious materials	.0000094
Stainless steel	• Different finishes and colors available • Excellent corrosion resistance • Self-cleaning, low maintenance • Does not stain adjacent surfaces • Very durable • Superior resistance to metal fatigue • May be used in contact with cementitious materials	.0000096
Terne-coated stainless	• Weathers to a uniform dark grey • Highly resistant to corrosion in industrial, chemical, and marine environments • Does not stain adjacent surfaces • May be used in contact with cementitious materials	.0000097
Galvanized steel	• Can be factory painted • Economical • Durability dependent on type and weight of zinc coating • Stain resistant • Zinc coating must be repaired when damaged, cut, or drilled • Do not use in contact with copper, redwood, or red cedar unless separated with a bituminous layer • Check with manufacturer of fire retardant or preservation treated wood for compatibility • Do not use in severely corrosive atmospheres	.0000067

Source: Adapted from SMACNA, *Architectural Sheet Metal Manual*, B1–B8.

2.7 TESTING AND MEASURING WATER LEAKAGE

Mock-ups of the wall should be tested for water leakage. The wall should include flashings, sealant joints, and typical openings, such as windows. The walls can be constructed on-site or in a testing laboratory. If the budget is tight, the mock-up can be a section of the wall constructed in place. It should be noted that a wall built for inspection may be very different from a wall constructed at the end of the day on the twentieth floor of the building while it is raining. For this reason on-site supervision and continued testing is critical. Joints at tranitions and openings, in particular, should be tested. At a minimum, on smaller projects, a window and wall interface should be tested in-place. The window may be watertight, but that says nothing about the joint between the window frame and the wall.

Testing for water ingress includes both static and dynamic methods. Mock-ups may be two stories or more in height and several feet in width depending on the testing facilities. It may be prudent to include a short section of the roof to ensure that the roof and wall interface is watertight. American Society for Testing and Materials (ASTM) Standard E1105 tests water penetration with uniform or cyclic static air pressure in the field. ASTM Standard E331 tests water penetration in the laboratory with uniform static air pressure.

Water ingress is more difficult to measure after construction of the interior is complete, although if a leak is copious, it may be measurable by strategically placed buckets. Much can be learned from observing a building. Some of the undesirable effects, such as efflorescence and mold, are very good indicators of moisture problems; without water, there is no mold, staining, organic growth, or efflorescence beyond the expected "building bloom." Water entering through joints, such as at the interface of a window and a wall, can be measured using a water spray rack (ASTM E331) or, more simply, by aiming a hose at the suspected site of the leak and observing the interior, remembering that water will often travel a great distance before it daylights. American Architectural Manufacturers Association (AAMA) 501.2 "Field Check for Metal Storefronts, Curtain Walls, and Sloped Glazing Systems for Water Leakage" is a calibrated but still inexpensive test.

Simple tests can be done in the office. For an empirical test of the watertightness of a water barrier, fill a jar with water, cover it with the barrier, secure it with tape or by other means, and invert it over a container. While this may not provide a definitive answer, and certainly it is not scientific, it lets you compare two materials. You can then check with the manufacturer to see if their data confirms your assessment. Figure 2.17 shows a simple method of comparing the absorption of different materials.

Using a moisture meter during construction can show if excess moisture is trapped in the wall. DC-resistance or dielectric meters will provide a good estimate of the moisture in wood. They can be used for lumber as well as plywood and OSB. The meter readings need to be corrected for the wood temperature and species. The moisture content of wood used in wall construction should be no higher than 19 percent, as it begins to decay at around 28–30 percent. The moisture in studs should be measured at approximately 12 inches and 48 inches (300 and 1220 mm) from the floor and at a minimum of two studs per exterior wall. On multistory construction, the lower floors are usually the wettest. Enclosing a wet wood frame, or any wet component, with nonpermeable layers is asking for problems.

FIGURE 2.17 A simple test using a plastic tube adhered to the surface with soft putty provides quantitative information on how fast a material will absorb water. For more information about this water absorption test, see: Kim Basham and John Meredith, "Measuring Water Penetration," *Masonry Construction Magazine* (November 1995): 539. Photo by G. Russell Heliker.

2.8 QUICK NOTES: WATER INGRESS

- Claddings and finishes and windows and doors will leak at some point.
- Water will always find the way into a wall through the smallest of openings but has more difficulty finding a way out.
- Sheet water barriers should be lapped or shingled with each other and with the flashing.
- Vertical laps should be sealed.
- Wall flashings should be metal and extend to the exterior with a drip edge.
- Methods of controlling water include the following:
    Face-sealed barrier walls
    Internal drainage plane walls
    Drainage cavity walls
    Pressure-equalized rain-screen walls
    Hybrid walls, which include face-sealed barrier panels with pressure-equalized (PE) joints, drained, or sealed joints
- Moisture trapped in the wall during construction will cause problems later, particularly if it is between components with low permeability.
- This book does not recommend sheathing, board insulations, or nonreinforced membranes and coatings as water barriers.

- Although a water barrier is forgiving of minor holes, such as those made with staples, they should be minimized whenever possible or sealed.
- The geometry of the exterior wall can help deter water and shed snow.
- Overhangs and drip edges are always a good idea.
- No water from the roof, parapet, or ground should be directed to the exterior wall.
- The way to avoid mold and mildew is to keep water out of the wall.

Finally, as noted by the contractor and author Michael Kubal, "As much as 90 percent of all water intrusion problems occur within 1 percent of the total building or structure exterior surface area.... [And] approximately 99 percent of waterproofing leaks are attributable to causes other than material or system failures."[9] In other words, the best way to avoid water entry problems is with good design, particularly at the joints at interfaces of components and systems.

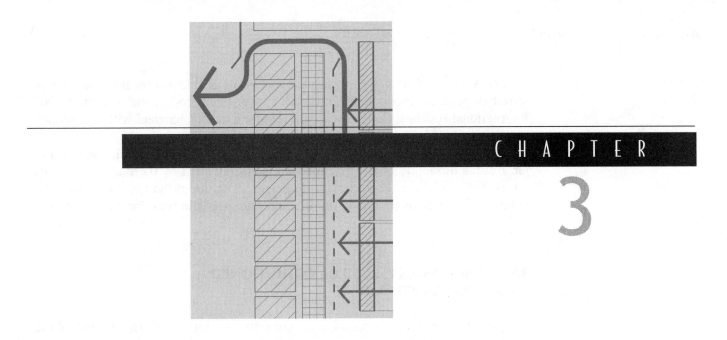

Air Barrier Systems, Vapor Retarders, and Insulation

3.1 STOPPING AIR AND CONTROLLING THERMAL AND VAPOR TRANSFER

Until the middle of the twentieth century exterior walls "leaked" air and had little insulation. Water vapor and warm or cool air easily moved from the inside to the outside and vice versa in wood framed walls. Many refer to this period as the problem-free days, but they were also the days of drafty interiors and substantial energy losses. Masonry walls had their own set of problems. While more airtight than wood framing, they still leaked, as there was little other than thickness to slow air movement. The masonry mass offered little thermal resistance; and while the thermal lag was helpful in cooling climates, it was less useful in heating climates, especially with air moving through the wall. (Advertisements for stuccoing over brick walls from the early twentieth century promised to eliminate drafts in a house.)

As higher levels of insulation were added to walls, condensation became a problem. In 1938, Professor F. B. Rowley of the University of Minnesota published a paper promoting the use of vapor barriers to eliminate condensation in walls.[1] Problems with wet insulation were becoming more common, and stopping the diffusion of vapor was deemed the solution. It took 30 years before it was clearly understood that diffusion is only a small part of the problem—most vapor is transferred through air movement. Outside Canada, many codes, including the 2003 International Building Code (IBC), still require a "vapor barrier" with no mention of an air barrier.

Comfort and energy savings are the primary reasons for controlling heat transfer. But the durability of the exterior wall is also affected by thermal changes and ultraviolet (UV) light. Protecting components from direct light and extreme temperature fluctuations increases the life and enhances the function of the exterior wall.

3.2 AIR MOVEMENT: LOSS OF CONDITIONED AND VAPOR-LADEN AIR

Air pressure differentials produce air currents; the most obvious is wind. Wind exerts a positive pressure on the windward side, resulting in infiltration of the interior, and a negative pressure on the leeward side, resulting in exfiltration of the interior. Gusting winds cause higher cyclic pressures. The natural phenomenon caused by warm air rising in a building is called the chimney or stack effect. In heating climates, the interior pressure increases at the upper levels as the warm air rises, causing cooler air to be drawn in at the lower levels. In cooling climates, with air-conditioned interiors, this effect is reversed. Positive and negative pressures are created also by mechanical ventilation systems. Fans may be used to pressurize a high-rise building to overcome the stack effect. Generally, negative pressure is desired in heating climates and positive pressure in cooling climates. Spaces with high relative humidity levels, such as swimming pools, require negative pressurization to stop vapor-laden air from moving through the wall. A poorly designed mechanical ventilation system can add to the problems instead of enhancing the wall's function. As so aptly stated by building scientist Joe Lstiburek, "to control the air, you must first enclose it. When you enclose the air, you must then control the mechanical system."[2] And it has to be controlled for the life of the building.

FIGURE 3.1 Airflow through the exterior wall is caused by one of three forces that create pressure differentials. Air movement only occurs if there is an opening or gap in the wall. Illustration from R. L. Quirouette, *Building Practice Note: The Difference Between a Vapour Barrier and an Air Barrier*, BPN 54 (Ottawa, Ont.: Division of Building Research, National Research Council of Canada, 1985. All rights reserved. Illustration reproduced with the consent of the National Research Council of Canada.

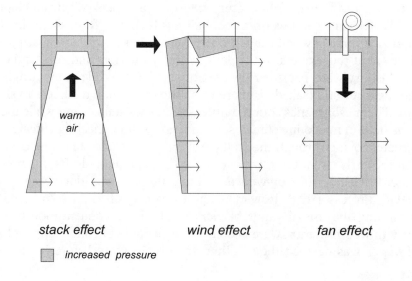

warm air

stack effect   wind effect   fan effect

increased pressure

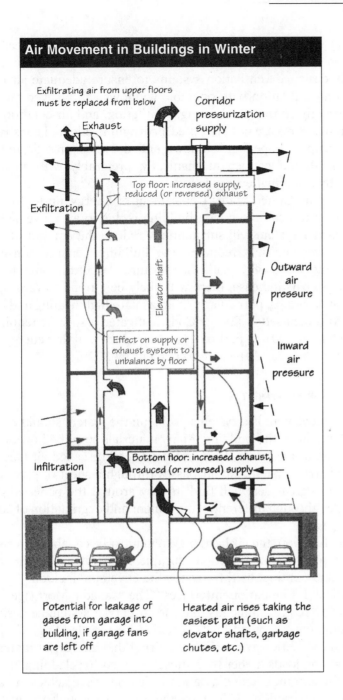

Air Movement in Buildings in Winter

Exfiltrating air from upper floors must be replaced from below

Corridor pressurization supply

Exhaust

Top floor: increased supply, reduced (or reversed) exhaust

Exfiltration

Elevator shaft

Outward air pressure

Effect on supply or exhaust system: to unbalance by floor

Inward air pressure

Bottom floor: increased exhaust, reduced (or reversed) supply

Infiltration

Potential for leakage of gases from garage into building, if garage fans are left off

Heated air rises taking the easiest path (such as elevator shafts, garbage chutes, etc.)

FIGURE 3.2 This diagram shows the complexities of air movement during the winter in a building located in a heating climate. Canada Mortgage and Housing Corporation (CMHC), *Healthy High-Rise.* All rights reserved. Illustration reproduced with the consent of Canada Mortgage and Housing Corporation, Ottawa, Ontario. All other uses and reproductions of this material are expressly prohibited.

Air currents carry water, water vapor, and conditioned air (heated and cooled); pollutants and sound are transported by air. Air barriers, more correctly termed air barrier systems, attempt to stop the flow of air through the wall. However, the movement of air through a wall has positive as well as detrimental effects. Air circulation is essential to our well being—buildings are required by code to bring in "make-up," or fresh, air. In heating climates, the movement of air through the drafty walls of the past helped to keep the wall dry. (It has been noted that walls are relatively moisture free if the construction leaks a lot of air or is very airtight.)[3] In cooling climates, airflow was the air conditioning.

Some are concerned that our buildings are too "airtight," that the air barrier system works too well. Commercial and institutional buildings with "sealed" envelopes that rely solely on mechanical ventilation, and well-sealed residential buildings often generate this concern. Exterior walls with no operable windows need carefully designed ventilation systems to ensure adequate air changes in all spaces. (Natural ventilation with operable windows can be even more difficult to implement properly so that the heating, ventilating, and air-conditioning (HVAC) system design pressures are not disrupted.) Airtight residential construction should not rely on occupants opening windows and doors to provide the required air exchange. This should happen mechanically, preferably with an air-to-air heat exchanger, so that minimal energy is lost.

According to the United States Department of Energy, up to 40 percent of the energy consumed to heat and cool a building is due to air movement. A properly installed air barrier system will substantially reduce the amount of air leakage of the building envelope, thus reducing the building's energy consumption. The National Building Code of Canada has required a continuous air barrier since 1985. As energy costs increase, there will likely be a trend toward tighter air barriers in the United States, particularly in areas with high heating and cooling loads. The State of Massachusetts's Energy Code instigated a specific requirement for an air barrier system in 2001 as part of a goal to reduce building energy consumption by 25 percent by the year 2010 and 50 percent by 2020.

3.2.1 STOPPING AIR MOVEMENT

Controlling air movement is a systems problem; the system should essentially form a balloon around the entire building. Many materials stop the flow of air; any leakage will be found at the joints. These materials can be called air barriers, but they are not an air barrier system. No air passes through a sheet of plywood or a stone panel; however, a great deal will find its way around the panel edges. Gaps will continue to open through differential movement and degradation of components as the building ages.

For optimal function, the air barrier system must be capable of resisting all wind loads, positive pressure, and suction; durable or maintainable for the life of the exterior wall; and continuous throughout the envelope, including at the wall and roof and wall and foundation interfaces. The Canada Mortgage and Housing Corporation (CMHC) recommends that the air barrier system be designed to withstand, at a minimum, the wind loads specified for the cladding. They further suggest that designers "seriously consider requiring that air barrier materials be capable of withstanding loads higher than those required for cladding."[4]

Although the automobile and aviation industries have achieved "airtight" construction, severe restriction of the movement of air through the wall rather than strict airtightness is a more obtainable goal for buildings. Building codes, energy codes, and trade association publications provide recommendations for maximum air leakage. The maximum recommended by the 1995 National Building Code of Canada is dependent on the relative humidity (RH) of the interior. The maximum is 0.1 L/(s·m^2) at 75 Pa air pressure differences when the interior RH is between 27 and 55 percent. If the RH is less than 27 percent, it increases to 0.15 and decreases to 0.05 with RH greater than 55 percent. The maximum air leakage rate of the air barrier material is 0.02 L/(s·m^2). The American Architectural Manufacturers Association has several recommendations for curtain walls, depending on the system. Their general recommendation suggests a maximum leakage rate of 0.3 L/(s·m²) at an air pressure difference of 75 Pa.[5] Many energy codes do not specify a maximum air leakage. Instead, they are descriptive, listing areas to be carefully sealed. The importance of recognizing the control of air movement as a systems problem cannot be overestimated. Words such as "continuous" or "complete" and "carefully seal" do not guarantee a continuous air barrier. The system needs to be detailed, specified, and then tested.

3.2.2 THE DIFFERENCE BETWEEN AN AIR BARRIER AND A VAPOR RETARDER

The terms *air barrier* and *vapor barrier* are often interchanged, perplexing the best of designers. To clarify the subject, the National Research Council of Canada published "The Difference Between a Vapour Barrier and an Air Barrier" in 1985.[6] Four years later, a similar article, "What You Ought to Know About Air Barriers and Vapor Barriers," was published in *Form and Function*.[7] Yet there is still confusion over the terms. A vapor retarder slows vapor flow by diffusion. A small crack here and there is less important than with an air barrier system. Put another way, a 95 percent complete vapor retarder will stop 95 percent of the vapor from diffusing through the wall. By contrast, an air barrier system stops the movement of air, which in turn stops the transfer of vapor-laden air leakage, by some accounts up to 98 percent of the total vapor transfer.[8] (The example in Figure 3.3 shows a 1:90 ratio.) To stop air movement, the air barrier system must be complete throughout the entire envelope, with a minimum of cracks or openings.

The problem of permeability was addressed in Canada in the 1950s with standards that later were referenced in the National Building Code. Vapor barriers were to have a permeance of less than .75 perm, while the permeance of breather-type weather resistant barriers—usually building paper—was to be greater than 3–5 perms. By the 1960s, Canadian researchers had determined that air leakage,

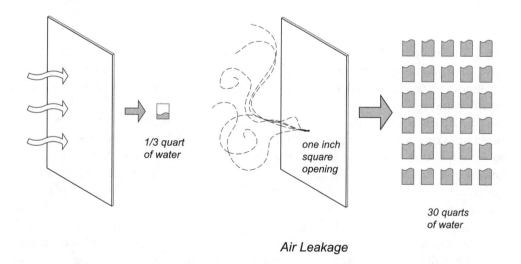

Air Leakage

FIGURE 3.3 Considerably more vapor is transported by air movement than by diffusion though a material. This example from the *Builder's Guide to Mixed Climates* notes that in most cold climates over an entire heating season, one-third of a quart of water can be collected by diffusion through a 4 × 8 sheet of gypsum board without a vapor diffusion retarder, whereas 30 quarts of water can be collected through air leakage that passes through a 1-inch-square hole. It is assumed that the interior temperature is 70°F with 40% relative humidity (RH). Illustration reproduced courtesy of Joseph Lstiburek.

Air Barrier or Vapor Retarder? Airtight or Breathable?

These terms have caused more confusion in understanding the function of the wall than perhaps any others. The key points to remember are as follows.

- Air carries heated and cooled air *and* water vapor.

- Vapor retarders stop water vapor that is transferred by *diffusion.*

- Much more water vapor passes through a wall through air leakage than by diffusion.

- Some materials function as both air barriers and vapor retarders.

- Stopping air requires a system that is continuous throughout the envelope, whereas vapor diffusion is more forgiving of small openings and gaps at transitions.

- A single sheet of material may stop air and be called an air barrier. But unless it is structurally supported and carefully taped and sealed to form a continuous barrier, it is not an *air barrier system.*

- When the term *breathable* is used it usually refers to the capacity of the wall to absorb and then release moisture, tempering the interior environment. It is *not* an indication of air moving through the wall. *Breathable* is sometimes used to define permeability.

not diffusion, was responsible for most vapor migration. To solve the problem, the term *continuous vapor barrier* was used.[9] In reality, stopping vapor migration through the wall focused on a single sheet of polyethylene, which is a vapor retarder and not necessarily an air barrier system.[10]

The oil embargo of the 1970s spurred the United States to cut energy usage. Building codes began to require a barrier to minimize the flow of air from the inside to the outside in colder climates to reduce the heat loss in residential construction. Unfortunately, this was frequently called a vapor barrier. The concept of using a single component as an air and vapor barrier gave rise to the popularity of polyethylene serving in both capacities, just as it was in Canada. It was not until much later that questions were asked, such as: does polyethylene perform well as part of an air barrier system? Is a very low-permeance vapor retarder always desirable on the interior of a wall? Much of this experimentation was happening in Canada, which can be primarily classified as a heating climate. Even so, the system proved problematic in some areas. Worse yet, these ideas were adopted in the United States, where there was greater potential for adverse results in mixed or cooling climates. If a vapor retarder was even warranted, using polyethylene in a cooling climate and many mixed climates put it on the wrong side of the wall.

3.2.3 Air Barrier Systems and Their Placement

The water barrier influences the choice of air barrier systems. Table 3.1 shows which systems are commonly used, depending on the selection of the water barrier and the climate.

Unlike a vapor retarder, the air barrier (if it is vapor permeable) can be placed anywhere to the inside of the drainage cavity (or plane), and redundancy is not a problem. Some argue that the air barrier should be to the exterior of the wall, as the number of penetrations will be fewer. Others argue for the interior, as it conceivably can be repaired or replaced, and it is protected from thermal extremes.

The following systems, listed in order of approximate cost, are commonly used as air barrier systems in walls. The cost takes into consideration the cost reduction with dual functions. For example, building wrap (BW) is also a water barrier, so the effective cost is only the taping and sealing of the joints.

- *Polyethylene, sealed.* Polyethylene is also a vapor retarder, so it should be used only in heating climates, and even here with caution. The sheets must be lapped one stud space and sealed. A minimum thickness of 6 mil is recommended, although the thicker membrane is more difficult to seal than thinner membranes.[11] All penetrations, including electrical junction boxes and window and doors, must be sealed to provide a continuous barrier. The barrier must be continuous across the floor structure, which can be a problem as the line of the air barrier moves from the interior of the wall to the exterior of the floor structure. Another type of air barrier material can be used at these difficult transitions. For example, the rim joists, in light-frame wood structures, can be wrapped at the exterior with a vapor permeable building wrap sealed to the polyethylene. Polyethylene is generally sealed with an acoustical caulking.

  Structurally supporting the film, by sandwiching it between rigid components, provides the highest level of airtightness but adds cost. Ronald Brand feels that "under no circumstances should [unsupported] polyethylene film be expected to serve as an air barrier. Its useful life is uncertain, it is not

TABLE 3.1 Common Air Barrier Systems

Water Barrier	Air Barrier Systems	Climate
Building paper and felt	• Polyethylene, sealed	Heating
	• Airtight drywall approach (ADA) or simple caulk and seal (SCS)	All climates
	• Spray polyurethane foam	All climates
Building wrap	• Building wrap, taped and supported	All climates
	• Polyethylene, sealed and supported	Heating
	• ADA or SCS	All climates
	• Spray polyurethane foam	All climates
Peel-and-stick membrane	• Peel-and-stick is an air barrier, but it must be sealed at all openings and transitions.	Insulation must be to the cold side.
Asphaltic sheet membrane and fluid applied membrane	• The membrane may be an air barrier, but it must be sealed at all openings and transitions.	Insulation must be to the cold side.

strong enough to withstand wind loads; it cannot be sealed to the structural members that must penetrate it, and it cannot be made to adhere to other parts of the structure. Even acoustical caulkings extend and extrude like bubble gum when subject to moderate wind pressure."[12]

- *Building wrap, taped.* Like polyethylene or any other flexible sheets, BWs must be taped at all transitions and openings, including windows, doors, and exterior electrical and mechanical penetrations. For the highest level of airtightness, they must be structurally supported, which is an added cost. At minimum, the support should be vertical spacers or strapping at 16 inches (400 mm) on center. If the furring strips cover the fasteners that attach the building wrap, it will perform better. Self-draining building wrap water barriers have a textured surface with small rivulets or channels for water drainage. These corrugated water barriers are harder to seal with tape, reducing their effectiveness as air barriers.

  Acting as a water barrier, a building wrap allows for construction to be quickly "closed in." All holes and tears must be sealed before covering the building wrap with cladding. As it is not a vapor retarder, it is suitable for all climates.

- *Airtight drywall approach (ADA).* A continuous line of airtightness at the interior gypsum board or drywall is achieved with compression seals, gaskets, or sealant installed or applied between the edges of the drywall, the frame, and any openings in the wall. Electrical boxes are sealed with integral airtight gaskets. Joints between framing members, such as the sill plate, the floor sheathing, and the floor joists, are sealed. Transitions at floors, ceilings, interior partitions, and all openings must be carefully detailed to assure that the air barrier system is complete. It relies on careful coordination of trades and continued surveillance to ensure that all seals are installed. Trades are becoming aware of the necessity and more skilled at sealing wood-framing transitions with sealants designed to inhibit airflow, according to Robert Taylor of the American Wood Council. This approach—ADA—is vapor permeable and suitable for all climates.

- *Simple caulk and seal (SCS).* Also called SimplexCS (pronounced "simplex"), this system is similar to ADA except that the sealing is done after the drywall is installed, using a sealant rather than gaskets. Spray polyurethane foam is often used to seal difficult areas. While SCS may not be as effective as ADA, it is simpler, and installation is less disruptive. Vigilance is still required to ensure an airtight application. SCS is vapor permeable and suitable for all climates.

- *Fluid applied membranes.* Some of these membranes are a water barrier but vapor permeable. Reinforcement is necessary in areas where differential movement might occur.

- *Asphaltic sheet membrane.* These membranes are also water and usually vapor barriers; transitions and laps need to be sealed. The self-adhesive peel-and-stick sheet membranes have an adhesive back, making them easier to seal, although care is still required for their installation. Thermal insulation must be installed to the "cold" side of these membranes unless they are vapor permeable. See Chapter 2 for more information.

- *Spray polyurethane foam (SPF).* Medium-density, closed-cell SPF and ½-pound, open-cell SPF are excellent air barriers as they expand to conform to the substrate. This expansion can be problematic around windows and doors with an

Tyvek, the Gore-Tex of the Building Industry

Building wraps, of which the best known is the SBPO Tyvek, work on the same principle as the fabric Gore-Tex. While Gore-Tex stops the wind and water, it lets water vapor, created by our bodies, escape through the fabric. Robert Gore, the coinventor of Gore-Tex, got the inspiration from a polymer for insulating wires from moisture, developed by his father, a chemical engineer with Dupont. Gore bonded the stretched polymer to cotton, creating Gore-Tex. It took a while to perfect the fabric—less-than-satisfied customers referred to earlier versions of the fabric as "pour-tex." Gore-Tex is now synonymous with keeping dry—from both the outside (water) and the inside (vapor). The secret with Gore-Tex, as with Tyvek, is in the size of the pores. A Gore-Tex pore is 700 times larger than a water vapor molecule, but it is thousands of times smaller than a drop of water.[1]

Tyvek has gone beyond providing a "Gore-Tex" wrap for our houses. It is favored by some artists as a painting surface; it is the indestructible material of many mailing envelopes; and it has even made its way into clothing, in the form of the Tyvek windbreakers handed out after marathons.

---

1. Steven Threndyle, "Six Degrees and Precipitation," *Living West* (November 1994): 30–31.

inexperienced installer. The ½-pound SPF expands to fill the space but exerts less pressure. Sheet membranes can be used to bridge transitions where the foam is not capable of withstanding the differential movement. Although SPF is costly, it becomes more competitive when also serving as the vapor retarder and water barrier. SPF can be used to seal difficult areas in tandem with another, less costly, air barrier sheet for lower budget projects. See 3.4., "Heat Transfer by Conduction and Radiation," for more information.

Exterior sheathing, sheet metal, and extruded polystyrene boards are good air barriers. They do not have the problems of structurally unsupported building wraps and polyethylene. The problem is sealing these materials at the transitions. They cannot be lapped like flexible sheet materials. They can be sealed but not necessarily at a reasonable cost with a reasonable assurance of long-term success.

- *Taped, rigid board insulation.* First introduced as EASE (External Airtight Sheathing Element),[13] some board insulations or their facings stop the passage of air. (Today EASE refers to a building wrap air barrier that is sandwiched between two layers of fiberboard sheathing.) Board insulations that shrink with aging should not be considered. One exception is Dow Styrofoam tongue-and-groove, extruded polystyrene insulation. XPS is relatively stable, and boards with overlapping joints on all six edges are available, increasing the possibility for airtightness, if carefully taped and sealed at transitions. Because XPS retards vapor, the use of additional insulation may cause problems and should be carefully assessed for the climate.

- *Sheet metal air barriers.* Relatively uncommon, sheet metal air barriers have the advantage of stiffness and provide a lightweight exterior sheathing for metal studs. Detailing is critical, and sealing between panels and at openings can be problematic. This may be a reasonable systems approach for a building that is prefabricated and has considerable repetition in its design.[14]
- *Taped exterior wood product sheathings (WPS).* Sealing the edges of sheathing materials slows down the drying of wet oriented-strand board (OSB) and plywood sheathing. Water swelling tendencies of WPS create a significant hurdle for sealing the edges. Installation recommendations call for a gap between these sheathing materials; this is specified to allow for differential movement, but it is also useful for drying the materials.
- *Taped nonpaper-faced gypsum sheathings.* This sheathing is generally taped with peel-and-stick membrane. It must be carefully primed, and the installation of the peel-and-stick is critical. Gypsum sheathings are often selected because of their high permeance for a sheathing material. Because most peel-and-stick is vapor retardant, the vapor resistance of the "whole" wall should be reviewed in relation to the location of thermal insulation.
- *Cladding panels.* These panels may stop all air movement; but again, the problem is at the joints. The joints will *not* remain airtight for the life of the cladding if they are face sealed.

3.2.4 INSTALLATION OF AIR BARRIER SYSTEMS

Good installation and design of an air barrier system is critical and equal in value to that of the water barrier for the durability of the exterior wall. As discussed above, any small opening in membrane air barriers can quickly turn into a larger opening. Aiming for a completely tight air barrier system will hopefully produce one that meets the expectations or code requirements governing minimum air movement. Each product will have requirements for minimum lapping and recommendations for sealants and tapes. With any tape, sealant, or foam, the following questions should be asked: Will the adhesion be as good in 30 or more years as it was at installation? And if it is not, what are the consequences? Over time air leakage will increase as sealants and tapes fail and materials move differentially, opening cracks in the wall. For a high performance air barrier system, very detailed specifications must be written showing how the air barrier bridges any transitions. On-site inspection along with testing is equally important.

3.2.5 TAPES AND SEALANTS

Most air barrier systems are comprised of sheet materials that rely on sealants, foams, or tapes to bridge the gaps at joints, penetrations, and openings as well as the transitions at floors, windows and doors, the roof, and areas below grade. With each application, the recommendations of both the substrate manufacturer and the air barrier manufacturer should be checked to ensure long-term durability; generally, the wider the tape the better the chance for long-term adhesion.

Some common tapes and sealants are listed below:

- *Tapes for insulation boards, sheathing, building wraps, and polyethylene.* Dow produces an air barrier tape that is compatible with their XPS and polyisocyanurate (ISO) products. Tuck Contractor's Sheathing Tape, the ubiquitous red tape, has been the common choice for taping building wraps.

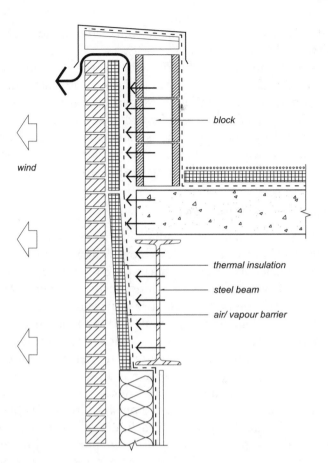

wind

block

thermal insulation

steel beam

air/ vapour barrier

FIGURE 3.4 Even rigid materials need to be attached to the structure, as illustrated in this example from the NRCC's *Building Practice Note: The Difference Between a Vapour Barrier and an Air Barrier.* Unable to stop negative wind pressure—positive wind pressure did not create a problem—the insulation dislodged at the parapet of this new shopping center exterior wall. In this case not only is the air barrier lost but also the thermal insulation. Richard L. Quirouette, *The Air Barrier Defined,* Building Science Insight (Ottawa, Ont.: Institute for Research in Construction, National Research Council of Canada). All rights reserved. Illustration reproduced with the consent of NRCC.

Dupont now manufactures a contractor's tape especially for Tyvek, claiming the "best Tyvek to Tyvek" adhesion. Dupont also manufactures butyl-backed FlexWrap and StraightFlash for sealing around openings and for use as flashing. 3M has developed tapes for sealing polyethylene, building wraps, sheathing, and polystyrene.

- *Peel-and-stick.* Available in 4-inch (100 mm) and wider strips, this is commonly used as a tape on a variety of substrates. A primer is usually required for peel-and-stick. Caution should be exercised, as peel-and-stick is usually a vapor retarder. It is not uncommon to see an extreme amount of peel-and-stick tape used on a permeable air barrier to make the system airtight. Has this crossed the line and become a vapor retarder as well? And is this a problem? If the headers are wrapped in peel-and-stick, how will any moisture escape? Peel-and-stick should not be used anywhere water might accumulate; also it should not be used in copious amounts as a tape for a vapor permeable air barrier, particularly over wood framing. The building envelope firm Morrison Hirshfield recommends that only sills be wrapped with impervious membranes; permeable building wraps or building paper should be used at jambs and heads to promote drying of wet wood frames.[15] Others recommend continuing the peel-and-stick up the jambs to a maximum height of 8 inches (200 mm). Bakor now has a vapor permeable peel-and-stick used primarily as a tape.

- *Acoustical sealants.* These are nonshrinking, nonhardening, nonmigrating, and highly elastic water-based sealants designed for sound control. They adhere well to polyethylene. U.S. Gypsum and Tremco both manufacture acoustical sealants. Different sealants may offer better adhesion between polyethylene and wood or metal.

- *ADA gaskets.* Polyvinyl chloride (PVC) or ethylene-propyline-diene monomer rubber (EPDM) preformed gaskets are installed during framing of the wall and prior to installation of the gypsum board.
- *Integral air-barrier gaskets for mechanical and electrical boxes.* The numerous and difficult to seal penetrations caused by electrical and mechanical equipment are the weak link of many air barrier systems. These proprietary preformed or integral gaskets help make the entire exterior wall airtight.

3.2.6 TESTING AND MEASURING AIR LEAKAGE

Leakage of air and the effectiveness of an air barrier is a systems problem, which means the "whole wall" must be tested. A "blower-door" is a unit that fits over an opening to a building such as a door or part of a building. A calibrated fan blows air into, or sucks air from, the space, creating positive or negative pressure. The volume of airflow and the interior air pressure is measured and computed to determine the air leakage of the air barrier system. ASTM Standard E1827 governs the use of blower doors to determine airtightness. Smoke tracers can help pinpoint the source of leaks, as can infrared thermography. Another on-site, qualitative test is ASTM Standard E1186, which delineates standard practices for detecting air leakage in building envelopes and air barrier systems. Overall air leakage through walls, windows, and doors can be determined on site with ASTM Standard E783.[16]

Laboratory tests include ASTM Standard E283, which is used to measure air leakage through wall assemblies under simulated pressure differentials. As this level of testing may not always be feasible, it is necessary to rely on results from other projects to ensure that a certain level of airtightness is maintained. Air leakage can also be estimated using the crack method.

3.2.7 QUICK NOTES: AIR MOVEMENT

- Air flows through an opening or crack in a wall due to air pressure differentials.
- Wind pressure changes as you move around a building and vertically on a building; the highest pressure will be at the corners and top of the building.
- In addition to wind, ventilation systems affect airflow, as does the natural tendency for warm air to rise (due to the stack effect).
- The design of HVAC systems should be closely coordinated to help control the direction and amount of air leakage.
- Air barriers can be placed anywhere to the inside of the drainage plane or cavity and can be redundant.
- An air barrier may also function as a water barrier, vapor retarder, or thermal insulation. Understanding all of its functions is critical.
- If the air barrier system is also a vapor retarder, it must be on the "warm" side of the wall.
- The air barrier system must be continuous throughout the envelope, from below grade through the exterior wall and roof. It must be well sealed at all connections, adjoining walls, and openings.
- To be effective, the air barrier should be structurally supported or of a rigid material; without this, small holes can become large openings very quickly.

- Building paper and felt and expanded polystyrene (EPS) are *not* considered air barriers.
- A pressure-equalized rain screen (PER) water management system relies on a complete air barrier system to maintain equal pressure between the cavity and the exterior.

3.3 VAPOR TRANSMISSION BY DIFFUSION

The diffusion of vapor is one of the trickiest elements to control. The vapor "drive" may be from the interior to the exterior during one season and then reverse during another season. Human occupation may change the amount of vapor from that expected by the original designer. This "drive," created by vapor pressure differentials, moves vapor through very small pores in the components by the mechanism of diffusion. Diffusion is dependent on both the air temperature and the concentration of water vapor in the air. Vapor retarders prevent the vapor from diffusing to cooler parts of the wall where it may condense. They do not necessarily stop the transmission of vapor by air leakage.

Water vapor comes from many interior sources, including: human metabolism; activities such as cooking, washing, and bathing; plants; manufacturing processes; and HVAC equipment. Residential buildings produce more humidity than commercial and institutional buildings in general. In hot humid climates, the vapor drive is typically from the exterior to the interior. In cold climates, it is the reverse. Understanding the direction of the vapor drive when selecting and placing a vapor retarder is critical. Vapor control for walls enclosing uses such as interior swimming pools, which produce extreme humidity, or museums, where the humidity has to be carefully regulated, should be designed by a specialist in this field.

Unless the humidity is severe, water vapor itself is relatively harmless; the problem occurs when it condenses or increases to the point of promoting corrosion, rot, or mold and mildew growth. (Metal corrosion can occur if the relative humidity is greater than 85–90 percent.)[17] As the amount of vapor in the air increases, the vapor drive increases, along with the risk of condensation. This is exacerbated if the temperature drops, as the cooler the air, the less water vapor it can hold. Full saturation occurs, and condensation as well, when the relative humidity is 100 percent. The temperature at which vapor condenses is called the dew point. However, vapor only condenses on colder surfaces, such as glass, that impede the flow of air. For example, in a heating climate, it does not condense in fiberglass insulation; it diffuses to the cooler surface of the WPS, where it will condense. Materials such as OSB, plywood, wood, gypsum sheathing, and brick may absorb some water if they are not fully saturated. This absorbed moisture is called bound water. When the RH drops, the bound water is released as water vapor.

Since the air barrier system is stopping most of the vapor transmission, why are we worrying about vapor movement by diffusion? A vapor retarder may not even be recommended for some climates. The problem is that all materials stop the diffusion of vapor to some extent, and some layers may act as vapor retarders whether intended or not. The most important task, in considering vapor diffusion, is determining the permeability of *all* components. Peeling paint on exterior cladding or disintegrated gypsum board beneath interior paint may be the result of these materials acting as vapor retarders in the wrong location.

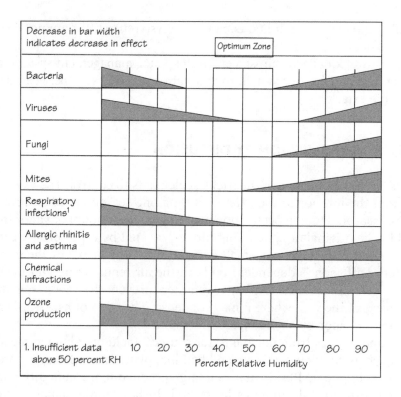

FIGURE 3.5 This graph shows that the optimum relative humidity for health is between 40% and 60%. Source: Canada Mortgage and Housing Corporation (CMHC), *Moisture in Atlantic Housing.* (Ottawa, Ont.: CMHC). All rights reserved. Reproduced with the consent of CMHC. All other uses and reproductions of this material are expressly prohibited.

3.3.1 VAPOR RETARDERS AND THEIR PLACEMENT

The ability of a component to retard the diffusion of vapor is measured in *perms* in the United States and by *permeance* in Canada: the lower the number, the less permeable the material. A material is generally considered a vapor retarder if its permeability is one perm (gr/h·ft²·in·Hg) or less in the United States. In Canada, the permeance of a vapor retarder should be less than 45 (ng/s·m²·Pa), which drops to 15 if the cladding has low vapor permeability. Common vapor retarders include polyethylene and vapor resistant paints. Components less likely to be identified as vapor retarders include some insulations, peel-and-stick, foils, paints, interior finishes, metal or vinyl sidings, and exterior sheathing.

A vapor diffusing retarder can be defined as having at least five times as much resistance as to the negative pressure, or "cool" side, all other components added together. CMHC, in its "best practice" guide for wood frame envelopes, gives a "rule of thumb" that the permeance of the materials to the cold side should be from 10 to 20 times that of the vapor retarder.[18] Unlike air barriers, a redundant vapor retarder, or one in the wrong location, may trap moisture. The resistance to permeance is measured for each material similar to the way in which thermal resistance is measured. *Rep,* the unit of permeability resistance, is the inverse of perms or permeance. Resistance of vapor through a wall and the location of the dew point can be graphed for specific conditions. This formula is useful for understanding the permeance of each component and the effect it may have on the wall's performance. But this gives only a rough approximation of what actually happens in a wall, as the permeability of most materials changes as they take on moisture. The interior and exterior environment produces innumerable combinations of temperatures, air pressures, precipitation, and vapor pressures over time. A more accurate reading can be obtained using one of the dynamic computer models (see Figure 1.7).

Perms, Metric Perms, or SI Permeance?

Much of the building envelope research comes from Canada, where SI units are used. Manufacturers sometimes list SI permeance or, more often, perms. This becomes confusing when the units are omitted or incorrectly identified. Both SI permeance and a perm indicate the permeability of a given material of a specific thickness measured by the passage of water vapor from one side of the material to the other during a specific time period under a specific pressure. One imperial perm equals 57.45 SI permeance. The common use of the term *permeability* means the ability of a material or component to allow the passage of water vapor by diffusion. This book uses this more inclusive definition. Strictly speaking, permeability, that is, ng/(s-m-Pa), refers to water vapor passage per unit thickness of a single material such as wood and should not be used when talking about components with more than one material such as plywood or gypsum sheathing.

Imperial perms are measured by the passage of one grain of water vapor per hour through one square foot of material at a pressure difference of one inch of mercury, gr/h-ft^2-in:Hg).

SI permeance is measured by the passage of one nanogram of water vapor per second through one square meter at a pressure difference of one pascal, ng/(s-m^2-Pa).

The resistance to water vapor is measured in *reps,* the inverse of imperial perms and SI permeance.

Metric perms were a short-lived idea where the area of the imperial perm was expressed in metric units. It is rare to find this unit measurement, but it does show up in older documents and some manufacturers' literature. More confusing is when the term *metric perm* is used for SI permeance to differentiate it from imperial perms.

Often a psychometric chart is used to determine the vapor pressure from the temperature and RH on both sides of the wall. Again, this gives only a rough approximation of what is occurring within the wall over time.

The vapor retarder is placed on the warm side of the insulation. The general rule of thumb is that the retarder may be placed anywhere up to the point where one-third of the thermal resistance of the wall is to the warm side. But herein lies the problem—the "warm" side of the insulation may change over the course of a year or even a day. In cold climates it is understood that the vapor retarder belongs on the interior of the wall. However, this may reverse during hot summer days, particularly if the interior space is air-conditioned. Refrigerant air-conditioning—unlike evaporative air-conditioning—reduces the amount of water vapor in the air, lowering the RH. This is not problematic if the reversal is short in duration and the temperature and vapor pressure differences not severe. In mixed climates, the placement of the vapor retarder presents a real challenge and may create more problems than it solves. The climate in Seattle, Washington, is cool enough during the summer that most residential buildings are not air-conditioned. This reduces the vapor drive in the summer. The temperate, and humid, winter climate does not contribute to large vapor pressure differences. Studies have suggested that a "vapor open" or "pass through" approach—that is, all components are permeable—may be more appropriate for this cool, wet climate.[19] This is good advice only if all the components are permeable, and the interior RH is less than 60 percent.

Some researchers recommend very low permeance vapor retarders be used in only the coldest of climates. Building scientist Joe Lstiburek states that "we may need vapor barriers in Canada, but we don't need them in the Lower 48." His response to code requirements for a vapor barrier on the warm side is: "Warm side when? In January or July?"[20] This is a point that should be seriously considered, particularly with mixed climates. The problems cited revolve around the inability of a wall to dry to the interior, particularly when polyethylene is the vapor retarder.[21] With a more permeable vapor retarder, or none at all, drying may occur in both directions. Some feel that a wall's ability to dry to the interior is limited at best, as interior surfaces are often painted or surfaced in ways that preclude such diffusion. This becomes more of a problem with time as the occupants repaint or resurface interior walls as well as exterior walls. A good air barrier system may increase the relative humidity of the interior, and therefore the vapor drive, in heating climates during the winter unless adequate air exchange is provided. This can be a problem with residential units that rely on the occupants to regulate ventilation, something they may be loathe to do during the cold months. A vapor retarder paint in heating climates will help control condensation within the wall but not on the wall surface. Condensation on the face of the wall or window can only be avoided by increasing the surface temperature of the wall or window or decreasing the interior relative humidity.

3.3.2 MATERIALS COMMONLY USED AS VAPOR RETARDERS

The following are listed in order of approximate cost for the added function of retarding vapor:

> *Vapor resistant paint.* Vapor resistant paints are available in both acrylic and oil bases. They should *not* be used in cooling climates.
>
> *Polyethylene.* Perhaps the most common vapor retarder is polyethylene. It is inexpensive and easy to install if it is not also part of an air barrier system, as it does not need to be continuous. Installed on the interior of the wall, it should *not* be used in cooling climates or most mixed climates.
>
> *Foil or asphaltic, adhered paper facing on fiberglass batt insulation.* As the insulation should be to the cold side of the facing, correct installation is critical. Some fiberglass comes encased in polyethylene, which is generally perforated on one side, so correct installation is also critical.
>
> *Foil backing on gypsum board.* Installed on the interior of the wall, this product should *not* be used in cooling climates and many mixed climates. Foil-faced board insulation can be used as a vapor retarder, depending on its placement in the wall and if other insulations are used.
>
> *Peel-and-stick.* A very good vapor barrier, peel-and-stick is placed on the exterior of buildings, as it also stops water. This may work for cooling climates

but *not* for heating climates unless the thermal insulation is to the exterior of the peel-and-stick material.

Spray polyurethane foam (SPF). Slowing heat transfer and vapor diffusion with a single material can work well, as the vapor retarder is always on the warm side whether the drive is from the interior or the exterior. Because there is some migration of vapor through SPF, a minimum thickness of 1½ inches (40 mm) is recommended.

3.3.3 OTHER MATERIALS WITH VAPOR RESISTANCE

Rigid insulation. Extruded polystyrene has low permeance. Expanded polystyrene is more vapor permeable.

Plywood and OSB. The permeability increases as the sheathing becomes saturated.

Smart Retarders

When the question is asked—"Warm side when? In January or July?"—what is needed is a "smart" retarder. Building scientist Joe Lstiburek cites one material that already performs in this manner. The Kraft paper that faces fiberglass insulation has a permeability of 1; in other words, it is a vapor retarder in a dry cup test. But this rises to 5 perms with the wet cup test. As the paper takes on moisture, it becomes more vapor permeable.[1] Plywood and building paper work in similar ways. Unfortunately, it is not enough of a change to solve the problems of a vapor barrier in the wrong place during some seasons, but it can help with drying.

Smart retarders are used in Europe. One of these retarders is a 2-mil, nylon-based monofilm made by the German company G+H ISOVER. Tests run on the film showed that the permeability ranges from 0.7 to 36 perms, depending on the vapor pressure. When the RH is low, say below 40 percent, the permeability is 1 perm. When it rises to 90 percent, the permeability rises to 36, allowing for passage of vapor and drying.[2] The material had originally been used for sausage casing.

In 2003 this product was introduced to the North American market by CertainTeed Coporation. MemBrain Smart Vapor Retarder is a 2-mil-thick, nylon film intended for use with unfaced insulation in wood- or steel-framed construction assemblies. Its permeance is 1 perm or less when tested with the dry cup method. This rises to 10 or more perms when tested with the wet cup method. As the RH rises, the pores in the material expand, and its permeability increases. This is again useful in that drying may occur in two directions.[3]

---

1. "Air Barriers vs. Vapor Barriers," Building Science Corporation, http://www.buildingscience.com
2. "Smart" Vapor Retarder Can Change Its Permeability," *Energy Design Update* 19, no. 2 (February 1999).
3. Randall K. Straight (CertainTeed Corporation), correspondence with author, August 2004.

Paints and finishes. Finishes not specified as vapor resistant may still have a very high resistance to vapor diffusion. This includes paints used on both the interior and the exterior. Vinyl wallpapers are notorious for causing problems in hot, humid areas. Often an interior designer makes the selection with little knowledge of the problems and no input from the architect. The architect should be very specific about the maximum (or minimum) vapor permeability required of all materials, including those selected primarily for aesthetics by interior designers or others.

Building paper and felt. These materials are resistant to vapor transfer, felt more so than building paper. However, the permeability of building paper increases as it becomes saturated, allowing for drying to both the inside and the outside by diffusion.

3.3.4 VAPOR MANAGEMENT

Vapor management should first focus on the completeness of the air barrier system and elimination of incorrectly placed vapor retarders. As previously discussed, selecting and placing the retarder is more difficult. The U.S. Department of Energy (DOE) recommends placing a vapor retarder on the interior for climates with 2,200 or more heating degree days (HDD) with an assumed base of 65°F. Below 1,900 HDD, the placement and even the use of a vapor retarder is debatable.[22] The requirements for a vapor retarder can be relaxed even in heating climates, according to researchers in Canada. They found that "for the more heavily populated areas of Canada, to control vapor diffusion alone, a water vapor retarder having a permeance of 200–400 ng/s-m^2-Pa (i.e., 3–6 perms) is completely adequate."[23]

This is an area where it is difficult to set hard-and-fast rules. The climate should be evaluated in light of the building occupancy and construction. For firms that work in a defined geographical region, determining the vapor drive in the winter and summer for certain building types needs to be done only once. This information can then be used to make judgments about the components of the wall.

3.3.5 TESTING AND MEASURING VAPOR DIFFUSION

Permeability is a property of the material. Manufacturers should be able to provide the permeability or the vapor resistance of their components. ASTM Standard E96 measures the water vapor transmission of materials such as paper, plastic films, gypsum and wood sheet materials, and plastics. The material is sealed over a cup that contains a desiccant (RH 0%) for the dry cup test or water (RH 100%) for the wet cup test. The surrounding atmosphere is maintained at 50 percent RH. The results can vary substantially between the two, as one is essentially measuring a wet material and the other a dry material, and the resistance of many materials changes as they take on moisture. Some manufacturers use the dry cup findings, as the permeability is lower. Moisture within a material can be measured with a moisture meter. Relative humidity in a space can be easily checked with a hygrometer.

3.3.6 QUICK NOTES: VAPOR TRANSFER

- A given volume of air at a given temperature can hold a given volume of water vapor before it condenses to water. The temperature at which it condenses is called the *dew point*.

- Cool air can hold less water vapor than warm air.
- The permeability of *all* components of the wall must be understood.
- There should be only one vapor retarder, which is defined as having a minimum of five times the vapor resistance of the total of the resistance of all materials to the cool side of the retarder.
- The vapor retarder should be to the warm side of the wall. In mixed climates with low vapor drive throughout the year, it may be best to minimize the resistance of all components.
- If the air temperature is below freezing the vapor changes very quickly to frost.
- Vapor diffusion resistance, measured in *reps,* is the inverse of permeability.
- Condensation occurs when warm, vapor-laden air meets a cold surface, which is why a complete air barrier is critical.

3.4 HEAT TRANSFER BY CONDUCTION AND RADIATION

The transfer of heat, whether from a hot exterior environment to an air-conditioned interior or from a heated space to the cold outdoors, occurs by convection, conduction, or radiation. Controlling this transfer is different for each of the mechanisms. Airflow, due to air pressure differences, causes the loss of conditioned air, either heated or cooled.

3.4.1 HEAT TRANSFER

Air flow or air leakage accounts for a large percentage of heat loss or gain. Whether induced by mechanical fans, the stack effect, or wind, it is controlled by air barrier systems. See 3.2 for more on these systems.

Convection is thermal transfer that occurs with the movement of air (or water). Convective currents can occur within fiberglass insulation and similar insulations if not properly installed. With any insulation that is permeable to air, one side should be placed tightly against a surface that acts as an air barrier. Airflow, caused by mechanical fans, is sometimes called forced convection.

It is *conduction*—the flow of heat through a solid material—that we usually associate with designing a wall for thermal comfort. *Thermal insulation* regulates the transfer of heat by conductance, measured by the U value. The resistance to this thermal transfer, the reciprocal of the U-value, is the R-value, or in SI units, the "RSI," of a wall. Determining the thermal resistance of a wall is a relatively straightforward calculation, as the values are additive. The R-value is the value readily available from manufacturers. It is also the single function of the exterior wall that the client understands.

Insulating materials historically were organic. Anything that could fill a cavity —sawdust, moss, seaweed, straw, and mineral fibers—was used. During the early twentieth century the ability to process solid materials such as minerals and glass into small fibers added to the range of options. Newsprint and wood were also shredded for insulation. After World War II, plastics, formed into boards or sprayed in place, opened up new insulating possibilities.

Research in insulation continues, often driven by environmental concerns with the manufacturing, installation, or long-term use of the product. Asbestos heads the list of problematic insulation materials of the past, along with formaldehyde foams. The safety of manufacturing and installing fiberglass has been questioned. But encapsulation of this product in thin polyethylene bags or Kraft paper limits the exposure during installation, and new "nonirritating" fibers have been introduced. (The International Agency for Research on Cancer, or IARC, has removed glass, rock, and slag wool fibers from its list of substances that are possibly carcinogenic to humans.[24]) The blowing agent used in the manufacture of plastic products is the center of present concerns. Manufacturers rushed first to eliminate chlorofluorocarbons (CFCs), and then hydrochlorofluorocarbons (HCFCs), to make the "green" products list. Today the "green" label may be a stronger governing factor in the popularity of insulation than the R-value.

3.4.2 INSULATING MATERIALS AND THEIR PLACEMENT

Most thermal insulation tries to capture air or other gases in small quantities. The material itself may have little insulating value. A good example is fiberglass. Plastic foams work on the same concept, capturing small bubbles of air or other gases. There are a number of safe and efficient forms of thermal insulation available for exterior walls. They come in batts or blankets, rigid and semirigid boards, loose fill, and sprayed- or foamed-in-place products. To maintain the resistance, the product must fill all voids and not settle, shrink, or lose its thermal resistance over time. Insulation also has the same potential problem as other wall components—it may be retarding vapor diffusion in the wrong location.

Glass and mineral fibers

Glass and mineral fibers are nonplastic, inorganic materials, most commonly used in *batts* or *blankets*. Batts may be "friction-fit" or enclosed in Kraft paper or polyethylene. Fibers can also be preformed into *semirigid boards* or *pipe insulation* with a binding resin or used as *loose fill*. BIBS (Blow-in Blanket System) is a patented process that mixes glass fibers with a binder. The product is sprayed into a wall cavity formed by the exterior sheathing and a nylon netting on the interior. Semirigid glass and mineral board insulation is frequently used in drainage cavities. The insulation is not harmed by the water, which drains through it.

Cellulose

Various forms of cellulose are also used as *loose fill* or *blown-in* insulation. They may be mixed with a binding agent. Some are blown-in under pressure between the exterior sheathing and a mesh-reinforced, plastic membrane on the inside of the stud cavity. Cellulose limits air movement more than fiberglass, particularly when installed under pressure.

Plastics

Sprayed or formed into boards, pellets, or other shapes, plastics offer a wide range of choices. Plastic insulations have problems with flame spread or smoke development to differing degrees, thus limiting their use without fire protection. Some plastics are permeable to water vapor, others function as a vapor barrier. Note that the term "closed-cell plastic foams" does not necessarily mean they are vapor impermeable.[25] The R-value of plastic foam changes with the modification of the blowing agents.

Expanding foams, such as SPF, are frequenetly used as air barrier systems.[26] Foams can be classified as follows:

Medium-density foam: closed cell, rigid, densities of 2 lbs/ft^3 (30–35 kg/m^3)
Semirigid foam: open cell, semirigid, densities of ½–1 lb/ft^3 (8–16 kg/m^3)
Sealing foam: bead applied, densities of 1–2½ lbs/ft^3 (16–40 kg/m^3), similar to medium-density foam but for use in cracks of ¼ inch (6 mm) and larger

Urethanes and *polyurethanes,* medium-density foams, were developed in the 1930s, but they were not used in building construction until the late 1950s. They adhere to almost all substrates and expand as they cure, making them an excellent air barrier.

The next generation of urethane was *polyisocyanurate* (or ISO). Manufactured in laminate form, it comes factory-faced with rigid boards, foils, or fiberglass felt. The R-value is higher than that for other board insulations, although the NRCA recommends using the five-year R-value, as the thermal resistance of the material decreases with age.[27] The facings can also function as a radiant barrier or a vapor retarder. Thermax, now manufactured by Dow, is a common ISO that has been on the market since the 1980s.

One of the newer insulations is the water blown, semirigid, ½ lb, open-cell SPF, developed in Canada in the 1980s and manufactured under the trade name of Icynene. It expands to fill the space, but it exerts less pressure than urethanes. Also produced by companies in the U.S., it is popular as a combination air barrier system and thermal insulation.

Polystyrene is expanded and then either extruded with a smooth skin surface or used as molded beads. *Extruded polystyrene* (XPS), best known by the product name Styrofoam, has the higher insulating value of the two and the greater density. It can be extruded with lapped joints or tongue-and-groove edges. Several companies manufacture XPS, sometimes called blue-board after the color of Styrofoam. The boards can be installed on the exterior or interior of the wall or fitted between studs. XPS comes in many densities, although a two-pound density is common for thermal insulation. A simpler manufacturing process produces *expanded (EPS)* or *molded polystyrene.* Molding plants, found in most states and provinces, produce a wide variety of products with different attributes. Individual manufacturers must be contacted to ensure that the product specified can be produced. Molded polystyrene is sometimes called bead board. It is often confused with the XPS trade name Styrofoam, as this is a common term used for the disposable coffee cups, which are in fact molded. (A more descriptive term is *MEPS,* for *molded expanded polystyrene.*) A common density for EPS is one pound. EPS is more vapor and air permeable, has a lower R-value, and is generally less impact resistant than XPS. But it is also less costly. While EPS and XPS can be wire cut, only EPS can be formed into shapes.

A *thermal break* is needed where a highly conductive material, such as metal, goes from the interior to the exterior. The vertical stripes seen on stucco applied over a metal-stud wall are often the result of differential thermal resistance. In a cool wet climate, the stucco over the studs will be warmer and drier than the insulated space between the studs, thereby supporting less organic growth. Using board insulation on the exterior of the stud wall, as a thermal break, would help eliminate striping. (It would be desirable to eliminate the organic growth; but drying the stucco through heat loss is not the way to achieve this.)

The thermal-resistive, plastic gasket in thermal-break windows slows the conduction of heat through the metal window frame, reducing the chance of condensation. The actual heat loss through the frame is minimal, as this is a very small percentage of the wall. The problem is the possibility of condensation on the *wrong* side of the wall.

3.4.3 WHERE AND WHEN TO MEASURE THERMAL RESISTANCE

The resistance of the entire exterior wall must be considered, not just the resistance of the thermal insulation or a section through a stud cavity. The most effective insulations are those that cover the exterior wall *without* the web of a concrete block, a column or beam, or a steel or wood stud acting as a thermal conductor. Not only is heat loss decreased, but the other components to the interior and the structure are protected against thermal extremes. It is important to "area-weight" the resistance for different components. For example, approximately 15 percent of a wood-stud wall is framing rather than a cavity to be filled with insulation. The thermal resistance of a metal-stud wall is compromised even more, as the steel acts as a kind of "fin radiator."

3.4.4 INSTALLATION OF INSULATION

Installation is a major factor in the efficacy of any system, and insulation is no exception. Sprayed-in-place insulations must be checked to ensure that they are the correct formula applied to the minimum specified thickness. Batts should completely fill the cavity, without gaps at the top or edges. Stapling the paper facing of batts to the side of the stud rather than the face unnecessarily compresses the insulation. Friction-fit fiberglass batts have the ability to completely fill a stud cavity. However, this is highly dependent on the installation. A poorly installed friction-fit batt may be less effective than a paper-faced batt properly installed. The size of batt should match the cavity size. A 6-inch (150 mm) batt made for steel studs will have less thermal resistance, when compressed in a 2 × 6 cavity, than the properly sized 5½-inch (140 mm) batt.

Insulations that expand as they cure must be detailed to avoid unwanted forces, or a product with less expansive properties should be specified. A case in point is spraying urethane between a window frame and the structure; too much of the wrong kind of insulation may lead to problems with the window. With the more generic insulations, such as EPS, care must be taken that the material specified is the material delivered to the site. Insulations applied wet should not be enclosed before they have released all moisture. A polyethylene vapor retarder placed over a wet, sprayed-in-place insulation spells disaster.

3.4.5 REFLECTIVE SURFACES AND GLASS

Reflective surfaces redirect electromagnetic waves back to their source. All bodies, including our own, will radiate heat to a cooler body. Using materials on walls that have a lower density, hence are closer to the air temperature in the room, will reduce this radiation from our bodies, making us feel warmer. An example is the perceived change that results from installing drapes over large expanses of glass in heating climates. Although the increased temperature of the room is minimal, the room is more comfortable because less heat from our bodies is radiating to the drapes than previously radiated to the cooler glass. This is one of the reasons that tapestries were hung on medieval masonry walls. Radiation is measured by emissivity, which refers to the ability of the surface to emit radiant energy. Emissivity is the ratio of the radiation absorbed by a material to the radiation absorbed by a blackbody. As the material reaches a blackbody, rated as 1.0, the majority of the radiation is absorbed and not reflected. The lower the number, the lower the absorption, and the greater the reflectivity—something understood by the public, as seen with the proliferation of low-E glass availability. Some define emissivity as radiation reflectivity; while it is an indicator of such, one must understand that the lower the number, the higher the reflectivity.

Reflective insulation, barriers, and coatings help to keep the heat on the side of the enclosure where it is desired. Radiant barriers consist of a thin sheet, usually aluminum, and sometimes reinforced for durability. It may also be a thin coating or paint applied to a substrate. Reflective paints, containing aluminum pigment, are available. The Reflective Insulation Manufacturers Association (RIMA) defines radiant barriers as those products with a surface emittance less than or equal to 0.1—a value met by highly polished aluminum but not by most aluminum paints. Reflective insulations include foil-faced foam boards and fiberglass batts. The reflective surfaces will have little effect if not facing an air space. In fact a sheet of aluminum, tightly sandwiched between two materials, may have the reverse effect, as it quickly conducts heat.

3.4.6 HEAT TRANSFER AND GLASS

Energy codes usually consider the overall heat loss or gain of a building. It is the rare client who desires less light-emitting but poorly insulating glass on a project. Innovations during the last 50 years have greatly increased the thermal resistance of glass units, making our "glass walls" possible. The first major change came with the introduction of double-insulating glass units. Further improvements include the use of inert gases, such as argon, in insulating glass units, and coatings that select the emissivity of the glass. Laminated glass with a thin layer of plastic, used for safety reasons, has a higher thermal resistance than glass with wire mesh that serves the same purpose.

Selective, low-emissivity coatings on glass reflect long-wave radiation while allowing the short-wave radiation to pass. This is why low-E glass can help keep a space warm during the winter in heating climates and also reduce solar and infrared radiation during the summer. These coatings, often titanium, can be either "soft" or "hard" coat, the latter being less effective but more durable. See Chapter 5 for more discussion on the different types of glass.

3.4.7 TESTING AND MEASURING HEAT IN A WALL

Infrared thermography scans are the most common method of testing for heat loss. Only the degree of heat in the wall is indicated, but repeated scanning and analysis can determine the method of heat loss. This is generally not part of normal construction testing. Conductance of heat through a wall can be graphed. The effect of radiation on the overall thermal performance can be calculated. Many manufacturers give general guidelines about the efficacy of their reflective products.

3.4.8 QUICK NOTES: THERMAL TRANSFER

- Thermal resistance should be measured for the whole wall, not just through the section with insulation.
- Insulation stops heat transfer by conductance.
- Loss of conditioned air is stopped by the air barrier system.
- Insulation applied to the exterior helps protect the structure and other wall components from differential thermal movement and premature aging.
- Thermal breaks in metal window frames are more important for decreasing the likelihood of condensation than for retarding thermal transfer.
- Environmental concerns are an important part of insulation selection.
- Cracks or gaps in the insulation can cause condensation problems, particularly if the air barrier fails.

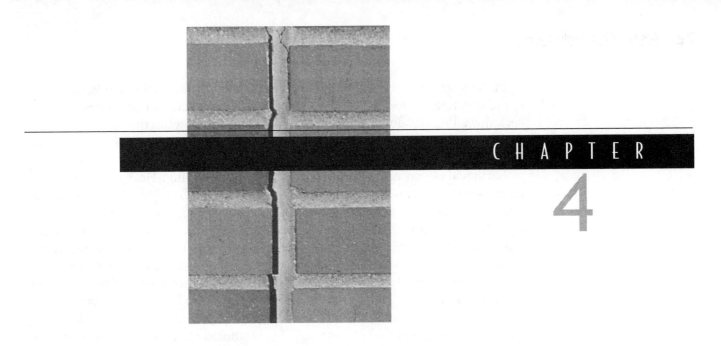

Sealant Joints

4.1 STRUCTURAL FORCES AND DIFFERENTIAL MOVEMENT

Buildings move. The structure and components of the exterior wall expand and contract, shrink and swell, exacerbated by climate and time. Wind and earthquakes induce lateral forces. Heavy, and not so heavy, claddings must be supported.

4.1.1 LATERAL FORCES

Cladding is often viewed as a finish material, selected only for its ability to weatherproof the building and provide the aesthetic face. Little attention is given to designing for lateral forces. Metal cladding or vinyl siding, attached directly to the frame or to furring channels, may easily withstand positive wind pressure; but negative pressure can "suck" these lightweight materials off the building. The attachment of the cladding must be designed to resist these pullout loads. A heavy cladding, in combination with a drainage cavity, substantially complicates the anchorage. Anchored brick veneer is a good example. Lateral loads are transferred to a backup wall with frequently spaced steel anchor ties that span a wide cavity. The ties must be stiff and strong enough to transfer the positive loads, while the fasteners that attach the anchor have to withstand pullout loads from what is often the flange of a light-gauge metal stud. Engineers do not normally design anchored brick veneer, because it is not seen as structural. Unfortunately, all too often, neither do architects, and prescriptive standards for anchored brick veneer do not cover all conditions.

Backup walls for the cladding must be capable of transferring the lateral loads to the concrete or steel structural frame. It is also critical that the stiffness of the backup wall is considered and differential movement between the backup wall and the structure accommodated. A structural engineer should design the connections and backup walls for heavy claddings.

Earthquakes can have two separate effects on cladding. Heavy cladding must resist inertia forces, which are similar to forces created by wind. Earthquakes also can cause forces on the building structure that can induce horizontal forces, creating what is called story drift. Whether it is a glass curtain wall or anchored brick veneer, vertical expansion joints are required to take up this in-plane racking movement. The width of these joints is usually greater than that required for expansion. It should be noted that unlike wind, seismic forces do not respect the boundaries of outside and inside. During a restoration project carried out by this author, three stories of brick veneer inside a lobby were suspected of being inadequately attached, causing a life-safety hazard.[1] This prompted the remark that this was one building where, contrary to conventional wisdom, you should run outside in case of an earthquake.

Hurricanes also cause excessive lateral forces. Not only are the wind and cyclic pressures due to gusting winds extreme, but these forces hurl debris against exterior walls. When Hurricane Andrew hit southern Florida in 1992, gusting winds were measured at 175 mph (78 m/s). Dade County became the first area in the United States to require exterior windows and doors to resist debris impact, a direct result of this third-strongest hurricane to hit the U.S. mainland in recorded history.[2]

4.1.2 Gravity Loads

Gravity loads, transferred from the cladding to the structure usually at each floor, are also substantial with heavy claddings. In the case of precast concrete panels, the connection between the cladding and structure can be cast anywhere in the panel. The panel can be attached at the floor beam or designed to span from column to column. Anchored brick veneer is another story. Modern brick veneer is typically laid in single-story panels with gravity loads supported on steel shelf angles. Detailing of this connection is difficult if the shelf angle is not positioned at a floor beam, a situation that can occur with ribbon or strip windows.

4.1.3 Differential Movement: Expansion and Contraction

Materials expand and contract due to thermal or moisture changes that induce forces within the material or at the interface with another material. Live and dead loads cause elastic deformation and creep. A concrete frame will contract or shorten due to hydration of the concrete, elastic deformation from initial loading of the structure, and creep, which causes deformations that continue over time. The speed of construction can affect differential movement. Concrete columns that are "loaded" prior to adequate curing experience even greater shortening due to elastic deformation. Fired-clay masonry "grows" in size due to initial moisture absorption and continues to grow with thermal and moisture changes. Some marble permanently deforms through a process called hysteresis. Metals expand and contract, depending on the type, thickness, and temperature.

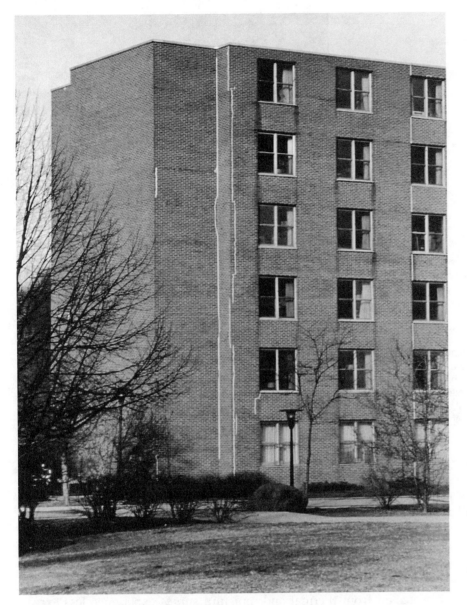

FIGURE 4.1 Buildings will form their own expansion joints if the architect does not design for differential movement. The vertical cracks, filled with white sealant applied by the maintenance crew, are a good indicator of where joints should have been located on this college dormitory. Photo by G. Russell Heliker.

FIGURE 4.2 The efflorescing salts that crystallized behind this antigraffiti sealer have not caused damage, but they have certainly affected aesthetics. Photo by G. Russell Heliker.

Water ingress creates additional movement problems. Organic materials swell and shrink as the moisture content changes. When the temperature drops below freezing, expansive forces are generated in wet materials, as water increases in volume when it freezes. With each freeze-thaw cycle, small cracks become larger, allowing for more water to enter, resulting in even greater forces the next time. Corrosion of steel produces forces, as the iron oxide takes up more volume than the steel it replaced; estimates suggest 8 to 10 times more volume. The frequent spalling of concrete at the location of rusting steel-reinforcing illustrates this point. Water moving through a porous material can deposit soluble salts just under a surface that has been treated with a waterproofing or antigraffiti sealer. When the salts crystallize under the sealer, they often form an unattractive chalky or milky appearance; at worst, they exert an expansive force.

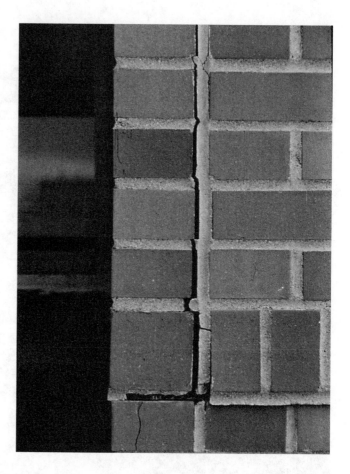

FIGURE 4.3 There were no horizontal or vertical joints for expansion on this nine-story brick-clad building. Growth of the brick veneer and shortening of the concrete frame created stresses in both directions. The veneer formed a vertical crack at the corner, where an expansion joint should have been located to accommodate the horizontal movement. The panels were tightly pinched between the steel shelf angles at each floor because of vertical movement, causing the veneer to "walk out" on the angle. Photo by G. Russell Heliker.

The designer must be aware of the potential differential expansion and contraction of all components in the exterior wall. The cladding will move differently from the structure, which will move differently from the backup wall. Metal panels on the sunny side of a building will move differently from panels in shadow. Joints and attachments must be designed to take up this differential movement. The amount of movement is dependent on the material, the climate, and the position in the wall. Components protected from thermal and moisture surges experience less expansion and contraction.

4.1.4 LIFE SAFETY

High winds, seismic activity, or differential movement due to thermal or moisture changes often trigger cladding failures. The heavier the cladding, the more likely its failure will endanger people. Such dangers have prompted local authorities to check periodically the stability of facades in some urban areas, as in Manhattan and Chicago. Frequently it is the heavy ornamental and functional pieces that pose the greatest danger. Parapets, chimneys, and cornices of terra-cotta, stone, and brick have all contributed substantially to the rubble found after an earthquake. While care must be taken with the attachment of all facades, it is especially important for heavier claddings. Equally critical is keeping water out of the wall, as failure can often be attributed to corroded metal attachments, fasteners, and anchors.

FIGURES 4.4 AND 4.5 Even lightweight claddings create havoc when they fail. Photos by Margarete von Adamic.

4.2 EXPANSION AND CONTROL JOINTS

Differential movement is accommodated with joints that allow the material to expand or contract without undue stress to the component or structure. Joints can be grouped into expansion joints and control joints. *Expansion joints* provide an empty space into which a material can expand. They should not be filled with "stuff" without a very good reason. Compressible fillers are often recommended for horizontal expansion joints (sometimes called "soft joints") in brick veneer. While the filler may keep most of the debris out of the joint, it offers no guarantee. One of the primary drawbacks to the use of compressible fillers is that the space cannot be inspected. An inspection should be made of all expansion joints — vertical and horizontal — prior to sealing them to ensure that there is no construction debris in the space. Compressible fillers also increase the minimum width of the joint, something many designers go to great lengths to avoid.

Anytime an element such as a hose bib or electrical fixture protrudes through the cladding, differential movement must be accommodated. Windows and doors have expansion joints on all but the bearing side. Most backup walls move differently from the structure, requiring an expansion joint at the top of the wall. This is also true anywhere two components join, whether it is an aluminum window wall frame next to a precast concrete panel or stone veneer meeting EIFS (Exterior Insulation and Finish Systems). Some claddings, such as brick veneer, will require expansion joints within the field of the cladding.

Cementitious materials such as concrete and stucco shrink, due to hydration, putting the material in tension. Cracking results as the material tries to pull apart. The solution is to control the cracking by inserting a weakened line in the plane of the material. The material will crack on this line, called a *control joint.* The joints do not stop the cracking, they just direct and consolidate it. In addition to the aesthetic advantage of controlling the cracking pattern, the control joint allows for application of a sealant to prevent water from entering.

The terms *control joint* and *expansion joint,* when discussing movement, should not be used interchangeably. Expansion joints belong in materials, such as fired-clay brick veneer, that expand. Control joints are used primarily with cementitious materials that contract. Many an expansion joint in brick veneer has been filled with mortar, possibly because the designer and contractor did not understand the difference. Using the more general term *movement joint* does not convey the necessary information about the joint's function.

This book does not cover the seismic or isolation joints that are necessary between parts of a building on larger projects. Both of these are enlarged versions of expansion joints. They should be free of all materials except those necessary to keep out water and support the loads. The sizing of these joints should be the responsibility of the structural engineer. However, sizing should be coordinated with the architect who will select the sealant to fill the joint. The architect should present the engineer with information on the sealant's movement capabilities. The engineer can then respond with the size of the joint and spacing for the given product. The following discussion focuses on expansion and control joints.

4.3 JOINT DESIGN

The first task in designing joints is to identify the locations where there is a change in plane, a change in materials, or an opening or transition that necessitates an expansion joint. Carefully redlining a building elevation and wall section provides an overview of the joints required. The substrates should also be identified, as a different surface preparation may be recommended for each. A structural engineer should be consulted on the width of expansion joints that involve seismic forces or differential movement between the structure and the cladding. Cementitious materials that require control joints need to be identified. The width of a control joint is less critical. If sealant is used to stop water and air entry, the joint must be of adequate dimension, both width and depth, to assure a good installation. Most liquid sealant manufacturers require ¼ inch (6 mm) adhesion on the substrate along with a 1:2 depth-to-width ratio. This translates to a minimum dimension of ½ inch (13 mm), after construction tolerances and clearances have been considered. The width of a joint should never be reduced for aesthetic reasons. The machinations some designers go through to reduce the size of a joint are of little consequence and can be fraught with problems. The width of the expansion joint must take into account the compressed dimension of the sealant and backer rod, any joint filler, story drift in areas of seismic risk, and construction tolerances and clearances.

A consultation with the structural engineer concerning spacing of expansion joints early in the design process is a good idea. The pattern created by the joints, whether they are control joints or expansion joints, is a key aesthetic element. The aesthetic design of the facade must be integrated with the functional spacing of the

FIGURE 4.6 Many facades have been changed when expansion joints are added to a brick-veneer wall without understanding the rhythm of the facade. Photo by G. Russell Heliker.

joints. Figure 4.6 is an example of what can happen when function and aesthetics are not integrated.

The problem of dealing with water that gets past the first seal can be solved with *two-stage drained sealant joints* (see Figure 4.8). The base of each drained area, between the two sealant joints, must end in flashing that extends to the exterior; otherwise this becomes a face-sealed system at some of the most critical junctures, for example, at a window head. It is often impossible to install the inner sealant from the interior, so the joint must be wide enough to allow careful installation of sealant from the exterior. This installation is difficult when the requirements for cleaning, priming, correct placement of backer rod, and tooling are con-

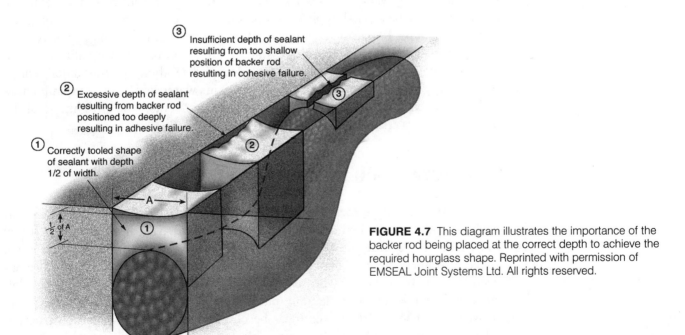

③ Insufficient depth of sealant resulting from too shallow position of backer rod resulting in cohesive failure.

② Excessive depth of sealant resulting from backer rod positioned too deeply resulting in adhesive failure.

① Correctly tooled shape of sealant with depth 1/2 of width.

A

½ of A

FIGURE 4.7 This diagram illustrates the importance of the backer rod being placed at the correct depth to achieve the required hourglass shape. Reprinted with permission of EMSEAL Joint Systems Ltd. All rights reserved.

Two-Stage Drained Sealant Joints

Water management of some cladding systems occurs at the joints. Precast concrete panels are a good example. Well-designed and carefully installed two-stage drained sealant joints can increase the long-term durability of the cladding system.

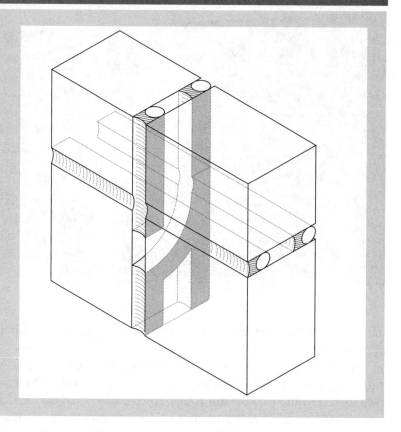

FIGURE 4.8 Canada Mortgage and Housing Corporation, *Rain Penetration Control: Applying Current Knowledge.* All rights reserved. Reproduced with the consent of Canada Mortgage and Housing Corporation. All other uses and reproductions of this material are expressly prohibited.

sidered. Three-quarters of an inch (19 mm) may be adequate for a two-stage joint, but an inch (25 mm) is better—and this is *after* construction tolerances have been considered. The success of this joint relies on workmanship; meticulous installation is mandatory. What looks workable on a drawing may not be in the field. The inner joint may be a good application for some of the precompressed, impregnated foam sealants. Repairing or replacing this system is difficult and expensive.

Some installations call for a two-stage joint to be pressure-equalized, which relies on the inner seal to act as an air barrier. The ability of this inner seal to remain airtight over time is doubtful; if it remains watertight, it offers redundancy. If the front seal has a large number of openings, or "vents," the airtightness of the inner seal is less critical.

4.4 CONSTRUCTION TOLERANCES

Construction is not perfect. Materials and systems have different tolerances that must be understood when designing the exterior wall. The distance a steel frame can be out of vertical and horizontal plumb is different from the distance for a concrete frame. These tolerances may be well understood by the structural engineer, but it is the designer who selects the cladding, which has its own set of tolerances. The tolerances of cladding panels in turn affect the design of the joints between the panels. All details must be checked against allowable construction tolerances. For example, if the joint between precast concrete panels is detailed at ¾ inch (19 mm) and the construction tolerance on placing the panels is ¼ inch (6 mm), the joint may end up being only ½ inch (13 mm). The architect, structural engineer, and contractor must agree on a set of workable construction tolerances. This is particularly critical to the performance of sealants intended to seal these gaps. When more than one of the subcontractors uses tolerance maximums, the joints may be narrower than the miniumum required for the specified sealant. Sealant innovator Lester Hensley uses the term *tolerance buildup* and notes that "improperly constructed joints cannot be properly sealed."[3]

4.5 JOINT COMPONENTS

Joint sealant has one purpose: to keep out water and air. It is the face seal between two materials. Unless a two-stage joint is designed or there is a drainage cavity to the interior of the sealant joint, there is no second line of defense. Numerous components in various applications can be used for one- and two-stage sealant joints. Some are applied hot or foamed-in-place, others are preformed tapes or precompressed, impregnated foam, but most are "gunned" in place. (To avoid confusion, the Sealant Waterproofing and Restoration Institute, or SWRI, uses the term *liquid sealant* for the "gunnable" sealants.) Silicones, polyurethanes, and polysulfides cure chemically, while latexes and most acrylics are water based. Butyls and some acrylics are solvent based. Water- and solvent-based products cure by "drying." They are generally less durable. Silicones or polyurethanes of single or multiple parts that must be mixed are the more durable liquid sealants for exterior applications. Butyl tapes have a place in lapped joints that see little movement and are not exposed to ultraviolet (UV) light. Some cladding systems have sealants designed specifically for their use.

Sealants are rated in terms of elongation capacity, modulus of elasticity, adhesion or bond, UV resistance, and hardness, as well as curing times, staining potential, compressibility, and durability. Elongation is expressed as a percentage of the sealant's original size. A sealant with 100 percent elongation will stretch to twice its original width. Modulus refers to the tensile strength of the sealant at a given elongation. The lower the number, the more elastic the sealant. High-modulus sealants are relatively rigid and will not perform well in joints that see significant movement. Selecting the right sealant for each application can be a formidable task. Sealants should be evaluated on watertightness and airtightness, measured by adhesion, cohesion, compressibility, and elasticity. Service life is based on UV resistance and general durability. Ease of application is also a consideration.[4]

Cost should *not* be a factor in selecting a sealant. Well designed and installed sealant joints require a small fraction of the building's budget, but they can save a substantial amount in maintenance and remediation during the exterior wall's life. ASTM C24 "Committee on Building Seals and Sealants" continues to develop a strong base of sealant standards. Thomas F. O'Connor, past chair of this committee, states that sealants are "approximately one percent of the construction cost" but are "90 percent of the problem" when a building develops leaks.[5] The cost of the sealant material is a small percentage—some estimate 15 percent—of the installed cost. It is a foolish decision not to use the highest-grade sealant appropriate for the installation.

Liquid silicone sealants are emerging as the favorite of the high performance sealants. Exceptional life, excellent UV protection, and high elasticity, along with good adhesion and wind resistance, make them a good choice. Although not as strong in adhesion as urethanes, their elasticity still makes them the better long-term option. In the 1970s Dow Corning introduced 790 Silicone Building Sealant, which was expressly designed for unprimed adhesion to most concrete and masonry substrates. Close to three decades of service have proven that silicones in general are longer lasting than urethanes. Staining of substrates can be a problem with silicone sealants, although some newer products are formulated to be stain resistant. Silicones cannot be painted but come in a variety of colors. Custom colors can be produced for large projects.[6]

Liquid urethane sealants have a reputation for excellent adhesion. Application of urethanes is more forgiving than application of silicones, and they may be a good choice when faced with a variety of substrates or a situation where the applicators' skill is questionable. However, urethanes will neither last as long nor provide as good a seal as properly applied silicone. More affected by UV light, age, and low temperatures, urethanes tend to become brittle and fail in cohesion. Urethanes can also have staining problems. The fast-curing urethanes tend to stain less but are harder and therefore less durable. The surface of urethane continues to dust as UV light corrodes it. As the dust is washed or blown away, the joint appears to be cleaner, sometimes noted as an advantage over silicone, even though the sealant is deteriorating.

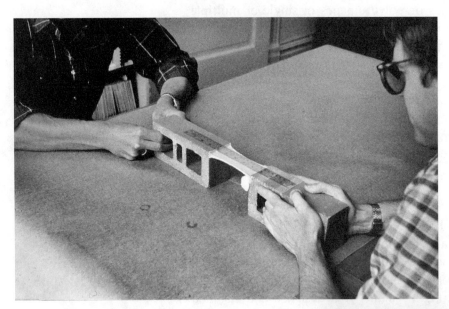

FIGURES 4.9, 4.10 Simple experiments can be done in the office. A pullout test indicates how a silicone sealant matched up with a one-part urethane sealant. Though not scientific, it shows what one would suspect. The bricks in Figure 4.10 are placed respective to the location where the sealant failure occurred. The urethane sealant (two bricks in the background) failed in cohesion, while the silicone sealant (two bricks in the foreground) failed in adhesion after elongating more than double the urethane. Photos by G. Russell Heliker.

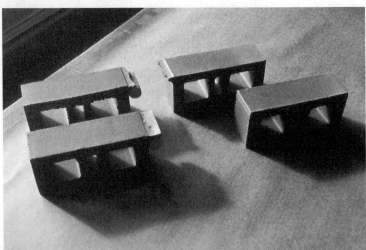

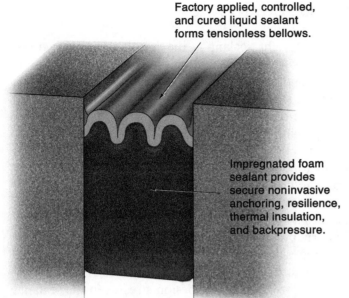

Factory applied, controlled, and cured liquid sealant forms tensionless bellows.

Impregnated foam sealant provides secure noninvasive anchoring, resilience, thermal insulation, and backpressure.

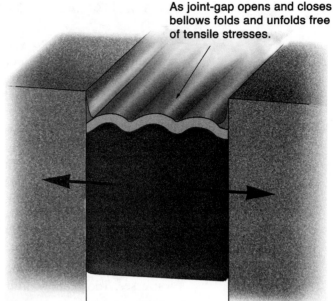

As joint-gap opens and closes bellows folds and unfolds free of tensile stresses.

Backer rods are generally of two types: closed-cell polyethylene and open-cell polyurethane. They come in a variety of dimensions as well as triangular shapes for fillet joints. They should be a minimum of 20 percent larger than the maximum width of the joint to ensure proper backing for the sealant. A closed-cell rod should be used unless the sealant manufacturer specifies open-cell rods. Open cell rods are for sealants that cure by reaction with moisture in the air. However, these rods will hold water, which can contribute to sealant failure. Care must be taken that closed-cell rods are not punctured, as the off-gassing can affect sealant curing. Impregnated foam sealants can be used in place of backer rods when the depth of the substrate is too shallow to receive both a sealant and a backer rod.

Bond breaker tapes are used wherever there is a possibility of adhesion of the sealant to substrates on three sides, which severely limits elongation of the sealant. The bond breaker tape should have good adhesive properties and not interfere with the sealant application.

Hybrid sealants or *preformed sealants* combine the sealant with the backing material (see Figure 4.11). This solves the problem of irregular depths of the backer rod with conventional installations. One proprietary system, Emseal COLORSEAL, is comprised of polyurethane foam impregnated with water-repelling adhesive agents. On top of this is bonded an accordion layer of silicone. The silicone protects the compressed foam below. Curing in the factory avoids the problems associated with weather and dirt. The silicone "bellows" are adhered to the substrate with a bead of silicone on both sides. The primary seal is the silicone bellows, while the expanded water resistant foam provides a secondary seal. As the sealant, including the silicone, is under compression, tension-adhesion failures are eliminated. Although it still relies on the site application of silicone sealant, a poor installation of this system may be better than a poor installation of liquid silicone. Is it worth the extra cost? Part of the decision may be based in aesthetics. The color selection is wide and can change within a single installation as the sealant passes from one substrate to another. It has a consistent profile, unlike the somewhat messy liquid sealants.

FIGURE 4.11
Precompressed, impregnated foam sealants are always in compression. They are a good choice for wider joints, joints of varying widths, hard to reach joints, and corners. Illustrations reprinted with permission of EMSEAL Joint Systems Ltd. All rights reserved.

4.6 INSTALLATION OF LIQUID SEALANTS

Equally important to selecting the right sealant is the installation. Extra time should be spent in detailing, specifying, and testing the sealant during the design phases with continued inspection and testing during construction. Primers are an integral component of many sealant systems, as are backer rods and bond breaker tapes. Failures often occur because of not using the specified primer, using the wrong primer, or not properly applying the primer.

The sealant manufacturers' directions, including surface preparation and climate control, should be carefully followed. Different substrates will require different primers and mechanical preparation. Sealants must have adhesion compatibility with the substrate. Concrete and masonry sealers or antigraffiti films can interfere with adhesion. The substrates should be completely dry and clean. Urethanes can pull away thin layers of poorly prepared substrates. Installation of the backer rod must be exact so that the correct shape of sealant can be obtained. If the backer rod is too deep, the sealant bead will be too deep, resulting in excessive adhesion stresses. Too shallow an installation will result in cohesion stresses in the sealant. Silicones are to be tooled to a 1:2 hourglass shape formed by the backer rod (see Figure 4.7). Urethanes sometimes require a thicker bead, up to a 1:1 ratio. Tooling should be done by a skilled applicator using a tooling stick with slight positive pressure to ensure good adhesion to the substrate and a concave profile. Proper tooling also gets rid of any air bubbles. Weather at the time of installation should be considered. Both temperature and relative humidity affect curing. Sealants generally should be installed when the temperature is above 40°F (4°C) and rising but not extremely hot. If the expansion joint is at its minimum width when the sealant is installed, the sealant may fail in colder weather, as the substrates contract. If the sealant is installed when the joint is at its widest width, the sealant may be overly compressed in hot weather.

Silicones cannot be painted, but as a general rule neither should other exterior sealants, unless a product specially recommended by the sealant manufacturer is used. Finding a paint with similar elongation capabilities and modulus of elasticity as the sealant, in addition to good adhesion properties, is very difficult. The impression of a mortar joint can be obtained by pressing sand into an uncured sealant. On-site experimentation will provide the best results. Many sealant decisions have been made based on the appearance of the sealant or its ability not to stain or attract dirt. While these aesthetic considerations are important, the ability of the sealant to function for its expected life should be given top priority. Also the results of a failed sealant joint usually has a worse effect on the wall's appearance than a slightly dirty, but functioning, sealant.

One-part sealants eliminate potential problems with improper mixing, and today they are the equal of two-part sealants. In the case of sealants, working with the old "tried and true" is safer than allowing a project to be used as a guinea pig for a new material or system.

4.7 MAINTENANCE

Replacing sealants is one of the givens with exterior wall maintenance. The "maintenance manual" should require an initial inspection of the sealant at five years and then every three years at a minimum. This can sometimes be coordinated with

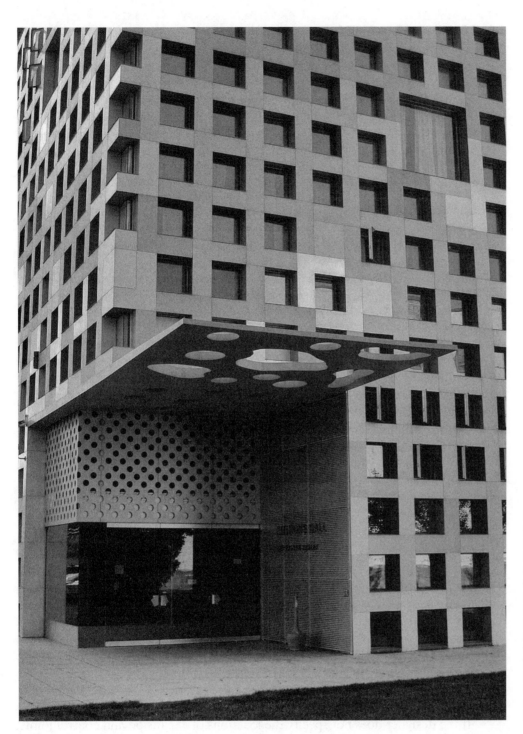

FIGURE 4.12 The exterior wall of the Massachusetts Institute of Technology's Simmons Hall (Steven Holl Architects, 2002) is a giant Vierendeel truss of pre-cast units covered with an aluminum skin. Typical dorm rooms have nine windows, each two feet square. The deep recess protects the windows from the weather, but the linear footage of sealant that will require maintenance is substantial compared to a more conventional design. Photo by Martin Lewis; © Martin Lewis.

other maintenance items, such as window cleaning. Sealant replacement should be a consideration in the design of the joint. Removing sealants can be difficult. For example, urethanes, with their excellent adhesion, can pull away the lamina on EIFS cladding when removed. Silicones can be more easily replaced, as silicone adheres to itself quite well. In areas where adhesion of the original sealant is good, it can be cut away, leaving a thin layer of silicone and, more importantly, an undamaged substrate.

4.8 TESTING SEALANTS

Most sealant manufacturers will run numerous tests on their products at no charge. They will do adhesion, compatibility, and stain testing (among others) on substrate samples provided to them. Specific installation and surface preparation and primer recommendations are made based on the tests. This testing should occur during the design phase so the requirements can be included in the specifications. As many different types of joints as feasible should be included in the construction mock-up of the exterior wall. Testing for water or air leakage should be focused on the joints, as this is most likely where failures will occur.

4.9 QUICK NOTES: SEALANT JOINTS

- Most materials change in size due to temperature and moisture differences.
- Freezing water, crystallized salts, and iron oxide create additional forces within a material.
- Expansion joints belong in materials that expand and contract. The primary components are a void or space and a seal to keep out the water.
- Control joints belong in cementitious materials that contract. They are a weakened line in the plane that directs and consolidates cracking and often incorporate a water seal.
- Low-modulus silicone is a good sealant choice.
- Liquid sealants should be applied in an hourglass shape. Three-sided adhesions should be avoided.
- The backer rod must be installed to a precise depth and the liquid sealant well tooled.
- Substrates should be dry and clean, and often require priming or other surface preparation.
- Durability of the sealant should take precedence over cost and aesthetics.
- Joint width must be designed for differential movement, particularly between the structure and the cladding, taking into account construction tolerances.
- Story drift is a consideration in determining the width of vertical expansion joints in seismic areas.
- Expansion joints should be a minimum of ½ inch (13 mm) *after* considering construction tolerances and clearances required for installation.
- Two-stage joints should be a minimum of ¾ inch (19 mm), or better yet one inch (25 mm), *after* considering construction tolerances.
- An important design task is identifying the locations of expansion and control joints.
- If the designer does not specify the locations of expansion and control joints, the contractor will. If the contractor does not determine the locations, the building will.

CHECKLIST
SELECTING AND POSITIONING BARRIERS AND RETARDERS

- Check and recheck the compatibility and durability of all exterior wall components.
- Allocate extra time to design the water management system and the air barrier system.
- Allocate an adequate portion of the construction budget to the water management system and the air barrier system. Consider the additional labor costs incurred with careful installation of these systems.
- Work with the mechanical engineer on the design of the HVAC systems early in the design process.
- Work with the structural engineer on lateral and gravity connections of the cladding and sizing and spacing of movement joints early in the design process.
- Review the drawings and specifications while asking the questions:
  Are all conditions covered in the detail drawings and specifications?
  Are any potential problems built into the wall?
  What will this wall look like in 25 years? Can the "maintenance manual" help mitigate any of the problems?

Water Barrier System

- Select the water management system based on the cladding, durability expectations, exposure, and climatic conditions.
- If a face-sealed barrier wall is selected, review ways to deflect water from the wall and decrease water penetration at the joints, or better yet, add a concealed water barrier with a drainage plane.
- If a pressure-equalized rainscreen is selected, check for completeness of the air barrier, size of the compartments, and size of the vents.
- Select a water barrier, flashings, and windows that meet the water control expectations including durability.
- Note the permeability of the water barrier.
- Determine flashing types and materials
- Check compatibility of water barrier with cladding, flashings, and substrates.
- Review the drawings and specifications to assure that the water barrier, including flashings, is continuous and difficult areas have been adequately detailed. In particular check all openings, penetrations, changes in plane, connection at the roof, and building corners.
- Specify testing procedures for water penetration including a mock-up wall.

Air Barrier System

- Determine the air barrier system based on the water barrier.
- Note the permeability of the air barrier.
- Review drawings to assure that the air barrier is continuous throughout the wall and roof and difficult areas have been adequately detailed and specified.
- Work with the mechanical engineer to design an HVAC system based on the effectiveness of the air barrier system.
- Specify testing procedures for air penetration.

(continued on following page)

CHECKLIST
SELECTING AND POSITIONING BARRIERS AND RETARDERS

Vapor Retarder

- Determine if a vapor retarder is needed and, if so, where it should be located in relation to the thermal insulation.
- Check for any unintended vapor retarders. Interior and exterior finishes are often culprits.
- Select the vapor retarder based on air barrier system and the interior and exterior climate.
- Review the permeability of the water barrier, air barrier, insulation, sheathing, and cladding.
- Review permeability of interior finishes with the interior designer.

Thermal Insulation

- Select the type of insulation(s) in consideration of vapor retarders, intended or unintended.
- Eliminate thermal breaks where possible.
- Note the permeability of the thermal insulation.
- Review drawings to assure that the thermal barrier is complete and difficult areas have been adequately detailed and specified.
- Work with the mechanical engineer to determine insulation levels, given the placement of vapor retarders; the extent of glass and types of glass units; and the HVAC systems appropriate for the insulation level.

Design for Structural Forces and Sealants

- Review drawings to determine the location of all expansion and control joints.
- Coordinate location and width of joints with structural engineer and the cladding manufacturer where appropriate.
- Add tolerances and clearances, as well as the compressed depth of the sealant and any other materials in the joint, to the joint width.
- Select the sealant for each joint and test for adhesion with substrates.
- Determine if water and/or air can be kept out of a joint without relying on sealant.
- Design lateral support of lightweight claddings for negative and positive wind pressure.
- Consider remediation possibilities when the sealant fails.
- Include a maintenance schedule for sealant inspection in the "maintenance manual."

The structural engineer should:
- check for differential movement between frame, backup walls, and cladding, along with seismic forces, to determine the width of expansion joints.
- design lateral connections and supports systems for heavy claddings.
- design heavy cladding panels such as precast or reinforced fired-clay brick.
- review drawings and specifications to assure that cladding and backup walls can withstand all lateral and gravity loading.

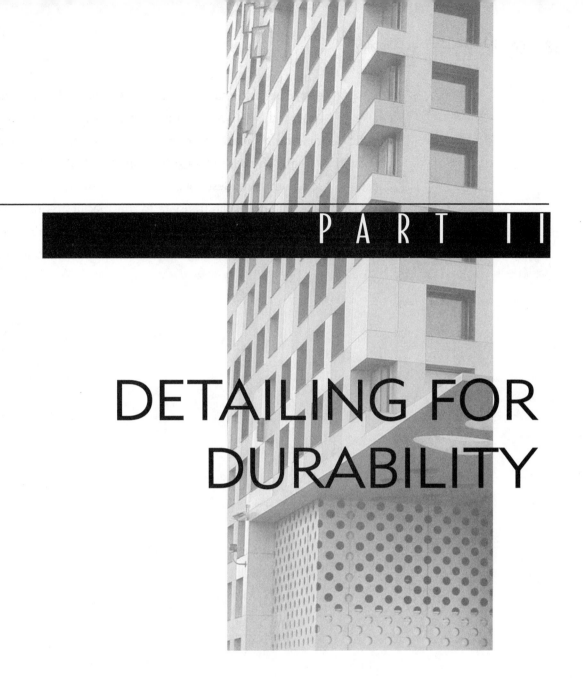

PART II

DETAILING FOR DURABILITY

DETAILING IS ONE OF THE MOST SIGNIFICANT TASKS in designing a building. It is fundamental to the continuing function and appearance of the exterior wall. Modern buildings are often described through their details—the fine grain of aesthetic design is played out in the details. Many building envelope failures can be traced to poor detailing or lack of detailing. Part II covers detailing of the exterior wall from its interface with the ground to its termination at the roof.

Given the multitude of wall components and different structural types, coupled with numerous cladding types, and mediated by climate and geography, the combinations seem limitless. To be useful this book must have broad coverage but be specific at the same time. Four wall types provide an overview of the challenges presented when detailing the exterior wall. Each set of details is for a specific cladding on a specific structural system, in a specific climate, with notation on how they might be adapted for other climates. Although generic in nature and chosen to provide the broadest coverage, the intention is that understanding the details for these wall types can translate to the specifics required for a particular project. Case studies and other examples show innovative applications of these ideas. Part III offers additional insights into the detailing of buildings.

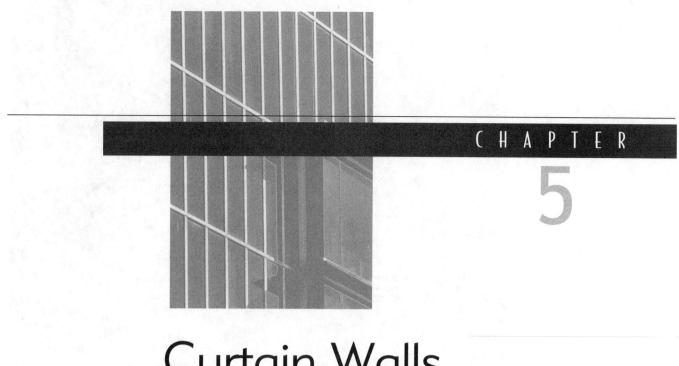

CHAPTER

5

Curtain Walls

5.1 THE DEVELOPMENT OF CURTAIN WALLS

In 1918, a seven-story facade of glass appeared on Sutter Street in San Francisco. The Hallidie Building, designed by James Polk, was one of the first applications of a pure curtain wall in North America. The multifloor wall of glass was suspended 39 inches (1 meter) in front of the reinforced concrete columns from the cantilevered concrete floor. Narrowing to a mere 3 inches (75 mm) at the glass skin, the cantilevered floor also provided a fire break. According to Kenneth Frampton, Polk's decision to break away from the heavy masonry of the Richardsonian architecture was influenced by a desire for natural light, a limited budget, and a need to facilitate erection of the building.[1] Facades changed forever with the introduction of the frame building, which permitted a light exterior wall of glass instead of the meager punched openings of masonry load-bearing walls. (Early curtain walls were typically of thick masonry, usually brick or terra-cotta, because building code officials were still fearful of fires. See Section 9.2.1.)

While the term *curtain wall* means any non-gravity-load-bearing wall, the metal and glass curtain wall is what first comes to mind. The importance of glass as a cladding material cannot be underestimated. With the exception of plastics, it is the only transparent cladding material, providing daylighting and connection with the outside. It is the rare client who desires (or the odd program that benefits

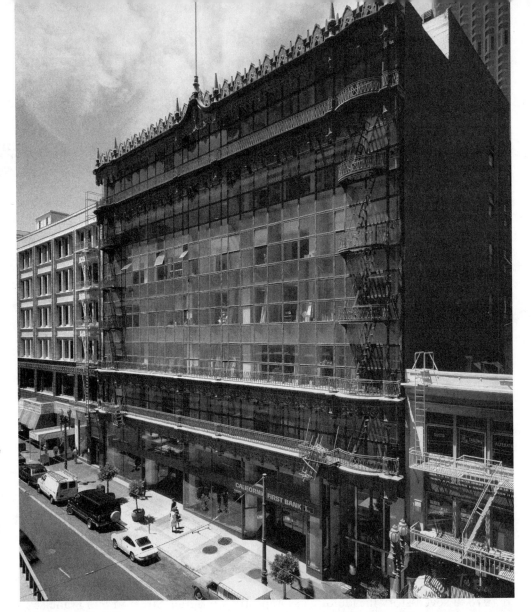

FIGURE 5.1 The facade of the Hallidie Building (James Polk, 1918) in San Francisco is one of the first glass curtain walls. (The facade is very similar to that of the Boley Clothing Company Building constructed in 1908 and credited by some as the first, true glass curtain wall in the U.S. (Louis Curtiss, St. Louis, Missouri.) (© 2004 Russell Abraham)

from) less light-transmitting glass on a project. The limitations generally come from energy codes such as ASHRAE 90.1.

Development of the extruded aluminum frames for these ethereal walls began in the 1950s. Bolting glass together with small metal "patches," a system called structural glass, was introduced in the 1960s. But the greatest change in the last fifty years took place in glazing technology. Prior to the introduction of float glass in 1959, glass was expensive, if not marred by imperfections. Today the glass curtain wall is the ubiquitous cladding of the office tower and the source of invention on projects around the globe. There seem to be no limits on the potential for innovation—glass cubes, curved glass, and floating and flying forms of transparent, reflective, translucent, colored, and patterned glass are becoming more commonplace. Glass, metal, and even stone claddings are part of new organic forms created digitally and seemingly unbound by conventional construction restrictions.

This chapter discusses metal curtain walls with panels of glass, metal, and stone. Because the framing and fitting systems are designed and developed by particular manufacturers, the discussion focuses on what architects need to know for a successful project—not on the specific detailing. Also discussed are precast concrete and glass fiber reinforced concrete panels.

Anchored brick veneer is a curtain wall that is not a product of a manufacturer. It is also a cladding with the potential for serious problems if not designed and constructed correctly, particularly if the backup wall is built of steel studs. The design of this curtain wall is covered in detail in Chapter 6 in reference to buildings up to 20 stories in height. This chapter provides an overview of the complexities of curtain wall design. Other information on curtain walls can be found in Chapter 7 (prefabricated EIFS panels), Chapter 9 (terra-cotta, marble, and brick veneer), and Chapter 10 (metal, glass, thin brick integrally cast in concrete panels, and double-skin facades).

5.2 ALUMINUM GLASS CURTAIN WALLS

The metal curtain wall business is rapidly changing. Large, global companies are supplanting smaller, local companies, as well as challenging the established larger, national companies. The cost difference between custom and off-the-shelf systems is narrowing. Custom systems are required for complex building forms or where a unique frame or panel profile is desired. The move is toward unitized systems over stick systems. Curtain walls are often designed for all seasons, with climatic changes generally noted only in increased thermal resistance of frames, panels, or glass units or in the reflectivity, emissivity, or heat absorption of the glass. Without the selective surfaces of glass and insulating glass units, today's transparent facades would not be practical in most parts of the world. While the present choices for economical glazing may seem limited, this might change within a few years as the more specialized types become more common.

Curtain Walls

AAMA defines a curtain wall as any building wall, of any material, that carries no superimposed vertical loads. This clearly divides walls into bearing and nonbearing. Anchored brick veneer and precast concrete panels are both examples of curtain walls. A metal curtain wall has a metal frame that supports panels of glass, metal, stone, or other cladding materials. The metal frame can be installed on-site with individual pieces (stick system), or units can be prefabricated in the factory (unit or unitized system). Finally, a window wall is a type of curtain wall that is installed between two floors or a floor and the roof.

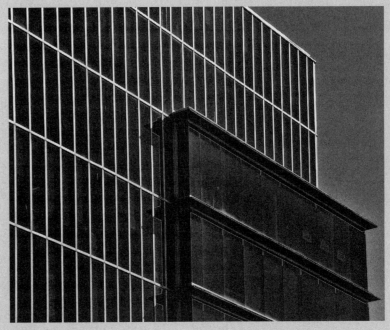

FIGURE 5.2 (Photo by G. Russell Heliker)

The development of the metal and glass curtain wall is intrinsically linked with heating, ventilating, and air-conditioning (HVAC) systems, prompted by more stringent energy codes and desired for comfort. In the more sophisticated examples, the curtain wall contributes to the building systems, providing daylighting, ventilation, and dynamic thermal transfer. Some predict that the era of the passive facade is ending, although North America has been slower to adopt alternatives than Europe.[2]

5.2.1 ALUMINUM FRAMES

Most curtain wall frames are extruded aluminum. The differences are in the amount of prefabrication. The American Architectural Manufacturers Association (AAMA) defines several wall systems in their *Curtain Wall Design Guide Manual*.[3] The most common aluminum frames are based on either the "stick system" or the "unit system." They have the following advantages and disadvantages.

The *stick system* is installed piece by piece on-site, including the glazing. Stick systems are purchased in 24- to 40-foot (7–12 m) lengths and cut on-site or in the shop—some may be partially assembled at the shop. Advantages of the stick system are the lower cost (although this gap is narrowing), including lower shipping and handling costs, flexibility, and the potential to adjust the curtain wall frame to the structural frame. Other advantages include getting the frame to the job site quickly, ease of handling and storing, and the ability to work on different areas of the building at the same time.[4] The disadvantage is field installation of the glazing, often by unskilled workers. A certain amount of control is lost when the curtain wall frame is installed on-site. These systems are more suitable for small projects.

The *unit,* or *unitized,* system is a series of prefabricated units that interlock with the adjacent frame and are often preglazed. They may be as high as three stories in height, but generally span just one floor, and range from 4 to 12 feet (1.2–3.6 m) in width.[5] The obvious advantage is the fabrication in a controlled environment. It is also easier to isolate the glass unit from structural movement, especially seismic, with unitized systems. With proper scheduling and lead time, the unitized system allows the building to be "closed in" more quickly. (The overall fabrication and installation time is often similar for stick and unitized systems. Stick systems can be delivered to the site more quickly but take longer to erect. Unitized systems require more lead time but are erected more quickly.) Some of the disadvantages of unitized systems include the increased cost and problems with transportation, protection of the units, and on-site storage. Because the units interlock with each other, installation must be sequential. "Leave-out" units are necessary to load construction materials into the interior of the building; these units, installed out of sequence, require special installation and joint design. Replacement of components can be more difficult. Unitized systems have more joints than stick systems. Where the rails and mullions of stick systems each have a joint to either side that seals the glass to the frame, unitized systems have an additional joint that seals the frame of one unit to the adjoining unit. However, installing and sealing the glazing unit in a controlled environment, as is possible with the unitized system, is superior to the field installation of glazing units with the stick system.

The *"unit-and-mullion" system,* sometimes called the semiunitized system, is a hybrid of the stick and unit systems. It is comprised of subframes, with fixed glazing, that are then attached to a stick system on site.

Window Walls

The curtain wall has become synonymous with the glass and metal cladding of high-rises. Everyone assumes that the cladding is a continuous curtain wall attached to the exterior of the structure. But is it? Careful detailing of a window wall, bearing on the floor slab, can make it appear as a continuous curtain wall. It is by definition a curtain wall —the difference is one of function. With a continuous curtain wall, all barriers and retarders can be continuous for the full height of the building. When the system bears on the floor slab, the continuity is broken and the water barrier, air barrier system, vapor retarder, and thermal insulation must be designed to wrap around the floor structure. The system is generally used to reduce costs. When used on mid- to high-rise construction it is especially critical that the window wall be capable of withstanding the wind and seismic loads. Because this is a marginal system, every attempt must be made to ensure that it is properly detailed, specified, and constructed. The design in Figure 5.3 shows how the continuity of the water and air barriers between two window wall units can be maintained at the floor slab. It is equally important that the window wall meet the requirements for the specific application. Oftentimes the units meet only the standards required for windows rather than for a window wall used on a high-rise building.

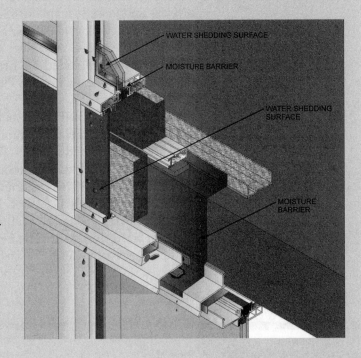

FIGURE 5.3 (Courtesy of RDH Building Engineering Ltd.)

Generally, the more that can be fabricated under controlled conditions, the more reliable the function and durability of the system. The trade-offs are usually higher cost and possible scheduling problems. The preference for a unitized system over a stick system is sometimes dependent on the local construction culture. Whether a customized system is worth the additional expense must be determined on a case-by-case basis. The custom systems become more economical the larger the project and the greater the repetition.

Another type of support offers a seemingly *frameless* wall of glass. Structural glass, also called bolt-fixed glass, is a series of glass units held together with "patches" or bolted connections that support the glass by direct bearing and friction. These fittings are usually stainless steel. Lateral support can be in the form of vertical glass fins (or mullions) or steel and cable tension structures taking the form of a vertical truss.

A frameless appearance can be acquired with fittings that are integral with laminated glass, such as the Pilkington Planar Integral. Another approach is an aluminum frame, such as the 1600 Wall System2 by Kawneer, that secures the glazing unit with structural sealant, hiding the frame behind. The frame or fittings become visible from the exterior when the exterior light level is lower than the interior.

5.2.2 GLASS TYPES

Alistair Pilkington is one of the individuals who deserves credit for our contemporary glass curtain walls. In 1952 he began to experiment with using molten tin to support, or float, the molten glass.[6] The tin was dead flat and so would be the glass. With the invention of *float glass,* in full production by 1959, high quality glass became economical. Pilkington has been an important player in the manufacturing of glass and glass systems for many years. By the mid-1850s, shortly after the construction of the Crystal Palace, 75 percent of all glass in England was manufactured by only three firms, and Pilkington was one of them.[7] Further developments by Pilkington have included the first structural or bolt-fixed glass system to be widely marketed—the Pilkington Planar—which can now accommodate triple-glazed insulating units.

Today the "incentive to expand the primary product range [in glass] is small," according to Michael Wigginton.[8] The developments in glass are enormous; but they are concentrated more on finishes and coatings, fittings and gases for insulated units, and small manipulations of float glass. Spurred by energy concerns, aesthetics, and safety concerns, much invention continues to occur within these areas. As Michael Flynn of Pei Cobb Freed & Partners states, "an architect's quest for glass that is truly clear, nonreflective, minimizes heat transfer, and resists impact, may not be so elusive.... 'The industry is not far from achieving this seemingly contradictory set of criteria.'"[9] The automotive business is at the forefront of much glass research, as the search for highly transparent, solar heat–reflective, impact resistant, and safe glass for windshields is ongoing.

Shiny Buildings

Curtain walls of highly reflective materials (both glass and metal) are becoming a concern. The reflected energy can add to the heat load of nearby buildings, while the glare can be an annoyance at best and hazardous to traffic at worst. Some cities in Asia, such as Singapore, are enacting legislation to control external reflectivity. Unfortunately, this can also limit the use of low-E glass.[1]

Tall buildings clad with glass also cause problems for migratory birds that use the stars to navigate at night and are confused by the lights of office towers. Chicago, which is in the flight path of 300 species, and Toronto, Ontario, have instituted programs to reduce the number of bird deaths from flying into glass walls (estimated by some to be as high as one billion birds a year in the United States). By turning off the upper floor lights in office towers during peak migration periods, the death rates have fallen sharply. Reflective glass and metal is a problem during the day, where reportedly 500 birds hit two mirrored towers in Toronto on a single morning.[2]

1. "Sealing the Building Envelope: Curtain Wall and Cladding in Hong Kong," *Curtain Wall & Cladding Supplement, Building Journal,* discussion with Bruce Wymond of Meindhardt Facade Technology. (http://www.building.com.hk)
2. "Birds and Buildings: Traffic Accidents," *The Economist* (May 8, 2004), p.31.

The following general information on glazing concentrates on aesthetics and energy. (Much of the information in this section comes from the Glass Association of North America's *GANA Glazing Manual,* a very good primer on glazing technology.)[10] It should be noted that each glass manufacturer's products will be slightly different.

Glass can be annealed; heat strengthened such that its bending strength is double that of annealed; or fully tempered, with four times the bending strength of annealed glass of the same size and thickness. These types can then be *laminated* with a plastic film between two lites for safety reasons or increased sound resistance. Lamination is also used to protect coatings. *Insulating units* of two or more lites held apart with a spacer, usually of aluminum or stainless steel, increase thermal resistance. The spacer contains a desiccant to keep the air space free of visible moisture. A single or double seal around the unit insures the space is hermetically sealed. *Warm-edge technology* recognizes the advantages of lower thermal conductance at the edge of insulating units by using low-conductance spacers. This not only decreases heat loss but helps control condensation. Many manufacturers provide units with warm-edge technology. Warm-edge technology spacers include "extruded butyl materials, foam rubber based materials, formed plastics and metal strip based products."[11] There is a great deal of research occurring in this area, and a number of spacers are available for use with insulated glass units. Each should be carefully evaluated by a consultant or manufacturer with expertise on edge seals, as each has advantages and disadvantages.

Float glass, the clearest of the glazing options, has a transmittance of 75 to 92 percent of visible light, depending on the thickness and composition. Unless low-iron glass is specified, float glass will usually have a slight greenish tint at thicknesses of ⅜ inch (10 mm) or greater. *Tinted or heat-absorbing glass* has a transmittance of 14 to 85 percent, depending on thickness and degree of tinting. According to GANA, typical colors available in North America are bronze, gray, dark gray, aquamarine, green, deep green, blue, and black, with colors such as rose and emerald green produced in Europe. The tinting absorbs, and thereby reduces, solar transmittance.

The reflection, absorption, and radiation of solar energy can also be controlled with coatings on glass, the most common being *solar-reflective glass* and low-emissivity (or *low-E*) glass. Depending on the climate, these coatings often pay for themselves in reduced sizing of HVAC systems and lowered operating costs. Reflective coatings come in silver, blue, gold, and copper colors. The ability to reflect light is often at the expense of visible light transmission—a complaint of some occupants in buildings with solar-reflective glass. The various metallic coatings of low-E glass are nearly invisible, according to GANA. Low-E glass reflects long-wave, infrared energy. Some coatings are also reflective of the entire infrared spectrum. Selecting the appropriate coating on the correct surface will depend on the climate.

When transparency or translucency is not desired, there are various ways of creating *opaque* or *spandral glass. Ceramic frit* is a ceramic coating fused to the base glass during the heat-treating process. The frit can be applied in thicker and also multiple layers to increase the opacity. It comes in a wide range of colors. Because pinholes are an acceptable part of the manufacturing process, fritted glass requires opaque backup construction. *Polyester* and *silicone films* and paints are other methods of creating opaque glass. Both also come in a wide range of colors. The

Self-Cleaning Glass

The glass industry is developing glazing with a photocatalytic coating that reacts with sunlight to break down and dislodge organic dirt. (The concept can work equally well with paints.) The Pilkington Activ self-cleaning glass is also hydrophilic; instead of remaining in droplets, rainwater spreads uniformly to wash away the dirt.

manufacturer should be consulted concerning contact with other materials, such as insulation, and the air-space requirements behind these films. Typically, manufacturers advise against adhering insulation directly to films. A *"shadow box"* creates the illusion of opacity with a dark metal pan or insulation board that is held back from the glass. Such boxes must be ventilated to avoid temperature buildup and condensation.

The efficiency of insulated glass units is enhanced by using these coatings and glasses in combination with warm-edge technology and low-conductance gases such as argon, krypton, or xenon. Coatings can create differential thermal stresses between the center of the glass and the edges, a possible source of failure if not designed correctly.

5.2.3 ENERGY CONCERNS

Many aluminum glass curtain walls are poorly designed with respect to thermal performance. Thermal breaks in the frame, if there are any, are often thin and compromised by cold air flow or thermal bridges from fasteners or adjacent construction. This break is important for reduction of condensation and also heat transfer.

Another concern is ensuring that the overall U- or R-value of the aluminum glass curtain wall is correctly calculated. Using information provided by manufacturers, architects and engineers often determine the thermal performance of the wall by using the U-values of the center of the glass panel and the center of the spandrel panel and area-weighting the two. "Even dated ASHRAE or AAMA references indicate this approach is incorrect and significantly overestimates the thermal resistance of the wall," according to Mark Brook (from the building facade engineering firm, Brook Van Dalen & Associates). The glass should be area-weighted based on the U-value at the edge of the glass and at the center. The thermal value of the frame of the vision and spandrel panels must also be included in the calculations.[12] The spandrel insulation and the air barrier system for the curtain wall should be detailed and specified by the architect to ensure that the intended R-value is obtained and the air barrier is continuous.

5.2.4 GLASS FAILURES

Glass breakage problems have plagued the building industry ever since glass became a popular cladding, according to Tom Schwartz of Simpson Gumpertz & Heger. Glass is unforgiving—it is very brittle and gives no warning before it fails. High-wind loading is generally not the cause of glass failures, as this is usually well considered during design. Hurricane Andrew is a case in point; the incidence of broken glass in downtown Miami was relatively low. Glass breakage problems are more often due to "impact damage, thermal stress on glass with damaged edges, and spontaneous fracture of fully tempered glass from nickel sulfide impurities."[13] Brook notes that thermal breakage is the most common and readily identifiable problem.[14]

Perhaps the most famous glass curtain wall failure occurred with the reflective glass cladding of the 790-foot John Hancock Tower in Boston, completed in 1973. Many of the 10,344 insulated glass units fractured, and all were eventually replaced with fully tempered monolithic glass. For years rumors abounded as to the failure mechanism. Some thought it was the excessive swaying of the building, others blamed the long, slender footprint or the settlement of the foundation. The disputes were finally settled and the cause of the failure made public during court testimony in 1990. The failure resulted primarily from the design of the insulating glass units themselves. The lead tape spacer, which separated the two lites of glass, bonded tenaciously to the glass. Stress at the soldered lead-to-glass bond line eventually led to bond failure. In the process of failure, the lead "ripped microscopically small pieces of glass from the glass surface," creating serious stress-concentrators along the edges that triggered the fractures under loads within the design ranges.[15] To avoid glass failures, the best advice may be to make sure the glass unit meets the expected (which may be higher than the required code) wind and impact loads, specify a glass type and a manufacturer with a long record of success, and use only qualified installers.

5.3 METAL- AND STONE-PANEL CURTAIN WALLS

If transparency or translucency is not desired, panels of a variety of materials, from terra-cotta to titanium can be used in curtain walls. Some of these panels are combined with glass units in the aluminum curtain-wall frame. Others are merely a screen for the rain, such as the open-joint systems or punched metal screens, while still other panels may be joined with sophisticated pressure-equalized joints. Stone can also be cast in concrete panels, supported by a light-gauge metal truss, or directly supported by an in-situ concrete or concrete masonry backup wall with clips. Metal can be fabricated in panels (sometimes with integral insulation), shingles, or laminated to sheathing for direct attachment to a light-gauge frame.

5.3.1 TYPES OF METAL AND FINISHES

An excellent reference on metals is *Architectural Metals: A Guide to Selection, Specification, and Performance,* by L. William Zahner. Much of the information in this section comes from this reference.

The two most common *aluminum* panels are *honeycomb backed* and *aluminum composite material (ACM).* An aluminum skin bonded to a stiffening layer or honeycomb of plastic, aluminum, or stiffened paper allows for varying panel thicknesses. This is an advantage when the structural or thermal properties need to be increased, but these systems require custom detailing. The more popular ACM can be formed into curves and is usually less costly and easier to install than other aluminum panels, as standard details have been developed for its thin profile.[16] Alucabond, made by Alcan, was introduced in North America from Europe in the late 1970s.

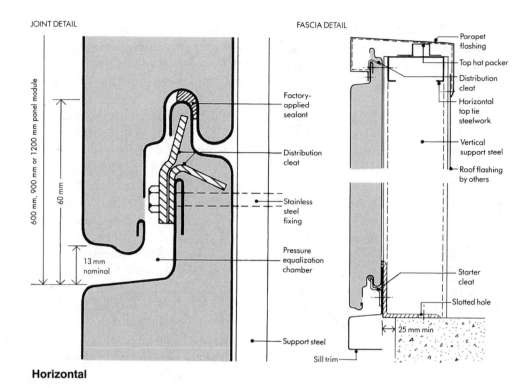

Horizontal

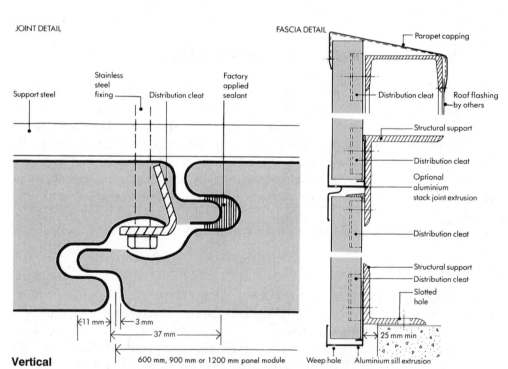

Vertical

FIGURE 5.4 The joint between Formawall 1000 panels by H.H. Robertson creates a pressure-equalization chamber (PEC) that stops the passage of both water and air. A 13-mm (½ in.) capillary break along with a sloped drain shelf assures that water drains to the exterior at the horizontal joints. For panels oriented horizontally, there is typically a factory-applied butyl sealant, which sits in the neck of the PEC. When the panels are joined on-site, this is compressed, which further precludes water ingress. The horizontal panel has a number of alternative vertical joint details—the most commonly used is sealed on-site with a backer rod and polyurethane sealant. The vertical joints have a factory applied sealant. (Courtesy of H. H. Robertson Asia/Pacific)

H. H. Robertson Formawall 1000 is an example of a foamed aluminum panel. The standard two-inch (50 mm) thick panels come clad with steel, Zincalume, or aluminum, with various finishes. The metal skin covers expanded or extruded polystyrene, polyurethane, or rock wool insulation. Panels up to 32 feet (10 m) in height are available as well as curved forms (see Figure 5.4).

Aluminum is corrosion resistant and comes with a variety of finishes in a wide range of colors. At minimum, aluminum should be protected with clear anodizing. Electrolic deposition of salts into the microscopic pores of the surface oxide of aluminum produces "striking reds" with copper salts and "deep blue tones" with cobalt salts.[17] The higher priced gold and silver salts will produce yellows and golds.[18]

Stainless steel is long-lasting and comes in a number of finishes, including highly reflective, matte, smooth, brushed, and embossed. Deep rich hues, which "no paint can even come close to," can be produced with a process called light interference on stainless steel and also titanium, according to L. William Zahner.[19] Various finishes can be factory applied, including a terne coating that has an appearance similar to lead. Terne is an alloy of lead and tin, with the tin helping to bond the lead to the steel. *Terne-coated stainless steel* is referred to by the initials TCS. For standard corrosion resistance, 304 alloy stainless steel is commonly used; 316 alloy, with molybdenum, can be specified for even greater corrosion protection in coastal areas or areas with high pollution levels. The primary disadvantage of stainless steel is the initial cost. However, the life-cycle cost makes it more economical when compared with less durable metals.

Steel with various finishes offers lower cost alternatives. Steel needs to be protected from corrosion, generally by a sacrificial zinc coating. Galvalume (another trade name is Zincalume) has a hot-dip zinc and aluminum coating and is produced by most major steel manufacturers. It offers better corrosion resistance than just galvanized metal. If the cut edges are protected, the Galvalum coating lasts five to ten times as long as the coating on G90 galvanized steel in salt spray tests.[20] The first commercial sheets were fabricated in 1972. An acrylic coating, part of Galvalume Plus, protects the sheets during transit and storage and eliminates the need for a varnishing oil that must be removed on-site. If a uniform appearance is desired, the product should be prepainted by the manufacturer, as even Galvalume Plus will exhibit the normal variations seen with all hot-dip products.

Sheet metal can be sprayed with paint as individual pieces or "coil coated" as flat material. The coil finish must be more flexible, with better adherence than a spray-applied coating, as the coil-coated metal is recoiled after it has been painted. Coil coating allows for better control of volatile organic compound (VOC) emissions than spray coatings.[21] There are a number of paints used on metals with a variety of primers. Fluorocarbons are considered by some to be the "premier exterior architectural coatings." Known by the registered name Kynar 500, they are manufactured by a number of companies. They resist fading and chalking and are "superior to all other coatings in weatherability."[22] They come in earth tones, to which metallic and clear coatings can be added with low to medium glosses.

Other coatings include thermoset acrylics, which are durable and come in a wide range of colors and glosses; however, the pieces cannot be postformed, as the acrylic finish is baked-on. They will fade to some degree. Various urethane coatings also come in a wide range of colors and glosses and have excellent chemical resistance. They will fade and chalk to a minor degree. Polyesters come in a variety of colors, as well as high glosses, and have good durability. Although fluorocarbons have better weathering characteristics, polyester coatings are widely used in

Europe in "high-quality architectural applications."[23] Urethane and polyester coatings can be enhanced with pearlescent additives that act as thin-film light interference. Metals can also have a porcelain enamel or ceramic coating.

Weathering steel in plate form has been used for cladding. The thinner sheet materials had durability problems and are no longer produced. Careful detailing, to ensure that the steel is always dry, by eliminating ponding opportunities and using a thickness of 0.032 inches (0.813 mm) or greater, has alleviated most of the earlier problems. Staining can be a major problem with the rich and changing texture of the self-arresting oxidation. Although oxidation will eventually be minimal, it will not be arrested if subjected to running water. The exterior wall must be detailed with this in mind. A house in Toronto, Ontario, by Shim-Sutcliffe Architects used 4.5 mm (0.17 in.) weathering steel as cladding.[24]

Zinc is well known for its high corrosion resistance. When combined with titanium (1%) and copper (1%), it is a malleable and strong metal with a natural blue-gray or pewter appearance. Zinc also comes in preweathered finishes to avoid the transition phase. Rheinzink now offers a preweathered graphite-gray, which is a darker variation than normally found with zinc. Zinc panels should be well ventilated on the nonexposed surfaces. Water from condensation or leaking can dissolve the metal relatively quickly.[25] The panel profile should not include ledges where water can pond.

Titanium is also a popular but costly metal, perhaps made most famous by Frank Gehry's Guggenheim Museum in Bilbao, Spain, which is clad in more than 10,000 square meters (107,340 sq ft) of the material. One of the attractive features of titanium is its low coefficient of thermal expansion, which is half of stainless steel and one-third of aluminum. It is more flexible and weighs less than steel, yet it is equal in tensile strength and is up to four times as hard as mild steel.[26] Titanium, the fourth most abundant metal on earth, was first available commercially in 1951.[27] The major drawback is the cost.

5.3.2 SPECIFYING METALS FOR CURTAIN-WALL PANELS

Specifications need to stipulate the specific metal (for example, there are many different types of stainless steel), the finish, and the gauge. A sample, cut in half and engraved with the signature of the architect and the supplier, will eliminate any misunderstanding later on. Some metals, such as stainless steel, need to be installed in order of fabrication, with the rolling direction indicated. This complicates erection but avoids unsuitable changes in the surface appearance of the curtain wall. The final consideration is called "flatness." This is dependent on the thickness of the material, the finish, the size and profile (or backing) of the panel, and the attachment.[28] Durability should be the overriding criteria in selecting the metal, finish, gauge, and profile, tempered by aesthetics and budget. Galvanic action between dissimilar metals should be considered when selecting fasteners for metal panels. If corrosion protection is obtained with zinc or other coatings, this must be repaired on-site when the metal is cut, drilled, or otherwise damaged. In addition to durability problems with corrosion, there is the visual problem of staining.

5.3.3 THIN STONE PANELS

There is an infinite variety of colors and patterns within natural stone. However, stone is a heterogeneous material with limited availability—it is *not* a product that can be ordered from samples. To ensure that a particular look is obtained for a project, the architect needs to visit the quarry and determine that there are adequate deposits of the desired stone and that the quarry is capable of fabricating the amount and quality needed. Then one must expect considerable variation within the fabricated panels. Stone should be tested from the specific area of the quarry to be used. Historical test data from the quarry should not be relied on.

Stone only makes sense as a contemporary cladding if the weight is reduced. New technology in stone cutting has led to its use as a lightweight curtain-wall material. Its use was further refined with design advances in finishing and fastening techniques through the 1980s. (In the 1980s the use of finished travertine and marble increased 800 percent and granite 2,000 percent.) [29] What is termed "thin stone" is stone cut in slices from 0.75 to 2.5 inches (19 to 64 mm). As the panels become thinner, the potential for failure increases.

Thin stone is attached to a backing system or frame. Alternative methods of attachment include stone-faced precast concrete panels, and stone attached to a steel truss or steel studs in a factory. Each system has had its share of problems. Stone is now attached to the mechanically precast concrete panel and a bond-breaker is placed between the two to accommodate differential expansion between the stone and concrete, which created problems in early systems. [30] Corrosion of carbon-steel anchorage fittings also caused many early problems. This has been corrected with the use of stainless-steel fittings. Potential corrosion is always a problem with light-gauge steel frame supports.

Further technology led to slicing stone as thin as ¼ inch (6 mm). The drive has not only been for lighter materials but for increased availability and reduced cost. Exotic stone, sliced in thin layers, can be adhered to a lesser quality stone. To decrease cost and weight, it can also be adhered to an aluminum honeycomb panel. Long-term durability should be carefully reviewed with these systems, particularly at the joints between panels.

5.3.4 TYPE OF STONE

Stone is selected on the basis of type, grade, and finish, all of which influence the durability as well as the appearance of the stone. Climate, including exposure to pollutants and freeze-thaw cycles, should be considered in the selection of the stone and the finish. Stones traditionally used on exteriors are granite, limestone, sandstone, and marble.

The igneous rock granite is recognized as the most stable and consistent of the four traditionally used stones. Durability is dependent on a number of items, including permeability and capillarity of the stone. Of the four, granite is the least permeable. [31] Hardness is usually not important for vertical applications, but it does affect the ease of fabrication. Generally the more silica, the more durable the stone—with granite having the highest silica content. [32] The design safety factors recommended by manufacturers and stone associations are highest for marble (6–12), followed by limestone (4–7) and then granite (2.5–4). [33]

Granite is more than 90 percent free quartz and feldspar. It generally has a polished, honed, or thermal finish. The thermal finish, created by running a flame over the surface, causing it to fracture, also reduces its strength. It also reduces the thickness by approximately ⅛ inch (3 mm). The reduced thickness should be used for strength calculations. Granite comes in a wide range of colors, from white to dark gray, and has a more homogeneous appearance than many stones. Trace minerals such as iron can cause staining and also exfoliation or spalling at the surface when they oxidize.

The quality of sandstone, a sedimentary rock, varies widely. Because of this variability, it is not used as frequently as other stones. It is generally more porous or permeable than other stones, causing durability problems. Freeze-thaw cycles can cause delamination of the layers of sandstone. Laying the stone with the bedding planes horizontal (perpendicular to gravity) alleviates some of these problems. When the bedding planes are vertical they can more easily delaminate, causing the face to spall. Deicing salts should not come in contact with sandstone, which is also more susceptible than other stones to damage by acids and other cleaners. (However, it is a good idea to keep acids and other cleaners away from all stone.) Sandstone is primarily grains of quartz cemented together with a binder. Silica, as a binder, forms the lightest color and hardest sandstone. If the binder is carbonate of lime, it is more easily worked and more gray in color, but it will have some of the problems of limestone. Iron oxide produces a reddish-brown color that is easily worked, while clay matter produces browns that are absorptive and susceptible to freeze-thaw damage.[34]

Sandstone finishes include smooth, slightly textured, and rough. While less expensive than marble or granite, it usually is more costly than limestone. Caution should be exercised when specifying this stone. Crucial information for all stone, but especially important for sandstone, is the track record of the quarry. Certification should be obtained from the quarry that the stone meets ASTM standards for its grade. Viewing a large sampling will help in understanding the range of color variations. Finally, the contractor buying the stone must be knowledgeable.[35]

Limestone, another sedimentary rock, often contains visible clues of its formation in ancient lake- or seabeds. Because it is a sedimentary rock, there is a direction to the grain. Although the grain direction is not as pronounced as with sandstone, it must be considered during quarrying and fabrication. Because it is a fairly uniform stone, it can be cut or machined in any direction without splitting. Limestone comes in ranges of almost white to gray, pinks, reds, blues, buff, and the whites and yellows of dolomite limestones. The more pure—that is, those of nearly all calcium carbonate—are the whitest and the most soluble. Dolomites are predominantly magnesium carbonate, making them generally harder and less soluble than other limestones.[36] Most "bluestone" is primarily calcium carbonate. The popular Canadian "tindal stone" is a limestone. Finishes include smooth, machine-pebbled, grooved, rock-faced, and other textures. Some limestones can be polished.

Marble comes in perhaps the widest variety of colors and patterns. Most of this metamorphic rock started out as limestone. Available in reds, greens, blues, blacks, and whites—impurities deposited during its formation create veining and "figures." Both marble and limestone are more prone to acid rain attack because of the carbonates in the stone. This phenomenon is sometimes called sugaring in marble, a descriptive term for the deterioration which can be seen on older marble statues. Some marbles permanently deform with thermal expansion. This permanent elongation, which causes a panel to bow, also increases its porosity and chance of failure. The irreversible process is called hysteresis. Dark-colored marbles can fade when exposed to ultraviolet light. Marble will also lose more strength when subjected to freeze-thaw cycles than granite or limestone. In general, marble and also travertine, another metamorphic stone, should be used very cautiously on exteriors.

Detailing Stone for Economy

To aid architects in designing for economy, the Indiana Limestone Institute of America made the following recommendations:

- Butt joints are usually more economical on smooth faces and quirk joints more economical on textured finishes, as only one face of the stone panel need be textured. (See Figure 5.5.)

- Keep return heads the same depth as the normal stone thickness. (See Figure 5.6.)

- Place design rustification on the side of the joint, not in the center. (See Figure 5.7.)

In addition, costs should be kept lower with repetition of stone panels whenever possible.[1]

---

1. This information is from *Indiana Limestone Handbook* (Bedford, Ind.: Indiana Limestone Institute of America, Inc., 2002) and Kenneth A. Hooker, "Working with Cut Limestone," *Magazine of Masonry Construction* (March 1993).

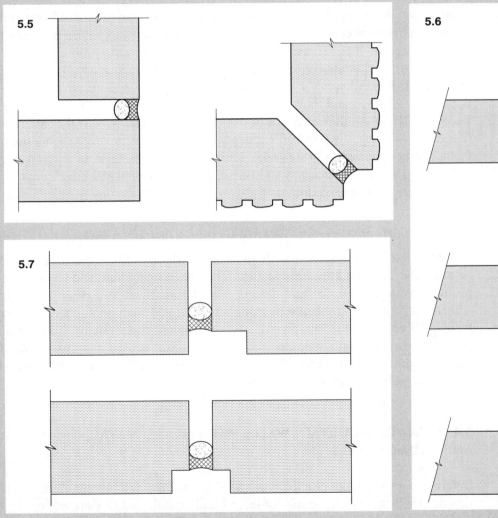

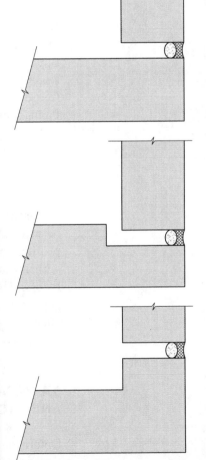

FIGURES 5.5, 5.6, 5.7 (Courtesy of Indiana Limestone Institute of America, Inc.)

5.3.5 SPECIFYING STONE PANELS

Selecting a stone, a finish, and a grade that are compatible with the durability expectations of the cladding occurs in tandem with finding a quarry and fabricator who can produce the selected stone. More so than with any other cladding material, availability is a key issue with stone. Talking with stone installers from similarly sized projects is useful. Ideally, the stone is selected by the architect and not through a low-bid process. Determining the thickness of the stone is also critical. The physical properties of the particular stone, finish, and thickness should be carefully reviewed and tested to ensure that the durability expectations will be met. The grade is selected in part on the finish and the visibility. A rough finish or a stone that is not visible at the pedestrian level can have more imperfections than a smooth finish at street level. Scheduling, storage, shipping, and handling are all important factors to consider with stone.

5.3.6 STONE FAILURES

Stone is a natural material with inherent weaknesses. These weaknesses are exacerbated as thinner and thinner panels are used with increased lateral loads and differential movement on higher stories, as well as increased exposure to freeze-thaw cycles and pollutants. There presently is no single test for durability of stone. Dissolving of carbonate-based stone by acids and damage through hysteresis are major problems. Chapter 9 discusses failures due to hysteresis on the Amoco Building in Chicago and Finlandia Hall in Helsinki, Finland. How much water the stone absorbs is another measure of durability for climates with the potential for freeze-thaw damage. A polished surface will absorb less moisture than a honed or flame-finished surface. Careful selection of an appropriate stone from a specific quarry, of a suitable dimension and finish, and a well-designed attachment system will produce a durable cladding.

5.3.7 FASTENING SYSTEMS FOR STONE PANELS

Fastening systems for stone panels must fulfill the function typical of any fitting between the cladding and the structure. The fastening system, and the stone panel profile, should be selected and designed by the architect and structural engineer with input from the stonemason, stone supplier, and manufacturer of the attachments. There are numerous proprietary stone anchorage systems. Today stone is generally attached with stainless steel fixings—302 or 304 is normally used for anchors embedded in stone. A number of good references on attaching stone veneer are published by trade associations.

5.4 DESIGNING CURTAIN WALLS WITH GLASS, METAL, AND STONE PANELS

Determining the energy efficiency of the glass curtain-wall system, detailing joints that do not leak, and designing for lateral and seismic stability are no longer solely the responsibility of the architect and consulting mechanical and structural engineers. The role of the architect has shifted to one of team management.

5.4.1 DESIGN TEAM

The architect, structural engineer, mechanical engineer, specialist facade designers, energy consultants; the glass, metal or stone fabricator, and the curtain wall manufacturer form the curtain-wall design team. They should all be on board from the proverbial sketch on the napkin. Depending on the project and cladding, other team members might include the specifications writer, testing laboratory, trade representatives, installers, and contractor or construction manager. As the AAMA noted: "Those less familiar with metal curtain wall construction, or perhaps using it for the first time, are likely to spend a great deal of time in minute detailing, only to discover later that some of the labor was wasted."[37] This is true for glass, metal, and stone panels, although the team members may be more difficult to identify when working with stone cladding than with off-the-shelf metal panels or glazing systems.

An understanding of the components of the curtain wall will help in understanding this complex mix of team members. Metal curtain walls are available to meet any aesthetic, budget, durability, or energy requirement. The stated intention of ASHRAE 90.1 Code is "to promote the application of cost-effective design practices and technologies that minimize energy consumption without sacrificing either the comfort or productivity of the occupants." This summarizes the function of curtain walls.

5.4.2 STRUCTURAL ENGINEERS AND CURTAIN-WALL CONSULTANTS

Wind and seismic loads, as well as differential movement and gravity loads, can be considerable on high-rise buildings and should not be discounted on low-rise buildings. A structural engineer should design—or approve of—all connections of the curtain wall to the structural frame and size all movement joints, based on thermal and moisture differential expansion and contraction, lateral loading, story

FIGURE 5.8 A steel band that encircles the interior concrete column and connects to the curtain-wall frame allows for differential vertical movement between the curtain wall and the structure but also provides lateral support. Photo by Linda Brock.

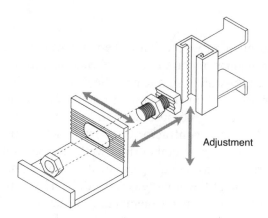

FIGURE 5.9 This wind and dead-load stone fixing allows for adjustments in the lateral, horizontal, and vertical directions, which is important when considering tolerances of the structural frame and clearances required during construction. After attachment there is no movement in the lateral direction. Differential movement between the stone panels and the structure is usually accommodated with vertical expansion joints to the sides of the panel and a horizontal expansion joint at the top of the panel. Illustration courtesy of Permasteelisa Cladding Technologies.

Adjustment

drift, elastic deformation, and creep. Shortening of concrete frames and slab deflection in combination with thermal expansion and contraction of the frame, fittings, and panels must be accommodated. Adjustability of the attachments in three directions accommodates fabrication and installation tolerances and clearances for both the fitting and frame and the structure. After the fitting and frame are attached and the panel installed, there should be no lateral movement. Differential vertical and horizontal movement must be accommodated between the panel and the structural frame. The joints between the panels and the curtain wall frame must be watertight and airtight.

Fabrication and installation tolerances and clearances, as well as the movement capabilities of the sealant, can add to the width of these joints. Story drift from seismic events requires wide joints to accommodate the movement. These joints *cannot* be minimized. The aesthetic concerns about wide joints should be mitigated by concerns over water leakage and, in extreme cases, life-safety problems created by undersized joints. Tolerances and clearances must be fully understood by the designers, the fabricators, the installers, and the contractor. Accommodating a slightly out-of plumb, two-story concrete frame is an entirely different story when the problem is on a 10- to 20-story building.

5.4.3 Keeping Out Water and Air

Many aluminum glass curtain-wall systems effectively rely on a face seal at the joints to keep out water, whether detailed as such or not. These are suitable only for low-rise buildings with overhangs that see little rain exposure. The minimum frame design should include horizontal sills that drain any interstitial water to the exterior through weep holes. The sills are dammed and sealed to the vertical mullions. Each unit should have three weep holes to avoid damming of water by the two setting blocks. Vertical mullions should drain at each floor and not, as one engineer put it, provide a vertical downspout for the whole facade. Some manufacturers have developed drainage sills that continue across the vertical mullion. Ideally the glazing pockets should be sloped to the weep holes. Minimizing the number of intermediate, horizontal mullions or rails also minimizes the potential for leakage. In other words, the larger the glass unit, the less chance of leakage.

Wet glazing, with liquid sealants, is more watertight than dry glazing with gaskets. However wet glazing is highly dependent on workmanship and must be done from the exterior. Structural silicone sealants should be factory applied, as surface preparation and workmanship is critical for long-term performance. The best protection against water entry is provided with a curtain-wall frame designed as a pressure-equalized rain screen. The liquid sealants and gaskets form the air barrier of such a system. However, according to building facade engineer Mark Brook, "contrary to the claims of many manufacturers, and the specifications of most architects, common North American curtain walls are not true pressure-equalized systems as currently defined in the literature."[38] While there is debate over whether these are truly pressure-equalized, they appear to be performing well.

The following recommendations from the engineering firm Simpson Gumpertz & Heger will help prevent glass breakage and keep water out of the aluminum glass and curtain-wall clad building:[39]

- Isolate curtain wall from building structure movement
- Isolate glass from curtain-wall frame movement
- Drain each glazing opening locally
- Slope glazing pocket and perimeter flashing sills to weep holes
- Keep water away from edges of insulating or laminated glass
- Wet seal for maximum watertightness
- Use backup flashing at the perimeter

Metal- and stone-panel curtain walls are often designed as a drainage cavity wall. Detailing of this cavity is the same as for any other cladding type. It is particularly important that metals such as zinc and porous stones rapidly shed any water that enters the cavity. Some joints between metal panels are designed as pressure-equalized joints. (See Figure 5.4.) In these cases there may not be an internal cavity with a water barrier. Without the redundancy of a drainage cavity, these systems are entirely dependent on the joint design. Some systems have "open" joints (see Chapters 7 and 9). Sealants used with stone should be carefully evaluated and tested. Some sealants leach into the stone, causing unsightly staining. Stone (and metal) panels should not continue below grade.

After ensuring that the curtain wall is watertight and airtight, the emphasis should shift to transitions to adjoining wall systems, the base of the building, and the roof and soffits. The curtain-wall manufacturer most likely will not design these interfaces—it is up to the architect. All of the rules for general joint design and flashing apply to these transitions.

5.4.4 MAINTENANCE

Facilitating the task of cleaning glass curtain walls is sometimes overlooked. The design of the window washing equipment should be part of the preliminary design. Sealant joints will need to be periodically checked and replaced on all curtain walls. Provisions must be provided for this important maintenance task. If a double-facade wall is being considered, the maintenance costs should be discussed with the client. Cleaning four surfaces instead of two, as well as maintaining any environmental controls within the glass facade, substantially increases the maintenance cost. In addition to sealant inspection, standard maintenance for stone and metal panels includes cleaning and periodic inspection of panels for damage. The "maintenance manual" should limit the use of chloride and any hydrochloride salts that might come in contact with most stone and some metals. Wood preservatives may also corrode some metals, such as zinc, and acid can etch metals such as aluminum.

METAL AND GLASS CUSTOM CURTAIN WALL WITH STONE VENEER

101 Second Street
San Francisco, California

Owner and developer: Meyers Development Company
Architect: Skidmore, Owings, Merrill, LLP, San Francisco
General contractor: Hathaway Dinwiddie Construction Company
Curtain wall design, fabrication, and installation:
Walters and Wolf Glass Company

FIGURES 5.10–FIGURE 5.18
Photos and drawings courtesy
of Walters and Wolf.

FIGURE 5.11

FIGURE 5.12

FIGURE 5.13

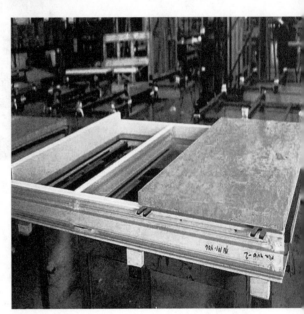

FIGURE 5.14

The 26-story 101 Second Street (Figure 5.10) was the first new office tower constructed in San Francisco in over a decade when it was completed in 1999. The custom glass and limestone curtain wall was designed, fabricated, and installed by Walters and Wolf Glass Company, Freemont, California, which specializes in custom curtain walls. The unitized panels were distributed and installed using a unique monorail system (Figures 5.11 and 5.12). After the architect's approval of a visual mock-up (Figure 5.13), the limestone was quarried in Spain, fabricated in Italy, and shipped to California for final assembly. The aluminum extrusions were fabricated in Walters and Wolf's northern California fabrication plant, where the units were also assembled and glazed (Figures 5.14). Walters and Wolf also con-

FIGURE 5.15

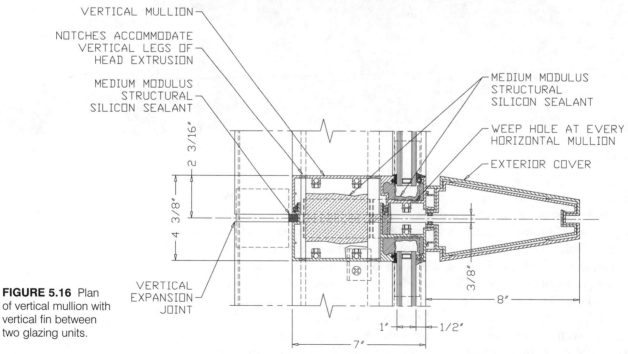

FIGURE 5.16 Plan of vertical mullion with vertical fin between two glazing units.

ducted a performance mock-up at their northern California test chamber, installing a full-size, two-story mock-up wall and testing it for both static and dynamic water penetration, lateral loading, and story drift (Figure 5.15). The 8-inch (200 mm), V-shaped, vertical fins are just two of the 77 custom parts that were created for this unique project. Differential movement and interstory drift movement were accommodated with ¾ inch (19 mm) horizontal expansion joints at the stack joints at each floor and ⅜ inch (10 mm) vertical expansion joints between units every 5 feet (1.5 meters) (Figures 5.16, 5.17, and 5.18).

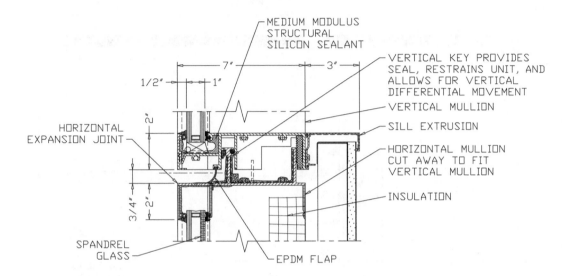

FIGURE 5.17 Stack joint at sill between a vision glazing unit and a spandrel glazing unit.

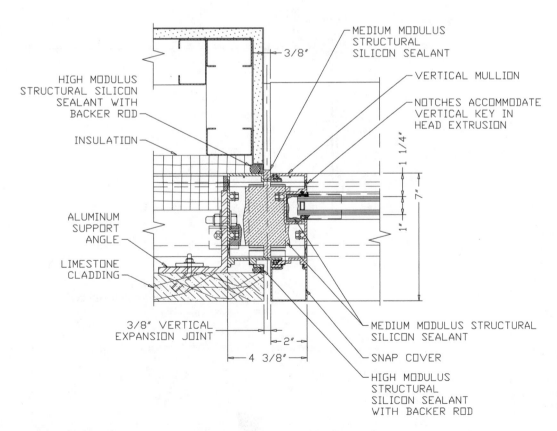

FIGURE 5.18 Window jamb at interface with limestone cladding.

5.6 PRECAST CONCRETE AND GLASS-FIBER REINFORCED CONCRETE PANELS

Precast concrete panels are a very durable and often economical cladding. They are, like other curtain walls, highly dependent on the ability of the precaster, both for the design and the fabrication of the panels. The concrete can be cast with a variety of finishes and in a variety of colors by using stone aggregates of different colors, types, and sizes. (When the granite selected for a large public project came in overbudget, the solution was to use precast concrete panels with a face mix that

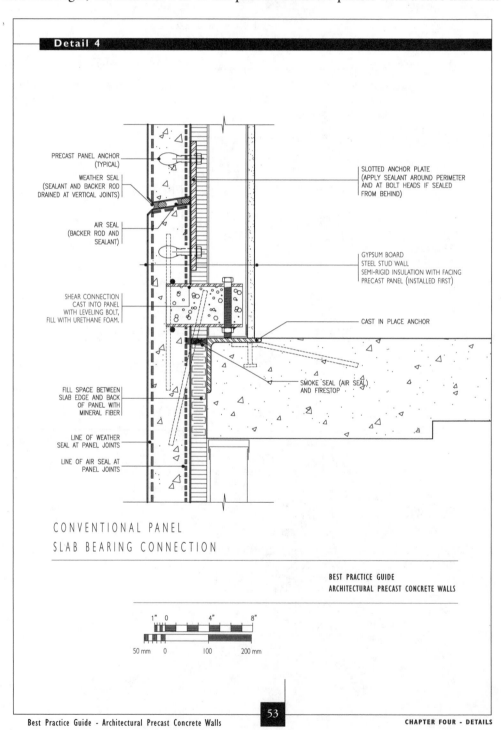

FIGURE 5.19 Precast concrete detail of a conventional panel with thermal insulation to the interior. Note the line of the air seal and the weather, or water, seal. Illustration from: Canada Mortgage and Housing Corporation (CMHC), *Architectural Precast Walls,* Best Practice Guide (Ottawa, Ont.: 2002). All rights reserved. Detailed illustration reproduced with the consent of CMHC. All other uses and reproductions of this material are expressly prohibited.

used the original granite ground to a fine aggregate.) Fired-clay and stone tiles can be cast integrally with the concrete (see Chapter 10). Assuming the fabricator is reputable, with experience in similarly sized projects, and the structural engineer is familiar with precast design, the detailing problems usually reside in the integration of the building envelope components. While the concrete may effectively stop the passage of air and water, the joints are where most problems occur. Concrete is a poor insulator, and adding thermal insulation presents another challenge. Figures 5.19–5.21 are details from the Canada Mortgage and Housing Corporation's Best Practice Guide, *Architectural Precast Walls*.[40] They show how

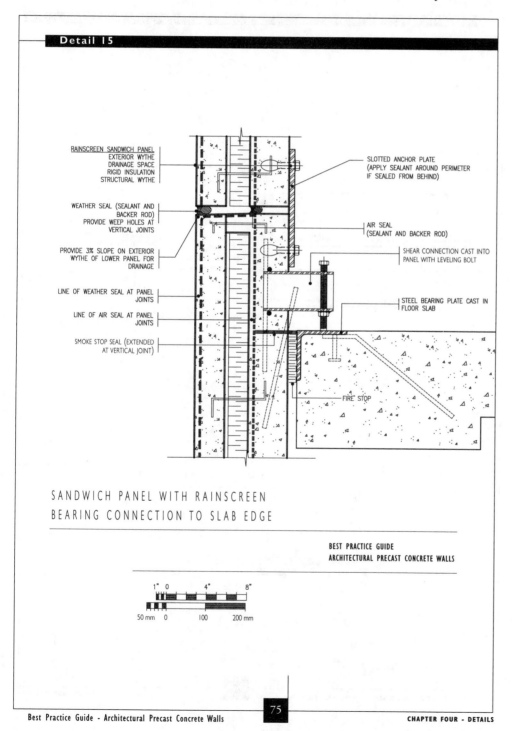

Detail 15

RAINSCREEN SANDWICH PANEL
EXTERIOR WYTHE
DRAINAGE SPACE
RIGID INSULATION
STRUCTURAL WYTHE

WEATHER SEAL (SEALANT AND BACKER ROD) PROVIDE WEEP HOLES AT VERTICAL JOINTS

PROVIDE 3% SLOPE ON EXTERIOR WYTHE OF LOWER PANEL FOR DRAINAGE

LINE OF WEATHER SEAL AT PANEL JOINTS

LINE OF AIR SEAL AT PANEL JOINTS

SMOKE STOP SEAL (EXTENDED AT VERTICAL JOINT)

SLOTTED ANCHOR PLATE (APPLY SEALANT AROUND PERIMETER IF SEALED FROM BEHIND)

AIR SEAL (SEALANT AND BACKER ROD)

SHEAR CONNECTION CAST INTO PANEL WITH LEVELING BOLT

STEEL BEARING PLATE CAST IN FLOOR SLAB

FIRE STOP

SANDWICH PANEL WITH RAINSCREEN
BEARING CONNECTION TO SLAB EDGE

BEST PRACTICE GUIDE
ARCHITECTURAL PRECAST CONCRETE WALLS

1"   0   4"   8"

50 mm   0   100   200 mm

FIGURE 5.20 Precast concrete detail shows a sandwich panel with integral thermal insulation. Note the line of the air seal and the weather, or water, seal. From CMHC's *Architectural Precast Walls*. All rights reserved. Detail illustration reproduced with the consent of CMHC. All other uses and reproductions of this material are expressly prohibited.

thermal insulation, a two-stage drained sealant joint, and an air barrier system can be accommodated with precast design.

Suffolk County House of Correction, designed by Stubbins Associates, is an example of a building clad with precast concrete panels with integral insulation (Figure 5.22). Two layers of colored concrete surround the thermal insulation. This design included two-stage drained joints between the panels. The inner seal continued the air barrier at the back face of the panels. Flashing integral with the insula-

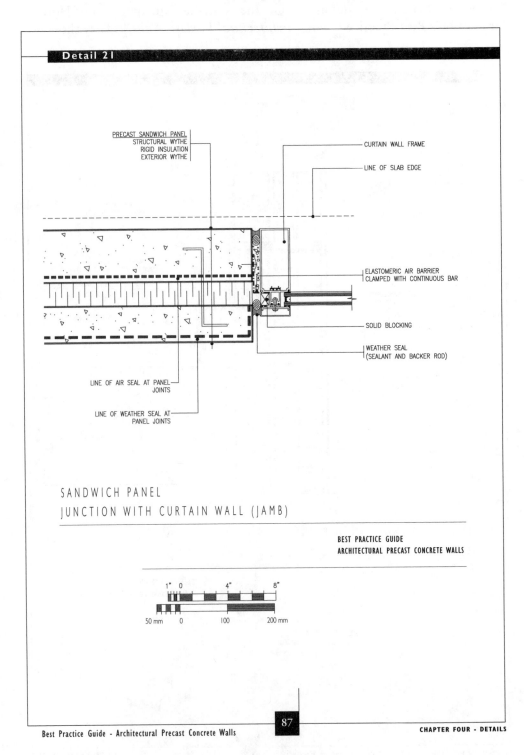

FIGURE 5.21 Precast concrete detail at the termination of a sandwich panel with integral thermal insulation. From CMHC's *Architectural Precast Walls*. All rights reserved. Detail illustration reproduced with the consent of CMHC. All other uses and reproductions of this material are expressly prohibited.

FIGURE 5.22 Suffolk County House of Correction (Stubbins Associates Inc., 1991). The contrast on the insulated precast panels is achieved solely with changes in the surface texture. (Photo by Edward Jacoby; © Edward Jacoby.)

tion weeped any condensation to the exterior. The contrast on the panels was achieved by applying a light sandblast on the lighter surfaces and using a retarder that exposed the aggregate for the rougher texture on what appears to be darker surfaces. The interior face of the precast panel was painted as the finish surface.

In the ongoing effort to find lighter-weight claddings, glass-fiber reinforced concrete (GFRC) was developed. This cementitious material with alkali-resistant glass fibers is sprayed onto a form, to a minimum depth of ½ inch (13 mm), called the backing. A face mix layer may also be used for color, texture, and increased durability. GFRC has a stiffening frame of light-gauge steel or structural steel, both with corrosion protection. Hot-dip galvanization of the frame after fabrication can cause distortion and is not recommended by the Precast/Prestressed Concrete Institute (PCI).[41] Another lightweight and less expensive system is the thin-shell concrete panels reinforced with reinforcing mesh on a light-gauge steel frame. GFRC panels usually weigh around 10 to 25 psf, while thin-shell panels are generally 35 to 40 psf.[42] The thinness of the concrete layer, particularly when coupled with a light-gauge steel frame, makes GFRC and thin-shell concrete panels potentially less durable than a precast concrete panel. While precast concrete may accommodate a certain amount of moisture, the exposed light-gauge steel framing of the thin-shell and GFRC panels cannot. A well-detailed and constructed double sealant joint is necessary at the panel joints, which can be a tricky proposition given the thinness of the panels. Even better is a drainage cavity behind the panel with a water barrier. An air barrier is critical to the success of all of these walls if they are to minimize the loss of not only conditioned air but pressure differentials that will suck water through the wall. While the decreased weight may compromise durability there are also advantages—for example, decreased shipping, handling, and erection costs. The fine grain of GFRC allows original stone or terra-cotta decorative work to be replicated as well as producing more intricate forms and shapes. PCI certifies GFRC manufacturing plants.

5.7 HOW TO STAY OUT OF TROUBLE WHEN DESIGNING CURTAIN WALLS

The key to success in designing the curtain walls discussed in this chapter is different from the systems detailed in the following chapters, with the exception of EIFS. For these curtain-wall systems, early consultation with manufacturers and installers is essential for success. A durable and economical exterior that meets the aesthetic criteria both in the short- and long-term can only be created with a good working team. Gehry Partner's Experience Music Project in Seattle, Arquitectonica's Westin New York at Times Square, and Mario Botta's San Francisco Museum of Modern Art (see Chapter 10) are all examples of successful team work between the owner, designers, manufacturers, and contractors.

5.7.1 STAYING ON BUDGET

The economics of the curtain wall are complex. Consultation with the manufacturer and installer will help select the most economical system for the required durability and desired aesthetic. Complete engineering of the system, along with very careful detailing of connections with other components prior to bidding, will help keep costs in check. Stephen Tanno, group director at Buro Happold Facade Engineering, thinks that with this team approach competitive bids should be within 10 percent of each other. He has seen bids 100 percent apart when much of the design is left for the shop drawing phase.[43] Skanska, the construction management firm for Frank Gehry's Stata Center for Computer Science at the Massachusetts Institute of Technology, (Figure 5.23) was hired during the schematic design phase to help with costs and constructability problems. The firm also held prebid meetings to explain the design and the construction of the Stata Center, which is Gehry's largest project to date and not lacking in curves and discombobulated shapes. The prebid meetings were credited with reducing the "fear factor" that might have inflated bids.[44] The design of the 51-story New York Times Headquarters includes the use of 1½ inch (38 mm) horizontal ceramic rods as part of the curtain-wall system. Four curtain-wall manufacturers were given $50,000 each to build a mock-up of the facade. These mock-ups provided the benefit of their different approaches. Incorporating this information into the bidding documents made the developer more confident about meeting the budget.[45]

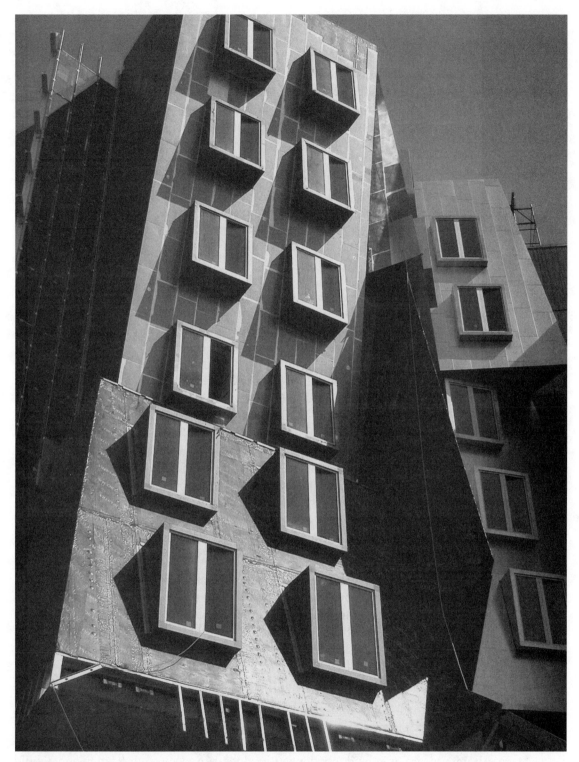

FIGURE 5.23 Curtain-wall design that includes sloping walls, projecting windows, and multiple corners is complicated. A team that included the architect, consultants, and construction manager as well as subcontractors worked together on MIT's Stata Center for Computer Science by Gehry Partners. Costs were kept in check partially by negotiating the contract for the structural steel and the metal skin.* (© Martin Lewis.)

---

*Nadine M. Post, "More Than an Academic Exercise," *Engineering News Record* (January 27, 2003), p.35.

The buildings mentioned here are all large projects with high public profiles. The more typical project involving a curtain wall may not have the funds for this kind of careful scrutiny during the design process. Often an owner requires that every component is bid, with the lowest bidder awarded the contract. However, the lessons of these projects still apply. Requiring a mock-up of a cladding system prior to construction can alleviate many problems and should be specified as part of the contractor's responsibility. (Constructing the mock-up during the design phase may save design time.) It is in the owner's best financial interest to preselect the installer and fabricator, or at least limit bids to by-invitation-only, for a complex curtain-wall system. It is not possible to separate the design of the more complicated claddings from their manufacturing and installation. Recognizing this fact may be the first step in good curtain-wall design. Utilizing a single curtain-wall company, such as discussed in Section 5.5, for the design, fabrication, and installation is one way to keep costs in check while maintaining quality.

5.7.2 DURABLE CURTAIN WALLS

With respect to curtain walls, there are a number of points of failure, including: the cladding panel, whether it is glass, metal, stone, concrete, or GFRC; the frame, with attachments, that secures the panel to the structure and transfers lateral loads; and the joints between panels or units. Finally, the transitions at the base of the wall, the roof, and to adjoining claddings are critical junctures, as are openings such as windows. Each of these poses different problems for different systems. The responsibility for the design of each is also different. For example, the joint between the glass unit and the aluminum curtain-wall frame is detailed by the manufacturer, whereas the joints between stone panels are designed on a project-by-project basis, usually by the architect. The higher the building, the more brittle the material (stone and glass), and the heavier the material the more serious the life-safety issues if the cladding fails. Curtain wall failures are not unlike those with other cladding types; the ingress of water heads the list of problems.

Dean Rutila of the engineering firm Simpson Gumpertz & Heger summarized widespread water leakage problems in curtain walls as attributable to:

- the failure of designers, contractors, managers, and oversight professionals to understand waterproofing design principles;
- failure in the communication of the waterproofing design through contract documents and constructor-produced design and submittal documents;
- the failure to verify the design through shop and erection drawings, testing, and inspection; and
- the fragmentation of responsibility combined with a lack of coordination.[46]

Following good water management design, the basics of which are contained in Chapter 2, is the starting point for keeping water out of the wall. The other key elements include keeping air from leaking through the wall; ensuring that the thermal requirements are met and condensation does not occur where damage would result; and accommodating differential movement. (See Chapters 3 and 4.) But Rutila's list makes it clear that beyond the initial design, when a curtain wall fails there are major problems in the communication of the design to other parties; in understanding the system; in the effectiveness of the ongoing checks and balances to ensure the system is installed and working as intended, and finally, in the establishment of a single line of responsibility. With design-build or construction management projects—or those with a single curtain-wall designer, fabricator, and erector—this responsibility may shift somewhat; however, the primary responsibility for overseeing the process from design through completion usually lies with the architect. Durability depends on quality design, components and assemblies, installation, and maintenance. And all of this relies on the successful coordination of many disparate parties. Finally, a key element of long-term durability is a good testing program that includes mock-up walls and ongoing testing throughout the construction process.

5.8 REFERENCES

GLASS AND METAL CURTAIN WALLS

Print Sources
1. *Curtain Wall Design Guide Manual,* AAMA Aluminum Curtain Wall Series, CW-DG-1 (Palatine, Il.: American Architectural Manufacturers Association, 1996).

2. *Installation of Aluminum Curtain Walls,* AAMA Aluminum Curtain Wall Series, CWG-1-89 (Palatine, Il.: American Architectural Manufacturers Association, 1996).

3. *Glass and Metal Curtain Walls: Best Practice Guide* (Ottawa, Ont.: Canada Mortgage and Housing Corporation, 2004).

4. *Glazing Manual* (Topeka, Kans.: The Glass Association of North America, 2004).

5. John Carmody, Stephen Selkowitz, Eleanor S. Lee, Darinsh Arasteh, and Todd Wilmert, *Window Systems for High-Performance Buildings* (New York: W. W. Norton & Company, 2004).

6. Michael Wigginton, *Glass in Architecture* (London: Phaidon Press, 2002; orig. 1996).

7. Johann Eisle and Ellen Kloft, ed., *High-Rise Manual: Typology and Design, Construction and Technology* (Boston: Birkhauser-Publishers for Architecture, 2003).

Online Sources
1. American Architectural Manufacturers Association (AAMA), http://www.aamanet.org

2. Glass Association of North America (GANA), http://www.glasswebsite.com

3. Insulating Glass Manufacturers Alliance, http://www.igmaonline.org

METAL PANELS

1. L. William Zahner, *Architectural Metals: A Guide to Selection, Specification, and Performance* (New York: John Wiley & Sons, 1995).

2. Annette LeCuyer, *Steel and Beyond: New Strategies for Metals in Architecture* (Boston: Birkhauser-Publishers for Architecture, 2003).

STONE PANELS

Print Sources

1. Michael D. Lewis, *Modern Stone Cladding: Design and Installation of Exterior Dimension Stone Systems,* MNL 21 (Philadelphia, Pa.: ASTM, 1995).

2. James E. Amrhein and Michael W. Merrigan, *Marble and Stone Slab Veneer* (Los Angeles: Masonry Institute of America, 1989).

3. *Indiana Limestone Handbook,* 21st ed. (Bedford, Ind.: Indiana Limestone Institute of America, 2002).

4. *Masonry Construction* (Addison, Ill., Hanley-Wood, Magazine Div.). This magazine contains articles on how to design, specify, test, install, and maintain masonry claddings.

5. Seymour A. Bortz, Don E. Shorts, and Gail R. Hush, "Anchoring Exterior Stone: An Overview of the Major Types of Anchors for Attaching Dimension Stone to Backups" (December 1990).

Online Sources

1. Marble Institute of America, http://www.marble-institute.com

2. National Building Granite Quarries Association, http://www.nbgqa.com

3. Indiana Limestone Institute of America, http://www.iliai.com

4. Canadian Stone Association, http://www.stone.ca

PRECAST CONCRETE AND GFRC PANELS

Print Sources

1. *Recommended Practice for Glass Fiber Reinforced Concrete Panels,* 4th ed. (Chicago: Precast/Prestressed Concrete Institute, 2001).

2. *Architectural Precast Concrete,* 2nd ed. (Chicago: Precast/Prestressed Concrete Institute).

3. *Architectural Precast Concrete—Color and Texture Selection Guide,* 2nd ed. (Chicago: Precast/Prestressed Concrete Institute).

4. *Architectural Precast Concrete Walls: Best Practice Guide* (Ottawa, Ont.: Canada Mortgage and Housing Corporation, 2002).

Online Sources

1. Precast/Prestressed Concrete Institute (PCI), http://www.pci.org

2. Canadian Precast/Prestressed Concrete Institute (CPCI), http://www.cpci.ca

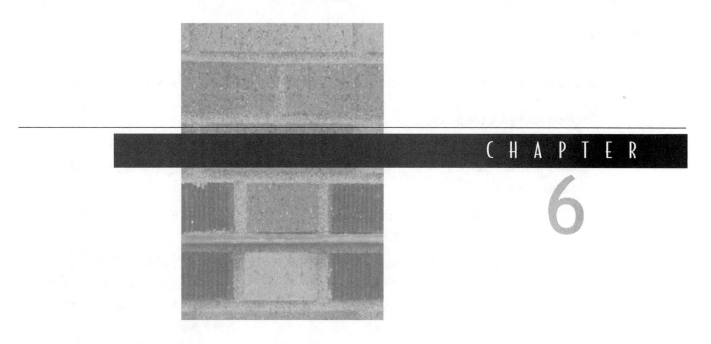

Anchored Brick Veneer

6.1 BRICK VENEER ANCHORED TO THE STEEL-STUD BACKUP WALLS OF A FOUR- TO TWENTY-STORY BUILDING*

Stone and brick masonry has a legacy of durability. Leon Battista Alberti, in his Ten Books on Architecture, commented that he "would be so bold as to state that there is no building material more suitable than brick, however you wish to employ it."[1] In North America, brick structures, often constructed after a town's first major fire, were a visible sign that the town had arrived. It was permanent, not to be swept away by the vagaries of climate or commerce.

The basic size of a brick has remained nearly the same for over 10,000 years. It still can be grasped by one hand, and its placement is still dependent on the skills of the mason, who still lays one brick at a time. However, the rise in the use of steel and concrete frame construction in the nineteenth century changed the use of fired clay or shale brick. It is no longer load bearing, nor has it been for most of the last century. It is now merely a veneer, a cladding, albeit a heavy one.

Brick veneer is now formed in laid-in-place panels separated by expansion joints that run up the sides and across the top of the panels to accommodate a host of differential movements. Usually, steel shelf angles, fixed to the building frame, support the dead weight of each panel. A backup wall, also fixed to the frame, sup-

*This chapter is based on the work of G. Russell Heliker and Phil Green, P.E.

121

Reducing Confusion

Some of the terms used in this chapter are so common that they cannot be replaced with more descriptive nomenclature, and sometimes the terminology may be confusing. The following definitions should help.

- *Anchored brick veneer (ABV) panels:* ABV panels are laid-in-place brick-veneer panels that are attached to a backup wall with veneer anchors.

- *Anchored brick veneer panels attached to steel-stud backup walls (ABV/SS):* ABV/SS walls are composed of laid-in-place ABV panels anchored to a backup wall composed of light-gauge, cold-formed steel framing, which is commonly called "light-gauge framing" or just "steel-stud construction." ABV/SS exterior walls must always be designed as drainage cavity walls (see definition below). (In other publications, ABV/SS is often abbreviated BV/SS.)

- *Brick and brickwork: Brick* and *brick unit* denote a brick masonry unit made of clay or shale usually formed from a rectangular prism while in a wet, plastic state and then fired in a kiln within closely controlled parameters. (These terms are not meant to describe concrete bricks, which are generally less common. Their characteristics, especially as they pertain to expansion and contraction, are so different that their use is specifically *not* covered in this chapter.) *Brickwork* is a composite material, made of brick units and mortar, that "courses out" so that in every 8 inches (200 mm) of height there are three horizontal courses of brick and mortar. (Another brick and mortar module courses at multiples of 3 inches (75 mm), e.g., four courses in every 12 inches (300 mm) of height.

- *Directions:* Figure 6.1 shows the three terms used to describe the direction of physical phenomena like forces, pressures, and expansion or contraction acting on or within a veneer panel. Of particular interest is the difference between "horizontal," which is in a direction along a level line within the plane of the veneer panel, and "lateral," which is in a direction perpendicular to the plane of the veneer panel. Lateral forces and pressures acting against an exterior wall are described as "positive"

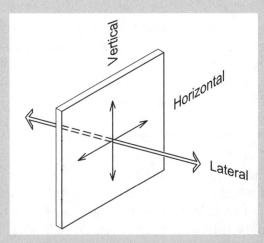

FIGURE 6.1 Brick-veneer panel showing directions used in text.

when they tend to push or pull the wall toward the building interior and "negative" when they act to force the wall toward the building exterior. Negative wind pressure acting from the exterior is sometimes called "suction." (Some publications refer to the lateral direction as *out-of-plane* or *transverse,* but for clarity these terms are seldom used in this chapter.)

- *Drainage cavity wall, drainage cavity, and free air space:* ABV/SS walls must always be designed as drainage cavity walls. The term *drainage cavity wall* is based on the method used to manage water (Section 6.6). The drainage cavity wall is not necessarily pressure equalized, so it is not synonymous with a "rain-screen wall." (See Sections 6.6.3 and 2.2 for a discussion of pressure equalization.) The term *drain screen* is also not as descriptive and is not used in this chapter.

  It is conventional to define the drainage cavity as the *entire* space between the interior face of the brick veneer and the exterior face of the steel-stud sheathing. Most of this space is taken up by the cavity insulation board and a two inch (50 mm) free air space. The free air space is actually the only part of the drainage cavity that is intended to drain water. The term *free air space* is used in this book to emphasize that it is to be free and clear of all mortar droppings and other debris so that water can *quickly* drain before it is absorbed by the veneer or makes its way to the interior (Figure 6.12). Other terms sometimes used to describe the free air space include *air space* and *air cavity.* They are not used in this book.

- *Shelf Angles and Loose Lintels:* Steel shelf angles and loose lintels support the dead weight of the veneer. Shelf angles are rigidly attached to the building frame and are, therefore, stationary. See Figure 6.11, at the foundation wall, Figure 6.13, at a typical concrete floor beam, and Figure 6.14, at roof level. (Shelf angles are also sometimes called *ledgers* or *ledger angles.* To avoid confusion these terms are not used in this book.)

  Loose lintels, on the other hand, are *never* attached to the building. They are solely supported by the brick veneer on both sides of an opening and move up and down with the veneer as it expands and contracts. They must, consequently, extend into the veneer at each end, even if it is necessary for them to cross a vertical expansion joint (Figure 6.19 and the lower portion of Figure 6.10).

- *Steel-stud wall cavity:* Not to be confused with the drainage cavity, the steel-stud wall cavity is the cavity within the steel-stud wall itself. It is often filled with fiberglass batt insulation. Unlike the drainage cavity, it will not tolerate even minimal amounts of water.

ports loads imposed on the veneer by natural forces, principally those caused by wind and earthquakes.

Brick veneer has the advantage of a very small module, often just 8 inches (200 mm). Laid-in-place brick veneer can better accommodate construction tolerances than most other claddings. Brick creates a distinct aesthetic, morphing from neo-colonial to University Gothic and later to accommodations of the modern move-mentist forms. In 2002, approximately 13 percent of exterior residential and non-residential wall construction was brick veneer in the United States.[2] It is, and will remain, a popular cladding. Besides aesthetics, long-term durability and low main-tenance needs are reasons often cited for choosing brick veneer. It is generally lower in cost than stone and many metal panel and concrete precast systems.

One distressing trend has been to promote brick veneer anchored to a steel-stud backup (ABV/SS) as a less expensive cladding in competition with systems such as Exterior Insulation and Finish Systems (EIFS) and stucco. Designed correctly, it is not inexpensive, but it can be economical. (A poorly designed brick veneer cladding is very expensive in the long run.) Brick veneer anchored to a steel-stud backup wall can be designed to last 50 years, and anchored to a concrete or rein-forced concrete masonry backup wall, perhaps 75 years or more.

This chapter describes Wall Type A, which is brick veneer anchored to steel-stud backup walls (ABV/SS) on a 4- to 20-story concrete frame, a common cladding for buildings of these heights. The differential movement between the concrete frame and the veneer presents a number of challenges for the designer. The ease of installation of a steel-stud backup wall makes it a more economical backup than reinforced concrete masonry for most projects. But it is also more vul-nerable to failure, adding another challenge for the architect. Because of these problems and resulting concerns about the potential for life safety, ABV/SS is one of the most difficult claddings to design and install. This book does not recommend its use above 20 stories.

6.2 WALL TYPE A: BRICK VENEER ANCHORED TO STEEL-STUD BACKUP

The suggested wall assembly for brick veneer anchored to a steel-stud backup wall with a drainage cavity in a heating climate is listed and described in Table 6.1 and the notes that follow. This is the assembly described and detailed in this chapter. Suggestions for assemblies in cooling and mixed climates are also given in Table 6.1.

More detailed information about the specific climatic conditions follows in Section 6.3. Details of the wall are included in the figures of Section 6.10. See Chapters 2 through 4 for more information on wall components related to climate.

6.3 CLIMATE

Some of the coldest and wettest North American climates were considered in the design presented in this chapter. The geographical area that encompasses these cli-mates is a broad horizontal band that stretches across the entire width of the north-ern United States and southern Canada, which is roughly bordered by the 40th and 50th parallels. A significant portion of the built environment of the United States and most of that in Canada falls between these lines of latitude.

TABLE 6.1 Building Envelope Components Based on Climate

Anchored Brick Veneer on a Steel-Stud Backup Wall (ABV/SS): Building of 4 to 20 stories			
Water Management System: Drainage Cavity Wall			
	Heating Climate (described in this chapter)	Mixed Climate	Cooling Climate
Water Barrier	SBPO (spun-bonded polyolefin), Nonperforated building wrap[1]	SBPO[5]	Peel-and-stick, self-adhesive membrane
Air Barrier System	Airtight drywall approach (ADA) or simple caulk and seal (SCS)[2]	ADA or SCS	Peel-and-stick, self-adhesive membrane
Vapor Retarder	Kraft paper face of fiberglass batt insulation[3]	Vapor retardant paint	Peel-and-stick, self-adhesive membrane[6]
Insulation	Extruded polystyrene (XPS) and fiberglass batt[4]	XPS and fiberglass batt[4]	Fiberglass batt
Backup Wall	6" (150 mm) steel-stud backup wall with nonpaper faced gypsum sheathing	6" (150 mm) steel-stud backup wall with nonpaper faced gypsum sheathing	6" (150 mm) steel-stud backup wall with nonpaper faced gypsum sheathing
Comments			Interior finishes should be *highly* vapor permeable

Notes:

1. The water barrier should be located where it is most protected: between the drainage cavity insulation board and the backup-wall sheathing. In this chapter, the water barrier is a heavy-duty, nonperforated spun-bonded polyolefin (SBPO) building wrap such as Tyvek Commercial Wrap. Attaching the cavity insulation board with insulation stops instead of using screws can considerably reduce the number of penetrations through the barrier (see Figures 6.18 and 6.19).

2. Since the SBPO building wrap retards movement of both liquid water and air, it seems logical to use, as both the water and air barrier. However, by the time hundreds or even thousands of the veneer anchor fasteners have penetrated the SBPO building wrap, the airtightness will be compromised, even if every attempt has been made to patch or seal these penetrations. This book recommends that the air barrier system be on the interior side of the backup wall using the airtight drywall approach (ADA) or the simple caulk and seal (SCS) method. In this location there are fewer penetrations, and it can be inspected as well as maintained over the years. Its function will be somewhat shared with the water barrier, which also represents a potential, if imperfect, air barrier. Two air barriers are better than one air barrier because the pressure drop across each of these barriers is additive.

3. The Kraft paper face on fiberglass batts is an acceptable vapor retarder. When there is a strong vapor drive from the interior to the exterior, as happens in severe heating climates, the resistance can be increased by the substitution of foil-faced batts or the addition of polyethylene sheeting or vapor retardant paint. See Chapter 3 for more information.

4. The location of insulation in relation to vapor retarders is critical. While its location is clear for the extreme heating climate with high vapor drives to the exterior, it needs to be reevaluated as the vapor drive lessens. Exterior steel stud flanges must be kept warm enough to avoid condensation. This requires a fine balance between the amount of insulation in the stud cavity and in the drainage cavity. Hiring a building envelope consultant to run a hygrothermal analysis of the wall is good insurance. Excessive use of nonpermeable peel-and-stick membrane on the permeable SBPO building wrap can cause condensation, as well. (See Section 3.2.5.)

5. In mixed climates (and some heating climates), some building scientists recommend the use of a less vapor-permeable water barrier, such as building paper or felt, particularly if the extruded polystyrene (XPS) cavity insulation board is eliminated.

6. There can be a strong vapor drive from the exterior to the interior in cooling climates, especially when interiors are air-conditioned. Because owners will inevitably add layers of paint and, possibly, vapor retarding wall coverings over the years, nonpermeable peel-and-stick is recommended as a vapor retarder on the exterior sheathing of the backup wall to prevent moisture-laden exterior air from entering the stud cavity.

6.3.1 Avoiding Saturated Brick Veneer

In most of these environments, brick veneer that becomes saturated during the winter often takes weeks—in the marine environment of the Pacific Northwest, sometimes months—to dry. This is because masonry dries most rapidly by evaporation, which is less efficient in cold weather. If its design causes brick veneer to become saturated whenever it rains or snows, its life will be shortened. Metal components—like veneer anchors, horizontal joint reinforcing, loose lintels and shelf angles, including those that are zinc-coated—will eventually corrode, sometimes causing loss of strength within 20 years. In addition, the expansive forces created during the formation of iron oxide (rust) may cause horizontal and stair-stepping cracks and spalling of brick units. Mortar will, as well, deteriorate more rapidly than normal due to freeze-thaw cycles, moving forward the date of the first repointing, an expensive maintenance procedure. Finally, freeze-thaw cycles can damage brickwork. However, in the absence of liquid water, freeze-thaw cycles do not harm masonry. (The advice given in Section 6.6 aims to mitigate these problems.)

6.3.2 Using Caution in Other Climates

Several severe climates exist outside of those described above. For example, the coastal regions of the southeastern and Gulf of Mexico states are occasionally subjected to rains driven by winds of hurricane force. The hottest and most humid areas of the southern United States have very high cooling loads in the summer, resulting in a predominately high vapor drive from building exterior to interior. The earthquakes of the very high seismic zones of California and Nevada can create lateral forces of extreme magnitude. The text and details of this chapter may not do justice to these conditions, and caution is advised. Some details will be useful and others will not. For instance, the recommendation that anchored brick veneer "spandrel panels," between horizontal ribbon windows, be supported both vertically and laterally by structural steel frames may be useful but not necessarily sufficient under extreme lateral loading or hours of high-velocity rain (see Figures 6.16 and 6.17). The table and accompanying notes in Section 6.2 should be carefully considered and Chapters 2 and 3 reviewed. In many cases, it may be prudent to have a building envelope specialist review the wall assemblage.

6.4 IS ABV/SS RISKY BUSINESS?

The advisability of using the ABV/SS system has been debated for several decades. At the time this book was was written, some observers of the debate, including the author, remained skeptical about the use of ABV/SS except on low-rise buildings where wind-driven rains are less severe and facade failures are usually less costly. On mid-rise buildings some would prefer a more substantial and stiffer backup wall such as a reinforced concrete masonry wall, which is considerably less flexible and potentially more durable.

In the United States, this debate probably peaked in 1991 with the publication of a paper by Clayford T. Grimm. Grimm, an engineer who wrote and lectured extensively on masonry for decades, was especially concerned about this system and concluded that "duty requires that the architect and engineer warn clients about the risks inherent in the use of the...[ABV/SS] wall system."[3] This remains good advice if the architect and engineer choose to use ABV/SS on mid-rise buildings, particularly in cold, wet, and windy climates and especially when the construction budget is tight.

However, because of its economy, the ease with which the ABV/SS system dovetails with the work of other subcontractors, and the help it offers in meeting tight construction schedules, this system remains popular. The more important reservations about this system and recommendations for reducing risks are summarized in the following section. These recommendations should be read carefully. However, following the advice of the next section will reduce risk, not eliminate it.

6.5 REDUCING RISK

When compared to anchored brick veneer (ABV) attached to reinforced concrete masonry or to cast-in-place concrete backup walls, the use of the ABV/SS system may result in decreased life for the reasons discussed in this section.

6.5.1 REDUCING CORROSION

The most obvious risk in the ABV/SS system is that the steel studs and lower tracks will corrode if rainwater or condensation causes more than occasional dampness within the steel-stud wall cavity. Even zinc-coated studs will lose strength if subjected to several years of moisture, because they are made of light-gauge steel. Once the sacrificial zinc coating has been breached, there is little steel to corrode before the integrity of the backup wall is compromised. (Field welds, which destroy nearby zinc coating and are often of low quality, should be avoided.)

Free-standing exterior walls
This book advises the use of reinforced concrete masonry or cast-in-place concrete backup walls for free-standing exterior ABV walls, including balcony and roof parapets (Figure 6.14). A better solution is to eliminate the ABV and use a more durable cladding, like metal panels for the parapet walls of mid-height buildings. In Figure 6.2, the parapet is not clad in brick veneer, and the illustrated ABV drainage cavity wall is nicely protected from rainwater by ample overhangs. (If ABV must be used on freestanding walls, see Section 6.8 for more information.)

Backup walls that support the weight of brick veneer
Some backup walls support the dead weight of the ABV as well as transfer lateral loads from the veneer panels to the building frame. Examples are the ABV spandrel backup walls positioned between horizontal ribbon windows (see the upper part of Figure 6.10 and Figures 6.16 and 6.17) and backup walls that are hung from the building frame to support ABV fascia panels.

FIGURE 6.2 Anchored-brick veneer supported by exposed floor slabs in a mild climate. (Shadows and sealant color hide the horizontal expansion joints that separate the brick veneer from the underside of each floor slab overhang.) Photo by G. Russell Heliker.

These walls should be constructed of zinc-coated structural steel. Hence, as recommended by one authority, the shelf angle in Figure 6.16 is supported by and welded or bolted to vertical structural-steel elements and not to steel studs.[4] Structural-steel backup walls can include steel-stud infill to support the sheathing and interior gypsum board; but as Figures 6.16 and 6.17 suggest, this may not be necessary.

Preventing the entry of water into the steel-wall stud cavity

The most important layer of defense against the intrusion of water into the stud-wall cavity is the 2-inches (50 mm) of free air space directly behind every panel of ABV/SS. 2 inches (50 mm) of free air space is easier to keep clean than 1 inch (25 mm) of free air space, and it helps avoid the problem shown in Figure 6.3. To function properly during periods of heavy, wind-driven rains it must be completely free of mortar droppings and other debris (Figure 6.5). For that reason, it is recommended that the architect specify full-brick cleanout holes at a maximum of 24 inches (600 mm) on center, along each shelf angle and loose lintel. Even the use of cleanouts does not ensure a mortar-free cavity without inspection, but it does make inspection at the base of the cavity easy and reliable. (In Figure 6.4, the cleanouts are at 16-inch (400 mm), centers. Note the wet mortar droppings that have not yet been cleaned from the base of this test panel.) Using proprietary products, like mats and mortar diverters, that are designed to prevent the consolidation of mortar droppings at the base of the free air space may keep this area clear; but they may also move the problem of mortar obstructions higher in the free air space. None of these products offer the reliability and "inspectability" of cleanouts. They also may give masons a false sense of security, resulting in sloppier work. (Some publications continue to show the base of the cavity filled with pea gravel. This classic "solution" to the problem has been shown to be the least effective.)

Keeping steel studs warm[5]

The installation of 1 to 2 inches (25 to 50 mm) of extruded polystyrene (XPS) drainage-cavity insulation board to the exterior of the water barrier is recommended to increase the temperature of the steel-stud system during winter, thereby decreasing the risk of condensation on the steel. Because extruded polystyrene is relatively tough, it also acts to protect the water barrier during the construction of the brickwork. The use of 1½ to 2 inches (38 to 50 mm) of a higher density XPS like Dow CavityMate Plus is recommended. XPS drainage-cavity products that have both higher density and higher R-values per inch of thickness are also recommended, especially in areas with severely cold winters. Figures in this chapter that show a steel-stud backup wall always detail a 6-inch (150 mm) steel-stud wall cavity with 4 inches (100 mm) of fiberglass batt insulation. This is to emphasize that the exterior flanges of the studs and tracks, which are somewhat cooled by the batt insulation, must be kept warm enough to avoid condensation within the steel-stud wall cavity. The balance between the steel-stud wall cavity insulation and XPS drainage-cavity insulation is critical; if there is too much insulation in the stud cavity or not enough in the drainage cavity, condensation will occur on the exterior flanges of the studs and tracks. (Also see Note 4, Table 6.1, Section 6.2.)

6.5.2 Choosing Reliable Fasteners

A less obvious, but arguably greater, risk to the ABV/SS wall system is the attachment of the veneer anchors to the steel-stud backup wall. This is typically accom-

FIGURE 6.4 Mortar cleanout holes at base of drainage cavity. Photo by G. Russell Heliker.

FIGURE 6.3 A minimal drainage cavity cannot accommodate an out-of-tolerance frame. At this bulge in a concrete frame, the masons reduced the depth of bricks to keep the exterior face of the ABV/SS plumb. The veneer was thereby weakened, and the drainage cavity eliminated. A drainage cavity with 2 inches (50 mm) of free air space and at least 1½ inches (38 mm) of drainage cavity insulation board would have accommodated this out-of-tolerance beam and even helped accommodate an out-of-plumb frame.

FIGURE 6.5 Mass of mortar droppings taken from the base of a 12-foot-high mock-up drainage cavity wall built without the use of mortar cleanout holes. The skilled masons who constructed this panel were advised to use any method and take whatever time was necessary to avoid this condition. Photo by G. Russell Heliker.

plished with self-drilling, self-tapping, sheet-metal screws that engage the steel studs by only one or two threads (depending on the steel-stud gauge and number of threads per inch). The screw threads and the mating steel of the stud are even more susceptible to corrosion if they have lost part of their corrosion-resistant plating during the self-tapping process. In addition, if the installer overtorques the screws, part of the stud material will be stripped away, reducing strength at the thread and stud interface. Finally, these screws are driven from the exterior of the steel-stud wall through the sheathing. If the installer misses the stud and does not realize this mistake and if the inspector does not catch the problem, then though it may appear to have succeeded, the attachment has failed. These risks are considerably reduced by the following recommendation.

Using more reliable fastening methods

The small bolts, nuts, and washers shown, for example, in Figure 6.12 can be used with any veneer anchor designed to be attached with screws to steel-stud flanges. Admirably, one brick-industry publication suggests this as an alternative method.[6] This chapter recommends it as a best choice. The fasteners should be stainless steel if the veneer anchor is stainless steel. A thin, nonmetallic washer should be used between the stainless-steel washer and the zinc-coated stud flange to reduce galvanic corrosion at this location.

One veneer anchor requires the use of a special web-mounted anchor section fastened to the steel-stud web (see Figure 6.19, below the sill). This method has the advantage of putting the fasteners into shear and, therefore, offers higher strength and potentially longer life. The fasteners, which are entirely within the relatively warm steel-stud cavity, can be zinc-coated, sheet-metal screws. The system requires vigilance in applying the water barrier, as it must be cut and fit around each anchor and then sealed to the anchor. See Section 6.9.5 for more information on two-piece, adjustable veneer anchors.

6.5.3 REDUCING CRACKS

The least obvious risk, and the most difficult to mitigate, is the differing stiffness of the steel-stud backup walls and the brick veneer panels. A brick veneer panel is relatively stiff and brittle, while a steel-stud backup wall is relatively flexible and elastic. Therefore, brick veneer cannot conform to the curvature of steel studs under lateral loading without first cracking horizontally along one or more of its bed joints. Figure 6.6 treats this situation schematically; cracks will probably not be so evenly spaced, and the extent of cracking will be roughly proportional to the flexibility of the steel-stud backup wall and the maximum lateral loads experienced to date.

Under high-wind loading, with substantial rainfall, the obvious risk is the entry of water into the brick veneer. However, very high lateral loading may result in further risk if extreme flexing of the veneer causes so many bed-joint cracks that some horizontal sections of veneer remain anchored by only a single horizontal row of veneer anchors between the horizontal cracks that define these sections. In this situation, the veneer may lose stability because of the unrestrained rotation of these sections.[7]

The stiffness of steel-stud walls is specified by limiting the lateral deflection of the studs when they are subjected to code-required lateral loading due to wind and seismic activity. For example, if the deflection is limited to L/600, then the maximum deflection of the stud (usually at midheight) is the height of the stud (L) divided by 600. Therefore, an 8-foot (2440 mm) tall steel-stud wall will deflect laterally 96 inches/600, or 0.16 inches (4.1 mm). Using a simple one-crack model, this deflection results in a maximum crack opening of .02 inches (0.5 mm) on the exterior face of the veneer. As assumed in Figure 6.6, there may be more than one horizontal crack, and the opening height of these cracks may be less than the maximum. However, these smaller cracks may still offer limited resistance to high velocity water molecules, although this will depend somewhat on the pressure difference across the veneer.

The only way of reducing the size and/or number of cracks is to limit deflection. For this reason, the specification of a lateral deflection limit is important, and it has been discussed for decades. Yet there is still no consensus among the recognized authorities. One U.S. industry publication recommends L/360, which is definitely not a conservative value, although these engineers hedge a bit by stating that

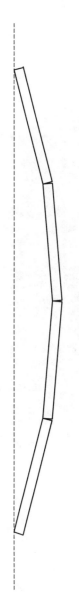

FIGURE 6.6 Simplified cracking model of ABV/SS under lateral loading. For clarity, deflection is exaggerated, and steel-stud backup wall is not shown.

"increasing the stiffness of the...[steel-stud backup] may be beneficial in that the amount of water allowed through cracks in the veneer would be reduced."[8] Another U.S. industry group makes a more conservative recommendation of limiting lateral deflection to L/600.[9] In Canada one of the most comprehensive and popular publications recommends L/720 and makes the following important observation about other contributors to lateral deflection in its guide specification: "More needs to be considered than the stiffness of the [steel] studs. The deflection experienced by the cladding depends not only on the bending of the studs, but also on the take-up of free play and lateral displacement in connections under load. Localized deformations can also contribute where the cladding is connected to the studs."[10] Consequently, depending on the magnitude of these other factors, the specification of L/720 may not always lead to a conservative result.

The following recommendations are made to mitigate the inevitable cracking that comes from combining two systems of such differing flexibility. The problem cannot be entirely eliminated without either abandoning the steel-stud backup wall or increasing its stiffness to the point that its superior economics begins to evaporate.

Using a single minimum stiffness throughout the building
In the United States, the maximum deflection of the steel-stud backup wall should be limited to L/600 or less. L/720 is recommended when additional contributors to lateral deflection cannot be tightly controlled, as may often be the case. In Canada, a maximum deflection of L/720 is advised.

Varying stiffness to fit lateral loading patterns
If it is known that wind-driven rains will be common, the architect's structural engineer may wish to decrease the maximum deflection of the steel-stud backup walls in the more exposed areas of the facade. L/1000 is not out of the question at higher floors, near corners, or in areas where a wind-tunnel effect is predicted to impact the facade. However, the varying stiffness of the steel-stud backup walls should not become so complicated that mistakes are made during construction. Moreover, the structural engineer also needs to review the differential movements between adjoining panels of ABV/SS that have differing stiffnesses.

6.5.4 USING THE TEAM APPROACH

A common difficulty in the design of ABV/SS system is the situation where the architect relies on the structural engineer to design the shelf angle and loose lintels but little else. The engineer is comfortable with this role, as the veneer is thought to be merely a cladding. Not versed in the structural complexities of ABV and its backup wall, the architect relies on prescriptive design guides. These are usually fairly generic, with little differentiation for a host of variables, including climate, exposure, the type of building frame, and building use.

Because the roles of the structural engineer and the architect are less clear with this system than they are in the design of other cladding types, it is imperative that the architect ensure that each component is well designed by the appropriate professional. Another consultant who should be involved in the design is the mechanical engineer, because HVAC-induced pressure differences can cause moisture to enter the wall. Additionally, all professionals should be involved at the earliest possible stage of the design to avoid conflicts between aesthetics and the realities imposed by the structure, HVAC systems, and environment.

6.6 REPELLING WATER

As discussed in Section 6.5.1, the entry of water into the steel-stud wall cavity is risky but avoidable. Water entry causes corrosion of the backup-wall components, and damage to interior finishes is not uncommon. This section describes how a layered approach to the design of the ABV/SS helps mitigate these problems. Two other issues associated with the avoidance of water entry into the system are discussed as well.

6.6.1 THE FOUR-LAYER DEFENSE

The philosophy behind a layered design recognizes that the individual layers cannot each prevent water entry on their own. Generally speaking, these are not redundant layers—each serves an important function and must be carefully detailed and constructed. This philosophy is especially important in the case of ABV/SS, a system that cannot tolerate liquid water on the face of steel-stud sheathing or, worse, in the steel-stud wall cavity and on its base track.

The first layer of defense

The first layer of defense is the brick veneer itself. At first glance, its purpose is simply to stop most rain water from entering the free air space. While that is important, the first layer also must slow the forward momentum of any water that is forced through the brickwork, causing it to have minimal velocity when it reaches the interior side of the brick veneer. Water that penetrates the brick veneer should, at most, ooze onto the interior surface of the brickwork. Otherwise, in a really heavy wind-driven rain, the amount of water flowing down the interior of the veneer can create a critical situation at the base of the free air space—although this will depend somewhat on the type and spacing of weep holes and the extent of obstructions at this location.

Therefore, the use of the superior water-shedding profile of a well-tooled concave mortar joint is advised (Figure 6.7). The concave profile can be tooled (or finished) by the mason to provide excellent consolidation and compaction behind the mortar surface. The result is a virtually watertight surface, free of pinholes and exposed aggregate (i.e., sand). Only in very dry climates should the V-joint be used, as it is difficult to finish properly. The other three joints shown in Figure 6.7 serve no purpose other than decoration and should only be used on interior brickwork. They cannot be properly finished and are often not tooled at all.

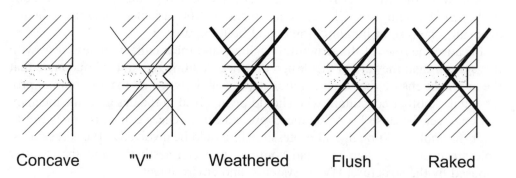

FIGURE 6.7
Mortar joint profiles.

Concave   "V"   Weathered   Flush   Raked

Mortar joints must also be free of shrinkage cracks and delaminations. Shrinkage cracks, which occur within the mortar, are minimized by the proper mixing and application of the mortar. Delaminations, which are thin cracks at the interface of mortar and brick, are caused by poor brick-to-mortar bond. (The strength of the brick-to-mortar bond is called flexural-bond strength and can be tested, if necessary.) Poor bonding is often due to a combination of improperly specified brick units, given the local climate, or poor workmanship. The problem can be especially acute during warm, sunny, or windy weather if the initial rate of absorption (IRA) of the brick units is too high or the units are not soaked in water for a sufficient time before they are laid.

At the top of many veneer panels are windowsills and other coverings that literally serve as a coping for the brick veneer below. These are part of the first layer of defense. They are especially vulnerable where the sill meets the brick veneer at the jamb. Sealant-joint performance is often quite poor at these locations due to high differential movement between the brickwork and the sill, incompatibility of the sealant with the sill metal and brickwork (including mortar), or the questionable reliability of sealant applied against rough, dirty brickwork. The sills in Figures 6.18 and 6.19 suggest two methods of dealing with this situation. In these examples, sheet metal counter flashing covers the lower few inches of the brick veneer return and laps upturned metal at the ends of a sheet metal sill (Figure 6.18) or laps an L-shaped flashing that interfaces with an elastomeric flashing under an extruded aluminum sill (Figure 6.19).

The second layer of defense

The second defense layer uses the force of gravity to direct and collect the water that has penetrated the veneer and provide for its exit through weep holes at the base of each panel. It includes the 2 inches of free air space; the shelf-angle or loose-lintel flashing; and full-height, head-joint weep holes (Figure 6.13). The goal of this second layer of defense is obtainable if the velocity of the water entering the free air space is minimal and the free air space is completely free and clear of mortar droppings and other debris. If the drainage cavity is specified to include less than 2 inches of free air space, the masons will have a difficult time keeping the free air space clear.

The third layer of defense

The water barrier, a thin membrane that is installed against the exterior steel stud-wall sheathing (e.g., SBPO membrane in Figures 6.11 and 6.12), is the third layer of defense. It may appear to be a redundant system that simply backs up the first two layers, and, to some extent, it is. However, it also prevents any condensation that has formed in the drainage cavity from soaking into the sheathing, slowly destroying it, and thereby allowing water to reach the steel studs and tracks. Any positive pressure difference between the drainage cavity and the stud-wall cavity will accelerate this process; without an effective air barrier, the job of the water barrier becomes more difficult. (Also see Note 2, Table 6.1, Section 6.2.)

The fourth layer of defense

If the shelf-angle or loose-lintel flashing fails, water is directed to the head of the window or door below. Therefore, window and door heads located below shelf angles and loose lintels should provide their own last layer of protection against water entry (Figures 6.17, 6.18, and 6.19). This is especially important in the case of ribbon windows where the failure of shelf-angle flashing can result in very costly repairs, including the removal of the spandrel veneer or the removal and modification (or replacement) of the windows.

The shelf angles themselves are not a substitute for this last layer of defense. Shelf angles are installed in relatively short segments, with a small gap between each to accommodate their horizontal, thermal expansion. If the shelf-angle flashing is breached, these gaps direct water into the areas directly below.

6.6.2 CAREFULLY DETAILING HORIZONTAL AND INCLINED SURFACES

Most vertical brick-veneer panels with properly tooled concave mortar joints and with relatively minor cracking do not become repeatedly saturated unless rainwater or snowmelt is directed onto or into the veneer by architectural details located above them. Typical offenders are parapet copings that are not designed to direct all water to the roof side, are not made of sheet metal, and do not incorporate even a small overhang on the exterior side. The water-shedding surfaces of window sills and belt courses that are not clad in metal and do not have a drip edge and a significant overhang are also typical offenders, the water-shedding surfaces of deeper details, like deep belt courses and shed roofs not entirely clad in metal and without gutters at the base of their slope.

The architectural details discussed in the previous paragraph are generally acceptable, if properly handled. However, another class of details should be eliminated altogether. These are the small horizontal ledges that are created when one or more horizontal brick courses are recessed or protruded to break up a boring facade or to provide ornamentation. These ledges are often less than ¾ inch (19 mm) deep and cannot usually be clad with sheet metal. Substitutes like mortar and sealant that are used to create a sloped surface usually fail and often make the situation worse. Small ledges allow a surprising amount of water into the masonry, causing saturation that sometimes results in unsightly stains of efflorescence, dirt, and organic matter below the ledges. (Efflorescence is a white stain that remains on the exterior surface after water has evaporated. It is usually composed of soluble salts that are dissolved and carried to the surface, including calcium carbonate, which is difficult to remove without harming the veneer. Unless it causes spalling when it is trapped under a clear coating or under the surface of a glazed brick, efflorescence may appear to be only an aesthetic problem. However, it is also a warning that too much water is making its way into the veneer. See Section 6.9.2 for information on efflorescence and clear coatings.)

The accent provided by these unnecessary ledges can be created by adding brick patterns, such as a single course of soldier, rowlock, or basket weave; by using different colored brick; or by using brick with a different surface finish, such as courses of rug-textured brick in a field of wire-cut brick units. The result can be a cleaner, subtler facade, with less potential for staining and accelerated deterioration. Using these techniques, freeze-thaw damage as well as corrosion of veneer anchors is reduced, thereby lengthening the life of the facade. If a highly ornamental cladding is desired, a combination of differing patterns, color, and texture can be employed. However, patterns created with stacked-bond courses are inherently weak and should be avoided. If their use cannot be avoided, they must be liberally reinforced with horizontal joint reinforcing. This is also true of multiple courses of soldier, rowlock, and basket-weave brickwork.

6.6.3 USING PRESSURE EQUALIZATION CAREFULLY

Attempts to reduce the amount of water entering the free air space of an ABV/SS system by using a fully effective pressure-equalization system (sometimes called a "rain screen") are not recommended by this book as they are not very practical or economical. ABV/SS is a complicated and fussy enough system without the additional components necessary to create a full-blown pressure-equalization system. An effective pressure-equalized system requires both an upper and lower row of closely spaced vents, liberally spaced vertical baffles, and a virtually perfect air barrier. Full-height, head-joint weep holes at 16 inches on center (Figure 6.12) may suffice for the lower row of vents, but some of the other components may simply add risk. Adding a row of head-joint vents at the top of veneer panels, even if covered with miniature louvers, may allow high-velocity, wind-driven water to cross the free air space unless sufficient back pressure is guaranteed by a system of almost perfectly spaced and installed vertical baffles and by fully effective air barriers throughout the facade.

If pressure equalization is attempted, this book recommends a scaled back system, which, although less effective, is also less costly and less risky. Creating an effective air barrier system and installing vertical baffles at corners (Figure 6.15) where pressure differences are usually the greatest should help promote pressure equalization (Note 2, Table 6.1, Section 6.2). Increasing the number of full-height weep holes by decreasing their spacing to 8 inches on center may also help pressures behind the veneer adjust more quickly. However, the use of an upper row of vents is not recommended. In addition to the risks discussed above, it is unlikely that an upper row of vents will promote significant drying of the cavity.[11]

6.7 ACCOMMODATING DIFFERENTIAL MOVEMENT WITH EXPANSION JOINTS

Anchored brick veneer panels are bordered above, and to each side, with expansion joints to separate the panels from each other, thereby accommodating growth in the height and width of the panels as well as accommodating movement of the building frame. Veneer panels are usually one story or less in height, and they are normally supported by rigidly attached shelf angles with the horizontal expansion joints directly beneath. As shown in Figure 6.10, expansion joints are located to create rectangular panels of ABV.

An expansion joint is an unobstructed air space that provides for expansion and contraction of the veneer panels. Movement joints in ABV are exclusively expansion joints. Control joints, which are solid joints that can only accommodate contraction, should never be used to separate panels of anchored brick veneer, because ABV undergoes considerable moisture expansion in addition to thermal expansion. ABV does not experience the significant shrinkage sometimes experienced by concrete brick and concrete masonry unit construction. See Chapter 4 for more information.

The incorrect sizing and location of expansion joints causes cracking, which weakens the veneer and lets water into the ABV/SS system. See Section 9.4 for a discussion of the failures of two ABV facades that lacked adequate expansion joints.

The proper location and spacing of expansion joints, especially vertical expansion joints, is part art and part science. The maximum spacing of expansion joints can be calculated using the latest version of the formula published by the Brick

Industry Association.[12] However, the rules of thumb in the following sections may suffice.

As expansion joints are virtually impossible to hide, the architect should begin considering their location during schematic design and have the patience to continue working with them throughout the design process.

6.7.1 USING VERTICAL EXPANSION JOINTS TO ACCOMMODATE HORIZONTAL EXPANSION

A lack of properly located vertical expansion joints has been observed in a distressing number of brick veneer facades across North America. The result is sometimes severe cracking, enough to lessen the ability of the veneer to handle lateral loads. One situation that can be particularly destabilizing is that of classic rotational corner cracking, as depicted in Figures 6.8 and 9.24.

Locating a single vertical expansion joint at corners
Brick veneer corners at offsets, returns, and building corners must be protected from horizontal expansion of the veneer panels by the use of vertical expansion joints (Figure 6.10). This was traditionally accomplished with two joints, one to each side of the corner, and each hopefully within two or three feet of the corner. However, protecting brick veneer panels at corners is best accomplished with a single vertical expansion joint located at the first head joint to one side of the corner (Figure 6.15). This single corner expansion joint accommodates expansion of the veneer panels on either side of the corner by eliminating the single, two-sided corner veneer panel altogether. The single vertical joint also eliminates the possibility of vertical corner cracking due to the differential flexing of the two sides of a single corner panel under high lateral loading, a potential concern given the flexibility of steel-stud backup walls. (Elimination of the two-sided corner panel also better protects the AVB/SS system from story drift, covered in Section 6.7.3.) The

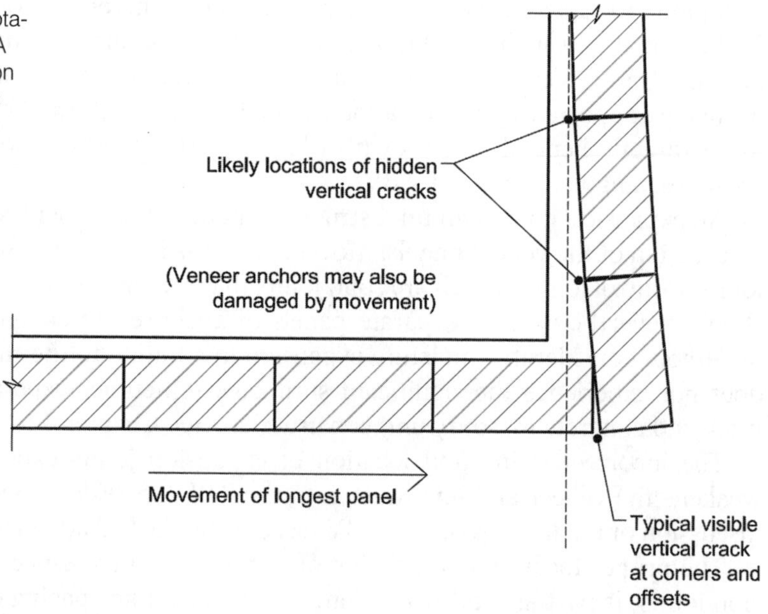

FIGURE 6.8 Classic rotational corner cracking. A lack of vertical expansion joints at or near corners causes this failure. Also see Figure 4.1.

Likely locations of hidden vertical cracks

(Veneer anchors may also be damaged by movement)

Movement of longest panel

Typical visible vertical crack at corners and offsets

Working with Patterns

There seems to be an almost universal move to minimize, camouflage, or otherwise deny the fact that ABV panels must be bound by expansion joints. Brickwork is no longer monolithic, and attempts to make it appear so are more likely to fail than attempts to detail the expansion joint locations as part of a well-designed geometric pattern.

The location of expansion joints should be considered during the preliminary design stage along with the location of all openings in, and projections from, the ABV panels; integration with other cladding materials; and the design of the brickwork surface. Working closely with the structural engineer to size and locate the joints allows for their incorporation into the overall exterior design. If expansion joints are located later in the design process, the result is often a compromised aesthetic (Figure 4.6). Locating expansion joints within the context of the exterior wall aesthetic should be the responsibility of the project's primary design architect, who will need the patience to continue working with them throughout the design process. Complicated facades require talented and tenacious designers; but if their work begins during schematic design and continues unabated, the task will be easier and the result will be an aesthetically and functionally successful facade (Figure 6.9).

Emphasizing the geometry of a well-designed panel system by using a standard 1-inch (25 mm) width for both horizontal *and* vertical expansion joints has several benefits. It creates consistency throughout the facade, makes sealant installation easier, and lowers the chance of an early sealant failure. A standard 1-inch (25 mm) expansion joint may be especially helpful in sunny climates at higher elevations where sealants lose elasticity more rapidly due to greater ultraviolet radiation. The wider the joint, the less stress a partially hardened sealant must endure and, consequently, the longer it will last. Owners will likely be amenable to this strategy, as the replacement of sealant joints is costly.

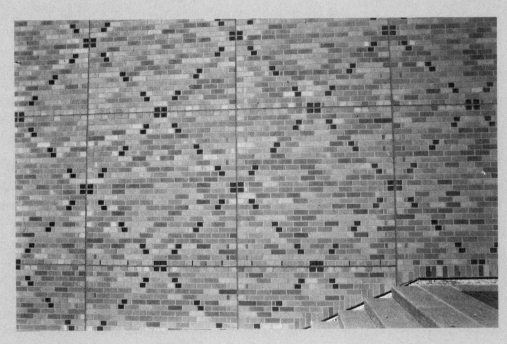

FIGURE 6.9 This brick facade shows how an adventurous designer overlaid a diamond pattern of contrasting brick on the rectangular grid of expansion joints. See Section 6.11 for more information on this project. Photo by Linda Brock.

single-joint design also reduces the amount of sealant that must eventually be replaced, an expensive maintenance procedure, especially above the first story.

Locating vertical expansion joints in anchored brick veneer walls without openings

In anchored brick veneer walls without penetrations like windows, doors, and other openings, vertical expansion joints should be spaced to create veneer panels that are not more than 25 feet (7.6 m) long.

Locating vertical expansion joints in anchored brick veneer walls with punched openings

To minimize cracking in walls that are interrupted by doors, windows, and other openings, vertical expansion joints are located to create rectangular veneer panels without openings (Figure 6.10). If oddly spaced or closely spaced openings occasionally make rectangles impossible, the spacing of the vertical expansion joints must be reduced. These veneer panels, which are usually some variation of an L or Ll, are susceptible to shear failures, which often take the form of stair-stepping cracks. These oddly shaped veneer panels should seldom exceed 15 feet (4.5 m) in length.

The location and spacing of vertical expansion joints is obviously simplified if the location and spacing of the openings are selected at the same time.

Sizing vertical expansion joints

The width of vertical expansion joints must accommodate moisture growth in addition to the maximum thermal expansion caused by exposure to direct sunlight during periods of high ambient temperatures. The temperature throughout the depth of darker bricks that receive solar radiation can be quite high, especially if the ambient temperature fails to drop significantly during the night.

Depending upon on the type of sealant and the manufacturer's recommendation, the width of the joint must be at least doubled to prevent premature failure of the joint sealant and extend its service life. Using the silicon joint sealant recommended in the next subsection, vertical expansion joints should not be less than ⅜ inch (10 mm) wide to separate panels up to 15 feet (4.5 m) wide; not less than ½ inch (13 mm) wide to separate panels 15 to 20 feet (4.5 to 6 m) in width; and not less than ⅝ inch (16 mm) wide to separate panels 20 to 25 feet (6 to 7.5 m) in width. If in doubt, the joint width at corners (Figure 6.15) should be increased. Corner joint sealant is not only susceptible to tension and compression (extrusion) failures but also to shear failures.

Specifying the most forgiving joint sealant with the longest life

Expansion joint sealant should be a high-quality, ultralow-modulus silicon, like Dow 790 by Dow Corning (not to be confused with Dow 795, which is a structural sealant with a higher modulus). To determine compatibility, the architect should specify preconstruction testing by the sealant manufacturer for compatibility and adhesion with all substrates. Based on these tests, the manufacturer will recommend a primer, if necessary. Preconstruction testing of the sealant and primer on a construction mock-up wall is essential, as is random field testing of fully cured joints.

The specifications should require that the expansion joints be formed against a board with a thickness of the specified joint width. After the brickwork on both sides of the board has been completed, the board is removed. The specifications should also require that the owner's representative be given notice when the joints are ready to be sealed so they can be inspected for deviations from the specified width and for the presence of mortar and other construction debris. Backer rods should not be installed until after the inspection, as they may hide mortar and debris.

6.7.2 USING HORIZONTAL EXPANSION JOINTS TO ACCOMMODATE VERTICAL EXPANSION OF ANCHORED BRICK VENEER PANELS AND SHORTENING OF THE BUILDING FRAME

There must be an unobstructed air space directly beneath shelf angles (Figure 6.13) and other supports and projections such as floor slabs (Figure 6.2) and concrete beams that are directly above the top of veneer panels. In addition to accommodating moisture and thermal expansion of the brick veneer panel, these horizontal expansion joints must also accommodate the shortening of the building frame. The unobstructed air space is closed from below by veneer panel expansion, and from above by frame shortening; these two movements are additive. (The failure to understand this concept has resulted in, arguably, the most expensive multistory, anchored brick veneer failures in North America. The literature on these failures can be fairly dry, but Barry P. LePatner and Sidney M. Johnson, a lawyer and an engineer, respectively, have published a nicely readable and well illustrated case study.)[13]

At first glance, the designer may dismiss differential movement due to the shortening of the building frame if only the elastic shortening of columns is considered. However, in the case of concrete frames, shortening of the columns is often magnified by concrete creep, a phenomenon that usually continues beyond the construction period. This movement is due to a number of technical factors in the specification and production of concrete. They cannot be reliably enough controlled to allow the designer to assume them away—creep must be accommodated, even though its magnitude is difficult to predict.

Sizing horizontal expansion joints
The unobstructed air space underneath shelf angles should not be less than ½ inch (13 mm) for single-story veneer panels (up to 12 feet high) (3.6 m) without approval from a structural engineer. The height of the horizontal sealant joints at the exterior of shelf angles is the height of the unobstructed air space plus the thickness of the steel shelf angle (Figure 6.13). Consequently, the total height of the sealant joint is only slightly less than one inch for single-story ABV panels. The use of a first course of "lipped" brick to reduce the height of the horizontal sealant joints should be avoided, as it complicates the configuration and installation of the shelf-angle flashing. It also makes the installation of the sealant more difficult and significantly reduces the height of the sealant joint and, therefore, its life. If the lipped brick is turned upside down with the lip facing upward and used as the highest course of brick, the potential for problems shifts to the unobstructed air space. In this position, the lip will shield the air space beneath the shelf angle from view, and the inspector will find it difficult to determine if it is truly unobstructed.

Providing for veneer expansion under window sills
Window sills are supported by the brick veneer, yet their design must accommodate upward expansion of the brick panel below. This means that the sill, or its attachment to the window frame, must be fairly flexible. The accommodation of this movement may be helped with the use of a sheet metal Z-section between the top of the brick veneer panel and the underside of the metal sill (Figure 6.18). Nonetheless the slope of sills should be designed for at least some brick veneer

expansion, which will force the outer edge of the sill upward a little and thereby decrease the slope of the sill. If a sill has such a limited slope that the back edge of the expanding brick veneer panel contacts its underside, the slope will quickly be reversed and water will pool against the window frame.

6.7.3 ACCOMMODATING DIFFERENTIAL MOVEMENTS CAUSED BY STORY DRIFT

As ABV panels are fairly rigid, they will not lean horizontally with the building frame as it flexes during high winds or seismic activity, unless a design flaw forces them to do so. Stair-stepping cracks will result if they are forced from a rectangular shape to that of a parallelogram.

Because the building frame leans during story drift and ABV panels must remain upright, the architect's structural engineer should analyze potential differential movements between the two. This analysis may result in recommendations to use a veneer anchor that allows very large, in-plane differential movements where veneer is attached to the building frame (Figure 6.15).

Protecting steel-stud backup walls

As the veneer panel must remain square and upright, so its backup wall must also remain in its as-built position. Otherwise, the veneer anchors that tie the two together may undergo significant shear, resulting in damage to the anchors and loss of strength. Therefore, the top of the steel-stud backup wall must be anchored with a slip joint that allows for both vertical and horizontal movement of the frame. Hence, this anchorage only constrains the steel-stud backup wall in the lateral direction. Two of these "deflection heads" are shown. Most details (e.g., Figure 6.13) show the traditional double-track deflection joint, whereas Figure 6.12 shows a story drift–clip head that is easier to install and open to visual inspection. However, the story drift–clip must have full-depth horizontal bracing within a few inches of the clip as determined by the structural engineer.

Protecting veneer panels at corners

On buildings with relatively flexible frames or in areas with high lateral loading, it is important to locate vertical expansion joints at the first head joint to one side of each corner (Figure 6.15). This is the safest configuration, as it reduces the possibility of veneer damage at corners due to story drift, but its location creates the need to position the joint so it faces the direction of the greatest expected building lean. This orientation may prevent the adjacent brick veneer panels from impacting during a major story-drift event. If this precaution is not sufficient to prevent impact, the structural engineer may need to increase the width of the joint. In extreme events, the sealant may be sacrificed, as it will probably be extruded from the joint.

If the structural engineer and architect cannot agree on the orientation and size of the sealant joint, then other solutions must be found. One publication apparently suggests that these corners be located away from pedestrian traffic.[14] This strategy is not recommended. A better solution is to eliminate ABV at these corners, with the substitution of a more forgiving cladding such as metal panels. Of course, the optimal solution is to stiffen the building frame sufficiently. If that cannot be accomplished, it is time to reexamine the use of anchored brick veneer on the building. Identifiable problems at corners and offsets are a warning that the ABV system needs a building-wide story-drift review.

6.8 DESIGNING PARAPET VENEER PANELS: A SPECIAL CASE

The use of parapets clad with anchored brick veneer is relatively risky, often unnecessary, and not recommended on taller buildings in northern climates. If they must be used and, to make matters more difficult, the parapet coping and its overhang must be deemphasized, then the following information and Figure 6.14 are offered in the interest of increasing what is sometimes a relatively short life. However, as discussed in Section 6.5.1, steel-stud backup walls should not be used. Instead, the backup walls for parapet veneer are constructed of reinforced concrete masonry or cast-in-place concrete. (Although not as common, the use of parapet backup walls made of reinforced, clay brick masonry reduces both vertical and horizontal differential movements, because the backup wall and its brick cladding are constructed of the same materials.)

6.8.1 MINIMIZING THE SIZE OF ANCHORED BRICK VENEER PANELS ON PARAPET WALLS

To reduce vertical movements that would interfere with the metal coping, and its vulnerable sealant joint, the parapet veneer panel should be limited to approximately 4 feet (1220 mm) in height. The horizontal distance between vertical expansion joints should never be greater than one-half of the distance between the vertical expansion joints that separate veneer panels lower on the building (Figure 6.10), because horizontal differential movement of parapet veneer is typically greater. Also, the sealant joint between the coping structure and the veneer will fail in shear if vertical expansion joints are not conservatively spaced. The roof slab must be sufficiently insulated to prevent it from expanding enough to harm the veneer or its backup wall, both of which should be supported by the structure and not by the slab.

6.8.2 DESIGNING COPINGS TO PROTECT ANCHORED BRICK VENEER

The vertical, outside face of a well-designed coping extends down the face of the veneer at least 6 inches (150 mm). The coping should be a corrosion-resistant metal with a reasonably small coefficient of thermal expansion, like Type 304 stainless steel or terne-coated stainless steel, if a duller (but more expensive) finish is desired. Standing seams should be specified and conservatively spaced due to the considerable expansion and contraction parapet copings undergo during 24-hour and seasonal temperature cycles. The coping structure should provide continuous support for the sheet metal. If this support is lacking, the rigors of roofing maintenance and reroofing projects will very likely decrease the life of the coping system. This usually becomes evident the first time a worker sits or stands on the coping. In section, the coping should be a "shed roof" with a minimum slope of 2 in 12 that directs all the water onto the roof and not onto the face of the parapet veneer, which will otherwise be constantly saturated. For this reason, gabled and mansard sections are not acceptable. Due to its exposure, parapet veneer needs all the help it can get.

The coping structure and its fasteners must be designed for the expected wind loading. For clarity, Figure 6.14 does not show the wood screws used in the assembly of the structure, which in this example is made of plywood and closely spaced 2x wood ribs.

The entire coping structure must be protected by a tough, long-life, elastomeric membrane, like a 45 mil, reinforced-EPDM sheet. Membrane seams should be minimized to promote long-term watertightness. The continuous metal cleat (exterior side) and the coping (roof side) should be attached with removable screws so the membrane can be replaced when necessary. The screws that attach the continuous cleat must not continue into the brickwork.

The coping design should include a well-defined drip edge, which overhangs the brick veneer by at least 2 inches (50 mm). If a drip edge with a substantial overhang is not included, rainwater and condensation that runs off the outside vertical face of the coping will be deposited on the first few feet of veneer below the coping. The drip edge and overhang distribute the water over a greater surface area below. If the overhang is 6 inches (150 mm) or more, this water may be spread over two or more stories of veneer, greatly increasing the efficiency of evaporation. Roof overhangs of a foot (300 mm) or more afford superior protection where it is most needed (Figure 6.2).

A long-life sealant should be specified where the coping overhang meets the veneer. Without sealant, wind-driven rain will be pushed up under the coping structure and saturate the masonry from the top down and the inside out.

The continuous cleat should also be continuous around corners. The gauge of the continuous cleat should be strong enough to handle expected wind loads and protect the outside coping face from distortion. If not, the face can become unsightly; and in the worst case, sections of the coping can be lost. The continuous cleat should be made of the same corrosion-resistant metal as the coping to avoid sacrificial corrosion between the two metals.

6.9 SUPPLEMENTAL INFORMATION ON ABV/SS COMPONENTS

This supplemental information on the selection and use of components is roughly ordered from the exterior to the interior. While the information in this section is important, the most critical information was often covered in preceding sections, especially Sections 6.5 through 6.7.

6.9.1 SUPPORTING WINDOWS, DOORS, AND CANTILEVERED ITEMS

Window and door frames transfer high lateral loads during windstorms and, consequently, are best attached directly to a strengthened backup wall. All window details in Section 6.10 show this arrangement. Whenever possible, it also makes sense to attach accessory items directly to the backup wall or building structure and, not to the brick veneer. This eliminates the need for a special provision to transfer these forces from the veneer to the backup wall. This is especially important when detailing cantilevered items like awnings and projecting signs and light fixtures, which can introduce large moments into the veneer. Their anchors should be rigid and penetrate the veneer to the building frame or to a backup wall strengthened for this purpose. These penetrations should be isolated from the veneer and carefully sealed, as they are likely sources of water.

6.9.2 USING CLEAR COATINGS SPARINGLY

The sealing of masonry with clear coatings that are designed to prevent water entry or make the removal of graffiti easier is often unsuccessful and sometimes only helps to create eyesores. (Figure 4.2 shows the results of an antigraffiti sealer with low permeability on stone.) This concern is especially appropriate when clear coatings are used to improve the performance of the brick veneer drainage cavity wall, which was developed to deal with water entry in an efficient manner and does not usually need the help or risk associated with clear coatings.[15]

The key in selecting a sealer is assuring that it is as permeable as possible. However, all sealers will reduce permeability and somewhat slow the drying of the brickwork by evaporation. Some may be responsible for the crystallization of soluble salts (cryptoflorescence) under the surface. Only the penetrating sealers — silane and siloxane — have acceptable water repellency and water vapor transmission in addition to a reasonably long life between expensive recoatings. Potentially, they also cause the least staining.[16]

If a sealer is needed for graffiti removal, it may be wise to consider a different, easier to clean cladding for these locations. For general water management, it is better to put extra effort into detailing the ABV/SS drainage cavity wall than to rely on questionable and high-maintenance products like clear coatings. In this regard, the information in Section 6.6.2 is especially appropriate.

6.9.3 SPECIFYING BRICK UNITS

Using a brick manufacturer and one of its standard brick colors with many years of proven experience in the local climate is a prudent decision. Although this simple rule of thumb does not eliminate the need for testing, it certainly reduces the chances of early failure.

In the United States, brick units made of fired clay or shale are usually specified by reference to ASTM C216, Grade SW. Regardless of climate and exposure, Grade MW should not be specified for units to be used on the exterior. In areas characterized by harsh winters, it is recommend that ASTM C216 be modified to make the referenced ASTM C67, 50-cycle freezing-and-thawing test a requirement in addition to the compressive strength, physical property requirement. If it is believed that the veneer will be saturated for lengthy periods during severe winters, then the specifier may wish to require the 50-cycle freezing-and-thawing test and all of the C216 physical property requirements. These tests must be run before construction of the veneer begins, which requires careful scheduling to avoid delaying construction. The tests should be made on a group of brick units randomly selected from the full color range manufactured for the specific project.

6.9.4 INCREASING VENEER ANCHOR RELIABILITY WITH HORIZONTAL JOINT REINFORCING

Single-wire, 9-gauge (W1.7, MW11), horizontal joint–reinforcing clipped to adjacent veneer anchors is a prescriptive code requirement in some geographic areas. It is also an inexpensive and simple way to increase the overall reliability of the veneer anchor system, where high lateral loading, uneven corrosion among anchors, or substandard construction is a possibility. Many problems of veneer design can be handled by the use of single-wire horizontal joint reinforcing. For example, the veneer anchor in the lower portion of Figure 6.15 must be located more than the recommended 6 inches (150 mm) from the end of the veneer panel. But the use of horizontal joint reinforcing mitigates this problem, especially if it is clipped to the veneer anchor as shown. Finally, should a catastrophic event cause the veneer panel to become unstable, the horizontal joint reinforcing that is clipped to the veneer anchors may help keep it on the building.

Sections of horizontal joint reinforcing should be as long as possible, and, if necessary, splices should lap at least 8 inches (200 mm). If the length of the veneer panels is short enough, splices can be eliminated altogether. Horizontal joint reinforcing should not pass through vertical expansion joints. Single-wire, horizontal joint reinforcing that is located no closer than one inch from the exterior face of the brickwork usually does not need to be stainless steel if every effort has been made to keep the veneer from becoming constantly saturated (Sections 6.6.2 and 6.8.2). Horizontal joint reinforcing must have a zinc coating of at least 1.5 ounces per square foot of surface area by hot-dipping after fabrication. If the veneer anchors are made of stainless steel, then the horizontal joint reinforcing must also be made of stainless steel, as zinc-coated steel should not come in contact with stainless steel.

6.9.5 USING EXCLUSIVELY TWO-PIECE, ADJUSTABLE VENEER ANCHORS

Two-piece, adjustable veneer anchors effectively deal with both horizontal and vertical differential movement between the veneer and its backup wall. Furthermore, in the case of ABV/SS, adjustable anchors are usually required by code.

An anchor section and a tie section

Four popular adjustable anchors are presented in this section. Each is composed of an inner "anchor section" that is fastened to the backup wall and an outer "tie section" (also called brick tie or simply tie) that mates with the anchor section and extends into the adjacent mortar bed joint. The tie section is often referred to by its shape and design (e.g., the "box wire tie" and "triangular wire tie" of Figure 6.15, the "triangular pintle wire tie" of Figure 6.13, and the "flat-plate pintle tie" of Figure 6.21).

Prong-type adjustable veneer anchors

The anchor section of this adjustable anchor is mounted after the extruded polystyrene cavity insulation board has been installed (e.g., Figures 6.14 and 6.15). It incorporates sharp prongs to penetrate insulation boards and gypsum or other soft sheathings. (It cannot be used with plywood or other hard sheathings.) Its thermal performance is relatively good because the geometry of the anchor section places most of its surface area against the exterior of the insulation board, and there is exceptionally little contact between the prongs and the backup wall. Another advantage is that the tie section is a standard triangular wire tie, which provides a very limited surface area on which mortar droppings can accumulate. Its third advantage is the relatively large amount of vertical adjustment it allows the mason and the large vertical differential movement it can accommodate. Against completely solid backup walls like concrete, concrete masonry, and structural steel, its anchor section can also be installed horizontally and be used with a ¼ inch (6 mm) (W5, MW32) diameter, triangular pintle wire tie (Figure 6.13). Therefore, its brick tie can be installed closer to the top or bottom of the veneer panel.

So that it can penetrate extruded polystyrene cavity insulation boards and soft sheathings, the prongs must be quite sharp. Therefore, they puncture the water barrier even when it is backed up by an impenetrable substrate such as concrete or structural steel. This problem can be somewhat mitigated by using a vertical strip of peel-and-stick, self-adhesive membrane under the anchor, as this membrane is somewhat self-repairing (e.g., under the lower anchor of Figure 6.15). This is certainly not a foolproof solution, and concern about potential for water entry into a steel-stud backup wall is warranted. The other difficulty occurs when the anchor section is installed over steel studs. There is no guarantee that the installer will know for sure that each of the prongs, at the top and bottom of the anchor section, actually engaged the stud flange. It is sometimes even difficult to detect this problem when trying to view it from the interior, because the prongs may not quite have penetrated the sheathing. Because of these disadvantages, the author is skeptical about the use of these anchors with ABV/SS; but as shown in several figures, it is acceptable for brick veneer over solid backup walls of concrete, concrete masonry, and structural steel.

Sheathing-mounted adjustable veneer anchors
The anchor section of this adjustable anchor is installed over the exterior sheathing of the backup wall before the extruded polystyrene drainage- cavity insulation board is installed (e.g., Figures 6.11, 6.18, 6.20, and 6.21). Therefore, its thermal characteristics are not likely to be as good as those of the prong-type adjustable anchor. In addition, because there is no direct contact between the anchor section and the steel stud, the sheathing actually supports the anchor section. If over the years the sheathing should become wet and lose its compressive strength, this anchor will no longer anchor the veneer tightly to the backup wall.

The tie section (Figure 6.21) of some sheathing-mounted adjustable anchors is a solid, flat-plate pintle tie that, when made of 12-gauge steel, is relatively strong compared to a triangular wire tie. However, it can capture a significant volume of mortar droppings, resulting in mortar bridges that cross the air space and allow water to breach the drainage cavity (Figure 6.11).

Steel-stud, web-mounted adjustable veneer anchors
The anchor section of the steel-stud, web-mounted adjustable anchor is a plate that is attached directly to the web of the steel stud (Figure 6.19). This anchor is becoming increasingly popular in Canada. Because of its solid, direct attachment to the stud, its use may become more common in the United States. It can be used with a standard, triangular wire tie, which discourages the formation of mortar bridges across the air cavity. However, a clear disadvantage of this system is that the steel-stud sheathing and the SBPO water barrier must be cut and fit around the anchor plates after they are installed. Each penetration through the water barrier must be repaired. In addition, if the sheathing is being used as part of the system by which the steel-stud wall is stabilized, then the engineer will have to determine if extra bracing is required due to the weakened sheathing. Arguably, the steel-stud, web-mounted adjustable anchor has the poorest thermal performance of the anchors discussed in this section.

Maximum span of the brick tie
One prescriptive code section used in the United States requires that the distance between the interior face of the brick veneer and the exterior face of the steel-stud framing be a maximum of 4½ inches (115 mm).[17] If the free air space is to be 2 inches (50 mm) deep, as recommended by this book (Section 6.5.1), and the exterior steel-stud wall sheeting is ½ inch thick, then the cavity insulation board is limited to 2 inches (50 mm). One problem with ignoring this limitation is that a standard ³⁄₁₆ inch (5 mm) (W2.8, MW18) diameter triangular wire tie may not be sufficiently stiff to span the greater distance. In this case an engineer should design the anchorage system to ensure that the brick tie will not deform excessively under compressive loads caused by lateral forces. Due to potentially large eccentricities where the box wire tie engages the anchor section, it will probably need to be ¼ inch (6 mm) (W5, MW32) in diameter, regardless of the span.

Reducing lateral deflection

The gauge is the thickness of the metal used to fabricate the sheet-steel portions of adjustable veneer anchors. Metal gauge is inversely proportional to the thickness of the metal. Hence, an adjustable anchor fabricated from 12-gauge steel is stronger and usually much stiffer than one of the same design made of 14-gauge steel. Stiffness is likely to be the most important criteria. Acceptable lateral deflection, under wind and seismic loading, will probably be exceeded before the components of the adjustable anchor actually fail by yielding. For this reason, the steel gauge should be reviewed by the structural engineer. If a structural engineer is not involved in the decision, the specification of 12-gauge steel is properly conservative. Of course, the amount of deflection will also depend on the spacing of the veneer anchors, as greater spacing will mean higher lateral loading on each anchor.

Lateral deflection of adjustable veneer anchors is further controlled by the specification of a maximum value for the clearance (mechanical play) at the connection between the tie section and the anchor section. The reality of manufacturing tolerances does not allow this value to be much less than 1/16 inch (1.6 mm), which has become a common specification in the United States.

Spacing adjustable veneer anchors

Adjustable veneer anchors for an ABV/SS system should be spaced at a maximum of 16 inches horizontally by 16 inches vertically. This is a properly conservative and convenient standard, and this book recommends its use, which will help mitigate problems caused by the occasional poorly installed veneer anchor. However, this spacing should not be used to compensate for poorly specified corrosion protection of the anchors and joint reinforcing or the specification of light gauge veneer anchors. (For a brick-and-mortar module that courses out in multiples of 3 inches (75 mm), an anchor spacing of 15 inches (375 mm), vertically, is recommended because of the flexibility of the steel-stud backup wall, although codes may allow a vertical spacing of up to 18 inches (450 mm).)

The first row of veneer anchors above a shelf angle (or other support) should be located in the second or third bed joint, above the supporting surface but not more than 8 inches above. The highest row of anchors should be in the second bed joint below the top of the veneer panel. The first anchor to each side of vertical expansion joints and openings for windows, doors, and mechanical penetrations should be not more than 6 inches from the joint or opening. If necessary, somewhat greater distances can be tolerated when accompanied by horizontal joint reinforcing (Figure 6.15).

Providing corrosion protection

As a minimum, adjustable veneer anchors should receive 1.5 ounces of zinc coating per square foot of surface area by hot-dipping after fabrication. However, in areas with a long season of cool, wet weather, this book recommends that at least the high-risk areas of ABV facades be attached with stainless-steel veneer anchors. These high-risk areas include the parapet veneer; the story of veneer directly beneath the parapet veneer; and the first story of veneer directly below window sills, sill courses, belt courses, and other surfaces inclined toward the exterior. Since 1994, stainless-steel veneer anchors ("connectors") have been required on Canadian buildings greater than 11 meters (36 feet) in height in areas of moderate or severe exposure as defined by the annual driving rain index for Canada. [18]

Type 304 stainless steel is acceptable for the typical facade; but Type 316 should be considered for corrosive atmospheres near saltwater or near heavy industrial activities. Type 304 stainless steel may not be a good choice if the masonry is going to be saturated for long periods.

Should all brick veneer anchors be made of stainless steel in climates characterized by long periods of cool, wet weather? Depending on the height and complexity of the facade, identifying the high-risk areas may be nothing more than informed guesswork. If in doubt, the architect may want to discuss this issue with the owner, as this may be a question of long-term durability and safety versus limited construction funding. The owner of some commercial buildings may opt for a shorter veneer life, whereas other commercial and institutional clients may require a longer life and greater reliability.

6.9.6 Designing Shelf Angles, Loose Lintels, and Floor Slabs That Support Anchored Brick Veneer Panels

The structural engineer should design the shelf angle and loose lintel systems (Figure 6.13 and Figure 6.19). Included in the structural work are the size and length of shelf-angle segments; shelf-angle welds, if any; shims and shim welds; horizontal shelf-angle fastener slots and fasteners, embed plates, or wedge pocket inserts and their spacing; and the location of the first fastener, embed, or insert at the ends of shelf-angle segments and at shelf-angle corners.

Shelf angles should be located at least as often as one per floor, vertically. Some sources allow up to 30 feet (9 meters) to the first shelf angle above a foundation brick ledge, which is much too liberal if this 30-foot panel includes parapet veneer (Section 6.8). Also, where ABV/SS panels are vertically continuous across one or more floors, under lateral loading the radius of curvature of the veneer panels at the intermediate floors is reduced. Consequently, the potential for horizontal cracking at these locations is substantially greater.

Loose lintels must be designed so they can thermally expand into the brickwork at each end. Loose-lintel flashing (Figure 6.19) extends into the veneer to just beyond each end of the loose lintel end, where it is upturned to form an end dam at a head joint. Beneath the flashing at each end of the loose lintel is a space that separates it from the abutting mortar joints. The expanding loose lintel slips beneath its flashing into the concealed space. (As there are often vertical expansion joints located above and near openings, the engineer must size loose lintels to carry the full weight of the brick.)

Warm versus cold shelf angles
The configuration of the shelf angle shown in Figure 6.13 is the traditional "warm" shelf angle that is part of countless installations across North America. It is called "warm" because it is warmed by the building frame. On the other hand, the loose lintel of Figure 6.19 is "cold," because it is insulated from the frame and remains relatively cool.

During the last decade, a small but increasing number of installations have used insulated or "cold" shelf angles to conserve energy by spacing the shelf angle away from the building frame and insulating between the two. Of course, insulated shelf angles lose more heat than insulated loose lintels because shelf angles must be solidly fixed to the building frame with steel extenders of fairly substantial cross section.

An insulated shelf angle may create unforeseen difficulties. In the years to come, architects and engineers may look back with some regret at having specified cold shelf angles in some climates. For example, although it is too early to know with certainty, climates that include periods of severe freezing rain (ice storms) may not be good candidates for cold shelf angles. The traditional, uninsulated warm shelf angle may help to clear ice from the base of the free air space, where it can block the drainage system, including the weep holes.[19]

A second problem created by insulated shelf angles is shared by the loose-lintel configuration of Figure 6.19. To allow room for the extruded polystyrene cavity insulation board, the loose lintel has been moved toward the exterior, and therefore its horizontal leg has been shortened. This decreases the depth of the free air space at the very critical area adjacent to the weep holes. Unless exceptional care is taken to keep this area clear of mortar droppings and other debris, it will funnel and pack this material into a mass just behind the weep holes. Accordingly, Figure 6.19 shows a compromise solution, whereby the lintel is insulated but with just one inch of drainage cavity insulation board.

A third difficulty is the connection of the insulated shelf angle to the structure by means of a structural-steel extender, welded to the back of the shelf angle and to a weld plate embedded or bolted to the building frame. This allows the cavity board insulation to be installed behind the vertical leg of the shelf angle, except at the tube extender. This design tends to require extensive field welding, which is expensive. Also, as all of this steel is heavily zinc-coated, the zinc must be removed before welding and then replaced. This is difficult and time consuming yet critical to restore the zinc to its original thickness at these locations. A possible solution is the use of one of the commercially available shelf-angle extender systems that have been specifically developed to attach cold shelf angles; but mortar funneled to the back of weep holes remains a potential problem.[20]

Avoiding corrosion

Stainless-steel shelf angles and loose lintels are usually not necessary if the angles are protected by well-designed, completely through-wall flashings (Figure 6.13) made of stainless steel. However, shelf angles should have a hot-dipped coating of at least 2.3 ounces of zinc per square foot of surface area. The hot dipping process should take place after the shelf-angle segments have been cut to length and after horizontal fastener slots have been punched.

Attaching uninsulated shelf angles

Shelf angles should be installed in segments, with a small gap between each to accommodate thermal expansion and contraction of the shelf angles. It makes sense that shelf-angle segments be laid out so that a gap falls at each vertical expansion joint.

The location of horizontal slots for shelf-angle fasteners should be dimensioned on the structural drawings. These horizontal slots allow for spacing tolerances between the fasteners and for thermal expansion of the shelf angles. As friction is not an acceptable way of supporting brick veneer panels, horizontal slots should not be oversized in the vertical direction to provide vertical adjustment. Nor should oversized circular holes or vertical slots be used for this purpose. Vertical adjustment is important, but it should be provided by some other method such as the wedge-pocket insert of Figure 6.13.

Cast-in-place wedge-pocket inserts (Figure 6.13) and weld plates (Figure 6.16) embedded in concrete beams provide adequate vertical adjustment, but they are sometimes improperly located or installed in the concrete formwork. The general contractor should carefully coordinate their location and installation, verifying that the concrete subcontractor has securely attached them to the forms so their outside face will be flush with the concrete face.

Floor slabs that support ABV/SS

Shelf angles usually support the dead weight of ABV panels—and that system is recommended. However, cantilevered floor slabs that support veneer panels have the advantage of overhanging and protecting the veneer below (Figure 6.2). But they also create problems. They are exposed to the exterior, resulting in energy loss and chilled floors in many climates. Vertical deflections of supporting slabs have damaged ABV panels. Therefore, if this system of support must be used, these slabs should be minimally cantilevered from the floor beams and columns at the point where they support the veneer panels, and they should be sufficiently thick and properly tied into continuous exterior floor beams. To prevent wind-driven water from entering the base of the ABV wall below the flashing pan (of similar configuration as that in Figure 6.13), the ABV and backup wall should rest on a minimum 2-inch high brick ledge that has been cast as part of the concrete slab so as to eliminate cold joints that would allow water to follow the slab to the interior. The top surface of cantilevered slabs must slope to the exterior to drain water away from the wall. It may be advisable to flash the entire top surface of slabs in metal, particularly in areas where there is snow buildup or wind-driven rains. (If snow is expected, large energy losses and cold floors should also be expected.)

6.9.7 STRUGGLING WITH SHELF-ANGLE AND LOOSE-LINTEL FLASHING

Shelf-angle flashing is one of the most important but fussiest and most frustrating components of the ABV/SS system. The following information should help, but preconstruction mock-ups by the subcontractor are essential. It is also recommended that, if in doubt, the architect have a mock-up built during the design development phase.

The shelf-angle flashing should be made of a corrosion-resistant metal like stainless steel or terne-coated stainless steel and should extend beyond the exterior face to form a drip edge (Figure 6.13). The Brick Industry Association (BIA) warns that "all flashing should extend beyond the face of the wall to form a drip. Termination of through-wall flashing behind the exterior face of the wall is a dangerous practice and is not recommended."[21]

Metallic flashings, such as those made of stainless steel and copper, should be separated from zinc-coated shelf angles to prevent sacrificial corrosion (Figure 6.13). The nonmetallic separation sheet should be thick enough to prevent perforation during installation. Copper flashing may not be a good choice if staining of the veneer beneath weep holes cannot be tolerated. Galvanized steel has the advantage of a low coefficient of thermal expansion, but it has low resistance to galvanic corrosion. Aluminum, which should not be used, has several disadvantages including low resistance to galvanic corrosion and a high coefficient of thermal expansion.

Shelf-angle flashing must include slip seams if its length becomes too great given its thermal expansion characteristics. These seams are difficult to detail and construct without interfering with the aesthetics of the exposed drip edge. A "hook seam" will theoretically give excellent performance. However, a sealed "butt seam," with a backup plate beneath, has half the thickness and may be easier to install.[22] The simplest way of dealing with seams is to eliminate them by reducing the distance between vertical expansion joints that separate brick veneer panels. Shelf-angle flashing need not pass through these expansion joints. Instead, a small "end dam" may be created where shelf-angle flashing terminates at the return edge of vertical expansion joints. (Behind the veneer, the end dam can simply be a 90-

degree upturn in the sheet metal; but under the veneer panel this bend is flattened into a hem.) As flashing must terminate at the ends of loose lintels, end dams that are upturned into head joints are important.

Figure 6.13 suggests a two-piece, stainless-steel flashing system that should make alignment of the drip edge much easier, thereby reducing visible distortion. It also ensures that the flashing will not be damaged by protrusions, like the exposed end of shelf-angle fasteners, or the cleaning of partly hardened mortar droppings from cleanout holes (Figure 6.4 and Section 6.5.1). The lower section, called the "flashing pan," must be turned up at the rear to prevent water from finding its way to the shelf angle. The drip edge is "hemmed" to further decrease distortion along its length. The top section, called the "cavity flashing," must be made of the same metal as the flashing pan. As it is a separate section, its depth can be adjusted to accommodate building frame tolerances. The two-piece, all-metal flashing system (suggested by Figure 6.13) is the result of a growing realization that one-piece systems are easy to detail but difficult to install without resulting in a degree of distortion and misalignment of the drip edge that is unacceptable to many architects.

A two-piece system that uses even the toughest reinforced elastomeric membrane for the cavity flashing does not offer sufficient puncture resistance if the cavity is to be cleaned during or after each day's work. The all-metal flashing system of Figures 6.13 and 6.19 seems to be the best solution to distorted drip edges and the expensive repairs that result if mortar droppings and other debris are not cleaned and subsequently block the exit of water. Most architects have not used the two-piece metal flashing, so it is important that they thoroughly understand it and carefully observe its installation during the construction of a design development mock-up panel. The building trades may also not be familiar with adjusting the two-piece all-metal system during installation or familiar with its durability—it is meant to be tough, not indestructible

6.9.8 EXTERIOR SHEATHING ON STEEL-STUD BACKUP WALLS

The sheathing that is fastened to the exterior of the steel-stud backup wall serves three functions: it provides a solid, continuous backing for the water barrier (Figure 6.12); it provides a strong, dense backing for sheathing-mounted adjustable veneer anchors; and it may be used to provide at least partial bracing of the steel studs.

Although this is old news, it bears repeating: traditional, paper-faced exterior gypsum sheathing should not be used in the drainage cavity environment. The use of fiberglass-faced sheathing, like Georgia-Pacific's DensGlass Gold, is recommended.

If the sheathing is used by the structural engineer as part of the system that braces the steel studs against rotation, then every attempt should be made to ensure its integrity. For example, if it is decided to use a web-mounted, adjustable veneer anchor, like the lower anchor in Figure 6.19, the engineer should be advised of this decision. Finally, wet or loose sheathing, obviously, makes poor bracing. One publication notes that standard fastening methods may not be adequate; so fasteners that attach the sheathing to the studs should be chosen to ensure "that cyclic loading will not render the sheathing ineffective as bracing."[23]

6.10 ABV DETAILS

Brick veneer anchored to a steel-stud backup wall with a drainage cavity is detailed in Figures 6.10–6.21. The details are based on a 4–20 story concrete frame building that is located in a heating climate.

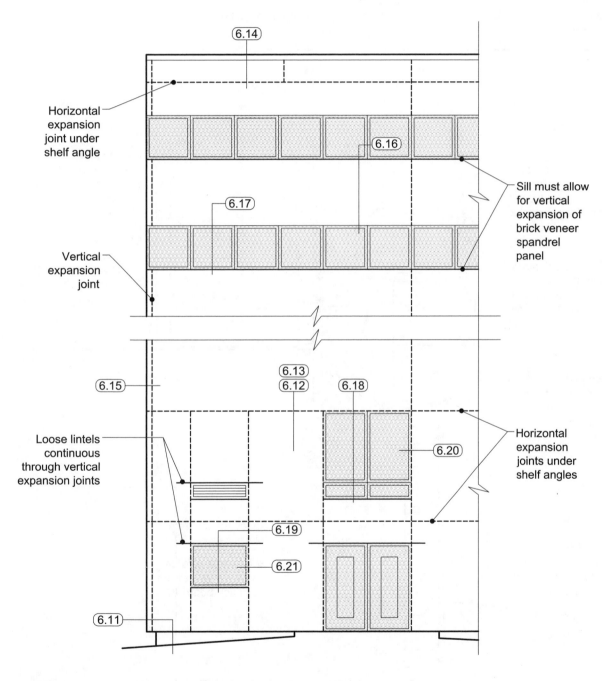

FIGURE 6.10 Locating expansion joints to create rectangular veneer panels.
Notes: This figure is referenced in 6.5.1, 6.7, 6.7.1, 6.8.1, and 6.9.1.

TYPICAL FOR ALL ANCHORED BRICK VENEER DETAILS
Heating Climate

Water Barrier:
Nonperforated SBPO

Vapor Retarder:
Kraft paper facing of fiberglass batt

Air Barrier:
Airtight drywall (ADA or SCS)
(not detailed)

Insulation:
XPS drainage cavity insulation board
Fiberglass batt

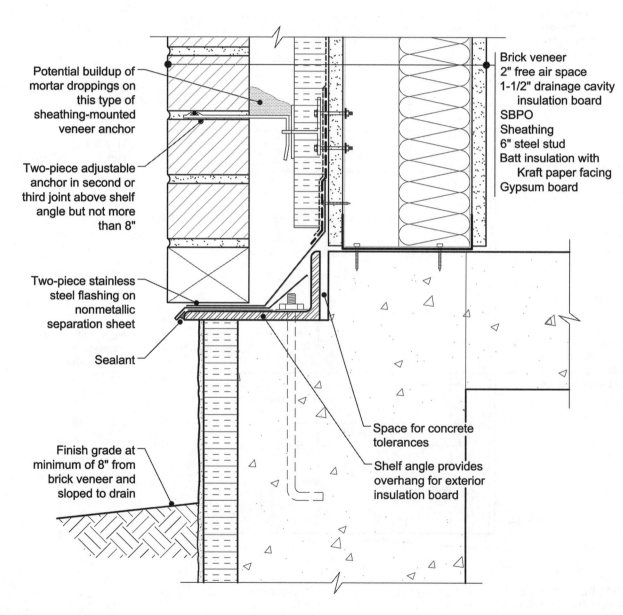

Potential buildup of mortar droppings on this type of sheathing-mounted veneer anchor

Two-piece adjustable anchor in second or third joint above shelf angle but not more than 8"

Two-piece stainless steel flashing on nonmetallic separation sheet

Sealant

Finish grade at minimum of 8" from brick veneer and sloped to drain

Brick veneer
2" free air space
1-1/2" drainage cavity insulation board
SBPO
Sheathing
6" steel stud
Batt insulation with Kraft paper facing
Gypsum board

Space for concrete tolerances

Shelf angle provides overhang for exterior insulation board

FIGURE 6.11 Typical ABV/SS wall components at base of building.
Notes: This figure is referenced in 6.6.1 and 6.9.5.

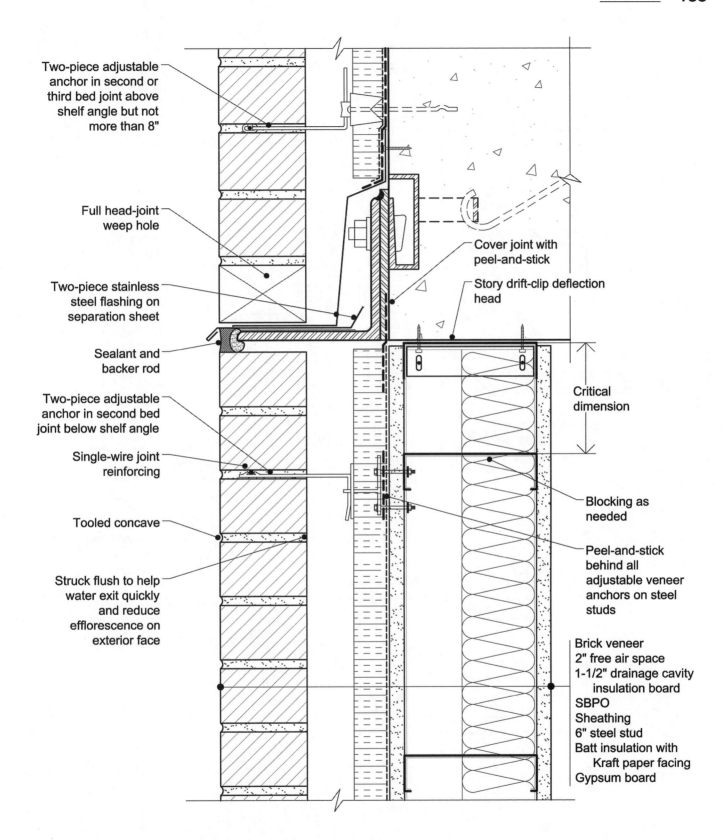

FIGURE 6.12 Typical ABV/SS wall components at intermediate floors.
Notes: This figure is referenced in 6.5.2, 6.6.1, 6.6.3, 6.7.3, and 6.9.8.

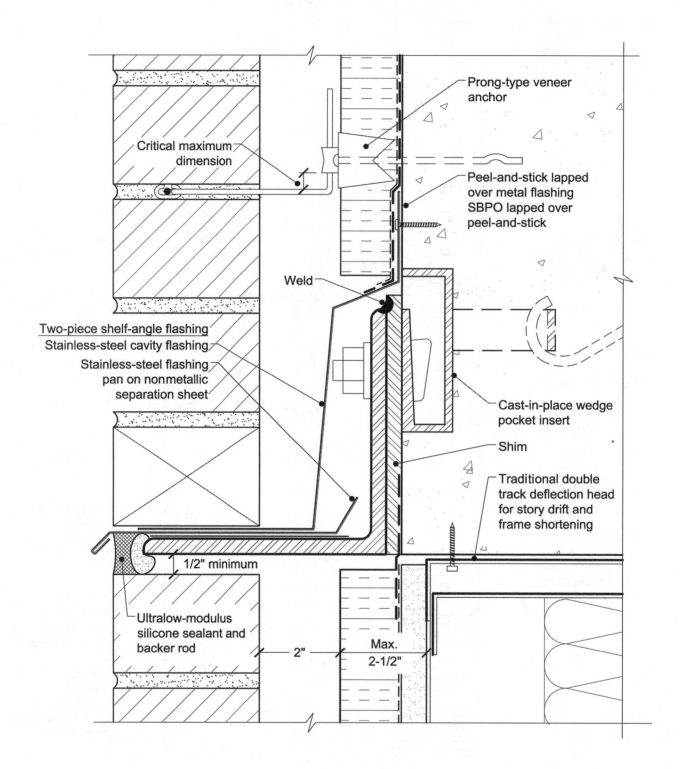

FIGURE 6.13 Typical ABV/SS wall components at concrete floor beams.
Notes: Shelf-angle flashing is similar at floor slabs that support ABV/SS, although caution is advised. This figure is referenced in 6.6.1, 6.7.2, 6.7.3, 6.9.5, 6.9.6, and 6.9.7.

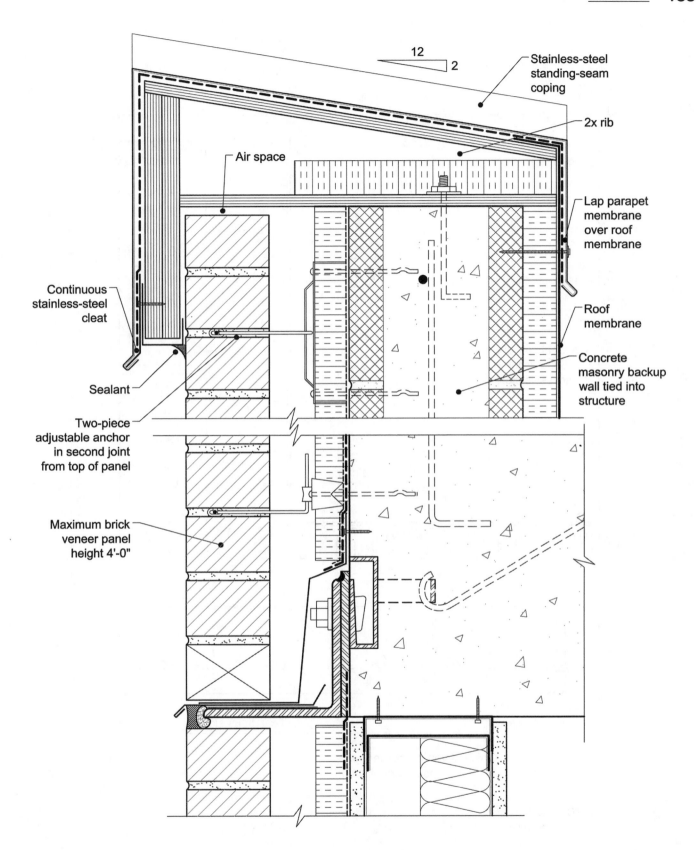

FIGURE 6.14 Typical ABV/CMU (concrete masonry units) wall components at parapet.
Notes: Coping has a minimum slope of 2 in 12. For clarity, screws and connectors used in the assembly of coping structure are not shown. This figure is referenced in 6.5.1, 6.6.1, 6.8, 6.8.2, and 6.9.5.

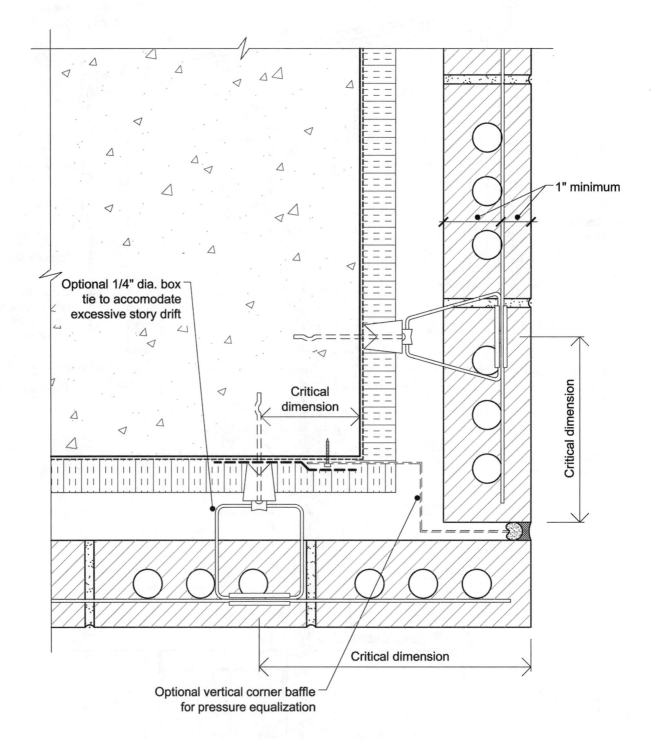

Optional 1/4" dia. box
tie to accomodate
excessive story drift

Critical
dimension

1" minimum

Critical dimension

Critical dimension

Optional vertical corner baffle
for pressure equalization

FIGURE 6.15 Typical ABV/SS components at corners, offsets and returns.
Notes: This figure is referenced in 6.6.3, 6.7.1, 6.7.3, 6.9.4, and 6.9.5.

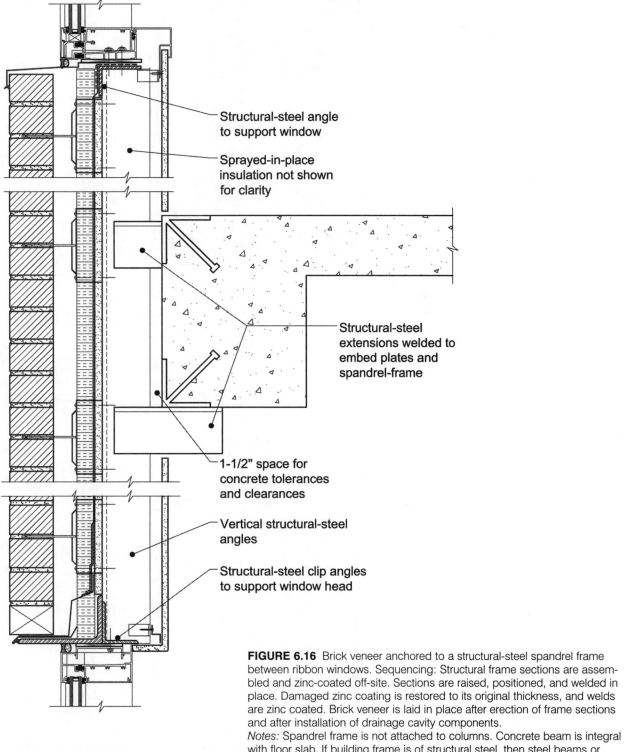

Structural-steel angle
to support window

Sprayed-in-place
insulation not shown
for clarity

Structural-steel
extensions welded to
embed plates and
spandrel-frame

1-1/2" space for
concrete tolerances
and clearances

Vertical structural-steel
angles

Structural-steel clip angles
to support window head

FIGURE 6.16 Brick veneer anchored to a structural-steel spandrel frame between ribbon windows. Sequencing: Structural frame sections are assembled and zinc-coated off-site. Sections are raised, positioned, and welded in place. Damaged zinc coating is restored to its original thickness, and welds are zinc coated. Brick veneer is laid in place after erection of frame sections and after installation of drainage cavity components.
Notes: Spandrel frame is not attached to columns. Concrete beam is integral with floor slab. If building frame is of structural steel, then steel beams or spandrel frame must be laterally braced against rotation. Systems that are completely panelized off-site may be an economical alternative, but positioning is critical to avoid noticeable irregularities where sections meet at vertical expansion joints. This figure is referenced in 6.3.2, 6.5.1, and 6.9.6.
Figures: See Figure 6.17 (ribbon window)

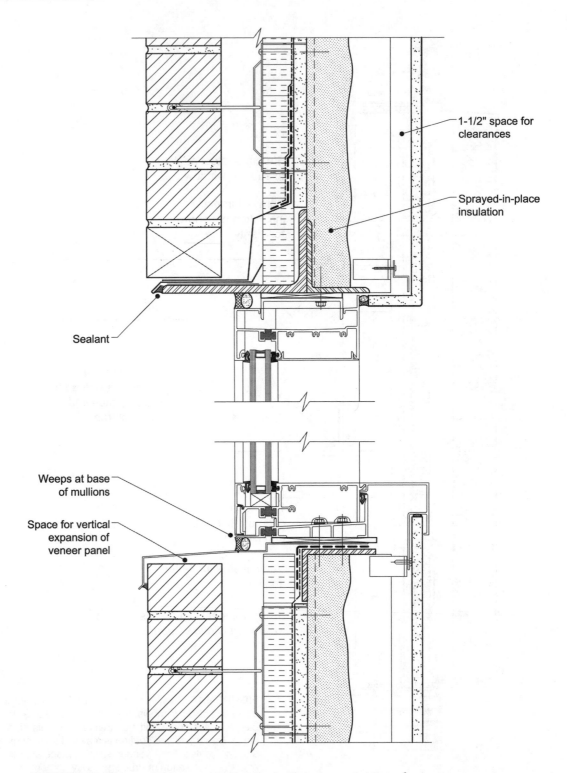

FIGURE 6.17 Ribbon window supported by structural-steel spandrel frame.[*]

Notes: This window head directs water entering from above into nearest mullion. It is then emptied from the base of the mullion through weeps onto the exterior sill. No fasteners attach to the underside of the shelf angle, eliminating the possibility that they will penetrate the shelf angle and its flashing. This figure is referenced in 6.5.1, 6.6.1, and 6.9.5.

Figures: See Figure 6.16 (structural-steel spandrel frame).

---

[*]Although the author is responsible for Figures 6.16 and 6.17, they were created with the help of the Walters and Wolf Glass Company, who should be contacted for design direction on actual projects. http:/www.waltersandwolf.com

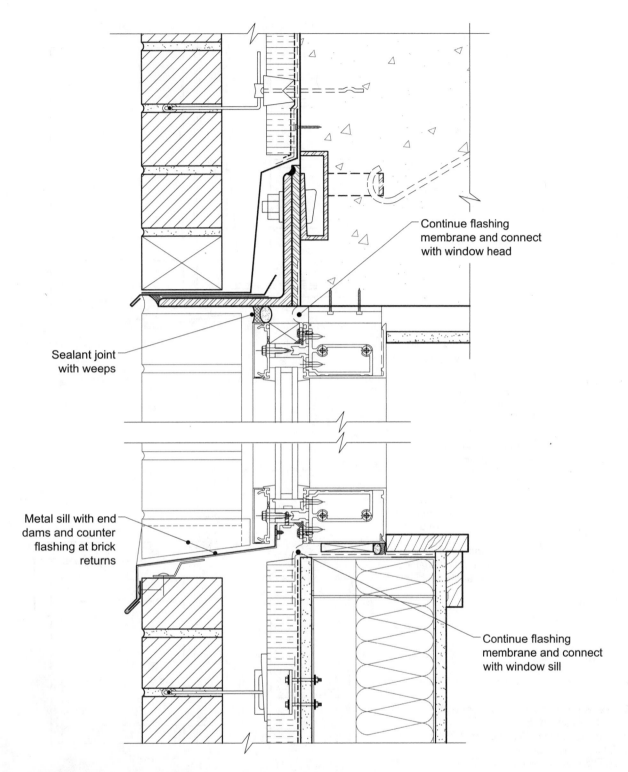

Continue flashing
membrane and connect
with window head

Sealant joint
with weeps

Metal sill with end
dams and counter
flashing at brick
returns

Continue flashing
membrane and connect
with window sill

FIGURE 6.18 Window anchored to a steel-stud wall and floor beam.*
Notes: No fasteners attach to the underside of the shelf angle, eliminating the possibility that they will penetrate the shelf angle and its flashing. This figure is referenced in 6.3.2, 6.6.1, 6.7.2, and in Table 6.1.
Figures: See Figure 6.20 (window jamb).

---

*Although the author is responsible for Figures 6.18 and 6.20, they were created with the help of the Kawneer Company, who should be contacted for design direction on actual projects. http://www.kawneer.com

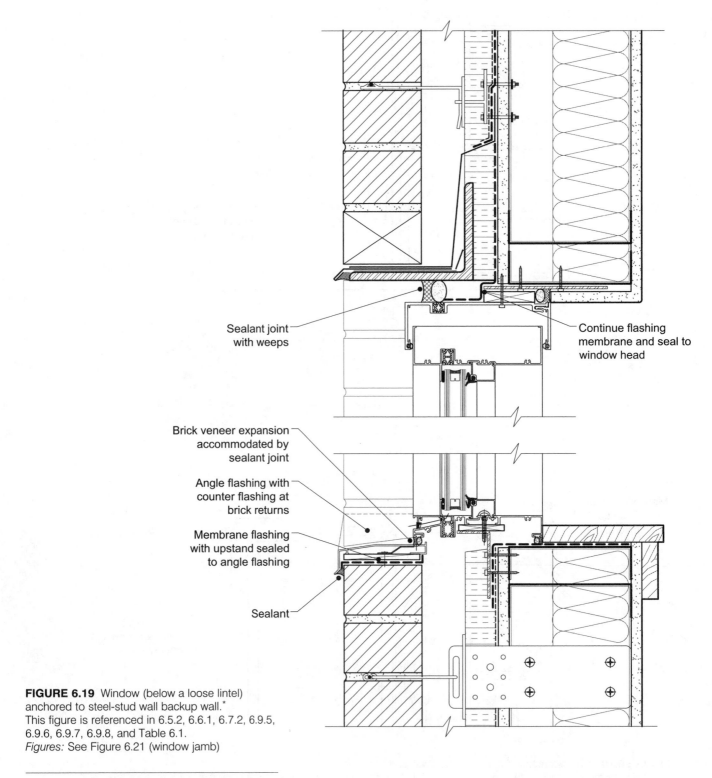

Sealant joint with weeps

Continue flashing membrane and seal to window head

Brick veneer expansion accommodated by sealant joint

Angle flashing with counter flashing at brick returns

Membrane flashing with upstand sealed to angle flashing

Sealant

FIGURE 6.19 Window (below a loose lintel) anchored to steel-stud wall backup wall.*
This figure is referenced in 6.5.2, 6.6.1, 6.7.2, 6.9.5, 6.9.6, 6.9.7, 6.9.8, and Table 6.1.
Figures: See Figure 6.21 (window jamb)

*Although the author is responsible for Figures 6.19 and 6.21, they were created with the help of Fulton Windows, who should be contacted for design direction on actual projects. http://www.fultonwindows.com

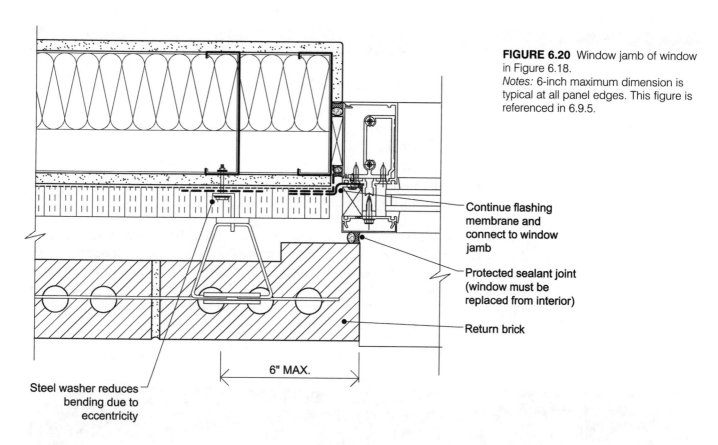

FIGURE 6.20 Window jamb of window in Figure 6.18.
Notes: 6-inch maximum dimension is typical at all panel edges. This figure is referenced in 6.9.5.

Continue flashing membrane and connect to window jamb

Protected sealant joint (window must be replaced from interior)

Return brick

6" MAX.

Steel washer reduces bending due to eccentricity

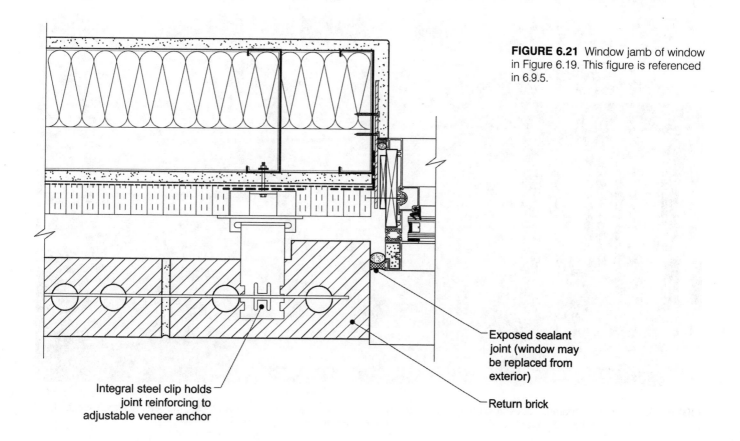

FIGURE 6.21 Window jamb of window in Figure 6.19. This figure is referenced in 6.9.5.

Exposed sealant joint (window may be replaced from exterior)

Return brick

Integral steel clip holds joint reinforcing to adjustable veneer anchor

6.11 CASE STUDY

ANCHORED BRICK VENEER RECLADDING PROJECT

Meany Hall for the Performing Arts
University of Washington
Seattle, Washington

Architect: Hewitt-Isley
Masonry consultant: Brock Associates
Masonry structural engineer: Phil Green, P. E.

This performing arts center was reclad with anchored brick veneer in the early 1990s. The detailing for the new veneer was similar to that shown in Section 6.10, except the backup wall was poured-in-place concrete, which reduced water entry concerns. Existing conditions, such as shelf angles located at different heights on various elevations, presented particular design challenges in addition to the technical problems.

FIGURE 6.22 It is not apparent that every other horizontal band is an expansion joint. On the long faces, the vertical expansion joints were located at 16-foot intervals, creating 12- by-16–foot veneer panels. Photo by Linda Brock.

Several design strategies were employed. First, the masonry consultant determined the minimum width and maximum spacing of expansion joints. Working with the architect, a grid of vertical and horizontal expansion joints was established. As the shelf angles, and hence the horizontal expansion joints, were typically spaced at 14-foot (4.26 m) intervals, the vertical expansion joints were placed at 14 feet on center, creating 14-foot square panels. Using a subgrid of 7-foot (2.13 m) squares drew attention away from the areas where the shelf angles had been moved up half a floor from their typical location. There was also a desire to change the scale of the brutalist forms so the building would better relate to the campus architecture. The architect used the necessity of expansion joints as a mechanism to create a more human scale.

Then the architect developed a variety of patterns, each relating to the different forms of the building, that overlaid the expansion-joint grid. Double, dark-colored, "clipped header" brick in a field of salmon-colored full-brick units were used as staccato "dots" to create lines or emphasize points. Three patterns were developed. The long expanses of veneer were accented with a double horizontal band of dark brick at 7-foot (2.13 m) intervals (Figure 6.22). The band drew attention away from the drip edge of the terne-coated, stainless-steel flashing and the horizontal expansion joint that occurred at every other dark band (Figure 6.23). After these bands turned the corner, they split at a diagonal, creating diamond patterns reminiscent of the "diaper or diamond patterns" in the Flemish bond used on nearby campus buildings. Each diamond was contained within either a 7-foot (2.13 m) square or, in the case of the tall, box-shaped fly gallery, a 14-foot (4.26 m) square. A textured pattern of double, dark brick "dots" was created by alternating a header and a stretcher brick at the narrow vertical recesses where the vertical location of the shelf angles had to be staggered. (A vertical expansion joint was required in each location where shelf angles were discontinuous around a corner.) These three surface designs can be seen in Figure 6.24.

FIGURE 6.23 The intermittently dark header brick courses not only draw the eye away from the horizontal expansion joint but seem to eliminate the dark slits created by full-height, head-joint weep holes. Next to the dark brick, the weep hole becomes part of the larger design. Photo by Linda Brock.

Using a single value and hue or color of brick for the field is very difficult, as subtle variations are common and can be quite visible in large fields of brick. To avoid these problems and create a more uniform background, a selection of differing colored brick was specified. Numerous mock-ups with simulated mortar joints were built on-site until the desired mix was determined (Figure 6.25). Another visual problem occurs when a diamond pattern is created with high contrast brick, as an optical illusion often causes the diamonds to appear as if they were "caving in" along the diagonal lines. To avoid this phenomenon, the dark brick of the diagonal lines were not contiguous.

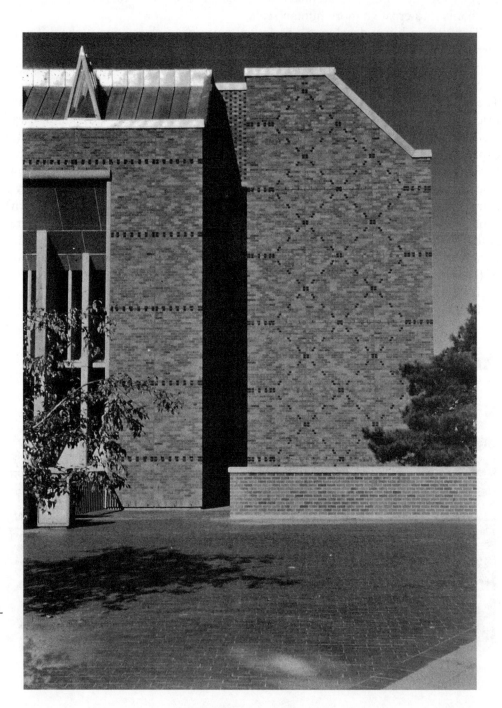

FIGURE 6.24 Three patterns are visible—the horizontal bands at 7-foot intervals, the diamond patterns in 7-foot squares, and the textured pattern in the vertical recess that separates the two forms. Photo by Linda Brock.

FIGURE 6.25 The mock-ups of the brick mix were kept on-site during construction. Photo by Linda Brock.

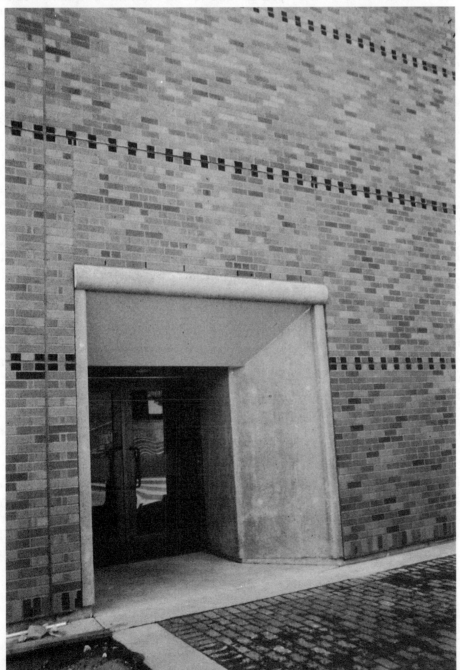

FIGURE 6.26 If this had been new construction, the door opening could have been moved to coincide with the vertical expansion joint to the left of the door jamb, avoiding the double joints only 12 inches apart. Photo by Linda Brock.

This project was made more difficult by the existing conditions. An example can be seen in Figure 6.26. If this was new construction, the door could easily have been located at the vertical expansion joint to the left. Instead, it fell 12 inches (300 mm) to the side, necessitating a second expansion joint along the jamb that carried through to the shelf angle above. (There is also a third vertical joint that follows the right-side jamb to the underside of the shelf angle.) However, this situation could just as easily arise with new construction if the expansion joints are not located during the preliminary design.

Because of extensive upfront design efforts looking at durability in combination with the aesthetics of the new veneer, construction went smoothly and the project came in under budget.[24]

6.12 OTHER SYSTEMS

Prefabricating brick veneer panels allows for increased quality control. According to the Brick Industry Association, these panels—sometimes called structural veneer or reinforced brick masonry—have "greatly increased resistance to forces that produce tensile and shear stresses. The reinforcement provides additional tensile strength, allowing better use of brick masonry's inherent compressive strength. The two materials complement each other, resulting in an excellent structural material."[25] The principles of prefabricated veneer panels are similar to those of precast concrete panels. A nominal 5-inch (125 mm)—or larger—hollow-core brick unit is recommended to increase the likelihood of fully consolidated grout. Any cracks in the grout increase the potential for corrosion of the steel reinforcing. Figure 6.27 shows the result of testing for grout consolidation for a reveneer project. Because of very restrictive existing conditions, 4-inch (100 mm) nominal brick with 2-inch (50 mm) grout cells were used in panels 13 feet (4 meters) high. Obtaining consolidation of the grout was very difficult. Extensive testing of different grout mixes, combined with lengthy wetting of the grout cells, and various methods of vibrating the grout produced a method that consolidated the grout throughout the height of the panel.

Avoiding the use of scaffolding and shortening the construction schedule are considerations for any project. A prefabricated panel that can be set in place with a crane may be a better choice for a dense urban area and a tight schedule. The cost of prefabricated panels decreases with increased repetition of panel sizes and configurations. Laying brick without the problems of inclement weather can produce a superior product. However, prefabrication is not a panacea, nor does brick in compression stop all water entry. A well-functioning drainage cavity, with a water barrier and metal flashing similar to that used for ABV, is required. Joints between panels should be carefully detailed. A thorough testing program and the selection of an experienced manufacturer and structural engineer are critical.

In an effort to make brick veneer lighter-weight and to reduce its cost, many thin-brick veneer systems have come on the market. Most fall into the category of "adhered veneer" or what some masons call "lick 'em and stick 'em." These brick "slices," or tiles, are typically from ⅜ inch to ½ inch (10 mm–13 mm) thick. They are snapped into styrene panels, glued to insulation or plywood, or held in place

FIGURE 6.27 Two prisms have been cut through the center to evaluate grout consolidation. Shrinkage cracks can be seen in the prism on the left. Photo by G. Russell Heliker.

with metal clips. These systems are lightweight and the brick is "real," but their long-term durability is questionable. The exceptions are the systems that consist of thin brick cast into concrete. This method can produce a panel that may be more durable than anchored brick veneer panels.[26] See Chapter 10 for a description of this method.

6.13 REFERENCES

ANCHORED BRICK VENEER

Print Sources

1. BIA Technical Notes on Brick Construction (Reston, Va.: Brick Industry Association).

2. Building Code Requirements for Masonry Structures, ACI 530-02 (Boulder, Colo.: The Masonry Society).

3. Best Practice Guide: Building Technology Brick Veneer Steel Stud (Ottawa, Ont.: Canada Mortgage and Housing Corporation, 1996).

4. Brick Veneer Concrete Masonry Unit Backing Best Practice Guide: Building Technology (Ottawa, Ont.: Canada Mortgage and Housing Corporation, 1997).

5. Barry B. LePatner and Sidney M. Johnson, Structural and Foundation Failures—A Casebook for Architects, Engineers, and Lawyers (New York: McGraw-Hill Book Company, 1982).

6. Masonry Construction (Addison, Ill.: Hanley-Wood Magazine, Div.).

7. Robert G. Drysdale, Ahmad A., Hamid, and Lawrie R. Baker, Masonry Structures: Behavior and Design (Englewood Cliffs, N.J.: Prentice Hall, 1994).

Online Sources

1. The Brick Industry Association (BIA), http://www.bia.org

Exterior Insulation Finish System (EIFS) and Concrete Masonry Walls

7.1 CONCRETE MASONRY WALLS

Concrete masonry walls are a development of the last century. Modern concrete block production began with the invention of the cast-iron block machine, which was patented in 1900 by S. Palmer.[1] Cast-iron molds formed blocks, with faces replicating everything from brick to cobblestones to intricately carved stone profiles. The molds and manual press were available from a variety of sources, including the early twentieth-century equivalent of Home Depot: the Sears, Roebuck Homebuilder's Catalog. Concrete block was advertised as "much cheaper than stone or brick" and "one of the most desirable and durable materials for building purposes."[2] Early blocks were often 24 or 32 inches (610 or 813 mm) in length. By 1930, industry standards prevailed, and 90 percent of the producers were using the present standard module of 16 inches in length and 8 inches in height.[3] The metric standard module is 400 mm in length and 200 mm in height.

Today reinforced concrete masonry walls and backup walls are an often-used construction method. Concrete masonry units (CMU), or concrete block, come with a variety of decorative surfaces. These architectural blocks include units with split or fluted-split faces, formed ribbed faces, and ground or honed faces (some polished to a highly reflective surface). Concrete masonry is usually selected because of economics, impact resistance, aesthetics, or fire separation requirements. Enhanced sound isolation is also a benefit. The single-wythe wall can be covered with any of the various claddings or left as an impact-resistant exterior face. A multi-wythe design, with a concrete or fired-clay face brick and a drainage cavity, substantially increases durability but also cost. This chapter discusses face-sealing the concrete masonry as the exterior finish and details Wall Type B, EIFS on Concrete Masonry with an Internal Drainage Plane. Case studies include a high-rise building clad with prefabricated EIFS panels and a concrete masonry building clad with open-joint calcium silicate panels.

7.1.1 CONTROLLING WATER INGRESS, AIR MOVEMENT, AND THERMAL TRANSFER

Water ingress, thermal transfer, air movement, and vapor diffusion need to be carefully considered with the concrete masonry wall. Concrete masonry is permeable to vapor, leaks both water and air, and is a poor insulator. There are a number of cementitious and asphaltic pargings as well as fluid-applied membranes, with reinforcing mats at the transitions, that do a good job of waterproofing the face of the concrete masonry wall. However, an exterior cladding is required over most of these surfaces. (Some of these water barriers can also act as the air barrier system and a vapor retarder.) Another option for the air barrier system is an interior gypsum board wall, using the airtight drywall approach (ADA) or simple caulk and

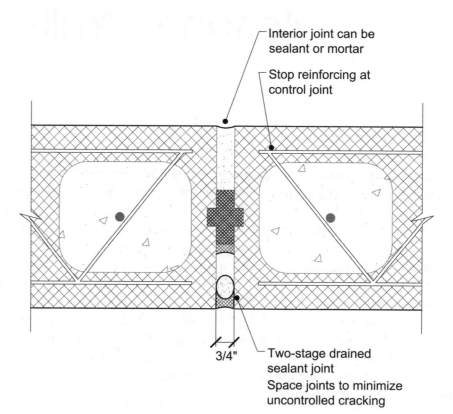

Interior joint can be sealant or mortar

Stop reinforcing at control joint

3/4"

Two-stage drained sealant joint
Space joints to minimize uncontrolled cracking

FIGURE 7.1 Two-stage, drained vertical control joint in concrete masonry. Locate weep holes at the base of the joint.

Keeping Water Out of Face-Sealed, Single-Wythe Masonry Walls

- Write specifications that ensure good workmanship and use of proper materials
- Emphasize a good bond between the block and the mortar
- Select a watertight joint profile (see Figure 6.7)
- Use flat-faced concrete block
- Deflect water with overhangs and drips on metal flashing
- Properly locate control joints and detail a two-stage drained sealant joint
- Include an air barrier system on the interior
- Specify an exterior water repellant
- Understand the permeability of all wall components in relation to the climate
- Design joints that keep water out of wall at openings and transitions

seal (SCS) detailing. Vapor diffusion can be retarded on the interior with paint or foil-backed gypsum board and on the exterior by a nonvapor-permeable water barrier. The location of the vapor retarder is dependent on the climate.

Concrete masonry walls will move; controlling the associated cracking with control joints is an important part of keeping the wall dry. (There should be a corresponding expansion joint in the cladding at each control joint in the concrete masonry.) The control joint should have a water stop and be sealed to the exterior. The joint reinforcing is stopped to both sides of the control joint (see Figure 7.1). Mortar droppings are not a problem here the way they are with fired-clay masonry expansion joints. General guidelines for placement of control joints are provided in the National Concrete Masonry Association's (NCMA) TEK 10-2B, *Control Joints for Concrete Masonry Walls—Empirical Method.*

Thermal insulation can be added to the exterior, to the interior, or within the block cells. Using standard block inserts or fill is not very effective as a majority of the cells may be grouted, and even if they are not, the webs of the block act as thermal bridges. There are specially formed masonry units that allow for increased insulation within the block. Some proprietary CMU have a continuous layer of 1¼ inch to 4 inches (32–100 mm) of molded, expanded polystyrene foam insulation, greatly enhancing the thermal resistance of the wall. Because of the reduced web thickness and limitations on placement of reinforcing, a structural engineer should review the design. Using a proprietary system to insulate within the block or insulating to the inside of the masonry wall produces an economical exterior wall, as cladding is not required.

Positioning the thermal insulation on the exterior wall provides the best thermal performance, as it shields the structure from temperature extremes and eliminates thermal bridges. But this method, like the water and air barriers applied to the exterior, requires an exterior cladding or surface finish to protect the insulation. EIFS has the advantage of adding insulation to the exterior of the wall with an inexpensive finish.

While a single-wythe masonry wall may not completely stop water, it is an excellent backup wall for any cladding. Should moisture get into the wall, it is capable of holding and releasing moisture with fewer detrimental effects than wood or light-gauge steel frame walls. Its rigidity provides good support for air and water barriers. It is commonly used with anchored brick veneer, providing a stiffer and potentially more durable backup wall than steel or wood studs.

7.1.2 New Developments in Concrete Masonry

Replacing lightweight aggregate with waste by-products such as wood fiber and cement with fly ash reduces the environmental cost of concrete masonry units. Autoclaved aerated concrete (AAC)—made of sand, cement, lime, and an expanding agent—is advertised as the new "green" concrete. AAC block walls weigh just slightly more than half of a conventional concrete masonry wall and have an R-value of 1.25 per inch (0.22 RSI) compared to 0.1 per inch (0.02 RSI) for conventional concrete. AAC is lightweight and can be sawn, nailed, and drilled like wood, and it comes in a variety of sizes. Developed in Sweden in 1914, AAC blocks are popular in Europe partially because of stringent energy codes. A cladding or finish is recommended to protect the exterior surface of ACC block walls.[4]

7.2 SINGLE-WYTHE CONCRETE MASONRY: FACE-SEALED BARRIER WALL

Single-wythe concrete masonry is often constructed as a face-sealed barrier wall, clad with a paint or sealer on projects with low budgets. It is the ubiquitous wall of shopping malls, motels, and schools. This wall type should be considered only when exposure is minimal—for example, when the wall is a single story protected by overhangs; the wind-driven rain index is low; and it has been determined that the wall can withstand periodic wetting. It is also dependent on the use and the expected life of the building. This may be a reasonable choice for a commercial building with a short projected life but not a university building with a life expectancy of 50 years or more. It is very difficult to waterproof a concrete masonry wall with fluid-applied sealers or paints. Using a low permeance paint can result in peeling paint with a vapor drive from the interior to the exterior, which is common in heating climates and in many mixed climates during the winter. For this reason NCMA advises against using impervious paints on exterior walls.[5] Some paints are durable and "breathable," but they will not bridge the cracks that will continue to open due to differential movement. Hydrophobic, penetrating water repellants, such as silanes and siloxanes, will help stop water at the face of the block and through the mortar; but again, the problem occurs at the inevitable cracks. Repellants can also be added to the block during production and to the mortar during mixing. Cement-based paints can increase the watertightness. Other paints are available that will fill small voids and irregularities, increasing the ability of the wall to shed water.

Hairline cracks or delaminations are common between the block and the mortar at joints. It is even more difficult to get good bond between the mortar and the block and, consequently, keep water out of the wall with masonry units that have an articulated face, such as fluted block. Delaminations can be minimized by using the lowest-strength mortar that is structurally acceptable, as it will provide the best bond with the concrete block. The watertightness of the concrete masonry wall can have as much to do with the masonry contractor as with the water repellant. Emphasis should be placed on specifying the materials and installation that will guarantee the most watertight finish. (This is not to say that the water repellant can be omitted.)

All openings and interfaces in the concrete masonry wall should be carefully detailed to assure that water is not directed into the wall. The geometry of the exterior wall can help direct water away; a simple overhang on a single-story wall is well worth the effort. Carefully placed and sealed control joints will help keep the wall dry. But when the inevitable happens and water gets into the wall, despite the best design and construction, the question must be asked: how will it get out? The architect should closely examine the permeability of the coating and any intentional or unintentional vapor retarders in relation to the climate. Trade associations can advise on how to make a concrete masonry wall as watertight as possible, while a structural engineer can limit uncontrolled movement of the masonry.

7.3 EXTERIOR INSULATION FINISH SYSTEM (EIFS)

Edwin Horbach, who had a background in chemistry and a love of the theater, developed the Exterior Insulation Finish System (EIFS) in Germany after World War II. While working for a building materials firm—having lost his job in the theater—a friend told him that he would "undoubtedly become a millionaire" were he to develop a system that affixed insulation to the exterior of the building with a flexible, attractive finish. After much experimentation, he settled on expanded polystyrene as the insulation. His concept, well suited to the reconstruction of war-torn areas, was developed during the 1950s. It came to the United

FIGURE 7.2 EIFS (Exterior Insulation and Finish Systems) with simple detailing is an economical cladding. Photo courtesy of Sto Corporation, 2004.

States in the late 1960s under the trade name Dryvit, for "quick dry."[6] Sto, another German company, introduced EIFS in 1963, bringing the product to North America in 1979. Basic EIFS has five components: the insulation board, the fastening system for the insulation board (adhesive or mechanical fasteners), the base coat, the reinforcing mesh, and a finish coat.

EIFS is still a popular cladding in Europe, where renovation is more prevalent than in North America. In Germany and Switzerland, 40 percent of all exterior walls were reportedly clad with some form of EIFS by the mid-1980s. Eighty percent of these installations were retrofits.[7] In Europe, EIFS is applied primarily over masonry walls. In the United States and Canada, it is more likely to be applied over a light-frame wall. The conventional application of EIFS in North America was a face-sealed barrier wall applied over paper-faced, exterior gypsum sheathing. Moisture will delaminate the paper face of the sheathing from the gypsum core. In response to these problems, the sheathing industry has developed more durable, nonpaper-faced gypsum sheathings, such as DensGlass Gold by Georgia-Pacific.

EIFS has many advantages. Adding thermal insulation to the exterior of a wall is a good idea in any climate. It is a relatively inexpensive cladding with a variety of textures and colors (one manufacturer has 800 standard colors) that can replicate finishes from stucco to brick to stone. Eighteen percent of nonresidential, new construction in the U.S. was clad with EIFS in 2002.[8]

The "finish" of EIFS, called the lamina, is the primary barrier to water. It is composed of a base coat with a reinforcing mesh, and a finish coat. There are two kinds of EIFS, generically called "soft coat" and "hard coat." The hard coat is a polymer-modified (PM) system with, typically, a minimum ³⁄₁₆ inch (5 mm) base coat that is applied to mechanically attached mesh and XPS insulation. It requires control joints similar to stucco and is more apt to develop hairline cracks. Because of this, some recommend an elastomeric finish that can bridge these small cracks. The soft coat is a polymer-based (PB) system with a total thickness of about ⅛ inch (3 mm). The insulation is fully adhered—the reinforcing mesh is embedded in the base coat. By far the most common EIFS application is the soft coat or PB system. The hard coat is generally only specified when impact resistance is important. (Even so, the soft coat, with the addition of a second layer of heavier reinforcing mesh, can exceed the impact resistance of some hard coats.) The discussion of EIFS in this chapter, unless otherwise noted, refers to the soft coat, polymer-based system.

The key to EIFS is in the system—all of the components should be from a single, reputable manufacturer. This is not the place to develop a new system using parts and pieces from different manufacturers. In fact, care must be taken to assure that this does not happen during construction. One problem faced by manufacturers is the use of look-alike, nonproprietary meshes. To assure that the proprietary mesh is used, some manufacturers print their logo on the mesh.

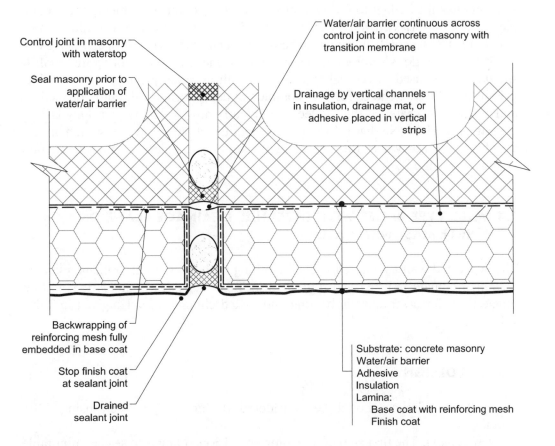

FIGURE 7.3 The five components of EIFS: finish coat, base coat, reinforcing mesh, EPS insulation, and adhesive. (The sealant at the concrete masonry is redundant and may not be needed if the water barrier membrane is continuous across the joint.)

7.3.1 LIFE EXPECTANCY OF EIFS

The durability of face-sealed EIFS is sometimes questioned, although there are projects from the 1970s that are exhibiting few problems. Water will most likely not penetrate the surface, which is watertight; the problems will occur at the openings and interfaces. Adding a drainage system prolongs the life of the cladding and the backup wall. Proprietary systems that incorporate drainage planes or drainage channels have gained in popularity. EIFS can also be installed with a drainage cavity and prefabricated in panels. In choosing a water management system, the complexity of the facade geometry, precipitation, driving-rain index, wall exposure, and moisture sensitivity of substrate should be considered. Life expectancies of 25 to 30 years are used when discussing EIFS. Longer life expectancies may be achieved with good design, proper installation and maintenance, and a drained system. The European Organization for Technical Approvals (EOTA) assumes an intended working life of at least 25 years for EIFS.[9] (European applications are typically over concrete and concrete masonry substrates, and there are differences in the materials and applications.)

To assure a more durable cladding, it is best to disregard the theatrical potential of EIFS, which allows for any shape that can be cut or formed in expanded polystyrene (EPS) insulation to become part of the building facade. Unless the building is in Las Vegas, where the climate is dry and the client may be willing to reclad in 20 years or less or the client absolutely demands a building in a rococo style and has the budget to flash all those small projections with metal, these complex facades are risky. (Much can be done with color to create three-dimensional effects.) EIFS is a good choice for an economical cladding when properly designed, but it has limitations—for example, it does *not* make a good roofing material. It should only be used in vertical applications with as much protection as possible. EIFS is not the best choice for very complex building forms with numerous ledges and nooks and crannies that collect water and snow—that is, if a long-lasting cladding is desired. Neither is EIFS a good cladding choice in an area with high levels of pollution or where the surface might see abuse, unless an impact resistant system is specified.

7.4 WALL TYPE B: EIFS WITH INTERNAL DRAINAGE PLANE ON CONCRETE MASONRY WALL

The suggested wall assembly for EIFS clothing with an internal drainage plane in a cooling climate is listed and described in Table 7.1 and the notes that follow. Suggestions for assemblies in heating and mixed climates are also given in Table 7.1.

7.5 EIFS DESIGN

The following issues should be considered during design when using EIFS cladding.

Design team: The first step in designing an EIFS cladding is to select a reputable manufacturer with long-term experience and make its representative part of the

TABLE 7.1 Building Envelope Components Based on Climate

EIFS on a Concrete Masonry Wall, Low-Rise Building, Water Management System: Internal Drainage Plane Wall[1]			
	Changes with heating climate	*Changes with mixed climate*	*Cooling climate (detailed)*
Water barrier[2]	Fluid-applied membrane on concrete masonry	Fluid-applied membrane	Fluid-applied membrane
Air barrier system	Fluid-applied membrane on concrete masonry	Fluid-applied membrane	Fluid-applied membrane
Vapor Retarder	Foil-backed gypsum board or fluid-applied membrane on concrete masonry	Depends on specific climate	Use a water and air barrier membrane that is vapor resistant[3]
Insulation[4]	4" (100 mm) or more expanded polystyrene (EPS)	2" (50 mm) or more EPS	2" (50 mm) or more EPS
Structure[5]	Reinforced concrete masonry	Reinforced concrete masonry	Reinforced concrete masonry
Comments	Finish coat should be vapor permeable	Finish coat should be vapor permeable	Interior finish should be vapor permeable but assume that owners will add coats of paint and possibly vinyl wall coverings in the future

Notes:

1. EIFS with drainage and a water barrier on the face of a concrete masonry wall was selected for detailing. Managing water with an internal drainage plane and an air barrier system for a low-rise concrete masonry structure provides a good, economical, and durable cladding. The added capital cost of the water barrier and drained system is small compared to the value of the increased durability and potentially lower operating costs. The detailing would be very similar for EIFS over wood or metal studs. It is even more important to use a drained system over these walls, because they are especially susceptible to water damage.

2. A complete water barrier system, including flashings, detailed such that water is *not* directed behind the EIFS at openings and interfaces, is an extremely important part of an EIFS-clad wall. The field of EIFS is relatively watertight; but water will enter at the numerous transitions, and it must be directed to the exterior. A water barrier on the exterior face of the concrete masonry and a proprietary system with drainage provides the internal drainage plane. Water drains to the exterior at each floor. Proprietary systems include drainage channels created by a vertical adhesive pattern, a drainage mat, or grooved, expanded polystyrene (EPS). All have their merits.

3. The EIFS is essentially a vapor retarder. In a cooling climate the actual vapor retarder belongs on the exterior of the water barrier. Caution must be taken that all materials to the interior of the water barrier have high vapor permeability. This is not the place to use nonpermeable vinyl wall coverings. This is an item that must be made clear in the maintenance manual. It must also be assumed that over the life of the building, owners will resurface the interior wall several times. As the designer has no control over the permeability of the paint or wall coverings chosen by the owner in the future, it is best to use a water and air barrier that is also vapor resistant.

4. Two inches (50 mm) of EPS with drainage provides the thermal insulation. Because the drainage plane is to the interior of the thermal insulation, air circulation would negatively affect the efficiency of the insulation. However, most EIFS with a drained system will not see air movement that equates to a loss of thermal resistance. In heating climates, the thickness of the insulation can be increased to 4 inches (100 mm) or more. This may also be merited in other climates, depending on the energy expenditure compared with the additional costs associated with a thicker wall.

5. Control joints in the concrete masonry need to be designed and sealed. Their location should be noted as locations for expansion joints in the EIFS. The masonry should be finished plumb and true to the exterior for the best EIFS application.

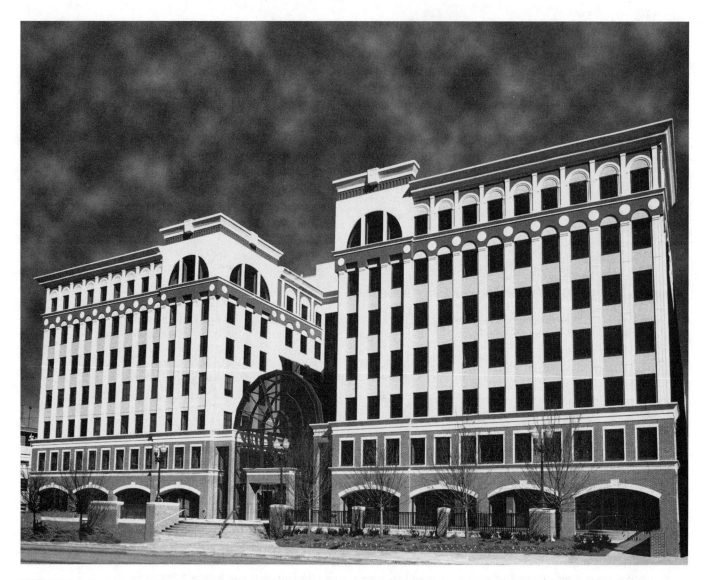

FIGURE 7.4 Corbelled shapes and cornices create depth on this hotel while providing protection for the surfaces below. The use of different colors effectively adds to the depth. Photo courtesy of Sto Corp.

design team. This is also the time to involve any third-party inspectors and possibly an installer. Emphasize the importance of keeping water out of the wall and solicit their input in achieving this goal. Following these recommendations can save headaches during construction and will help prevent future problems with EIFS cladding.

Building form: From broad overhangs to small projections, the building form plays an important role in making the exterior wall watertight. All nonvertical surfaces should be flashed with metal. Two exceptions may be those details that are shielded by an overhang and small "plant-on" shapes that are applied over the base coat. (Ornamental features installed on top of the base coat allow continuity of the lamina but may present a fire safety issue. Designing the shape such that the surfaces at the top and bottom allow for the required field-mesh overlap and joining can prevent these problems.) Limiting these plant-ons to areas where they are protected or to a thickness of one inch (25 mm), with a 6/12 slope, will enhance watertightness. A manufacturer may state that a product can be used on a 6/12 slope for a distance of 12 inches (300 mm) and may even show EIFS used for a parapet coping. This may work in a very dry climate or where the detail is protected; but it is not good practice if the detail sees any water or snow or if the client expects a long-lasting cladding with minimal maintenance. (Fluid-applied flashings can be used to stop water on an EIFS sill, but they do not protect the finish, which will deteriorate if continually wet. This is a maintenance item, as the finish can be reapplied.) See Chapter 9 for a discussion of EIFS and color.

Good EIFS Design

- Provide an internal drainage plane, not a face-sealed barrier wall (possible exceptions are EIFS over concrete masonry on buildings with low exposure)

- Involve a reputable manufacturer during design phase

- Write specifications that require (1) good quality EIFS materials from a single reputable EIFS manufacturer and (2) installation by a knowledgeable contractor

- Use EIFS only in vertical applications unless protected by an overhang or flashed with metal

- Provide a solid, moisture-resistant substrate

- Select a water barrier that is compatible with the EIFS adhesive

- Minimize cracking by properly applying and preparing the insulation board

- Understand the function of expansion joints and aesthetic reveals—locate and design accordingly

- Use two-stage drained sealant joints

- Use closed-cell backer rods with low-modulus silicone sealants

- Minimize the number of aesthetic reveals

- Keep the dew point out of the backup wall

- Accommodate drainage, however minimal, at each floor with flashing and weep holes

- Design a complete air barrier system

- Carefully specify and detail the windows and other openings

- Design joints to keep water out of the wall at transitions

Joints and reveals: Architectural reveals and expansion joints become part of the exterior wall design. Reducing the number of architectural reveals, except as required to provide a place to stop and start base and finish coats, will add to the durability. These aesthetic reveals can cause problems, as they are more prone to cracking. Determining the location of all expansion joints and reveals during the design phase eliminates surprises during construction. This requires coordination, as the reveals should not line up with the insulation joints or with light frame walls, and the insulation joints should not line up with the sheathing joints. The location of expansion joints is determined primarily by the structure, including the backup wall.

Surface finishes: The smoother the surface, the less dust will accumulate and organic growth occur. (Some finishes are now designed with additives, such as silicone, that resist dirt pickup.) However, the less texture, the more the chance that the edges of the insulation board will "telegraph" through the finish coats. If a smoother texture is desired, even more emphasis must be placed on preparing the insulation, particularly on large uninterrupted surfaces. A surface with greater texture will appear more uniform and, counterintuitively, may appear smoother than a smooth finish.

Impact resistance: A more impact resistant surface, such as precast concrete panels or brick veneer, may be advisable at the ground floor, depending on the building's use. Impact resistant panels to either side of an entry, or an extended concrete foundation wall to protect the first few feet, may be all that is needed. If the budget or design does not allow for using another material, a hardcoat (or polymer-modified [PM] EIFS) or a heavier reinforcing mesh should be selected for high-abuse areas. (The EIFS industry recommends using a heavier mesh on all ground floor applications.) In addition to damage from landscape equipment and normal ground floor wear and tear, window washing and facade maintenance need to be considered. Additional reinforcing may be required in some locations to avoid damage during normal maintenance of the exterior wall.

Durability: EIFS is probably not going to last as long as well-designed precast concrete panels; but carefully designed and installed, EIFS is a good and economical cladding choice. As with most claddings, the problems are more often at the openings and interfaces. Joints between panels would ideally be two-stage sealant joints that drain. Identifying every transition, and then designing a watertight detail, is the beginning of a durable EIFS cladding. The architect must design these interfaces between EIFS and other components and carefully review all of the manufacturer's standard details to ensure that they cover the specific installation. The final step lies with the application. Working closely with the manufacturer during design and installation and using third-party inspection will help ensure a good application.

7.6 EIFS INSTALLATION

The EIFS manufacturer should be the single source for all components of the EIFS. The company should be responsible for compatibility of the components, including the substrate and the water and air barrier, testing of the system, and fire ratings.

Coordination of the installation is absolutely necessary. Large-scale detail drawings will help those on-site understand the means for managing water and controlling air movement. A preconstruction meeting, along with the construction of a mock-up wall, will bring everyone together to test sequencing of the trades and installation of the EIFS. A window and other critical transitions and details should be included. The mock-up wall should then be tested for watertightness and airtightness. This is the place for the EIFS installer, along with those installing flashings, windows, and other components, to determine if the entire wall system really works—and if it does not work, how it can be fixed. This will cost a small fraction of what it costs to tear down part of the wall if a problem is discovered later. Most likely some part of the mock-up will fail the first time, which is something that may distress the owners, but they should be assured by knowing that the problem is being fixed. If the mock-up is located off-site, a panel should be produced on-site to serve as the sample for color and texture of the EIFS.

The following information comes from manufacturers, trade associations, and articles about EIFS. While each system will vary somewhat and backup walls may be different, the basics are the same. The following is not intended to be a "how to apply EIFS guide" but rather to serve as a resource to use in conjunction with the manufacturer's recommendations. A designer cannot detail a system without understanding that system. If any of the recommendations are contrary to that of the manufacturer, a solution should be determined that satisfies everyone, keeping in mind that it is the EIFS manufacturer and installer who warranties the system.

7.6.1 ATTACHING THE INSULATION

Prior to attaching the insulation, the EIFS installer should approve the water barrier. If the water barrier is installed by the EIFS applicator, the substrate should be approved prior to applying the water barrier. Some of the new liquid-applied acrylic, polymer-based coatings act as a water barrier *and* adhesive for the insulation. Extensive field testing of these systems, including a comprehensive set of details by the manufacturer that shows continuity of the water barrier, should precede any decision to use the system.[10]

The quality of the EPS insulation is important. There should be good "bead fusion" to resist the passage of water. The board should meet the applicable standards. The recommended density is one pound, defined as a minimum of 0.95 lbs and maximum of 1.25 lbs.

Adhesives should be applied as per the manufacturer's directions. The EIFS manufacturer should verify the compatibility of the adhesive with the water and air barrier and specify the percentage of the insulation that should be physically bonded to the substrate.

Attachment with mechanical fasteners should be carefully reviewed. According to Kevin Day, a building science specialist who has evaluated EIFS for a number of years, they are generally "not recommended for polymer based systems."[11] Mechanical fasteners are a thermal bridge that can cause shadowing on the exterior of the wall. Adhesively attached EIFS performs better with negative wind pressure, or suction, than mechanically fastened EIFS.

The EPS boards are installed in a running bond and interlocked at inside and outside corners. If the insulation has drainage grooves, it is critical that all grooves run vertically. (In frame construction, the joints of the EPS should not be in line with the sheathing joints.) Using a short starter row of 12-inch (300 mm) board will offset the joints—the minimum offset recommended by some manufacturers

FIGURE 7.5 Configuration of EPS insulation board and reinforcing mesh.

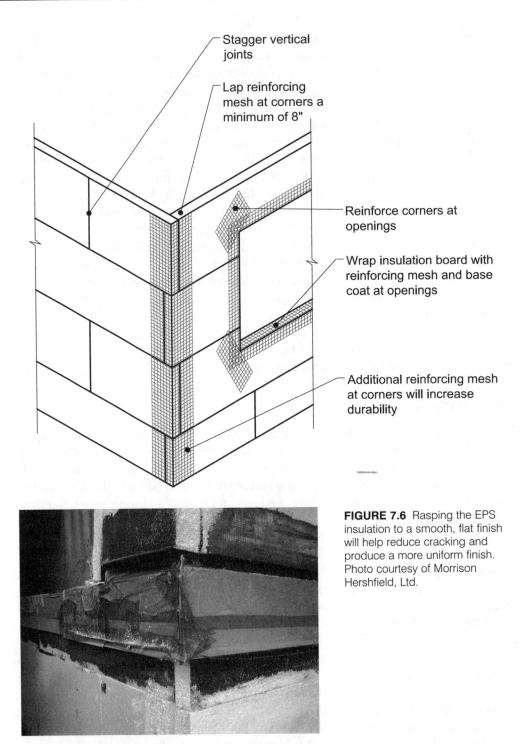

Stagger vertical joints

Lap reinforcing mesh at corners a minimum of 8"

Reinforce corners at openings

Wrap insulation board with reinforcing mesh and base coat at openings

Additional reinforcing mesh at corners will increase durability

FIGURE 7.6 Rasping the EPS insulation to a smooth, flat finish will help reduce cracking and produce a more uniform finish. Photo courtesy of Morrison Hershfield, Ltd.

is 8 inches (200 mm). No joints should be within 6 inches (150 mm) of the corners of openings. L shapes are used around windows and other openings to reduce stress at the corners (see Figure 7.5). Decorative or architectural reveals should not be in line with the EPS joints or line up with window or door openings, as this creates a weakened line in the plane, encouraging cracking.

After adhering the insulation, any small gaps or holes should be filled with slivers of EPS or spray foam and the entire surface rasped to ensure smoothness. (See

Figure 7.6.) The insulation must be flush and tight to avoid joint lines in the EPS telegraphing through the finish coat. A smooth surface also reduces stress on the lamina, which will reduce cracking.

7.6.2 APPLYING THE BASE COAT WITH REINFORCING MESH

Reinforcing mesh should be continuous and lapped a minimum of 2½ inches (64 mm) with an 8-inch (200 mm) overlap at corners. No joints in the field mesh should occur within 8 inches of an outside corner. Some manufacturers may require a greater overlap. Additional reinforcing mesh should be used anywhere the cladding will be stressed from differential movement or impact. This includes using additional mesh on all four sides of an opening for a window with additional diagonal pieces at the corners. Specify heavy or high-impact mesh for areas that might see abuse from adjacent recreational activities, walkways, roads, or landscaping and maintenance activities.

The more cement in the base coat, the more brittle it will become with age. More cement also means higher alkalinity, which can weaken the mesh, although today most mesh is alkaline resistant. A base coat that contains no more than 33 percent cement by dry weight is recommended by some and is more in line with European applications.[12] According to Peter Cuyler of Dryvit, the addition of 50 percent portland cement by weight in a wet polymer environment is considered ideal.[13] There are also synthetic base coats with no cement.

The base coat should be applied in two applications, with the first curing before the second is applied. This assures that the mesh is completely embedded in the base coat. The minimum thickness should not be less than ¹⁄₁₆ inch (1.5 mm), when measured between the mesh grid. Some recommend a thicker base of ³⁄₃₂ inch (2.5 mm) (dry).[14] No mesh color should be visible (slight telegraphing of the mesh may be visible) when the base coat is completed. The insulation boards should be backwrapped at terminations, with the mesh fully embedded in the base coat.

Some EIFS manufacturers produce waterproof base coats that can act as integral flashing. (These are examples of wet polymer technology where 50 percent portland cement is added.) They should be carefully reviewed for long-term durability. Metal is a better choice where long-term watertightness is an issue, and a drip edge is important to protect the wall below.

7.6.3 JOINTS AND REVEALS

EIFS has expansion joints, often mistakenly referred to as control joints. It also has aesthetic reveals. Understanding the purpose of each is important. Expansion joints should be located anywhere movement of the substrate is expected, including at all control joints in the concrete masonry wall. Expansion joints control cracking of the lamina due to stresses created by the backup wall and thermal movement. (See 7.10 for joints in light-frame walls.) Additional joints may be warranted on long uninterrupted stretches of EIFS, depending on the substrate, solar exposure, and color of the EIFS. Stephen Ruggiero, engineer and principal of Simpson Gumpertz & Heger, recommends a vertical expansion joint spaced approximately 60 feet (18 meters) on center for dark colored facades that face south and west.[15]

The EIFS Industry Members' Association (or EIMA) recommends that joint width be a minimum of four times the anticipated movement but not less than ¾ inch (19 mm) unless movement has been "determined to be negligible."[16] If the joint is solely to control cracking, the width can be reduced to ½ inch (13 mm). Carefully applied two-stage drained sealant joints are recommended to help keep water out of the wall. They require a minimum ¾ inch (19 mm) and preferably one-inch (25 mm) wide joint.

Architectural reveals provide a starting and stopping place for applying the lamina. (Expansion joints also fulfill this function.) The only other purpose of the reveals is aesthetic. While an expansion joint will help control cracking, aesthetic reveals should never be used for this purpose. Architectural reveals should be carefully designed to ensure that there is no cracking of the lamina by (1) using half-round or trapezoidal grooves and (2) continuing the mesh under the aesthetic joints. V-shaped reveals should be avoided, as it is too easy to get a buildup of material in the bottom of the V, which can lead to surface cracking (see Figure 7.7). A minimum of ¾ inch (19 mm) insulation is required at the low point of the reveal. Because rasping can reduce the thickness of the insulation, this should be called out on the drawings as a minimum of 1 inch (25 mm) (see Figure 7.7).

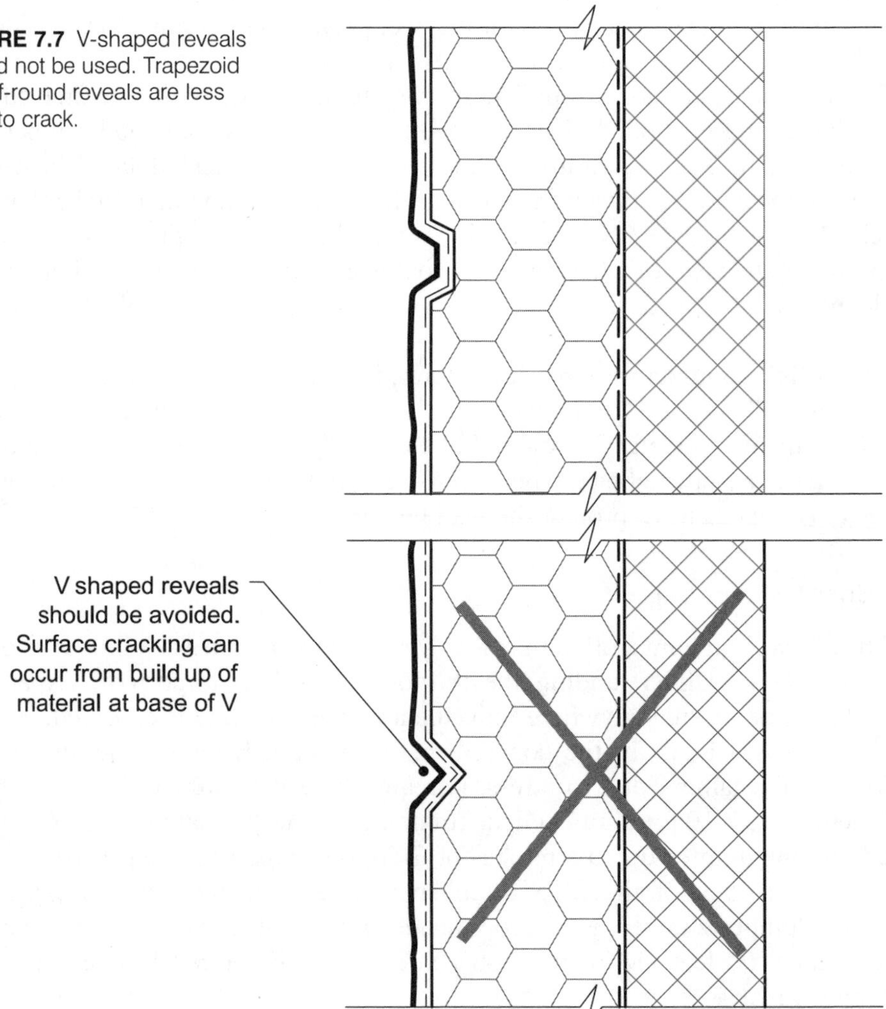

FIGURE 7.7 V-shaped reveals should not be used. Trapezoid or half-round reveals are less likely to crack.

V shaped reveals should be avoided. Surface cracking can occur from build up of material at base of V

The attachment of signage, ladders, and the like through EIFS can be a source of water entry. Using circular standoff mounts, which can be sealed around the perimeter, reduces this risk.[17]

When selecting the joint sealant, replacement should be considered. It has been noted that it is "practically impossible" to remove urethane sealants without damaging the lamina.[18] A Canada Mortgage and Housing Corporation (CMHC) study of moving joints showed that multipart urethane sealants tend to pull off the entire lamina, in addition to damaging the board insulation.[19] Building scientist Kevin Day recommends the use of a minimum base coat at sealant joints of 2.0–4.0 mm ($\frac{3}{32}$ to $\frac{5}{32}$) to reduce the potential for damage during sealant removal.[20] Silicone sealants and the preformed joint sealants, with acrylic impregnated expanding foam, that are sealed at the face with a thin bead of silicone may be a better choice than urethanes.[21] Silicone can be cut away when it needs replacing, leaving a thin layer on the substrate, as silicone seals well to itself. (This, of course, is only if the adhesion of the original sealant is still good.) Backer rods should be closed-cell foam that does not absorb water, as water retention at the joint will weaken the lamina. The sealant should be bonded to the base coat, and *not* the finish coat. Whatever sealant is used, compatibility should be tested and warranted by the sealant manufacturer. Most likely a primer will be recommended. The sealants should meet ASTM Standard C1382-97.

7.6.4 FINISH COAT

A primer for the finish coat is generally recommended to increase resistance to water, although it may not be required for the newer noncementitious bases. Color-matched to the finish coat, the primer will also help ensure color consistency, extend coverage of the finish coats, and cool the wall during installations in hot weather. The finish coat should *not* be continuous at the termination edges that receive the sealant.

7.6.5 CRITICAL INSPECTION POINTS

Problems with EIFS usually originate with the installation, not with the materials. Third-party inspection will help ensure a high-quality job. Critical inspection points include the following.

- Substrate: ready for application of water barrier.
- Air barrier system: complete.
- Water barrier and flashings: complete and ready for application of insulation.
- Insulation: good adhesion.
- Insulation: proper preparation for base coat application.
- Drainage: water poured behind the insulation should flow directly to the exterior if the system, including flashings, is working properly.
- Base coat: installed in two coats with a *minimum* thickness of $\frac{1}{16}$ inch (1.6 mm), or manufacturer's tested thickness for use in noncombustible construction; there should not be any excess, as it promotes cracking.
- Reinforcing mesh: completely embedded in base coat, with no mesh—identified by the color—visible.
- Sealant joints: adequate backup, good adhesion, and proper application.

7.7 MAINTENANCE

Sealant joints should be checked at least every three years and most likely will need replacing within 10 to 15 years.[22] Failed joints should be replaced immediately. Care must be taken when removing failed sealants so as not to damage the lamina. The lamina should be periodically checked for cracks, and any damage should be repaired immediately to avoid unnecessary water ingress. Washing the exterior every two to five years will help maintain the appearance. Paint approved by the EIFS manufacturer can be used for refinishing the EIFS.

7.8 EIFS CONCERNS

Failures with the construction of wood-framed detached houses in Wilmington, North Carolina, clad with face-sealed barrier wall EIFS, made headlines in the 1990s. The failures were not the fault of the EIFS cladding but a combination of problems that included leaky windows and lack of required flashings. (See Chapter 9 for more discussion about EIFS.)

Failures of this scope are less common in the nonresidential market. The industry attributes this to differences between the residential and the commercial market. Architects typically design commercial projects. This can result in drawings and specifications that lead to better installations by prequalified applicators. Also, the installation is often more closely monitored by the architectural firm.[23] But this does not mean that nonresidential EIFS installations have been problem-free. And it assumes that architects are conscientious in their detailing, specifying, and monitoring of the system, which is not always the case.

As with all claddings, the first goal is to keep water out of the wall with good detailing. The second goal is to direct any interstitial water that gets behind the EIFS cladding to the exterior with a drainage plane or cavity and flashings. If water gets behind the water barrier, the only recourse is evaporation before damage occurs. In this case, a concrete masonry backup wall adds considerably to the durability. However, even a continually damp concrete masonry wall will cause problems, from degradation of interior finishes to the propagation of mold and mildew or corrosion of steel reinforcing.

The problems attributed to EIFS can be overcome with conscientious design, a good product with good installation, and proper maintenance. The increased cost for such detailing should be small in comparison with the increased durability. A talented designer should be able to produce detailing that will keep water out of the wall while maintaining the desired aesthetic. (Some EIFS manufacturers are concerned that using a drained system gives the designer a false sense of security that may result in less attention paid to detailing and specifying windows, for example.)

The final step in overcoming these problems is to insist on a drained system with two-stage drained sealant joints as the minimum. The National Association of Home Builders recommends using a drainage path when EIFS is installed over wood sheathing.[24] As stated by Steve Ruggiero, the barrier concept itself is "conceptually flawed...building owners take on significant risks when using it in places with frequent rains."[25] But again, even a perfect EIFS cladding with drainage cannot compensate for a window that directs water to the stud cavity or the concrete masonry, nor can any other cladding.

7.9 DETAILS: EIFS

EIFS cladding with an internal drainage plane attached to a concrete masonry wall is detailed in Figures 7.8 to 7.12. The details are based on a building that is located in a cooling climate.

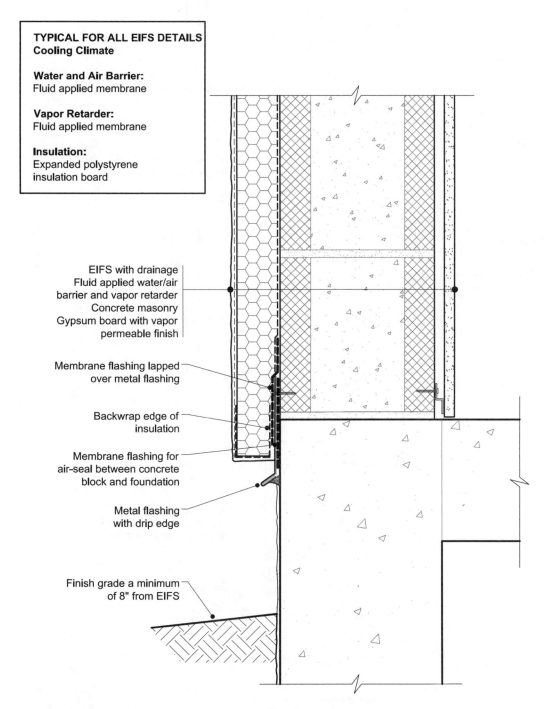

TYPICAL FOR ALL EIFS DETAILS
Cooling Climate

Water and Air Barrier:
Fluid applied membrane

Vapor Retarder:
Fluid applied membrane

Insulation:
Expanded polystyrene
insulation board

EIFS with drainage
Fluid applied water/air
barrier and vapor retarder
Concrete masonry
Gypsum board with vapor
permeable finish

Membrane flashing lapped
over metal flashing

Backwrap edge of
insulation

Membrane flashing for
air-seal between concrete
block and foundation

Metal flashing
with drip edge

Finish grade a minimum
of 8" from EIFS

FIGURE 7.8 EIFS at the foundation. The metal flashing accommodates drainage. Depending on the proprietary system, the drainage plane may be created with channels cut in the EPS board, vertical ribbons of adhesive, or a drainage mat.

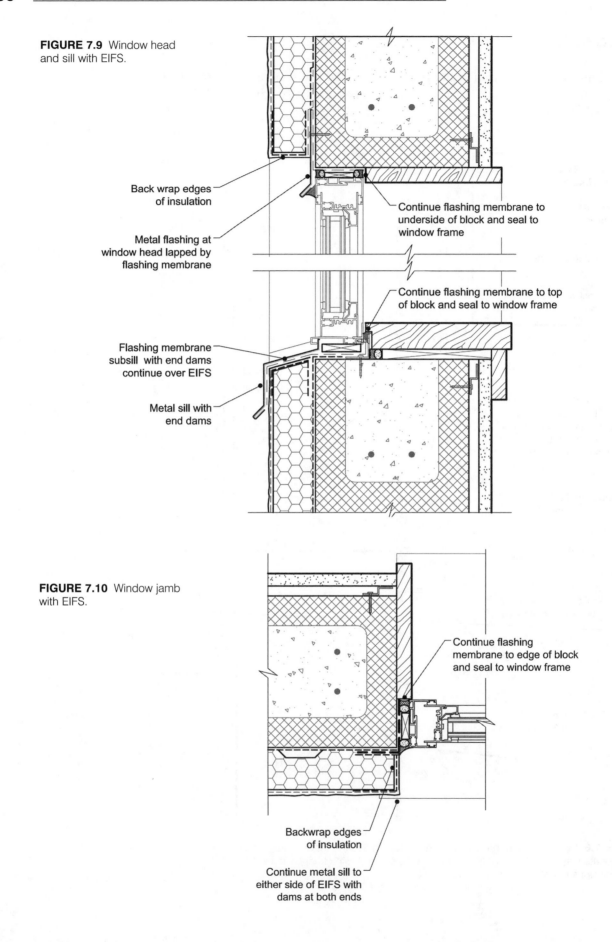

FIGURE 7.9 Window head and sill with EIFS.

Back wrap edges of insulation

Metal flashing at window head lapped by flashing membrane

Continue flashing membrane to underside of block and seal to window frame

Continue flashing membrane to top of block and seal to window frame

Flashing membrane subsill with end dams continue over EIFS

Metal sill with end dams

FIGURE 7.10 Window jamb with EIFS.

Continue flashing membrane to edge of block and seal to window frame

Backwrap edges of insulation

Continue metal sill to either side of EIFS with dams at both ends

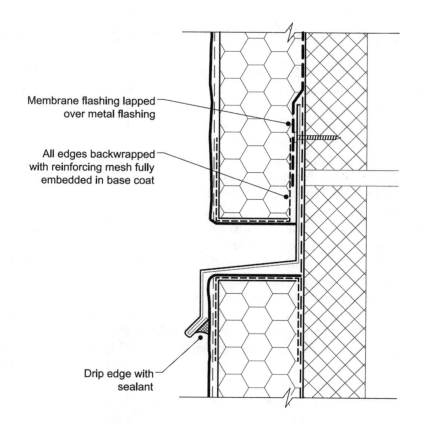

Membrane flashing lapped over metal flashing

All edges backwrapped with reinforcing mesh fully embedded in base coat

Drip edge with sealant

FIGURE 7.11 Drainage of EIFS at each floor. Each proprietary system has different draining details. The horizontal surface of the EIFS below should be flashed with metal.

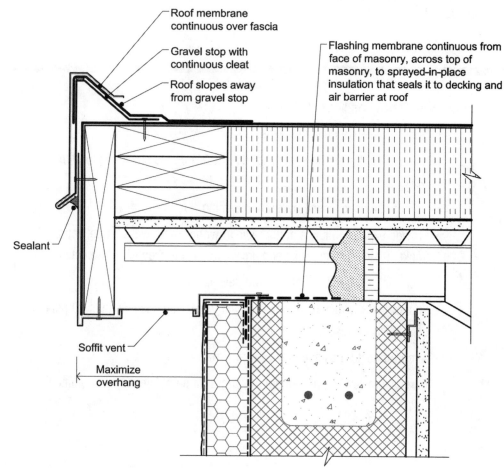

Roof membrane continuous over fascia

Gravel stop with continuous cleat

Roof slopes away from gravel stop

Flashing membrane continuous from face of masonry, across top of masonry, to sprayed-in-place insulation that seals it to decking and air barrier at roof

Sealant

Soffit vent

Maximize overhang

FIGURE 7.12 EIFS at the roof. Maintaining the air barrier through the roof assembly is a detail often overlooked.

7.10 EIFS OVER LIGHT-GAUGE STEEL OR WOOD STUD WALLS

The detailing for installing EIFS over metal or wood studs is similar to the detailing over concrete masonry. The main difference between the two types of backup walls is the vulnerability of the light frame to moisture. The face-sealed barrier wall water management system should never be used for EIFS over steel- or wood-stud walls, regardless of the climate or exposure of the wall.

At a minimum, the exterior sheathing over metal studs should be a nonpaper-faced gypsum sheathing, such as DensGlass Gold. A water barrier should be applied over the sheathing, whether it is plywood, oriented-strand board (OSB), or a nonpaper-faced gypsum or cementitious board. Even a minimum drainage plane to the exterior can help to reduce problems should moisture penetration occur. An air barrier system is also necessary to prevent the suction of moisture through the wall from air pressure differentials. Expansion joints should be located wherever movement is expected in the metal-stud wall or the structural frame. Wood-frame construction requires expansion joints at each floor to compensate for shrinkage of the frame. If additional insulation is added to the cavity in heating and mixed climates, the assemblage should be checked to ensure that the dew point is located to the outside of the stud cavity. This can be critical with wood-framed walls, as the plywood or OSB acts as a vapor retarder. The stiffness of the backup wall is less important than with rigid claddings such as brick veneer. L(wall height in inches)/240–360 is an acceptable stiffness according to Kevin Day.[26] All of the recommendations given for EIFS over concrete masonry should be considered.

EIFS over Metal or Wood Studs

- Detail an internal drainage plane.

- Use a water barrier on sheathing; do not rely on the sheathing to stop water.

- Do not use paper-faced gypsum sheathing.

- Provide expansion joints at floor line in wood-frame walls, at deflection tracks in steel-frame walls, and anywhere else movement is expected.

- Keep the dew point out of the stud cavity.

- Ensure that the moisture content of the wood frame is less than 19 percent when enclosed.

- Accommodate drainage, however minimal, at each floor.

- Carefully review the placement of vapor retarders, intentional or unintentional.

7.11 CASE STUDY

PREFABRICATED-EIFS PANELS ON HIGH-RISE BUILDING

Site: Treo Project
San Diego, California
Architect: Carrier Johnson
Developer: Intergulf Development
Cladding: Rainscreen Prefabricated-EIFS panels with preinstalled windows[27]
Manufacturer: Lakeview/Centura Building Systems
EIFS system: Sto Essence Plus

FIGURES 7.13–7.17 Photos and drawings courtesy of Lakeview/Centura Building Systems.

FIGURE 7.14

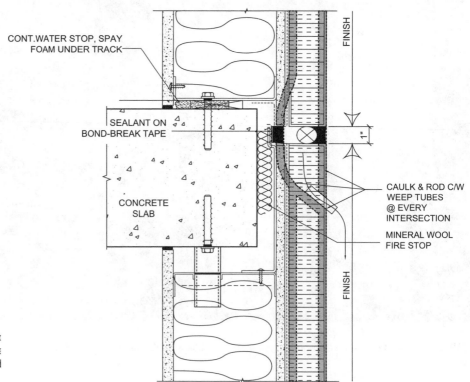

CONT.WATER STOP, SPAY
FOAM UNDER TRACK

FINISH

SEALANT ON
BOND-BREAK TAPE

1"

CONCRETE
SLAB

CAULK & ROD C/W
WEEP TUBES
@ EVERY
INTERSECTION

MINERAL WOOL
FIRE STOP

FINISH

FIGURE 7.15 Horizo
joint at typical slab se
Note the two-stage d
joint.

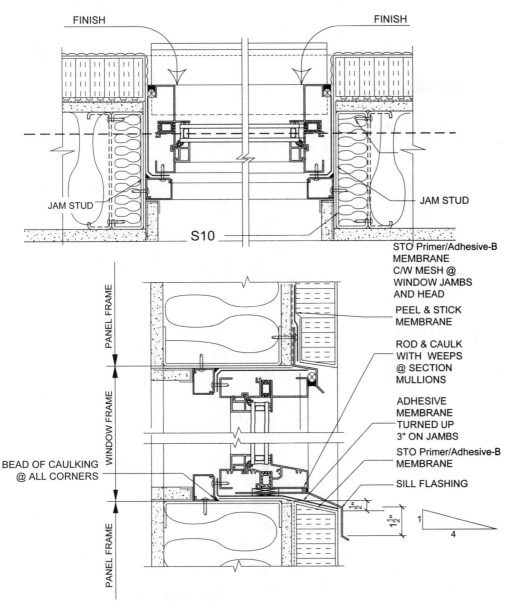

FIGURE 7.16 Window details.

FINISH

FINISH

JAM STUD

JAM STUD

S10

STO Primer/Adhesive-B
MEMBRANE
C/W MESH @
WINDOW JAMBS
AND HEAD

PEEL & STICK
MEMBRANE

ROD & CAULK
WITH WEEPS
@ SECTION
MULLIONS

ADHESIVE
MEMBRANE
TURNED UP
3" ON JAMBS

STO Primer/Adhesive-B
MEMBRANE

SILL FLASHING

PANEL FRAME

WINDOW FRAME

PANEL FRAME

BEAD OF CAULKING
@ ALL CORNERS

Most claddings benefit from prefabrication, and EIFS is no exception. Eliminating rain and wind assures a superior installation of not only the EIFS but also the various barriers and retarders that are part of the prefabricated panel. Windows and other components can be installed as part of the panel, increasing the quality of construction and durability of the wall. Scaffolding can be eliminated, as the panels can be installed from the interior. Prefabrication allows the panels to be quickly erected; enclosing a building during periods of inclement weather when a site application of EIFS may not be an option.

The panels for this 26-story housing project were fabricated in Vancouver, British Columbia, and then shipped to the site in San Diego, California (Figure 7.13). The story-high panels incorporate an EIFS drained system by Sto with an integral light-gauge, steel-stud backup wall and windows (Figure 7.14). Maintaining concrete tolerances of ± ½ inch (13 mm) for both columns and slabs

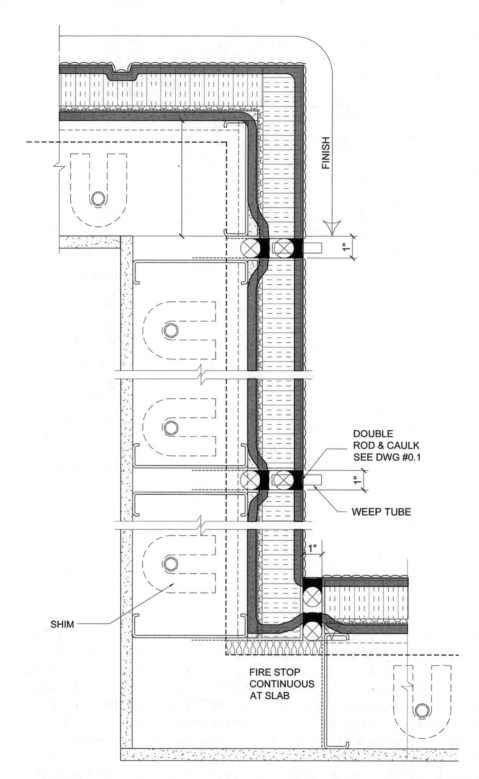

FIGURE 7.17 Vertical panel joints and inside corner joint. Note prefabricated corner panel.

Design of Prefabricated EIFS Panels

- Involve a reputable EIFS manufacturer at the beginning of the design phase.

- Involve a reputable EIFS curtain-wall fabricator at the beginning of the design phase.

- Accommodate drainage at the base of each panel and at each floor line.

- Design a complete air barrier system.

- Include windows and other openings in prefabricated panels where possible.

- Focus attention on the design of two-stage vertical sealant joints between panels and drainage of horizontal joints.

- Establish tolerances and clearances for the panels and the structure.

- Verify with a structural engineer that the lateral loading of the curtain-wall panel has been accommodated.

- Verify with a structural engineer that differential movement between the structural frame and the curtain-wall panel has been accommodated.

- Follow all other EIFS guidelines.

- Keep water out of the wall at transitions.

ensured the panels would fit. The continuous water and air barriers were sealed after installation of the panel. Carefully detailed two-stage, drained joints, one inch (25 mm) wide, continues the water protection at the exterior (Figures 7.15 and 7.17). Acoustical sealant at the top and bottom of the steel-stud wall seals the gypsum board to the concrete slab. A slip joint at the top of the steel stud wall accommodates shortening of the concrete frame (Figure 7.15). At the windows, a water barrier membrane forms a sill flashing pan, turning up at the corners and at the back (Figure 7.16). A metal sill flashing with a drip edge further protects the sill. The metal flashing at the window head diverts water from the window.

7.12 CASE STUDY

OPEN-JOINT CALCIUM SILICATE PANELS ON CONCRETE MASONRY

Site: Ecole Gabrielle-Roy
    Surrey, British Columbia
Architect: Marceau Evans Architects
Design team: Greg Johnson, principal-in-charge;
    Marie-Odile Marceau, principal;
    Craig Burns, intern architect-in-charge;
    and Leung Chow
Owner: Conseil Scolaire Francophone
General contractor: DGS Construction
Cladding: Lam Metals Contracting, Ltd; Super Panel
    by German Construction Systems Inc.

FIGURES 7.18–7.24 Photos and drawings courtesy of Marceau Evans Architects.

FIGURE 7.19

Schools are notorious for having low budgets, coupled with a need for long-lasting, durable walls. This French regional school with community support space, located in southern British Columbia, was no exception (Figures 7.18 and 7.19). The concrete masonry structure provides a durable interior wall. On the exterior, the calcium silicate cladding, installed with 10 mm (⅜ inch) open joints, is graffiti and impact resistant. There is no question that this is a durable system and that a particular aesthetic has been achieved. What may be surprising is that it is also economical. The cladding met the strict budget requirements of the owner in addition to providing a long life and an appearance that challenges the concrete masonry facade so typical of schools. Maintenance is a concern and a budget item for any school. If a panel is damaged, it can easily be replaced. With no sealant joints between the panels, a primary maintenance item has been eliminated.

The "back ventilated" or "open joint" wall is one of the more interesting cladding ideas to come from Europe. In addition to eliminating a good deal of maintenance, the large vent or openings means that the pressure differences are reduced between the cavity and the exterior, even with a less than perfect air barrier. (A terra-cotta cladding with open joints is described in 9.2.5.)

Medium-density sprayed polyurethane foam (SPF) on the exterior of the concrete masonry wall provides an excellent air barrier and insulation where it does the most good; it also ensures that most water is stopped before entering the wall. Galvanized Z-girts provide a drainage cavity between the insulation and the calci-

FIGURE 7.20

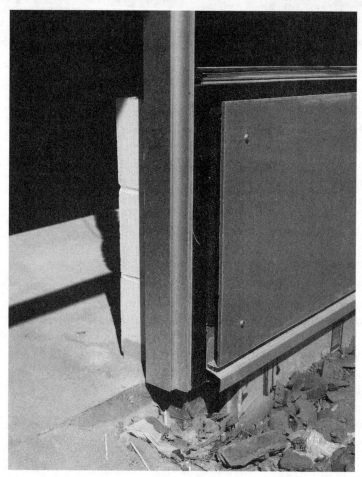

FIGURE 7.21

um silicate panels. A black coating on the urethane foam is for protection of the foam and appearances at the open joint. Careful planning resulted in crisp detailing with carefully aligned joints (Figures 7.20 and 7.21).

Using a curtain wall section for the windows substantially increased the durability of this wall. (This is the reverse of saving money by using windows for curtain walls on high-rise buildings as noted in Chapter 5.) Curtain wall sections are typically specified for mid- to high-rise buildings. They were used at Gabrielle-Roy to simplify the air and water barrier transition details between the window and the masonry structure. This also simplified the sequence of construction, as the flashing, insulation, and cladding could be completed independent of the glazing. The sophisticated section with a thermal break increases the watertightness and airtightness of the transition between the window and the concrete masonry wall. The SPF offers many advantages but also challenges. Overspray is difficult to remove, requiring extensive masking of adjacent surfaces. It is difficult to control around small details. The tolerance of the foam is ±5 mm (3⁄16 inch), which had to be accounted for in the design.

A full-scale mock-up from base to parapet, including a window head, sill, and jamb, was constructed in-place on the building prior to installation of the cladding. This mock-up enabled input from the various trades involved and resulted in minor modifications that simplified the assembly and ensured that the

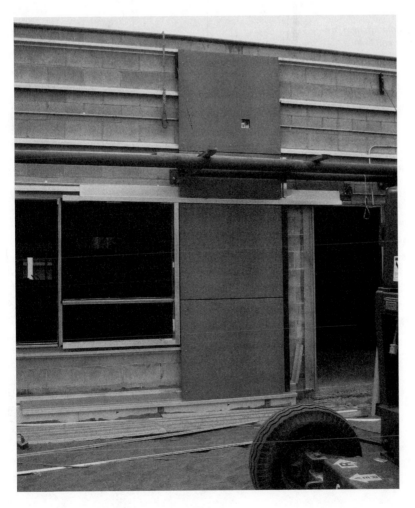

FIGURE 7.22

FIGURE 7.23 Wall sections showing parapet coping, curtain wall section, base detail, and horizontal panel joint.

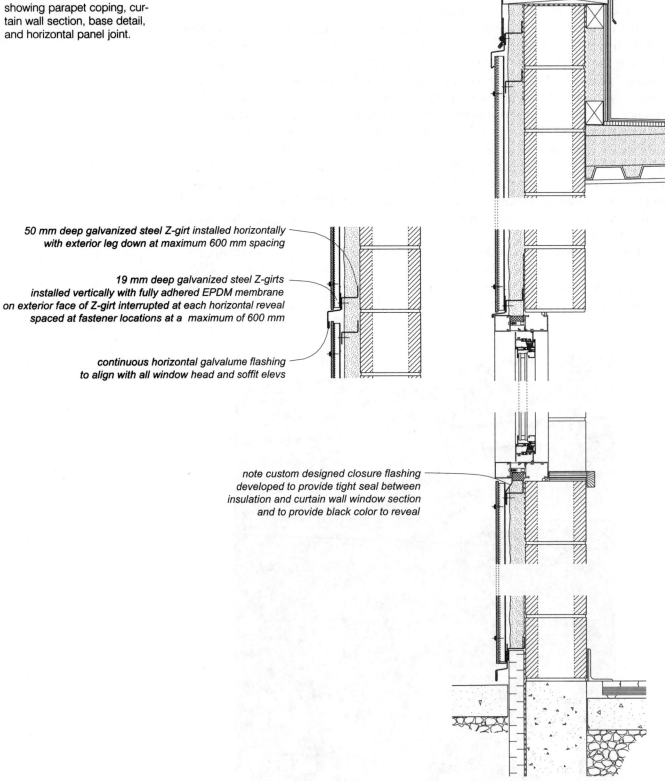

50 mm deep galvanized steel Z-girt installed horizontally with exterior leg down at maximum 600 mm spacing

19 mm deep galvanized steel Z-girts installed vertically with fully adhered EPDM membrane on exterior face of Z-girt interrupted at each horizontal reveal spaced at fastener locations at a maximum of 600 mm

continuous horizontal galvalume flashing to align with all window head and soffit elevs

note custom designed closure flashing developed to provide tight seal between insulation and curtain wall window section and to provide black color to reveal

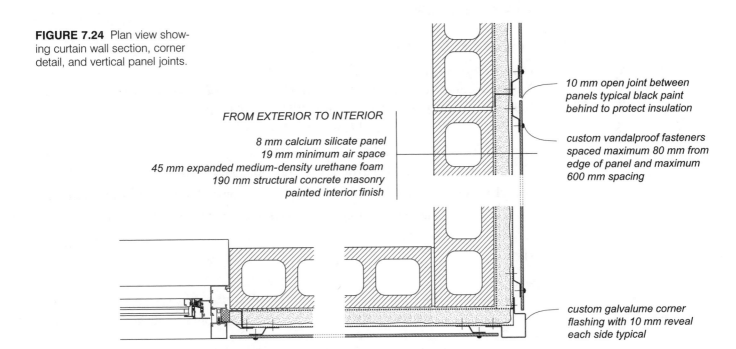

FIGURE 7.24 Plan view showing curtain wall section, corner detail, and vertical panel joints.

FROM EXTERIOR TO INTERIOR

8 mm calcium silicate panel
19 mm minimum air space
45 mm expanded medium-density urethane foam
190 mm structural concrete masonry
painted interior finish

10 mm open joint between panels typical black paint behind to protect insulation

custom vandalproof fasteners spaced maximum 80 mm from edge of panel and maximum 600 mm spacing

custom galvalume corner flashing with 10 mm reveal each side typical

desired architectural effect was obtained (Figure 7.22). The process of reviewing and modifying the full-scale mock-up enabled the architect to fine-tune the dimensions of the cladding details and establish a standard for quality and workmanship. Initially, there was resistance to spending time working out the details on the mock-up wall, but the subcontractors later commented that the installation went very smoothly and quickly after the problems were resolved on the mock-up.

Watertightness in the open-joint system occurs at the face of the backup wall, enabling a particular aesthetic of open reveals (Figures 7.23 and 7.24). It is relatively low-cost, given the increase in durability, which is the definition of economical. Specific considerations include accommodating differential expansion and durability concerns. For example, the spacing of the metal supports may be decreased in areas where more impact resistance is warranted. Detailing a metal backing for the open joints might increase the life of the urethane foam insulation, and applying a water barrier membrane to the exterior of the concrete masonry would ensure that no water ever entered the wall in areas with high exposure to wind-driven rain. This system could be as easily installed over a light frame of steel or wood studs, and a variety of materials for the panels might be substituted. Finally, this is a cladding system that requires careful detailing and installation. While it may be more forgiving than some systems in terms of water entry, the aesthetics will suffer unless time is spent understanding and detailing the system and testing those details on a mock-up.

7.13 REFERENCES

CONCRETE MASONRY WALLS

Print and Online Sources

National Concrete Masonry Association, *NCMA TEKs* (Herndon, Va.: National Concrete Masonry Association), http://www.ncma.org

1. TEK 2-3A: Architectural Concrete Masonry Units
2. TEK 6-11: Insulating Concrete Masonry Walls
3. TEK 10-1A: Crack Control in Concrete Masonry Walls
4. TEK 10-1B: Control Joints for Concrete Masonry Walls—Empirical Method
5. TEK 19-2A: Design for Dry Single-Wythe Concrete Masonry Walls

EIFS

Print Sources

1. *Exterior Insulation and Finish Systems, Best Practice Guide: Building Technology* (Ottawa, Ont.: Canada Mortgage and Housing Corporation, 2003).
2. Ian R. Chin, T. S. Thompson, and B. K. Rouse, "Exterior Insulation and Finish Systems (EIFS) Water Resistance/Leakage," in *Water Problems in Building Exterior Walls: Evaluation, Prevention and Repair,* eds. Jon M. Boyed and Michael J. Scheffler, ASTM STP 1352 (Philadelphia, Pa.: American Society for Testing and Materials, 1999), 3–16.
3. John Edgar, "Practical EIFS Detailing: Don't Rely on the Second Line of Defense," *Construction Canada* (November 2003).
4. Kevin C. Day, "Exterior Insulation Finish Systems: Designing for a Predictable Service Life," *Construction Canada* (March 2002): 6–13.
5. J. B. Posey and Jacques Rousseau, "Avoiding Problems with EIFS," *Canadian Architect* (February 1996): 32.
6. S. S. Ruggiero, and J. C. Meyers, "Design and Construction of Watertight Exterior Building Walls," *Water in Exterior Building Walls: Problems and Solutions,* ed. Thomas A. Schwartz, ASTM STP 1107 (Philadelphia, Pa.: American Society for Testing and Materials, 1991), 11–39.

Online Sources

1. EIFS Industry Members' Association (EIMA): http://www.eima.com
2. "Guide to Exterior Insulation and Finish Systems Construction" (Morrow, Ga.: EIMA, 2000). http://www.eima.com/Guide_to_EIFS.pdf

Wood-Frame Construction: Stucco and Fiber-Cement Siding

8.1 WOOD-FRAME CONSTRUCTION

Light wood-frame construction—alternatively called western platform, stick-built, and in other countries 2 x 4 construction—is the one structural system that originated in the United States and Canada. Derived from timber framing (now termed heavy timber framing) and later balloon framing, its development was prompted by a desire for a more efficient construction system and later fueled by dwindling forest reserves. Technological advances—such as the manufacturing of inexpensive, machine-made nails—combined with the development of the circular saw and later the band saw to produce this infinitely adaptable structural system. Softwood plywood made its debut at the Portland, Oregon, Lewis and Clark Expedition Centennial in 1905, and the platform for light wood-frame construction was literally set.[1] Visual grading of lumber was developed in the late 1920s, with machine stress ratings prominent by the early 1960s. Today lumber is graded by machine, using gamma radiation to nondestructively evaluate each piece. Grading allows for the most efficient use of small-dimension lumber. Countries as distinct as Finland and Chile are considering 2 x 4 light wood framing as a sustainable construction type for housing. Although masonry and concrete are common and often preferred materials, both countries are interested in utilizing their forests as a renewable resource for housing construction.

There is a certain genius in the simplicity of light wood-frame construction. Accommodating a wide range of styles and supported by a large and mobile labor force, it is almost synonymous with housing construction. Architects design only a small percentage of detached, single-family units, but they are responsible for the design of most low-rise multifamily housing, and much of this is light wood-frame construction. It is also an economical choice that offers design flexibility for industrial, commercial, and institutional buildings when permitted by codes.

Keeping Wood Framing Dry[1]

- Use lumber kiln-dried after any preservative treatment.

- Protect wood (framing and sheathing) from rain and snow on the construction site.

- Leave a minimum ⅛-inch (3 mm) gap around oriented-strand board (OSB) and plywood sheathing.

- Install the roof membrane as soon as possible.

- Install the water barrier and windows as soon as possible.

- Install the cladding, vapor retarder, nonpermeable insulation, and interior finishes as late as possible to promote drying to the inside and the outside.

- Do not overuse vapor-impermeable membranes, such as peel-and-stick, particularly at heads of openings.

- Separate wood from concrete.

- Do not pour concrete toppings against framing members. Use polyethylene or similar material to isolate framing from the topping.

- Dehumidify slowly, using a forced-air furnace temporarily installed for this purpose. It should *not* be fueled with propane or other fuels that create moisture.

- Check framing and sheathing to assure moisture content is consistently less than 19 percent before enclosing with any component, particularly components with low permeability.

1. Canada Mortgage and Housing Corporation, *Guidelines for On-Site Measurement of Moisture in Wood Building Materials*, Technical Series 03-112 (Ottawa, Ont.: CMHC, June 2003).

Vapor Diffusion Ports

Should there be moisture in the stud cavity, "vapor diffusion ports" may help in drying. These 3-inch (75 mm) diameter holes cut near the base and top of the stud cavity, through the exterior sheathing, promote drying of the stud cavity when used in combination with vapor permeable building wraps.[1]

1. CMHC, *Evaluation of Vapour Diffusion Ports on Drying of Wood-Frame Walls under Controlled Conditions,* Technical Series 02-130, Research Highlights (Ottawa, Ont.: CHMC, 2003).

FIGURE 8.1 Vapor diffusion ports.

By far the largest percentage of new construction is housing, and the majority is detached single-family units or small buildings of four or fewer units. Because of this, better and more complete references exist concerning wood frame construction than perhaps any other construction type. Much of the research on the building envelope comes from housing organizations such as the National the Association of Home Builders (NAHB) and Canada Mortgage and Housing Corporation (CMHC). Research on the building envelope by the Oak Ridge National Laboratories (ORNL), National Institute of Building Sciences (NIBS), and National Research Council of Canada (NRCC) is also largely associated with housing. Housing tends to have more problems partly because of higher interior relative humidity (RH) levels, often lower-quality heating, ventilation, and air-conditioning (HVAC) systems, and a propensity for geometrically complex facades. Although moisture problems, translated into mold and mildew, are not exclusive to wood framing, this is the focus of much of the present research.

The advantage of light wood-framing is the flexibility of the system in combination with a readily available work force. The stud cavity allows for the use of economical insulations, whether in batt form or blown in. With the addition of a drainage cavity and closely spaced vertical furring, wood framing lends itself to the compartmentalization required for pressure-equalized rain-screen (PER) walls. The disadvantage of wood frames is the need to keep the lumber and sheathing "dry," defined by water composing no more than 19 percent of the weight of the

Light-Gauge Steel Framing

Light-gauge steel framing is constructed very similarly to wood frame. Corrosion is a problem, especially at the fastening sites, but metal studs do not promote the growth of mold. Steel is lighter-weight and quicker to erect, and construction tolerances can be minimized. The "greenness" of the two systems continues to be debated, with steel promoted as a recycled material and wood as a renewable material. Often the choice between wood and metal studs is due to restrictions on combustible construction, although the behavior of wood-stud assemblies is remarkably similar to that of equivalent steel-stud assemblies when subjected to standard time-temperature fire exposures.[1] Steel-stud backup or infill walls are commonly used in concrete- and steel-framed buildings.

Perhaps the most critical difference is in the conduction of heat through a steel stud versus a wood stud. To solve the problem of thermal bridging with steel studs, insulation can be added to the exterior of the steel-stud wall. The simplified prescriptive requirements for detached and small residential buildings of the 2003 International Energy Conservation Code are an increased overall R-value and the use of exterior, thermal-insulating sheathing for steel-stud assemblies. For example, R-13 is the minimum R-value for a wood-framed wall, where the heating degree days (HDD) are between 2000 and 3999, and no sheathing insulation is required. The minimum for a steel-stud wall in the same HDD range is one of the following combinations of cavity plus sheathing insulation: R-11 (cavity) + R-5 (sheathing); R-15 (cavity) + R-4 (sheathing); or R-21 (cavity) + R-3 (sheathing). With the R-5 insulating sheathing, the total required resistance is R-16. This increases to R-24 when the insulating sheathing is only R-3, almost double that required by the wood-stud wall.

Both wood and steel systems can be easily prefabricated in modules or wall panels, with factory construction potentially providing a higher-quality wall. Prefabrication becomes more economical the greater the repetition.

---

1. N. Benichou, M. A. Sultan, and V. R. Kodur, "Fire Resistance Performance of Lightweight Framed Wall Assemblies: Effects of Various Parameters, Key Design Considerations and Numerical Modeling," *National Research Council Canada Report*, NRCC 45688 (Ottawa, Ont.: 2003).

lumber or sheathing. Whether the moisture comes from construction materials or processes, rain penetration, snowmelt, or vapor drive from the interior or exterior, the results are the same.

A variety of claddings are associated with wood frames and the residential market. These include stucco and sidings of wood, hardboard, fiber-cement, and vinyl. While these claddings represented only 11 percent of the square footage of the nonresidential market, they accounted for 76 percent of all wall claddings used in the U.S. in 2002.[2] (The size of the housing market is illustrated with the use of vinyl siding. In 2002 vinyl siding accounted for slightly over 4 percent of the total square footage of cladding used on nonresidential, new construction in the U.S.; but this jumps to 42 percent of all construction with the addition of the housing market.[3]) The selection of cladding in the residential market can be somewhat fickle. Preferences for a certain style change, as does the importance of features such as low maintenance. Failures often shift the popularity of a particular cladding, whether or not it was the source of the problems. The claddings associated with wood framing can be applied over concrete masonry walls or light-gauge steel-stud walls. This chapter details Wall Type C: Three-Coat Stucco on Wood Frame with Internal Plane, and Wall Type D: Fiber-Cement Board Siding with Drainage Cavity. The use of the drainage cavity does not imply that it is necessary when using fiber-cement siding or any other siding. The combination is used solely to illustrate detailing of a drainage cavity. (Included is a case study that uses medium-density overlay (MDO) plywood and cedar siding as cladding.)

8.2 STUCCO

Stucco has been used since antiquity as a rendering on substrates, from stone to the "daub" in wattle and daub. It weatherproofed the exterior wall and provided a smooth surface for painting, whether a single color or a decorative pattern. Stucco applied over a brick or rubble wall could be lined to resemble stone—an economical substitute for the real thing. Historical references giving specific instructions abound. One reference from the first century recommends three coats of sand mortar and two of marble mortar with the addition of powdered earthenware in the first coat when exposed to damp conditions or sea air.[4]

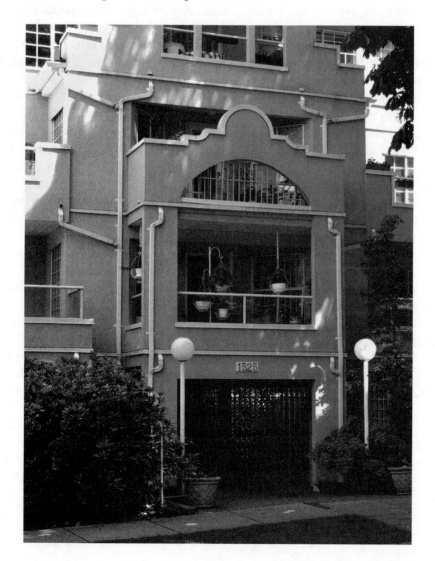

FIGURE 8.2 Metal flashing on all nonvertical surfaces and drainage at each floor protects this stucco clad building in an area that sees wind-driven rains during the winter months. Photo by G. Russell Heliker.

Once limited to trowel-applied finishes of lime, gypsum, or cement, the definition of *stucco* has expanded to include acrylics and polymer-modified (PM) base coats in modern times. The term *synthetic stucco* refers to Exterior Insulation Finish Systems (EIFS).

Traditional or conventional stucco—more correctly called portland cement plaster—relies on skilled tradespeople who understand the proper mixing and application given particular climatic conditions. The three-coat system of cementitious materials has developed through empirical research. It has had a long and successful history in North America and continues to perform well in many climates and markets. In instances where stucco has fallen into disfavor, it is usually related to poor construction and detailing rather than the system itself.

When it is well detailed and applied, stucco is a long-lasting and durable cladding. The ⅞-inch (22 mm) stucco is impact resistant and fire resistant. As a plastic material, it can conform to almost any form or detail offering aesthetic variety. It is one of the few materials that provide a monolithic appearance while relating to a historic past. However, as with many of our contemporary cladding systems, changes have occurred that challenge durability.

Traditional stucco is *not* face sealed. An internal drainage plane with building paper or felt is the typical water management system used with stucco. Stucco can also be applied with a drainage cavity for increased water protection. (Whether there is a drainage cavity, or a drainage plane, does not seem to affect the drying rate if water gets into the wood-stud cavity.[5]) Stucco is vapor permeable. Although good workmanship promotes high water resistance, it will get wet; but it will also dry.

Problems can occur when the finish coat is *not* vapor permeable, as is the case with some synthetic finish coats. Water from leaks at openings and interfaces will get in behind the finish coat but cannot get out. Many acrylic finishes are vapor permeable; but the question is—to what extent? A synthetic finish has a more intense and consistent color, is more water resistant, and stays cleaner. The downside is a greater potential for water damage due to the decreased drying potential to the exterior. Because the majority of water leakage occurs at transitions rather than through the stucco cladding, increased watertightness of the finish coat should not be at the expense of permeability.

Thin-coat systems, called both "one-coat" and "two-coat," were introduced in the mid-1980s. The base coat is similar in materials to that of traditional stucco, but it is only ⅜ inch (10 mm) in total depth with some systems. Proprietary systems may include polymer-modified base coats with acrylic finish coats. Each manufacturer has specific recommendations for the use of their product. The advantages of these systems are reduced weight (they are usually thinner), reduced labor costs (although some argue that the overall cost is not significantly less),[6] and greater water resistance than traditional stucco. But again the problem usually is not water entering through the surface of the stucco cladding but rather at transitions—windows leak and sealant joints fail. The new modified systems are sometimes used in areas that do not have a stucco tradition and thus lack the skilled tradespeople. However, proper curing time, often determined by the applicator, is even more critical with the acrylic-modified products. The durability of two-coat systems, including their drying capacity, should be carefully checked. The manufacturer's installation methods and warranties should be carefully reviewed. Nonproprietary, field mixed and applied one-coat systems should be avoided.

Stucco applied directly over studs, with no sheathing, is accepted by some building codes. Called open-stud construction, it is "an approved method, [but] not recommended for best performance" by the Northwest Wall and Ceiling Bureau (NWCB).[7] (This method has been commonly used in wood frame construction in California and is allowed under the National Building Code of Canada.) The backing support is provided by horizontal line wires over which building paper with metal lath is installed. More recently, paper-backed lath has been used, which can be more difficult to integrate with flashings, according to Mark Fowler, an architectural consultant with the NWCB. The line-wire and open-stud method depends greatly on the skill of the installers, as do all stucco applications. The thickness is difficult to control without a solid backing. Uneven thicknesses can lead to cracking. Because this method is usually chosen to reduce costs, it may be more likely that paper-backed lath will be used and that the installation will not be by the most skilled of craftspeople.

One of the methods of detailing a drainage cavity for stucco cladding essentially uses the open-stud construction over wood furring. NWCB calls it an "open-framed rain-screen construction." Caution is advised when using either of the "open" systems because of the absence of a solid backing for the stucco. The "drainage medium construction" system includes a drainage mat, generally, sandwiched between two water barriers. The effectiveness of this system relies on the stiffness of the drainage mat for the reasons stated above.

Stucco cladding is more durable over a solid substrate. With drainage cavity construction this can be provided with cement-and-asphalt impregnated thin sheathing boards, sometimes called "breather boards" or "rain screen boards." The rigid boards are manufactured for this purpose and fastened to the vertical furring. This is termed "semi-rigid rain-screen construction" by the NWCB. Another option

---

Stucco Substrates

- *Metal Studs with Sheathing*: Light-gauge steel framing is similar to wood framing. The lath and accessories are attached with screws through the sheathing to the metal-stud flange. There should be a minimum of three full threads exposed past the framing member.[1]

- *Concrete masonry:* An excellent substrate for stucco. For best water resistance use a three-coat system with an internal drainage plane. The two-coat system can be applied over concrete block without lath, although it will not be as watertight and should be reserved for drier areas with less exposure. (See Chapter 7 for information on concrete masonry walls.) Stucco applied over concrete masonry needs fewer control joints than when applied over wood or metal framing.[2]

- *Concrete*: A finish coat over concrete is usually done for aesthetic reasons—it is not meant to "true up" the surface. If more than a thin coat is applied, lath may be necessary. A better choice may be one of the proprietary, cementitious, permeable coatings developed specifically for bonding to concrete.

1. Northwest Wall and Ceiling Bureau (NWCB), *Stucco Resource Guide*, 3rd ed. (Seattle, Wash.: 1997), p.52.
2. Ibid, 142.

is "sheathed rain-screen construction," which uses rigid sheathing fastened to the furring. This is the most rigid and, consequently, the most durable; but it is also the most costly. If stucco is considered above the height limits of wood-frame construction or is located in a high exposure area with significant wind-driven rain, a drainage cavity or an enhanced drainage plane should be considered.

TABLE 8.1 Building Envelope Components Based on Climate

	Stucco on Wood-Frame Construction: Low-Rise Building Water Management System: Internal Drainage Plane Wall		
	Heating climate	*Mixed climate (detailed)*	*Cooling climate*
Water barrier system	2 layers, 30-minute grade D building paper	2 layers, 30-minute grade D building paper[1]	2 layers, 30-minute grade D building paper
Air barrier system	Airtight dry wall approach (ADA) or simple caulk and seal (SCS)	ADA or SCS[2]	ADA or SCS
Vapor retarder	4 mil polyethylene	Vapor retardant paint	Plywood
Insulation	Fiberglass batt and rigid board insulation or sprayed-in-place insulation in stud cavity to obtain higher R-value[3]	Fiberglass batt	Fiberglass batt
Structure	2 x 6 wood framing with plywood or OSB sheathing	2 x 6 wood framing with plywood or OSB sheathing	2 x 6 wood framing with plywood or OSB sheathing
Comments	Stucco should be vapor permeable	Stucco should be vapor permeable May consider a more vapor permeable sheathing depending on conditions	Interior finish must be highly vapor permeable

Notes:

1. Building paper and felt play a complex role in managing water with stucco claddings. Not only do they stop water, but with the curing of the stucco, they create a drainage plane. Building paper or felt absorbs water from the wet stucco application. When the stucco and the paper or felt dries, small drainage channels (reported by some to be $1/8$ inch (3 mm) in depth) are left on the back face of the stucco.[8] There is some concern that the heavier papers/felts may be counterproductive, as neither "wrinkle" as much during the drying of the stucco, and they may also retard evaporation.[9] The double layer of water barriers provides a secondary drainage plane for any moisture that may make it through the first. Some new proprietary water barriers, such as StuccoWrap by Tyvek, have a crinkled surface with small channels for water drainage. The other important component of the water management system is the weep screed, at the base of each stucco panel, which allows water to drain to the exterior at each floor.

There is much debate over the use of plastic building wraps with stucco. A study in Seattle by the Oak Ridge National Laboratory found that stucco bonded better to building wrap than to building paper. The better the bond, the less drainage. However, the study also stated that the corrugated, or crinkled, nonperforated building wrap drained very well. Single layers of sheathing membranes (water barriers) did not drain well.[10] NWCB requires that building wraps be designed specifically for use with stucco. Their "guide specification" also requires that two layers of grade D paper or building wrap or one layer of 60-minute building paper be used over wood sheathing. If a combination is used, the building wrap should be the first layer.[11] One stucco contractor says he uses two layers of 15-minute paper in the interior of Southern California, double 30-minute paper in Salt Lake City, Utah, and double 60-minute paper in Galveston Bay, Texas, presumably driven by degree of wetting and the potential for postwetting drying.[12]

2. Well-detailed stucco stops all air movement; but the leakage, as with many materials, occurs at the joints and transitions. A complete air barrier system is required.

3. Many sprayed-in-place insulations qualify as air barriers with careful detailing at the transitions.

8.3 WALL TYPE C: THREE-COAT STUCCO ON WOOD FRAME WITH INTERNAL DRAINAGE PLANE

The suggested wall assembly for stucco cladding with an internal drainage plane in a mixed climate is listed and described in Table 8.1 and the notes that follow. Suggestions for assemblies in heating and cooling climates are also given in Table 8.1.

8.4 STUCCO DESIGN

The following issues should be considered during design when using stucco cladding.

Design team: Traditional stucco claddings do not rely on proprietary materials. In designing stucco cladding, the best sources for information are trade associations and knowledgeable tradespeople.

Building form: The building form should work to deflect water from the face of the stucco. As suggested by A. J. Downing in 1850, there are a "few simple rules...necessary to insure success in stuccoing....The first of these rules is, not to use stucco except on buildings with projecting roofs, in order to prevent the possibility of the wall getting saturated at the eaves."[13] As with EIFS, stucco does not make a good roofing material. Nonvertical surfaces should be flashed with metal unless shielded by an overhang. (See Figures 8.3 and 8.4.) Shapes called "plant-ons" can be cut from expanded polystyrene (EPS) board. Applied over the stucco base coat, they are an EIFS, requiring an acrylic finish over both the plant-on and the stucco. Overhangs or metal flashing should protect these projecting details.

Control joints: Control joints determine panel size. ASTM C1063 calls for a maximum wall panel size of 144 square feet (13.4 sq m) with a length-to-width ratio of no more than 2.5 to 1 and a maximum dimension of 18 feet (5.5 m) in either direction. Others state that the panel size should be between 100 and 144 square feet (9.3–13.4 sq m) with maximum spacing of no more than 10 to 12 feet (3–3.7 m) in either direction, essentially forming a square.[14] Violating these ratios is a common problem, which can result in the cracking of long, slender panels.[15] The disadvantage of smaller panels is the greater likelihood of water leakage at the control joints. The location of the control joints is decided by the architect and becomes part of the surface design. Control joints direct or "control" the cracking of the stucco as well as provide a screed for leveling the cement plaster and a place to start and stop the work. The Portland Cement Association (PCA) specifically states, "The location of the control joints should be determined by the designer, not the applicator."[16] If the stucco contractor determines the placement of control joints, they most likely will be located to maximize function. The designer can use the control joints as both a functional and an aesthetic element.

Expansion Joints: Allowing for differential movement, expansion joints are required where movement is anticipated: where stucco meets another material, where the substrate materials change, and at floor lines with structures that see shrinkage (wood) or shortening (concrete). The importance of expansion joints is stated in the NWCB *Stucco Resource Guide,* with the admonition that "expansion joints govern over control joints."[17] The *Stucco Resource Guide* further states that

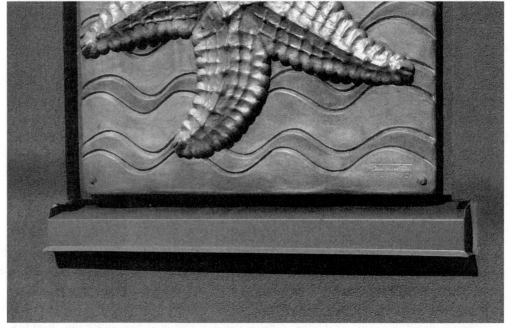

FIGURES 8.3, 8.4 The original design of the sill at the base of these recessed decorative panels had no protection, as shown in Figure 8.3. The EIFS cladding was removed, due to water entry problems, and replaced with traditional stucco with a drainage cavity. (The problem was not inherently with the EIFS—it was with the poor detailing. Neither stucco nor EIFS makes a good roofing material.) The new metal sill flashing with end dams directs all water away from the wall (Figure 8.4). Photos by G. Russell Heliker.

"the selection of the proper expansion joint is *not the responsibility of the contractor.*"[18] This means that it is the *responsibility of the architect.* The profile of these joints and their location are also design elements.

Appearance: Traditional stucco with a cementitious finish coat is not meant to look like plastic. It has a time-honored appearance that indicates the density of a carefully hand-applied material. It is not perfect. Even the best of applications may see a few hairline cracks or other surface imperfections, and the color will not be as consistent as that provided by an acrylic finish coat. Dark colors, particularly reds, are more prone to spottiness, although manufacturers are developing stronger and more stable cement colors.[19] If a more monolithic surface or an intense color is desired, an EIFS cladding may be a better choice.

Stucco lends itself to a wide and varied assortment of textures, from dashed finishes to those with embedded materials such as crushed stone. The finish coat can be applied in multiple layers to create high-relief textures. The heavier the texture, the more inconsistencies are camouflaged. Smoother surfaces accumulate less dust and organic growth. However, a smooth troweled finish coat is not recommended, as the cement-rich thin surface has a tendency to develop fine hairline cracks. A fine sand-float, properly applied, can meet the performance and aesthetic objectives of a flat finish.

The skill of the applicator is reflected in the appearance of the stucco. Prior to starting the stucco application, the contractor should construct a sample panel that will be left on site for comparison until the project is completed. This can be part of the mock-up wall.

Durability: Writing specifications and bidding documents that ensure installation by skilled and knowledgeable tradespeople is absolutely critical. This is a cladding system whose watertightness is more dependent on the skill of the applicators than the materials, just as with brick veneer. The stucco contractor should be licensed, bonded, and insured with documentable experience in quality work of a similar scope. The applicators should be properly trained, with experience on similar projects. Stucco contractors who do not meet these requirements should not be bidding on the work.

Reducing Cracks in Stucco

- Carefully locate control joints and expansion joints.

- Choose a rigid and dimensionally stable backup wall—stucco on concrete masonry will have the fewest cracks.

- Divert water from face of stucco wherever possible to stop hairline cracks from becoming larger in areas with freeze-thaw cycles.

- Design details and write specifications to ensure that:

    1. Lath is continuous and lapped where required. (Smaller openings in the lath provide greater crack resistance.)

    2. Recommended trim pieces are used at panel terminations and corners.

    3. Base and finish coats are of minimum and consistent thickness.

    4. Close attention is paid to weather and appropriate measures are taken, particularly in near-freezing temperatures and hot, dry conditions.

    5. Brown coat is trowel-floated.

- Find a good applicator!

8.5 STUCCO APPLICATION

The following information is not intended to be a "how to apply stucco guide," but rather a resource to use in conjunction with industry recommendations. It enables the designer to understand the critical points of stucco installation to ensure a durable and aesthetically pleasing application.

A successful stucco job requires a solid, rigid, durable, and watertight substrate — the more dimensionally stable the substrate, the less chance of cracking. A thorough examination of the wall prior to attaching the trim and lath should reveal a watertight surface with all joints and transitions flashed such that water is directed to the exterior of the cladding when possible and if that is not possible, to the exterior of the drainage plane. The water barrier should lap horizontally, and vertical laps should be taped and staggered.[20] If there is a chance that any materials might bond to the stucco, a separation sheet of Kraft paper can be used. Flashing should be in place and lapped by the water barrier. Head flashing at windows should have end dams and upturned back edges. Flangeless windows should be installed with sill-pan flashing that includes an upturned back edge and end dams. The stucco contractor should verify that conditions are acceptable and the wall is watertight before beginning work.

8.5.1 STUCCO ACCESSORIES AND LATH

Trim accessories are galvanized steel, zinc (alloy), polyvinyl chloride (PVC), or anodized aluminum. Panel terminations should have a "lip" that goes over the edge and embeds in the stucco. Trim should be installed in the longest pieces possible. Use trim at all external corners. Inside corner trim is not recommended unless the intersecting wall is a dissimilar material.

Lath is diamond-mesh (expanded metal) or welded wire, generally of 16-gauge wire with openings not exceeding 2 x 2 inches (50 x 50 mm). It is galvanized and available with self-furring crimps and paper backing. The self-furring lugs of the lath hold it away from the substrate ¼ inch (6 mm). Another option is to use special furring nails. Woven wire lath is also available. Whatever system is used, the lath needs to be completely embedded in the scratch coat.

The *weep screed* is an integral component of the drainage plane. Ideally, it should be sloped to drain and installed at each floor line. If there are no holes in the screed, it should be site-drilled. An ineffective screed at the base of a stucco panel turns an internal drainage plane wall into a face-sealed barrier wall. Horizontal control and expansion joints should also have a sloped top flange with drainage holes.[21]

The designer and the stucco installer need to understand the difference between *control joints* and *expansion joints*. Control joints can be one piece, but expansion joints should be two-piece or incorporate an accordion-pleat to maximize the movement potential. The lath is stopped at expansion joints and tied to the top of the two flanges. There is controversy over whether the lath can be continuous behind control joints. ASTM does not differentiate between expansion and control joints, requiring the lath to be cut at all joints and wire tied to both sides. This allows the joint to move with the stucco, as it is not rigidly attached to the framing.

Adequate attachment of trim accessories and lath to the substrate is very important. Testing may be required to assure the pullout strength of fasteners. The fasteners should penetrate a minimum of ¾ inch (19 mm) into the wood frame (not including the sheathing) and be ⅜ inch (10 mm) from the edges. Each staple, screw, or nail produces a hole through which water can enter. No area should have more than the required number of fasteners. Studs should be located prior to attaching the lath—they should not be located with the drill or staple gun. The attachment of signage, ladders, and the like through stucco can be sources of water entry. Using stand-off mounts that can be sealed around the perimeter reduces this risk.[22]

With some modifications, the stucco can help mitigate damage associated with seismic events. One possiblity is to use galvanized staples instead of nails to attach the lath so that the lath does not "move off" the nail head during an earthquake.[23]

8.5.2 THREE-COAT STUCCO

Stucco can be hand applied or machine applied (for larger projects). The *base coat* consists of the scratch coat and the brown coat. The first coat—the scratch coat with its roughened surface—should be a minimum depth of ⅜ inch (10 mm) to completely embed the lath. The brown coat will bring the total depth of the base coat to a minimum of ¾ inch (19 mm). This second coat can be applied over a damp scratch coat, when the scratch coat is able to resist the application without cracking. This is called "double-backing." The delay produces better bond and better curing of the scratch coat. Minimizing the time between coats speeds up construction; however, it can also cause problems, depending on the weather. Improper application of the first and second coats can result in the base coat slumping while curing. The International Building Code (IBC) requires a minimum of 48 hours between the scratch and brown coats with a reduction to 24 hours with moist curing. The application time between the two base coats has shortened over the past two decades—a seven-day wait used to be the standard recommendation. Determining the best time is highly dependent on the climate and the extent to which curing is controlled. It should *not* be based on a completion schedule.

After the brown coat has set but while still moist, it should be "trowel-floated" to make the base coat more dense. This increases the water resistance, reduces surface cracking, and provides a good surface for the finish coat.

The addition of polypropylene, nylon, or alkali-resistant glass fibers is recommended in the base coat but not the finish coat.[24] Admixtures for air-entraining, water-reducing, or cure-accelerating may be added, following association guidelines and approvals. Detergents and chlorides should never be used. Requiring the use of "standard measuring devices," or batching containers instead of shovels, will help assure a proper mix.

Moist curing of the base coat is recommended for the first two days, with a total curing time of seven days. Moist-curing occurs only after the base coat has set and is hard. The stucco is sprayed with a fine mist of clean water that does not saturate the stucco. Moist curing helps prevent "craze cracking," and it is necessary when the temperature is greater than 77°F (25°C) or the relative humidity (RH) is less than 70 percent, and it is windy. Extremely hot, dry, and windy conditions may also require plastic sheets to retard evaporation.

The primary decision with the *finish coat* is whether it will be cementitious or acrylic. Both have advantages and disadvantages, as noted above. For the best overall durability of the wall, the *portland cement–plaster finish coat* may be the best choice. It can be mixed on site or premixed by a manufacturer of finish coats. The manufactured finish coats will produce more uniform color than the "job-site stucco" finish coat, but there will still be inconsistencies due to climatic conditions and the application. The portland cement–plaster finish coat is applied to a dampened base coat, to a minimum depth of ⅛ inch (3 mm). Application should start at the top and work down, with no cold joints or scaffold lines. Moist-curing of the finish coat is not recommended—except in extreme cases of hot, dry, and windy weather—as it can cause discoloration.

An *acrylic finish coat* should be a 100 percent acrylic polymer base recommended by the trade association. Because of the thinness of the layer, it is critical that the base coat be floated. The temperature should be 40°F (5°C) and rising for a minimum of 24 hours when application begins. A wet edge should be maintained at all times and the finish protected until dry. The most uniform color is achieved by troweling on the acrylic finish, followed by a sprayed-on coat. Again, acrylic finishes will produce more consistent colors, but they may not be the most durable because of the decreased permeability.

8.5.3 CLIMATE

The weather conditions during application play a critical role in the durability of stucco. As one contractor stated, "If you want stucco that will last 100 years, pray for a period of cool, damp days—temperatures in the 50s [10°C] and 60s, [16°C] no wind, and high humidity."[25] If this is not the prevailing weather, measures should be taken to protect the stucco from temperature extremes and dry, windy conditions. The NWCB *Stucco Resource Guide* recommends a temperature of 35°F (2°C) and rising. The Portland Cement Association recommends a minimum of 40°F (5°C), as does the IBC. The National Building Code of Canada calls for 50°F (10°C) during application and for 48 hours afterwards.[26] Under no circumstances should stucco be applied to any frozen surface or surfaces containing frost. It should also be protected from excessive evaporation in warm, dry, and windy conditions. The better the curing environment, the more durable the stucco.

8.6 MAINTENANCE

Stucco surfaces can be washed to remove dirt and organic growth. Painting may reduce the permeability of the surface and should be carefully reviewed. Failures have occurred because of the application of multiple layers of so-called breathable coatings. Paints may also hide discolorations that indicate a problem with the wood structure.[27]

8.7 CONCERNS WITH STUCCO

Stucco has all the potential problems of other cladding systems, exacerbated by the need for skilled applicators. Carefully detailing and specifying stucco and selecting qualified installers should eliminate the problems sometimes attributed to this material. Stucco cladding will perform better over a rigid backup wall such as concrete masonry. The minimum industry recommendation for out-of-plane deflection of the backup wall is L (wall height in inches)/360.

Recognizing the limitations of stucco is important. Whether it is a suitable cladding for higher than four- to six-story buildings is one question—the higher the building, the greater the potential for application problems. For higher buildings it may be advisable to select a cladding more resistant to wind and wind-driven rain or to consider prefabricated stucco panels. In areas that see a great deal of rain, using a true drainage cavity will increase durability *if* a rigid backup is provided for the stucco.

Understanding the nature of stucco diminishes the problems associated with it. Stucco takes on water, which means in a damp climate, particularly in the shade, it will support organic growth on the surface. This will not happen in a hot, dry climate. Stucco may not be the best way to obtain the desert look in a rain forest climate. This is not to say that stucco should not be used in areas with high moisture exposure. Stucco is a traditional cladding material of the British Isles, which certainly sees its share of rainy weather.

Inconsistencies with the color of stucco and hairline cracks are normal. Color is affected by the curing time. An unevenly dampened brown coat or cold joints in the brown coat can cause color variations, as can adding water to the plaster surface while texturing the finish coat. Other color variations can be attributed to overfloating the brown coat. A final thin coat, sometimes called a fog coat, can help correct color variations.[28] Finding a good installer is the best way to diminish hairline cracks and minimize color variations.

FIGURE 8.5 This dryer vent has metal head and sill flashing. Another option for dryer vents is shown in Figure 8.14. Photo courtesy of Morrison Hershfield, Ltd.

8.8 DETAILS: STUCCO

Stucco cladding with an internal drainage plane attached to a light wood-frame wall is detailed in Figures 8.6–8.15. The details are based on a low-rise building located in a mixed climate.

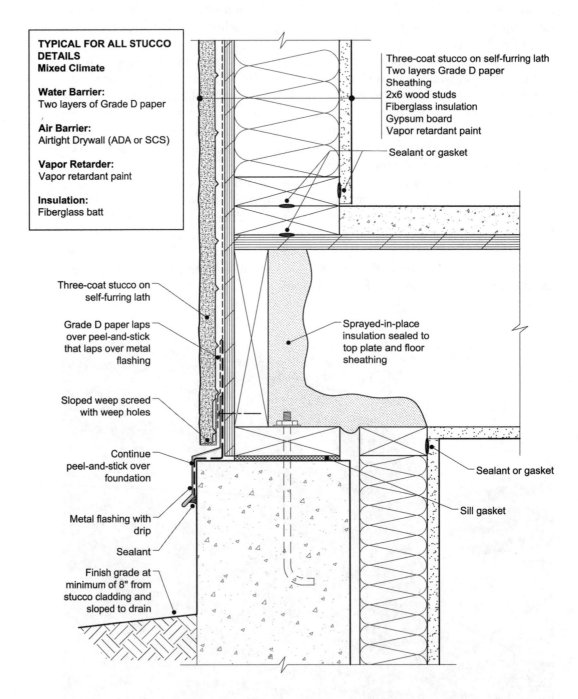

TYPICAL FOR ALL STUCCO DETAILS
Mixed Climate

Water Barrier:
Two layers of Grade D paper

Air Barrier:
Airtight Drywall (ADA or SCS)

Vapor Retarder:
Vapor retardant paint

Insulation:
Fiberglass batt

Three-coat stucco on self-furring lath
Two layers Grade D paper
Sheathing
2x6 wood studs
Fiberglass insulation
Gypsum board
Vapor retardant paint

Sealant or gasket

Three-coat stucco on self-furring lath

Grade D paper laps over peel-and-stick that laps over metal flashing

Sloped weep screed with weep holes

Continue peel-and-stick over foundation

Metal flashing with drip

Sealant

Finish grade at minimum of 8" from stucco cladding and sloped to drain

Sprayed-in-place insulation sealed to top plate and floor sheathing

Sealant or gasket

Sill gasket

FIGURE 8.6 Stucco cladding at foundation. This detail shows the stucco face flush with the concrete foundation. A preferable, and simpler, approach is for the exterior sheathing and the foundation wall to be in the same plane. If the sheathing is stepped back, as shown, it is imperative that the foundation wall be flashed with metal.

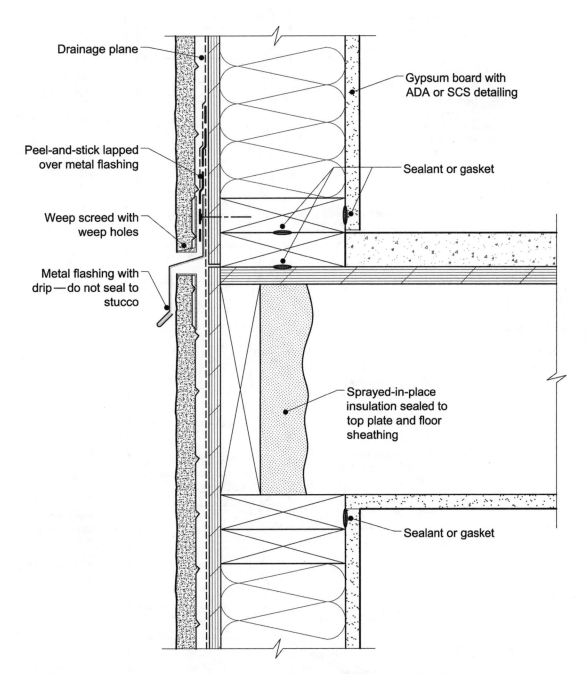

Drainage plane

Peel-and-stick lapped over metal flashing

Weep screed with weep holes

Metal flashing with drip—do not seal to stucco

Gypsum board with ADA or SCS detailing

Sealant or gasket

Sprayed-in-place insulation sealed to top plate and floor sheathing

Sealant or gasket

FIGURE 8.7 Through-wall flashing at each floor. In areas that see little rain, a simple expansion joint at the floor line may be adequate. See enlarged detail on Figure 8.11.

FIGURE 8.8 Counter-flashing at roof. Whether the roof is low-sloped or pitched, using a two-piece flashing makes reroofing much simpler. The stucco cladding should outlast the roof membrane or shingles.

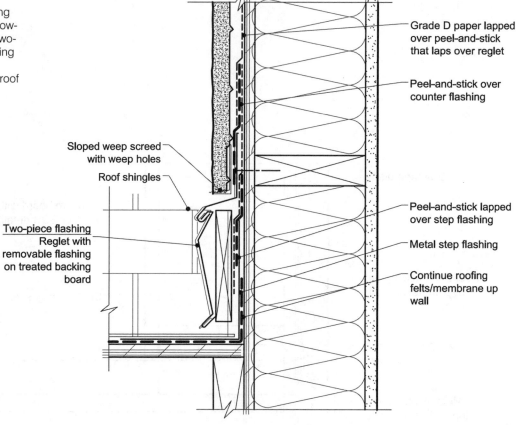

Grade D paper lapped over peel-and-stick that laps over reglet

Peel-and-stick over counter flashing

Sloped weep screed with weep holes

Roof shingles

Two-piece flashing Reglet with removable flashing on treated backing board

Peel-and-stick lapped over step flashing

Metal step flashing

Continue roofing felts/membrane up wall

FIGURE 8.9 Counter-flashing at roof.

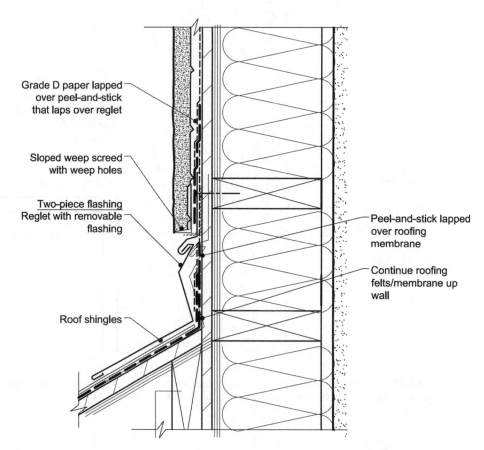

Grade D paper lapped over peel-and-stick that laps over reglet

Sloped weep screed with weep holes

Two-piece flashing Reglet with removable flashing

Peel-and-stick lapped over roofing membrane

Continue roofing felts/membrane up wall

Roof shingles

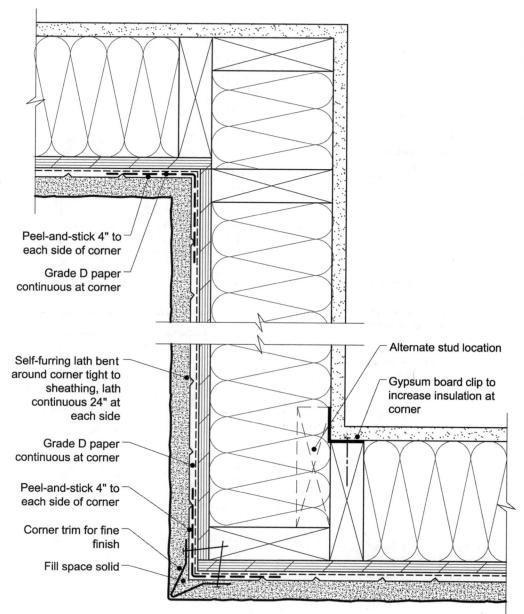

Peel-and-stick 4" to
each side of corner

Grade D paper
continuous at corner

Self-furring lath bent
around corner tight to
sheathing, lath
continuous 24" at
each side

Grade D paper
continuous at corner

Peel-and-stick 4" to
each side of corner

Corner trim for fine
finish

Fill space solid

Alternate stud location

Gypsum board clip to
increase insulation at
corner

FIGURE 8.10 Minimizing studs
at inside and outside corners
gives more space for insulation.
Using a peel-and-stick self-
adhesive membrane at the corners helps keep them watertight.

FIGURE 8.11 Horizontal joints. The upper, flashed expansion joint is preferable when the wall will be repeatedly wet, as it assures that the water is deflected away from the stucco below. In dryer areas, a two-piece reveal that allows for expansion and contraction may be adequate.

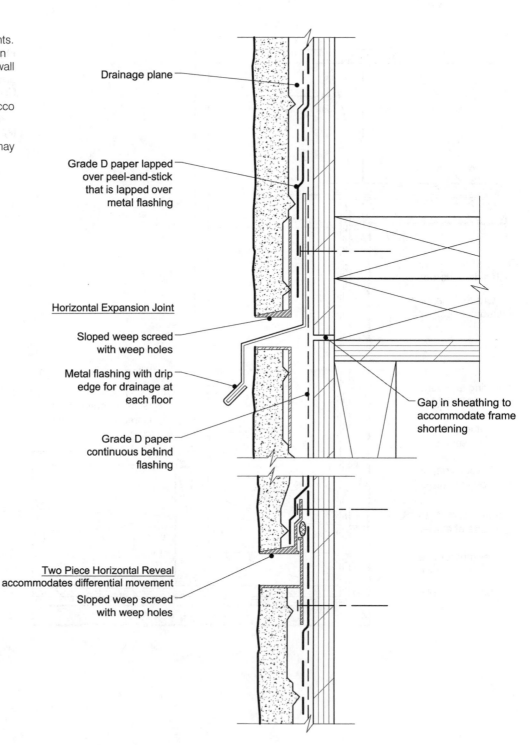

Drainage plane

Grade D paper lapped over peel-and-stick that is lapped over metal flashing

Horizontal Expansion Joint

Sloped weep screed with weep holes

Metal flashing with drip edge for drainage at each floor

Grade D paper continuous behind flashing

Gap in sheathing to accommodate frame shortening

Two Piece Horizontal Reveal accommodates differential movement

Sloped weep screed with weep holes

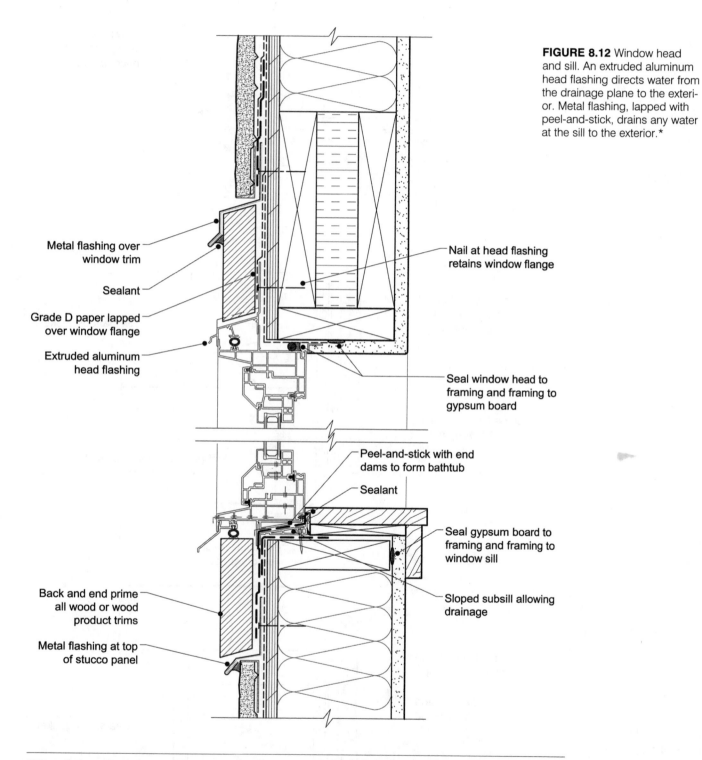

FIGURE 8.12 Window head and sill. An extruded aluminum head flashing directs water from the drainage plane to the exterior. Metal flashing, lapped with peel-and-stick, drains any water at the sill to the exterior.*

Metal flashing over window trim

Sealant

Grade D paper lapped over window flange

Extruded aluminum head flashing

Nail at head flashing retains window flange

Seal window head to framing and framing to gypsum board

Peel-and-stick with end dams to form bathtub

Sealant

Seal gypsum board to framing and framing to window sill

Sloped subsill allowing drainage

Back and end prime all wood or wood product trims

Metal flashing at top of stucco panel

*Although the author is responsible for Figure 8.12, it was created with the help of the Walters and Wolf Glass Company, who should be contacted for design direction on actual projects. http://www.waltersandwolf.com

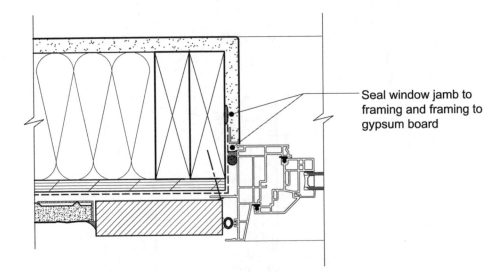

Seal window jamb to framing and framing to gypsum board

FIGURE 8.13 Window jamb.

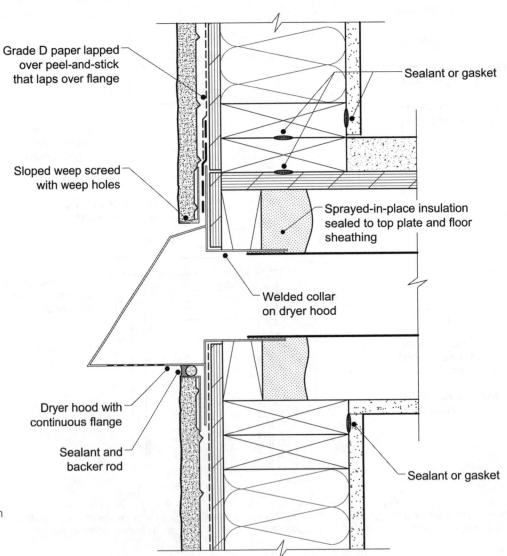

Grade D paper lapped over peel-and-stick that laps over flange

Sealant or gasket

Sloped weep screed with weep holes

Sprayed-in-place insulation sealed to top plate and floor sheathing

Welded collar on dryer hood

Dryer hood with continuous flange

Sealant and backer rod

Sealant or gasket

FIGURE 8.14 This dryer vent has a welded collar flashed with peel-and-stick self-adhesive membrane at the top.

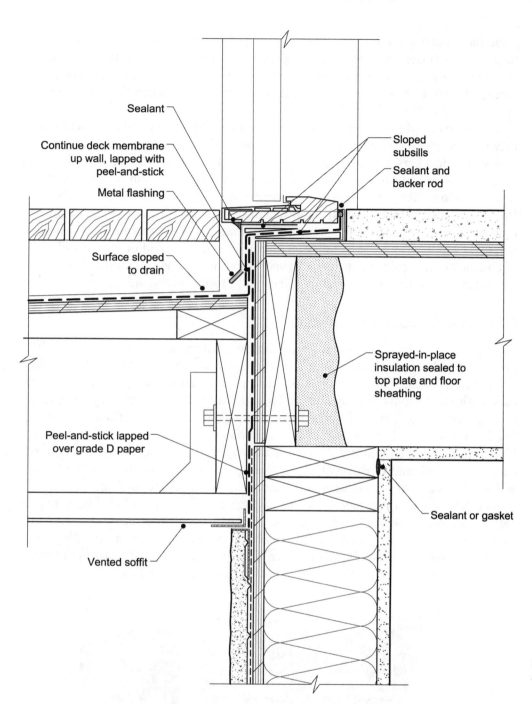

FIGURE 8.15 Accessible entry at balcony.

8.9 FIBER-CEMENT CLADDING

Wood and wood products constituted over a quarter of all claddings on residential and nonresidential new construction in the United States in 2002. Almost half of the claddings used were fiber-cement sidings.[29] A favored material, wood is becoming increasingly scarce, especially the more water resistant and durable species such as redwood and cedar. Fiber-cement products were introduced to overcome the shortages of economical wood sidings, the environmental problems associated with cement asbestos products, and the durability problems found with some hardboard sidings. James Hardie Siding Products, the first manufacturer of fiber-cement board in North America, had its beginnings in 1903 when James Hardie imported a new French product called "Fibro Cement" to Australia. It was reportedly able to resist "fire, frost, acid, and ants." Manufacturing of Hardie products in the U.S. began in 1989.[30]

Fiber-cement products resist rotting; they are more impact resistant than wood; they take on less moisture than wood; they are resistant to termites and fungus as well as woodpeckers, the nemeses of wood and EIFS; and they are noncombustible. Fiber-cement boards are proprietary mixes but generally contain portland cement, sand, cellulose fiber, and additives. Some may contain clay (although not the Hardie products). Fiber cement is autoclaved (cured with pressurized steam) to produce a more dimensionally stable product than wood or vinyl siding. Each manufacturer will have specific installation instructions that should be closely followed. The installation requirements may change from one product to another because of the differences with the proprietary mixes and profiles of the siding.

8.9.1 DRAINAGE CAVITY WITH SIDINGS

For maximum protection from water, a drainage cavity may be used with siding. The cavity, drained at each floor, helps assure that any water that penetrates the cladding will drain to the exterior. "One-by" (1x) furring, attached vertically to the studs, creates a ¾-inch (19 mm) drainage cavity. (See Figures 8.16, 8.19, and 8.20.) A variation on vertical furring is diagonal furring that permits two directions of cladding finish (vertical or horizontal) while maintaining the desired drainage cavity. Horizontal furring should not be used, unless applied as a second layer over vertical furring. Claddings must be capable of spanning the distance between the furring without buckling, or a solid substrate must be attached to the furring.

The detailing of a drainage cavity wall is similar for all types of cladding, including stucco. A drainage space can also be created with a proprietary mat, typically ¼ inch (6 mm) or so in thickness. This can be an economical way of providing additional drainage for certain types of siding. Care must be taken in fastening through this nonsolid mat layer, particularly when using pneumatic nailers.

FIGURE 8.16 This closely spaced vertical furring provides a drainage cavity and structural support for the SBPO building wrap air barrier system. Photo courtesy of Morrison Hershfield, Ltd.

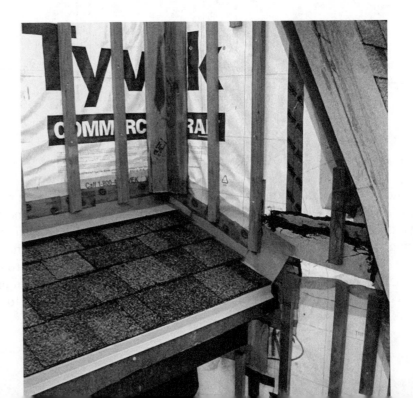

Vinyl Siding

Vinyl siding has come a long way since the early 1960s products that faded, cracked, and looked like what they were —plastic. The fact that 42 percent of the square footage of all wall cladding used in the U.S. in 2002 was vinyl siding attests to its popularity. While still not the aesthetic choice of some designers, the durability of the product has improved considerably. The low-maintenance feature is attractive to owners, and some manufacturers are offering 50-year limited materials warranties. Vinyl is a PVC resin with inorganic color pigments, ultraviolet (UV) stabilizers, and various minor components such as processing lubricants. Usually the outer 20 percent, called the "cap-stock," provides the primary UV-resistant surface. This two-layer process is produced through coextrusion in an effort to reduce costs.[2] Horizontal siding is available in a number of patterns, colors, and textures. Each manufacturer has a unique locking system that attaches one siding piece to another. PATH (Partnership for Advancing Technology in Housing) lists five grades of vinyl siding based on thickness. Those at the "super premium" thickness of 0.048 inches (1.2 mm) or greater can cost 50 to 100 percent more than those at the "super economy" thickness of 0.035 to 0.040 inch (0.1 to 1 mm) thicknesses. Most of the material sold is in the 0.040 to 0.042 inch (1 to 1.1 mm) range.[3]

If vinyl siding is a consideration, the following should be carefully reviewed:

- Specify vinyl siding that has been certified to meet or exceed ASTM D3679 through an independent, third-party inspection program sponsored by the Vinyl Siding Institute.

- One of the biggest considerations with vinyl siding is that of thermal expansion. A 12-foot length of siding can expand ½ inch from winter to summer. Installation of siding panels, trim, and accessories must be designed with this in mind. One contractor said to "think of vinyl...products as being hung, not fastened in place."[4] The architect should be aware of the limitations of the particular product and ensure that installation is by a qualified contractor in accordance with the siding manufacturer and ASTM D4756 requirements.

- Weathering of vinyl can result in dusting or chalking of the surface. While this occurs to a much lesser extent than it once did, darker colors may show this more readily. It is also climate and air pollution dependent. One industry representative says that 80 percent of their chalking occurs in the northeast. They see little in the south, where there is a lot of sunlight.

- Vinyl, like most polymers, becomes brittle at lower temperatures—the colder it gets, the less impact resistance. According to the Vinyl Siding Institute, while the thickness of the vinyl affects impact resistance, other factors, such as the characteristics of embossing patterns, may be of equal or greater importance.

- Wind resistance varies from product to product, but a reinforced nail hem created by folding over the vinyl is more capable of resisting wind uplift.[5]

- Water can enter the wall through laps and joints. Better than average care should be taken to ensure a good, complete water barrier and complete flashing at all transitions. Most vinyl siding also drains very well because of the multitude of openings. If a drainage cavity is considered in areas that see a lot of rain, the thickness of the vinyl will determine its spanning ability. It may be necessary to use wider furring strips or space them at 8 inches or 12 inches to counteract the "waviness" created when siding spans too great a distance, or consider diagonal furring.

1. 2002 Drucker Report (Bloomfield Hills, Mich.: Drucker Worldwide, 2002).
2. Martin Holladay, "Builder's Guide to Vinyl Siding," *Journal of Light Construction* (June 2000).
3. PATH, *The Rehab Guide to Exterior Walls*.
4. George Schambach, "Durable Details for Vinyl Siding," *Journal of Light Construction* (June 1997).
5. Martin Holladay, "Builder's Guide to Vinyl Siding," *Journal of Light Construction* (June 2000).

TABLE 8.2 Building Envelope Components Based On Climate

Fiber-Cement Board Siding on Wood-Frame Construction: Low-Rise Building *Water Management System: Drainage Cavity Wall[1]*		
	Heating climate	**Mixed climate (detailed)**	**Cooling climate**
Water barrier	SBPO building wrap	SBPO building wrap	SBPO building wrap
Air barrier system	Sealed SBPO[2]	Sealed SBPO	Sealed SBPO
Vapor retarder	4 mil polyethylene	Vapor retardant paint	Plywood
Insulation	Fiberglass blanket and rigid board insulation or sprayed-in-place insulation to obtain higher R-value[3]	Fiberglass blanket friction fit	Fiberglass blanket
Structure	2 x 6 wood framing with plywood or OSB sheathing	2 x 6 wood framing with plywood or OSB sheathing	2 x 6 wood framing with plywood or OSB sheathing
Comments		May consider a more vapor permeable sheathing, depending on conditions	Interior finish must be highly vapor permeable

Notes:

1. The drainage cavity is detailed for a building with high exposure to rain. In other areas, a drainage plane is adequate for water management.

2. Taping and sealing the SBPO building wrap as an air barrier system only works if it is supported. Furring channels, at a maximum of 12 inches (300 mm) on center, that cover the staples and any laps, should offer adequate resistance for a low-rise building. This spacing must be coordinated with the stud spacing and the maximum spanning distance of the siding. With studs at 16 inches (400 mm) on center, a spacing of 8 inches (200 mm) on center would be used.

3. Some sprayed-in-place insulations qualify as air barrier systems if transitions are carefully detailed.

8.10 WALL TYPE D: FIBER-CEMENT BOARD SIDING WITH DRAINAGE CAVITY

The suggested wall assembly for fiber-cement siding attached to a light wood-frame wall with a drainage cavity is listed and described in Table 8.2 and the notes that follow. The wall assembly is designed for a building in a mixed climate with high exposure to rain. Suggestions for assemblies in heating and cooling climates are also given in Table 8.2.

8.11 FIBER-CEMENT SIDING DESIGN

The following issues should be considered during design when using fiber-cement siding.

Design team: Because fiber-cement sidings are products with different compositions, the manufacturer's requirements should be closely reviewed. Specific questions can be directed to the manufacturer's representative. Some manufacturers offer a 50-year limited materials warranty for specific products. Be sure the design detailing does not jeopardize the warranty.

Appearance: Fiber-cement siding comes in a variety of styles and sizes (some meant to imitate wood siding or shingles), as well as sheets up to 4 by 10 feet (1220 x 3000 mm). Siding is usually limited to 12-foot (3.6 m) lengths because of its weight. Most manufacturers offer a sealed and primed product and factory-

FIGURE 8.17 The metal head and sill flashings of the windows in this wood-clad wall are carefully detailed to keep water out of the wall, off the windows, and away from the cladding. The through-wall metal flashing at each floor, with the extensive overhang, also helps protect the cladding. However, this is not its only purpose. The building is located in Finland, where masonry is the preferred material for multistory residential structures, and the metal deflectors serve to stop flame spread. Photo by Linda Brock.

applied finishes. Fiber cement takes paint very well. It should not be left unpaint-ed. One Japanese manufacturer, Nichina Corporation, distributing in the U.S. and Canada, produces ½- to 1-inch (19–25 mm) thick fiber-cement panels that replicate brick and stone in addition to its imitation shake panels. They are designed for the heat and humidity of Japan, as well as the country's rigorous seismic and fire reg-ulations. The panels are shiplapped on all four sides and attached to a metal clip that is fastened to the stud, providing a narrow drainage cavity between the panel and the water barrier.

Nails are not countersunk in fiber-cement siding, as this decreases the holding power. The visible head may be objectionable to some. This can be avoided with blind nailing; see comments under Section 8.12.

Mitered corners require significant skill from the installer. Staggered, lapped joints at corners are acceptable but may let in more water, and their construction is more time consuming than using corner boards. Two-piece corner trim boards will eliminate the visible vertical sealant joint by allowing the siding to slip behind the top piece. (See Figure 8.20.)

Durability: Because of the cement content, fiber-cement board should not be in contact with aluminum windows or trim unless anodized. Even when anodized, the fiber-cement should be primed on all faces in contact with the aluminum. Vertical joints at trim or other fixed objects should be sealed, and nonlapping horizontal joints flashed with metal. A factory sealed and primed product will offer the best weather protection. All cut edges, including on prefinished boards, should be primed prior to installation. No fiber-cement product should be tightly butted with itself or another material. At all vertical joints there should be a ⅛-inch (3-mm) gap. Fiber-cement siding should be kept 8 inches (200 mm) from finish grade, 2 inches (50 mm) from the roof surface, and separated from concrete.

8.12 FIBER-CEMENT SIDING INSTALLATION

While very similar to natural wood sidings, fiber-cement siding has some different installation requirements. It is heavier and produces a lot of fine dust when it is cut. When using a circular saw, fiber-cement siding should always be cut outdoors in well-ventilated areas using a blade designed specifically for fiber-cement dust reduction, such as the four-tooth polycrystalline, diamond-tipped Hardiblade. Mechanical shears are convenient and necessary for irregular cuts, but they can crush the fiber and cut only one board at a time. The guillotine or shear cutters also tend to crush the board more than a diamond-tipped blade.

Fiber cement is more brittle than wood, and some manufacturers may recom-mend predrilling of fastener holes near the edges if hand-nailed. Fasteners should be hot-dipped galvanized or stainless steel and penetrate the framing a minimum of 1¼ inch (32 mm) for nails and ¾ inch (19 mm) for screws. Staples are *not* rec-ommended. (Steel studs should be minimum 20-gauge, at 16 inches (400 mm) on center. Screws should have a minimum three-thread engagement.) Care must be taken to ensure good anchorage. Some contractors prefer to use roofing nails with the larger head, especially if blind nailing. Fasteners are to be ⅜ inch (10 mm) from the edge of the fiber-cement board, and a ⅛ inch (3 mm) gap should be main-tained between the board ends. Nails should not be angled, meaning the construction tolerances are very tight when nailing to the 1½-inch (38 mm) face of a wood stud. Nails have no purchase in the fiber cement, so all fasteners need to have solid backing. Some manufacturers provide a metal joiner for butt joints between studs.

Blind fastening of lap siding allows for differential movement of the siding. The stud and furring spacing should be limited to 16 inches (400 mm) on center. Blind fastening is not permitted by some manufacturers for the wider siding boards. In areas where wind uplift may be a problem, face nailing is recommended. Siding should overlap a minimum of 1¼ inch (32 mm).

8.13 MAINTENANCE

Fiber-cement siding must be repainted and the sealant replaced just like any other sidings of wood or wood products. Because it is dimensionally stable and more moisture resistant than wood or other wood products, it should require repainting less frequently. A factory-applied high quality primer, careful priming of all cut edges, careful sealing at joints, and two, high-quality topcoats should assure a long-lasting finish.

8.14 CONCERNS WITH FIBER-CEMENT CLADDINGS

Fiber-cement siding is a good, economical choice for low-rise buildings. It is more durable than hardboard siding and more dimensionally stable than wood siding. Installation can be more difficult than with wood for those not used to working with the material. And while a poor installation may not cause the fiber-cement siding to fail, the appearance may suffer. As one builder commented, "When extreme care is taken in installation,... [fiber cement sidings] can look really good —so good that you will not be able to tell that it is not real wood. When improperly installed,... [fiber cement sidings] can look horrible, like any other poorly installed siding materials, but at least it won't rot!"[31] The concerns with cutting and installing fiber-cement are usually expressed in comparison with wood. This is a cement-based material, which is why it lasts so long, but it requires a slightly different set of skills and tools. As builders become more familiar with the product, the installation problems and costs should decrease. "Working with new materials requires patience and an open mind. Everything doesn't work as easily as wood," notes Paul Fissette, director of building materials and wood technology, University of Massachusetts, Amherst.[32]

Another concern is the production of dust containing silica, as it can be a hazard when the material is cut or drilled using improper methods and tools. (Silica is a very common mineral found in concrete, tiles, brick, and glass, as well as fiber cement.) Just as with the other building products, the silica in fiber cement is encapsulated within the product and poses no problems before or after installation. Manufacturers provide extensive information on eliminating the health hazards during installation that should be closely followed. New equipment, including more saws that create less dust and longer lasting saw blades, is being developed to meet these concerns.

8.15 DETAILS: FIBER-CEMENT SIDING

Fiber-cement siding attached to a light wood-frame wall with a drainage cavity is detailed in Figures 8.18–8.20. The details are based on a low-rise building located in a mixed climate with high exposure to rain.

TYPICAL FOR ALL SIDING DETAILS
Mixed Climate

Water Barrier:
Non-perforated SBPO

Vapor Retarder:
Vapor retardant paint

Air Barrier:
Non-perforated, sealed SBPO

Insulation:
Fiberglass batt

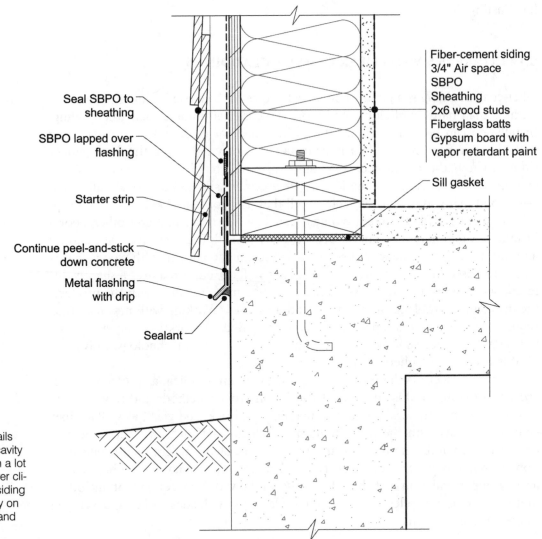

Seal SBPO to sheathing

SBPO lapped over flashing

Starter strip

Continue peel-and-stick down concrete

Metal flashing with drip

Sealant

Fiber-cement siding
3/4" Air space
SBPO
Sheathing
2x6 wood studs
Fiberglass batts
Gypsum board with vapor retardant paint

Sill gasket

FIGURE 8.18 These details show a ¾-inch drainage cavity appropriate for areas with a lot of wind-driven rain. In dryer climates, the cement-fiber siding would be installed directly on the SBPO building wrap and sheathing.

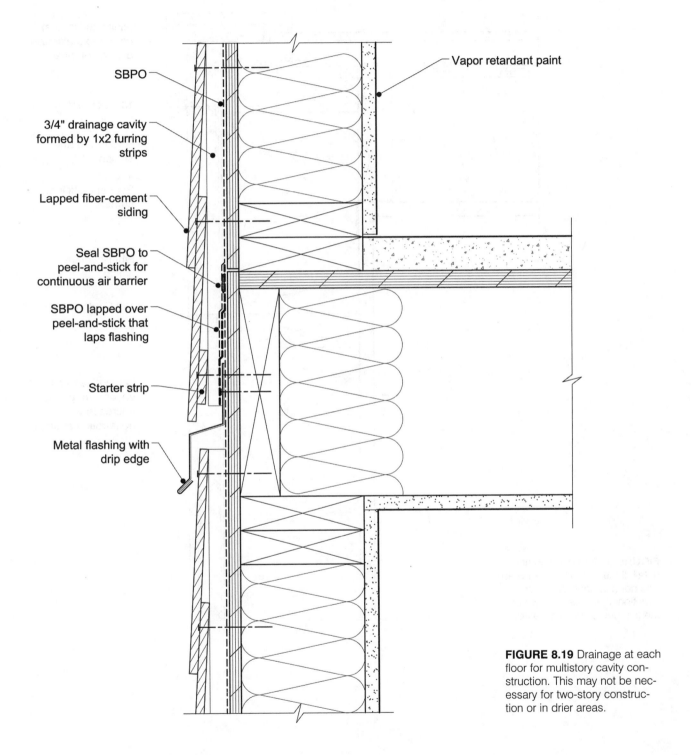

SBPO

3/4" drainage cavity
formed by 1x2 furring
strips

Lapped fiber-cement
siding

Seal SBPO to
peel-and-stick for
continuous air barrier

SBPO lapped over
peel-and-stick that
laps flashing

Starter strip

Metal flashing with
drip edge

Vapor retardant paint

FIGURE 8.19 Drainage at each
floor for multistory cavity construction. This may not be necessary for two-story construction or in drier areas.

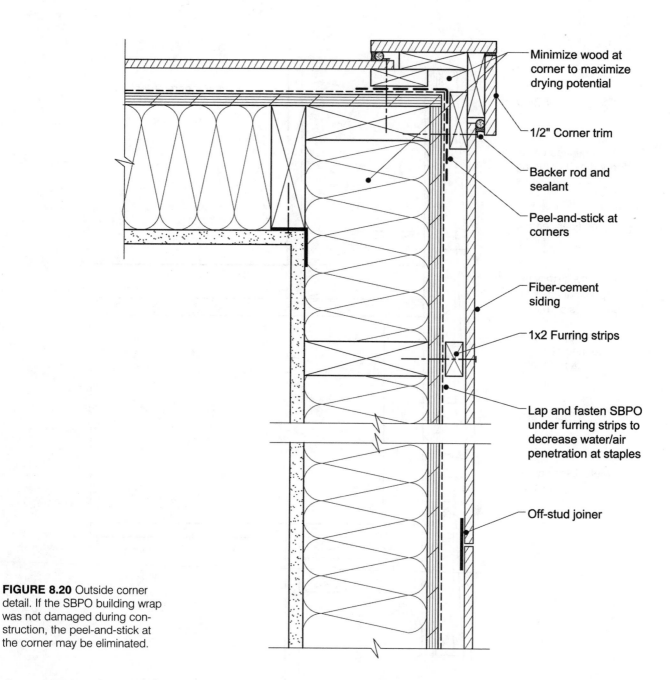

Minimize wood at corner to maximize drying potential

1/2" Corner trim

Backer rod and sealant

Peel-and-stick at corners

Fiber-cement siding

1x2 Furring strips

Lap and fasten SBPO under furring strips to decrease water/air penetration at staples

Off-stud joiner

FIGURE 8.20 Outside corner detail. If the SBPO building wrap was not damaged during construction, the peel-and-stick at the corner may be eliminated.

8.16 CASE STUDY

MDO PLYWOOD PANELS AND CEDAR SIDING

Site: Olympic College, Shelton Campus, Phase I
Shelton, Washington
Architect: Miller/Hull Partnership, LLP
Design team: Bob Hull, Scott Wolf, Sian Roberts, and Norm Strong
Owner: Olympic College
General contractor: Construction Enterprises and Contractors, Inc.

FIGURES 8.21–8.28 Photos and original drawings courtesy of the Miller/Hull Partnership.

FIGURE 8.22

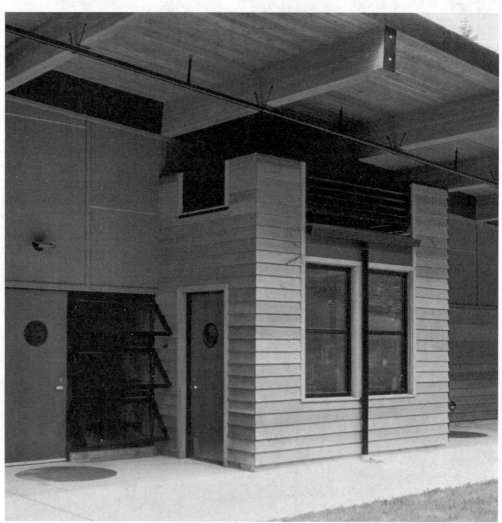

FIGURE 8.23

The Olympic College, Shelton Campus, located on a wooded site, is guided by environmentally conscious strategies in site planning and building design and through its use of locally produced wood materials. Local manufacturers in this timber-based economic area in western Washington donated glue-laminated beams, tongue-and-groove decking, and cedar siding for use in the Phase I building. Miller/Hull used these resources to create an environmentally responsible building within a very limited budget.

The 8,000-square-foot Phase I building responds to the scale of an anticipated 20,000-square-foot Phase II building with a roof that slopes up toward the main entrance, giving the project a larger "presence" than its size suggests (Figure 8.21).[33] At the opposite end, a day-care center, with its covered play area screened by a latticework of wood covered with translucent panels, acts as a large lantern in the forest. Instructional spaces and individual faculty and student offices are organized along a south-facing, 14-foot (4.3 m) wide, covered but open-air walkway that looks out to the adjacent forest (Figure 8.22).

This project met the community's requirements for the beginnings of this satellite college. It adhered to a very tight budget, with a building that makes an environmental statement, and won an American Institute of Architects National Honor Award. Less obvious accomplishments are the small, cost-effective details that contribute to the aesthetic design but also enhance the durability of the exterior wall. Three such examples are the protection of the ends of the glue-laminated beams, the metal corner trim for the cedar siding, and the medium-density overlay (MDO) plywood cladding.

Situating the corridor on the exterior of the building provides much more efficient use of the square footage in this temperate climate (the net to gross square footage is 92 percent). Not only does the broad overhang, created with the cantilevered glue-laminated beams, protect the occupants from the weather, it also protects the exterior wall. A slight overhang of the roof, in addition to a ½-inch (12 mm) steel plate over a membrane, protects the end of each glue-laminated

FIGURE 8.24

FIGURE 8.25

FIGURE 8.26

beam (Figures 8.23 and 8.27). Ends of glue-laminated beams are often left exposed, sometimes with disastrous results as water enters the end grain of the wood.

The donated horizontal, beveled cedar siding is used sparingly at the base and at the projecting office boxes to bring the warmth of the wood roof to a human scale. Turning corners with beveled wood siding is a challenge. The easiest solution is to use vertical corner trim boards, but this is not always the desired aesthetic.

Mitering beveled siding is difficult. The cut is a double miter and the joints usually open up, even if initially glued or sealed, creating both a durability and an appearance problem. Miller/Hull's design of a simple metal corner flashing provides a watertight corner. The siding is installed with a ⅛-inch (3 mm) gap between the flashing and the end of the siding, which is then sealed. The prefinished, black metal flashing creates a crisp corner that will be maintained even as the wood inevitably shrinks and swells (Figures 8.24, 8.25, and 8.28).

Engineered wood products stretch natural wood resources and are usually less costly. The budget required an inexpensive cladding for the remainder of the building. This was accomplished with a manufactured wood sheathing—painted MDO (medium-density overlay), exterior-grade plywood. The water resistance of the material is very good. Careful detailing of horizontal metal Z-flashing at the staggered horizontal joints directs any water to the exterior at the bottom of each panel. Typically measuring 4 feet by 7 feet (1.2 x 2.1 meters), the panels maintain

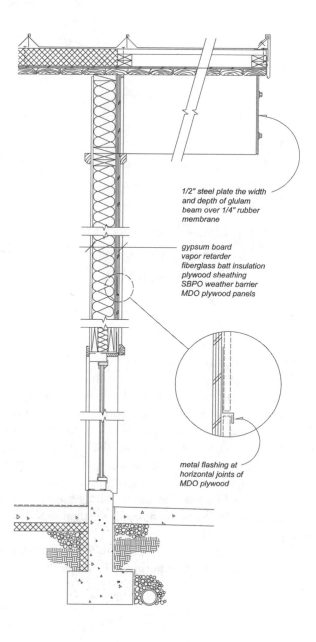

1/2" steel plate the width
and depth of glulam
beam over 1/4" rubber
membrane

gypsum board
vapor retarder
fiberglass batt insulation
plywood sheathing
SBPO weather barrier
MDO plywood panels

metal flashing at
horizontal joints of
MDO plywood

FIGURE 8.27 Wall section showing horizontal joint between medium-density overlay (MDO) panels and protection of glue-laminated beams.

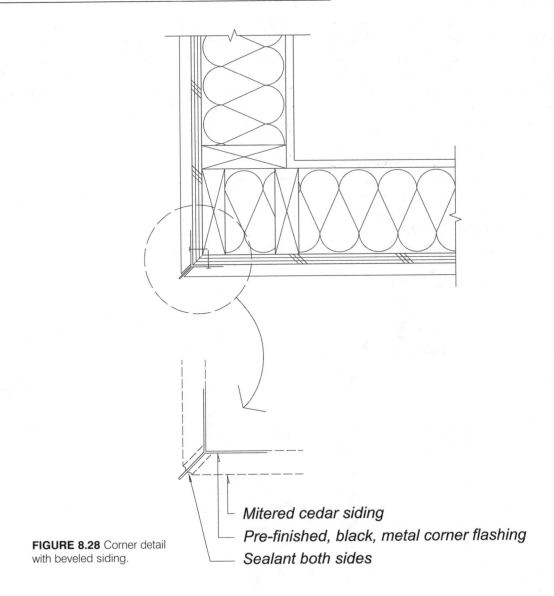

FIGURE 8.28 Corner detail with beveled siding.

Mitered cedar siding
Pre-finished, black, metal corner flashing
Sealant both sides

a module carried throughout the building. The MDO panels are surface-fastened, creating a finely articulated pattern. The ½ inch (12 mm) hex-headed screws have integral rubber and metal washers to seal out water. The panels are edge-nailed, and then covered with painted, vertical wood battens (Figures 8.26 and 8.27).

Overlaid plywood has a lower vapor permeance than nonoverlaid. (According to APA, the Engineered Wood Association, the permeance of ⅜ inch exterior plywood, with no surface finish, is 0.8 perms compared to 0.3 perms for the same plywood with MDO on one side.[34]) This should be considered when determining the placement of vapor retarders and the water management system. For more exposed areas, construction of a drainage cavity with vertical wood battens would increase the longevity of this panel siding.

This project, like the case study in Section 7.12, shows how simple materials, when combined with thoughtful detailing, can create both a durable and aesthetically pleasing facade.

8.17 REFERENCES

WOOD FRAME CONSTRUCTION

Print Sources

1. Canada Mortgage and Housing Corporation (CMHC), *Wood Frame Envelopes, Best Practice Guide: Building Technology* (Ottawa, Ont.: CMHC, 1999).

2. Canada Mortgage and Housing Corporation (CMHC), *Wood Frame Envelopes in the Coastal Climate of British Columbia, Best Practice Guide: Building Technology* (Ottawa, Ont.: CMHC, 2001).

These Best Practice Guides contain detailing for stucco and vinyl siding:

3. Joseph W. Lstiburek and John Carmody, *Moisture Control Handbook: Principles and Practices for Residential and Small Commercial Buildings* (New York: John Wiley & Sons, Inc. 1994). See update from Lstiburek at http:// www.buildingscience.com

4. Joseph W. Lstiburek and John Carmody, "Controlling Moisture in Mixed Climates," *Journal of Light Construction* (August 1997).

5. Lstiburek, Joseph W., *Builder's Guide to Mixed Climates: Details for Design and Construction.* (Newtown, Conn.: Taunton Press, 2000).

Also available from Taunton Press: "Mixed-Humid Climate," "Hot-Dry/Mixed-Dry Climate," "Hot-Humid Climate," and "Cold Climate."

Online Sources

1. American Wood Council, http://www.awc.org

2. Building Science Corporation, http://www.buildingscience.com

3. Canada Mortgage and Housing Corporation, http://www.cmhc.ca

4. Canadian Wood Council, http://www.cwc.ca

5. Engineered Wood Association (APA), http://www.apawood.org

6. Journal of Light Construction, http://www.jlconline.com

7. National Association of Home Builders, http://www.nahb.org

8. Partnership for Advancing Technology in Housing, http://www.pathnet.org PATH, a private-public effort, is managed and supported by the Department of Housing and Urban Development (HUD). Other partners include the Department of Energy and Commerce, Environmental Protection Agency (EPA), and the Federal Emergency Management Agency (FEMA).

STUCCO

Print Sources

1. Portland Cement Association, *Portland Cement Plaster/Stucco Manual*, 5th ed. (Skokie, Ill.: Portland Cement Association, 2003).

2. Northwest Wall and Ceiling Bureau (NWCB), *Stucco Resource Guide*, 3rd ed. (Seattle, Wash.: NWCB, 1997).

3. British Columbia Wall and Ceiling Association (BCWCA), *Portland Cement Plaster/Stucco Resource Guide 2003 Edition* (Vancouver, B.C.: BCWCA, 2003).

4. McCoy, Dennis, "A Close Look at Stucco," *Journal of Light Construction* (September 2003).

5. Francesco J. Spagna and Stephen S. Ruggiero, "Stucco Cladding—Lessons Learned From Problematic Facades," *Performance of Exterior Building Walls*, ASTM STP 1422 (West Conshohocken, Pa.: 2003).

Online Sources
1. Portland Cement Association, http://www.cement.org

2. Northwest Wall and Ceiling Bureau, http://www.nwcb.org

3. British Columbia Wall and Ceiling Association, http://www.bcwca.org

4. Association of Wall and Ceiling Industries, http://www.awci.org

5. Stucco Manufacturers Association (SMA), a trade association that promotes three-coat colored cementitious stucco, http://www.stuccomfgassoc.com

SIDINGS

Print Sources
1. Tim Uhler, "Installing Fiber-Cement Siding," *Journal of Light Construction* (December 2003).

2. Martin Holladay, "Builder's Guide to Vinyl Siding," *Journal of Light Construction* (June 2000).

3. Engineered Wood Association (APA), "HDO/MDO Plywood: Product Guide" (Tacoma, Wash.: APA, 2002).

Online Sources
1. Engineered Wood Association (APA), http://www.apawood.org

2. James Hardie Building Products, http://www.jameshardie.com

3. Vinyl Siding Institute, http://www.vinylsiding.org

PART III

ADVANCING THE ENVELOPE

IT IS NOT THE ORDINARY WALL THAT CATCHES OUR ATTENTION. Even those with careful detailing may not engage us in the first reading. It is the extraordinary wall that captures our interest. A wall may be extraordinary in form, in materials, or in its failures.

Design is advanced by experimenting with forms and materials and by examining failures. All of the materials used in the exterior wall have gone through periods of invention and have sustained failures. This process will continue with existing materials and those not yet developed. By understanding the constraints and the opportunities of the successful and the not-so-successful walls, the designer begins to develop a sense of when to advance the envelope and when caution is appropriate.

These issues are discussed in Part III. Successes and failures of cladding systems are investigated within the parameters of time, culture, and economics. The thin wall, the thick wall, and the double wall are explored. Also included are studies of the wall as a painter's canvas and cases where the wall and the roof are indistinguishable. The very ordinary construction of light wood framing is discussed in terms of durability and sustainability. An endemic failure of condominiums is contrasted with two houses that work—one in Hokkaido, Japan, and the other in Vancouver, British Columbia.

Terra-Cotta, EIFS, Stone, and Brick: Are They Durable?

9.1 TRUTH IN MATERIALS

What we venerate as "durable" materials, such as marble and terra-cotta, may prove otherwise under certain circumstances. Exterior Insulation and Finish System (EIFS), as with any cladding system, can be designed as an economical choice, when the life cycle cost is considered, or as an expensive failure. Brick veneer may appear to have stabilized, but continuous moisture growth and a period of abornormally high temperatures can cause additional differential movement that threatens life-safety long after the problems were first noted. Cladding materials are neither good nor bad; it is how they are detailed and constructed that determines a cladding's success or failure. This chapter discusses the durability of terra-cotta, EIFS, stone, and brick.

Vernacular design uses local materials, detailed to meet local climatic conditions and aesthetic intentions. The search for imitative materials began when the simple constraints of vernacular architecture were abandoned. The facade of public buildings, in particular, required materials such as stone that gives the building and society, an impression of stability. Shortage (or expense) of materials necessitated the production of less expensive and sometimes imitative substitutes. An early example of imitation can be found on brick buildings in Rome. Brick, a much-used vernacular material as clay beds are usually plentiful, did not always produce the desired "look." Where brick was not deemed an appropriate "face," other materials were substituted. The Roman emperor Augustus (69 BC–27 AD) is alleged to have found Rome a city of brick and left it a city of marble. This may be in reference to the common practice during this period of cladding brick structures with marble.[1] During the early nineteenth century, many of the brick buildings in London were stuccoed and lined to resemble stones. John Nash, the architect responsible, is claimed to have found a city of "all brick" and left it a city of "all plaster."[2] These two examples are from times when stone was the preferred material for public buildings, but when economics did not allow for the use of stone as the structure, in the first case, or as cladding, in the second case.

There is much discussion about "truth" in materials, about an architecture of "reality," especially as it relates to surface design.[3] We want materials that are recognizable, that have a sense of permanency, that transcend style—that is, materials that are enhanced rather than diminished by time. We do not want to be deceived. "Architectural deceit" was defined by John Ruskin in 1848 as "the suggestion of a mode of structure or support, other than the true one; ...the painting of surfaces to represent some other material than that of which they actually consist; ...and...the use of cast or machine-made ornaments of any kind."[4] Michael Benedikt, in *For an Architecture of Reality,* states that "technically speaking, a material is fake when it displays some but not all of the qualities of the material we take it to be."[5] In particular, Benedikt explains that "veneers are fake if and when they suggest solidity and consistency of material throughout the piece."[6]

Ruskin and Benedikt also discuss certain exceptions for veneers. Ruskin, in his chapter, "The Lamp of Truth," writes that "it is well known, that what is meant by a church's being built of marble is, in nearly all cases, only that a veneering of marble has been fastened on the rough brick wall."[7] Ruskin was most likely speaking of his colleagues, not the general public, for whom it may have come as a surprise that the marble was only a thin cladding, just as many today are unaware that the brick on a building is only cladding, serving a purpose similar to that of vinyl siding. Benedikt allows for veneers that express the structure by using the material in a thickness that pays homage to the material. But he states that materials that have no tactile, visual, or kinesthetic qualities or are not what they appear to be should not be used.[8] EIFS and historic terra-cotta would likely fail these tests for authenticity in materials. But so would a great number of other materials, including many brick and stone claddings. And whether they are "authentic" or not has little to do with their durability.

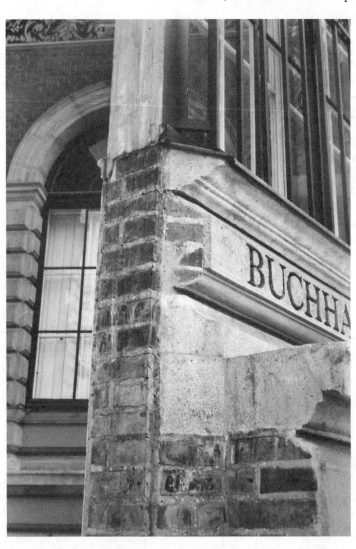

FIGURE 9.1 What appears to be stone is merely brick and concrete rendered to look like stone on this nineteenth-century wall section that was removed from a building during its restoration. Note that the window sill is flashed with metal. Photo by Linda Brock.

9.2 THE GREAT IMPOSTORS: EIFS AND TERRA-COTTA

What do terra-cotta and EIFS have in common? EIFS in the 1980s and terra-cotta at the end of the nineteenth century were marketed as economical solutions to emerging problems. And both were great impostors—they could be made to look like almost anything. Economics, styles of ornamentation, and building codes each played a role in the popularity of these claddings.

At the end of the nineteenth century, a new, "fire-proof" material was required to clad the new skyscrapers, or "sky-supporters" and "cloud-scrapers," as they were originally called.[9] During the latter part of the twentieth century, the 1970s oil embargo brought about concerns over the expenditure of energy, and the result was an emphasis on adding insulation to buildings. In addition to meeting the code requirements regarding fire in the case of terra-cotta and energy in the case of EIFS, weight and cost, as always, were preoccupations in the development of these claddings.

9.2.1 Terra-Cotta

The emergence of steel, "skeletal" frames, coupled with the invention of the elevator, gave rise to increasingly higher buildings. Earlier load-bearing masonry buildings, such as the Monadnock Building, Chicago (designed by Burnham and Root, 1889–1891), with its 6-foot (1830 mm) base, tapering to an 18-inch (457 mm) wall at the 28th story, were no longer economical. (See Figure 9.2.) The new steel frame needed a new cladding that was lightweight (complementing the lightweight structure), inexpensive, and met the fire code requirements. This was the era of the "fireproof" building, following catastrophic fires in Chicago (1871) and Boston (1872). What better material than terra-cotta? Its first use as fireproofing in New York was on the Potter Building, built in 1886. The round cast-iron columns were surrounded with four curved pieces of terra-cotta that were hollow on the interior.[10] Later, pieces were designed to carefully surround the new steel I- and W- shaped columns and beams. The backup wall on the early high-rises was usually of masonry. This was prompted partially by codes that were still concerned with fire and that required a minimum thickness for curtain walls. In New York City, the revised 1892 codes listed a minimum of 12 inches (300 mm) of noncombustible material for the top 50 feet (15.2 meters), with 4 inches (100 mm) added for each 50 feet below.[11] Thus the curtain wall at the base of a 200-foot (61 meter) high building would be 2 feet (600 mm) thick.

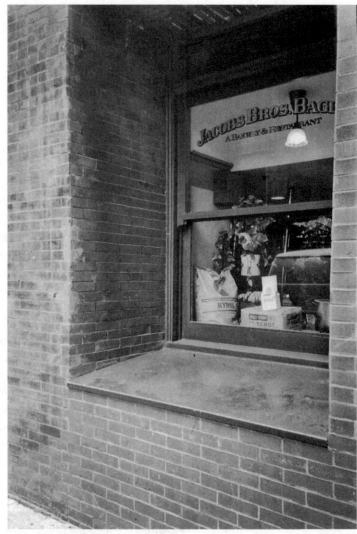

FIGURE 9.2 The walls at the base of the load-bearing brick Monadnock Building (Burnham and Root, 1889–1891) are close to six feet deep. The metal sill has protected the solid masonry below for over a century. Photo by Linda Brock.

With the new polychrome glazes, the fired-clay of terra-cotta could be made to replicate any stone or other material the architect desired. When compared with stone, particularly if the stone was intricately carved, terra-cotta was more economical and lighter-weight. Construction began on Burnham and Root's Reliance Building (Chicago, 1890–1895) a year after the Monadnock, to which it bears a striking resemblance in form. But the facade is very different. It appears much lighter, designed with more glass than was possible with the punched windows of masonry walls. The white terra-cotta shimmers in the sun, further emphasizing the light weight of the curtain wall. Terra-cotta was perceived as a modern, durable cladding that required little maintenance. The cladding on the Reliance Building was described in the 1894 *Economist* as "an innovation. It is indestructible and as hard and as smooth as any porcelain ware. It will be washed by every rainstorm and may if necessary be scrubbed like a dinner plate."[12] Unfortunately, the Reliance Building facade was showing distress by the 1920s. In 1994–1995, the entire curtain wall—terra-cotta and windows—was restored. The original terra-cotta cornice, which was torn off in the 1940s, was replaced with a cast aluminum replica. Boston Valley Terra Cotta produced 2,030 new hand-pressed terra-cotta pieces from 225 new molds. Another 1,000 pieces of the original 14,300 terra-cotta pieces were removed and reattached. The original anchoring system was replicated, using stainless steel fittings in place of the wrought iron.[13]

Clad with terra-cotta, a building could resemble an ancient temple constructed of granite for a fraction of the cost and far removed from its precedent in both distance and time. A negative plaster mold was made of clay or a wood reproduction of ornate stone carvings. Clay was then pressed by hand into the plaster mold. As the clay dried, it shrank. It was removed from the mold, and the piece was "burnished" to provide a dense outer surface. Glazes were applied and the piece was fired in a kiln. (As the clay body also shrinks significantly during the firing, the molds must be sized accordingly. The glazes and slips must "fit" the clay body, as they shrink at a different rate than the clay body during firing.) This is called hand-pressed terra-cotta and was popular until the 1920s, when production of the less expensive, and more modern, extruded pieces began. Producing hand-pressed terra-cotta was (and is) extremely skill-dependent, perhaps more so than any other manufactured product that relies on the skills of individuals for quality.

The United States National Bank in Portland, Oregon (designed by A. E. Doyle, 1917–1925), based on a Roman temple, is a good example of hand-pressed terra-cotta.[14] (See Figures 9.3 and 9.4.) The building, including the 54-foot (16.5 m) Corinthian columns, is clad in terra-cotta with a light pinkish-gray, matte finish. Gladding McBean and Company (the only manufacturer of the period still in production today) developed the glaze, which very closely replicates granite, for this particular project. The columns were described at the time as "symbolizing 'the soaring power of finance in a wealthy civilization.'"[15] Doyle also designed the Bank of California (1925) across the street, but this time the style was Italian Renaissance Palatial clad with a sandy-pink, glazed terra-cotta.[16] Gladding McBean

FIGURES 9.3 AND 9.4 United States National Bank in Portland, Oregon (A. E. Doyle, 1917–1925), based on a Roman temple, is a good example of hand-pressed terra-cotta. The building, including the 54-foot Corinthian columns, is clad in terra-cotta with a light pinkish-gray, matte finish. Gladding, McBean and Company developed the glaze, which very closely replicates granite, specifically for this project. See Virginia Guest Ferriday, *Last of the Handmade Buildings: Glazed Terra Cotta in Downtown Portland* (Portland, Ore.: Mark Pub., 1984), 25. Photos by Linda Brock.

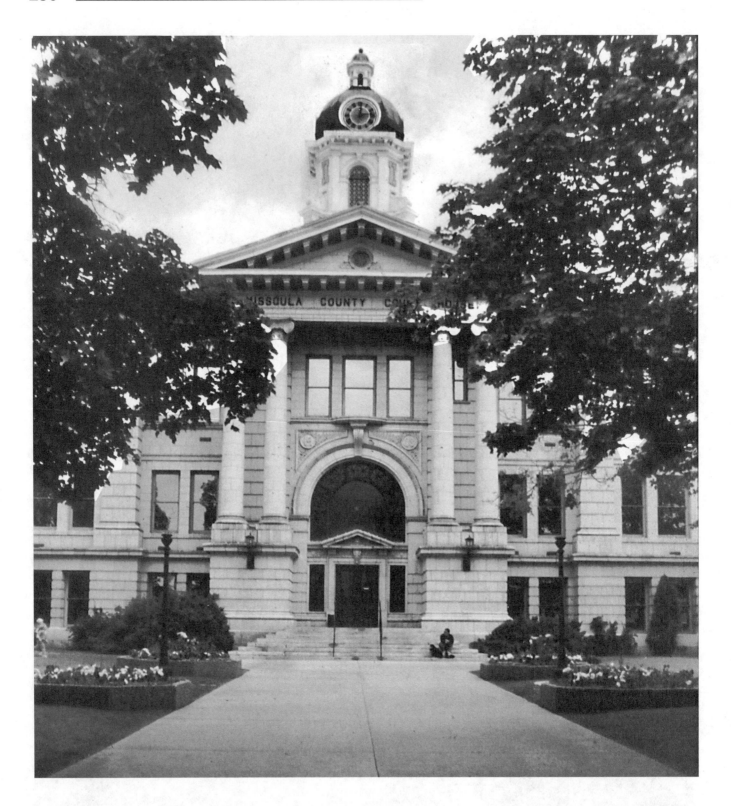

FIGURES 9.5, 9.6, 9.7 At the beginning of the twentieth century, cities and towns across the United States were clad with stock and custom terra-cotta, resembling everything from sandstone to Carrara marble. Terra-cotta allowed smaller communities on the rail lines, such as Missoula, Montana, to have their own great "stone" courthouses. Spalled areas (Figure 9.7) offer one of the clues that this is not granite, which it closely resembles. For those who could not afford terra-cotta and where fire codes were not a problem, the same look could be acquired with painted sheet metal, albeit with substantially less durability and higher maintenance. Photos by Linda Brock and G. Russell Heliker.

FIGURE 9.7

FIGURE 9.6

did not produce this terra-cotta, and the granite imitation is not the quality of the U.S. National Bank.

Although we like to view terra-cotta as a durable cladding, made of a substantial material, it has seen its share of failures, as noted with the Reliance Building. Because of the historic value and beauty of buildings clad with terra-cotta, they are often restored at extraordinary expense. If it is not feasible to reproduce or repair the terra-cotta pieces, other materials—from fiberglass resin to precast concrete—are substituted.

The failure mechanism for historic terra-cotta was water entry from the outside. While the glazed face of the terra-cotta may have been waterproof, the joints between the units were not. And the glazed face was only waterproof as long as it did not crack or craze. If the glazed skin was not bound tightly to the clay body,

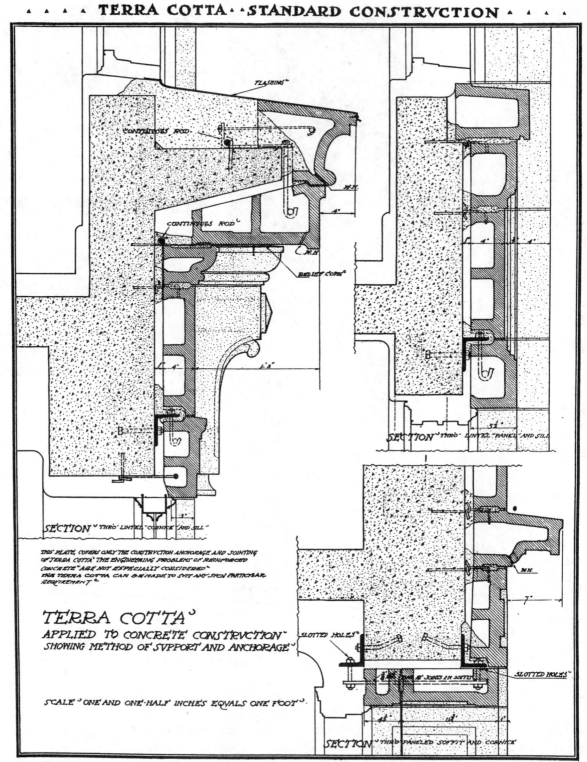

FIGURE 9.8 The 1927 revised edition of *Terra Cotta: Standard Construction,* published by the National Terra Cotta Society, noted several "important" changes, including the addition of flashing and drips, provisions for expansion joints, recognition of volume changes of concrete structures, and corrosion protection of anchoring systems. Illustration courtesy of Gladding McBean and Company.

expansion of the clay would result in cracking or crazing of the glaze. Once this occurred, the freeze-thaw of water within the cracks accelerated the process. Corrosion of the metal connectors would also cause expansion and cracking of the terra-cotta piece. As the mortar joint that separated the units broke down, water entered behind the terra-cotta, corroding the anchor and its attachment. Although some drawings from this period called for "nonrusting" metals to be used for the ties, it was generally mild steel or wrought iron that attached the terra-cotta to the building. Lateral forces make these marginally attached or nonattached pieces very susceptible to failure, particularly with the high wind loads found on upper stories. Sometimes it is only the friction at the mortar joint or the adhesion of remedial sealant that keeps the pieces in place on older facades. Drainage of the cavity behind the terra-cotta, if there was a cavity, was typically not part of the design. Generally, little thought was given to differential movement.

The Woolworth Building (designed by Cass Gilbert, 1913), located near New York City's City Hall, was touted as a "Temple of Commerce." At just under 800 feet, it was the world's tallest building until 1931. But problems were noted with the terra-cotta cladding before the construction was even complete, according to the Ehrenkrantz Group, the architectural firm in charge of the restoration.[17] With no allowance for differential expansion between the frame, the backup wall of fired-clay masonry, and the terra-cotta (coupled with extensive cracking and crazing of the glazing), problems were inevitable. By 1978, continuous pointing, caulking, and patching of the facade was not keeping pace with the deterioration. The patches were also unsightly. A restoration team inspected each of the nearly 400,000 terra-cotta pieces for cracks that might be indicative of more serious problems. Restoration of the "structural integrity of the cladding and ornament" in order to "ensure street safety" was the primary consideration of Woolworth's management.[18] Furthermore, they wanted a solution that could be replicated in the event of future failures. Wiss, Janney, Elstner Associates, the consulting engineers, designed a retrofit that would safely secure the cladding while balancing accurate preservation with economics. The surfaces of some pieces were repaired in place and some were reanchored with stainless steel pins set in epoxy; but 26,000 terra-cotta pieces had to be replaced. (See Figures 9.10–9.13.) The cost of terra-cotta replacements in the 1980s was prohibitive. After exploring and testing "dozens of materials and coatings," a dense concrete was developed specifically for the project that closely matched the color of the glazed terra-cotta. New plaster models were produced for decorative pieces, using rubber forms pulled from the existing terra-cotta pieces on the building. The plaster models were fine-tuned to sharpen profiles and to hold critical dimensions. Production molds were then made using various combinations of cast rubber, wood, metal, and fiberglass. Simple flat or corner units were measured and production forms made accordingly. A surface coating on the concrete, with added color, produced a similar reflectivity to the original and reduced water absorption.[19] The final rehabilitation of the cladding cost more than the construction of the original building, but a landmark was restored.

FIGURE 9.9 Drawing of the Woolworth Building (Cass Gilbert, 1913), from a postcard. The caption on the postcard read, "The Cathedral of Commerce... the tallest and most beautiful office building in the world. (Height 792 feet 1 inch—sixty stories)."

FIGURE 9.10

FIGURE 9.11

FIGURE 9.12

FIGURE 9.13

FIGURE 9.10–9.13 During restoration of the Woolworth Building, 26,000 terra-cotta units had to be replaced. As hand-pressed terra-cotta was too costly, a dense concrete unit was developed that closely matched the variegated creamy glaze of the original. Figure 9.11 shows the steel grid that was used in areas where several pieces were replaced. Figures 9.12 and 9.13 show the fitting of new concrete units with original terra-cotta pieces. The color matching followed the fitting. Figure 9.13 shows the new concrete units before the surface coating was added. Photos by Timothy Allanbrook, courtesy of Wiss, Janney, Elstner & Associates, Inc., and Ehrenkrantz, Eckstut & Kuhn Architects.

9.2.2 EXTERIOR INSULATION AND FINISH SYSTEMS (EIFS)

In the 1980s, EIFS offered a cost-effective solution to increasing energy code requirements. In addition to providing insulation on the exterior of the wall, where it was most effective, the insulation could be carved with a hot wire or molded into elaborate Corinthian columns, if one so desired. Just as with terra-cotta, the color palette was immense and the cost was right. It was often the cladding of choice for residential projects, from single-family homes to multifamily developments, easily producing popular postmodern detailing with little added expense. The "finish" stopped all water from entering the wall. The idea of a cladding that needed little maintenance and completely sealed out the rain was attractive to the general public, as well as to designers.

However, just as with terra-cotta, it did not always work that way. Water got in from a myriad of sources due to poor detailing. One of the first notable failures was the EIFS-clad public housing projects in Massachusetts in the 1980s. The systems were usually face-sealed and applied over a backup wall of gypsum sheathing on steel studs. As water entered the wall, the paper face of the sheathing delaminated, and the studs and fasteners corroded. Kenney Associates, with the cooperation of the Department of Housing and Urban Development (HUD), investigated 50 residential and nonresidential projects clad with EIFS during this period. Paper-faced gypsum sheathing was the substrate for the majority of the projects. A visual survey of the EIFS surface indicated that 73 percent had cracks large enough to allow water ingress, which may partially be accounted for by the fact that the base coat on 64 percent of the buildings was less thick than the manufacturer's standard. The sealant had failed on 52 percent.[20]

In the 1990s, the notable failures were on wood-framed, detached houses in Wilmington, North Carolina, with its hot and humid summers and mild but often wet winters. The failure mechanism was similar—water got into the stud cavity. Drying to the interior, where there was a 6-mil polyethylene vapor retarder, was limited. The water entered through "window frames and accessories, missing or incorrect roof/wall flashings, and faulty or missing sealants," according to building scientist Rick Quirouette, who investigated the failures. He further stated, "We have not yet found any cases of moisture problems due to rain penetration through the face of the EIFS cladding."[21] But to the general public, this was an EIFS failure.

As with failures of any cladding system, the question of liability arises. The cost of the failure may be borne by the owners, builders, suppliers and manufacturers, designers, general public, or a combination. If there is a dispute, legal fees often increase this cost substantially. Bad publicity and problems obtaining warranties and liability insurance are also consequences. When the backup wall is masonry, some moisture in the wall will be tolerated. But steel studs with paper-faced gypsum sheathing or wood studs with wood sheathing offer little resistance, especially where there is high exposure to wind-driven rain. They cannot tolerate additional moisture for long periods of time. Mold and mildew can be problems, feeding off the paper of the gypsum sheathing or the wood sheathing and framing.

To a lesser degree, water can enter at base coats delaminated from the insulation and at cracks in the lamina.[22] A Canada Mortgage and Housing Corporaton (CMHC) study showed that after moisture ingress, most problems were due to impact damage of the lamina and coatings that were not the required minimum thickness.[23] Kenney states that nearly 80 percent of the samples tested had a base coat thickness "substantially" less than that required by the specifications.[24] Although there is little evidence to show that a thin coat promotes water entry, a thin coat is more likely to crack and less likely to encapsulate the mesh. Another study, referring to HUD standards, noted thin base coats, exposed mesh, sealant failure, and cracking at V-shaped reveals, openings, and board joints.[25] These all point to problems with the installation of the EIFS, not with the EIFS product.

9.2.3 LESSONS LEARNED FROM TERRA-COTTA AND EIFS FAILURES

Some of the problems with historic terra-cotta are shared with EIFS-clad buildings. The simple lessons of these failures are as follows:

- Water will get beyond the face of any cladding, and it needs a path to get back out.
- Face-sealed barrier walls are risky even if the backup wall and structure can withstand moisture.
- Materials will move differently based on moisture content and thermal expansion.
- Proper installation and the use of systems from reputable manufacturers are critical.

Water will enter the wall usually at failed joints, transitions, and openings. All materials that might encounter moisture must be corrosion and rot resistant. Differential air pressures will "drive" water through the wall, if not mitigated by a good air barrier system. And even the best design, using the most durable materials, will fail if not constructed properly.

The other issue is one of life safety. This is where EIFS has a clear advantage. EIFS failures do not pose life-safety hazards as serious as failures with heavier claddings, such as terra-cotta, stone, or anchored brick veneer. One EIFS manufacturer even advertises that rock and brick "hurt when it fell [assuming these are claddings of the past] on you," but EIFS "doesn't hurt at all." The higher the building, the greater the exposure and the more likely a failure will occur. With heavy claddings, this can become a catastrophic failure.

9.2.4 THE FUTURE OF TERRA-COTTA CLADDINGS

Terra-cotta—literally, baked earth—is a durable and aesthetically pleasing material, when used properly. Relating to a masonry past, it has recently generated interest as a contemporary cladding system. Terra-cotta is still available as a hand-pressed cladding with minimum 1-inch (25 mm) thick walls. The units are a minimum depth of 4 inches (100 mm). These custom pieces are used in both new construction and historical restoration projects. Gladding McBean has produced such architectural terra-cotta continuously since 1875. These are not inexpensive cladding systems, but they are durable. Newer methods of attachment use stainless-steel fittings and anchors. Today terra-cotta is a recognized material—it has a beauty of its own that cannot be replicated. Often hand-pressed terra-cotta pieces are used as decorative elements (for example, door or window surrounds) in a field of less expensive cladding, such as anchored brick veneer. Terra-cotta pieces are also extruded in a process similar to the manufacture of extruded clay brick. These extruded pieces are more economical and more "modern," as the articulation is unidirectional.

Presently many of the extruded systems come from Europe. The Alphaton Terracotta Rainscreen System by Moeding and distributed by Shildan USA was used on the Glassworks Condominium Homes in San Francisco. Moeding is a German company that has been making terra-cotta building products for over 250 years. The Alphaton system has been widely used since 1984. The facade tiles come in five surface finishes and twenty colors. The relatively small size of the tiles simplifies installation. The 30-mm (1.2 in.) thick tiles come in heights (the extruded dimension) of 150–250 mm (5.9–9.8 in.), with 225 mm (8.9 in.) being the most economical. Lengths vary from 150 to 500 mm (5.9–19.7 in.), with 450 mm (17.7 in.) being the most economical. Exact lengths can be cut easily on the jobsite.

The future will hopefully offer a greater selection of more economical terra-cotta systems as the usage increases. It may be that a designer will be able to select a system off the web the same way a designer selected terra-cotta pieces from a stock catalogue a hundred years ago. And while we may not be able to afford either the labor or the weight of finely carved stone on buildings, hopefully hand-pressed or extruded terra-cotta will continue to provide this aesthetic.

9.2.5 THE GLASSWORKS CONDOMINIUM HOMES

Brand + Allen Architects designed the Glassworks Condominium Homes, a 120,000-square-foot mixed-use project, developed by Catellus and constructed by McCarthy Building Companies.

Completed in 2003, the building utilizes an aluminum and glass conventional curtain wall with back-ventilated terra-cotta tile cladding—the Alphaton Terracotta Rainscreen System.

The backup wall for the terra-cotta tiles on this cast-in-place concrete frame building, is a conventional steel-stud wall sheathed with silicone treated gypsum exterior sheathing (DensGlass Gold). A self-adhesive sheet (peel-and-stick) membrane (Perma Barrier by W. R. Grace) provides a complete water and air barrier system, as well as a vapor retarder on the outside of the sheathing. All insulation is within the metal-stud cavity. Simpson Gumpertz & Heger, the curtain wall consultant, modeled vapor movement through the assembly to ensure that condensation would not occur on the inside face of the peel-and-stick membrane in the temperate San Francisco climate. If insulation is required to the exterior of the peel-and-stick, as it would be in a cooling climate and some mixed climates, rigid board insulation can be used between the fittings that attach the horizontal supporting structure to the backup wall.

Typical tiles are 430 mm (16.9 in.) long by 225 mm (8.9 in.) high and 30 mm (1.18 in.) thick. The tiles are extruded with cores, making them lighter and more dimensionally stable through the firing process. Mitered tiles are used at corners. The tiles are attached to a horizontal aluminum support structure with aluminum clips called tile holders. These holders engage both the top and base rims of the tiles such that an air gap of 8 mm (.32 in.) is left between the tiles and the bearing profile for capillary separation. This allows any condensed water running down the back of the tiles to exit at the base of each tile. Vertical aluminum panel dividers prevent lateral displacement, penetration of wind-driven rain, and rattling of the tiles due to wind. A 5-mm (.2 in.) wide continuous horizontal gap between each tile helps pressure-equalize the cavity behind the tiles, which is 40 mm (1.57 in.) wide. The cross section of this vent corresponds to 25 percent of the facade surface area. Because the tiles overlap, most wind-driven rain is stopped at the face.

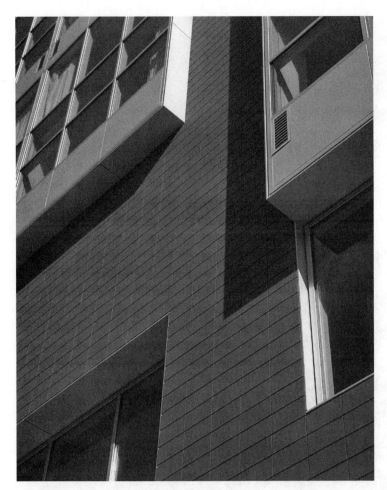

FIGURE 9.14 Terra-cotta and metal transitions on the Glassworks Condominium Homes. Reproduced courtesy of Brand + Allen Architects, Inc.; photo by Adrian Velicescu.

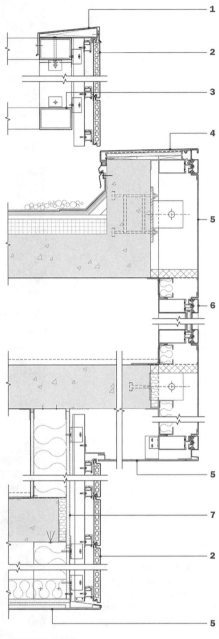

SECTION DETAIL

1. *16 ga. coil coated alum. coping*
2. *30 mm clay tile Alum. extrusion Alum. fixing clip Double alum. angles*
3. *Tube stl. frame*
4. *3/16" alum. plate*
5. *Prefinished alum. composite panel*
6. *Alum. window curtain wall Insulated glazing unit*
7. *Membrane 5/8" exterior sheathing*

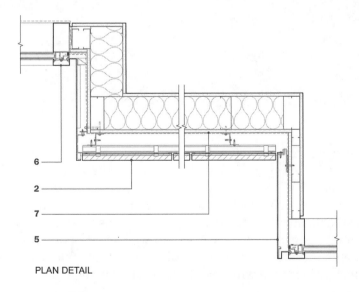

PLAN DETAIL

FIGURE 9.15 Plan and section details of the terra-cotta tile cladding. Drawing courtesy of Brand + Allen Architects, Inc.

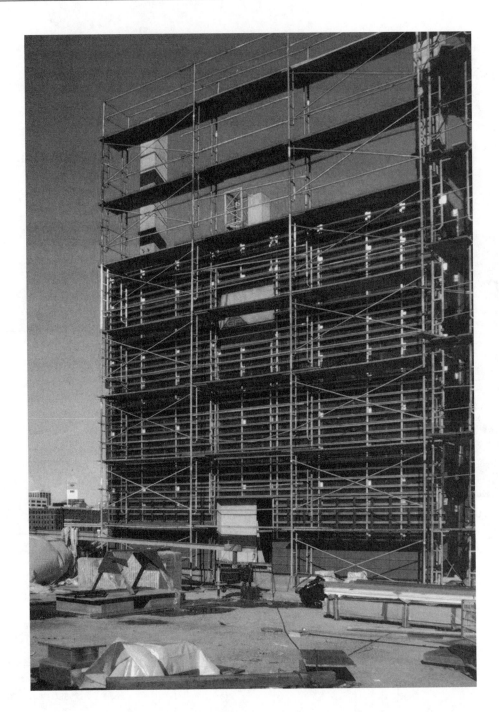

FIGURE 9.16 Installation of aluminum supporting structure over self-adhesive membrane. Reproduced courtesy of Brand + Allen Architects, Inc.; photo by Adrian Velicescu.

The self-adhesive sheet membrane is also protected from deterioration by ultraviolet (UV) light and weathering. Damaged tiles can be removed and easily replaced, although individual tiles cannot be removed without destroying the tile. Installation of this system should be relatively straightforward with careful upfront planning and detailing. Careful detailing will also ensure that the aesthetic of the geometric pattern is maintained. A mock-up wall should point out problems that might arise with the coordination of the different trades. Tolerances for terra-cotta tiles are much tighter than with some other claddings and must be accommodated.

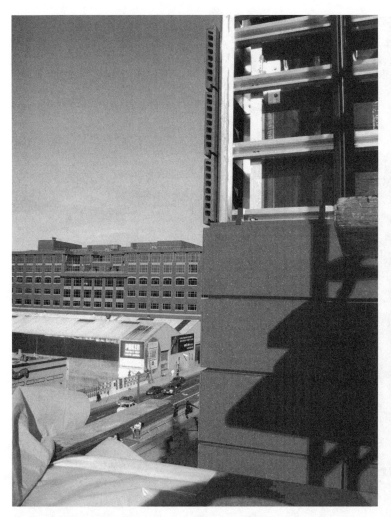

FIGURE 9.17 Installation of individual terra-cotta tiles showing vertical panel dividers and horizontal supporting structure. Reproduced courtesy of Brand + Allen Architects, Inc.; photo by Adrian Velicescu.

FIGURE 9.18 Construction of cladding at window opening. Reproduced courtesy of Brand + Allen Architects, Inc.; photo by Adrian Velicescu.

In concept, this is a simple system. First, the building is completely waterproofed (and made airtight). Then a screen for the rain is installed with a cavity to drain any interstitial water. The large vent openings (25 percent of the facade) help with pressure equalization, while the overlapping configuration of the joint deflects wind-driven rain and protects insulation or membranes within the cavity from ultraviolet light, weathering, or vandalism. Critical detailing areas are at the transitions to other cladding systems and at the roof and base as well as at openings.

9.2.6 THE FUTURE OF EIFS

The industry responded to the failures associated with EIFS with several innovations. More water resistant gypsum sheathings were developed; the first was DensGlass Gold. A variety of proprietary EIFs products that drain are now available, and the industry continues to research new ones. The system discussed in Chapter 7 offers a cost-effective, durable exterior wall. EIFS manufacturers have

FIGURE 9.19 St. Mary's Catholic Church (Michael Graves & Associates, 2002) in Rockledge, Florida, offers a new interpretation of EIFS. The panelized system saved the contractor up to two months in construction time over conventionally applied EIFS. Photo courtesy of Sto Corp.

developed water and air barriers, such as Sto Gold, to which EIFS can be bonded. Prefabrication of EIFS panels can increase the durability.

EIFS needs to find its place as an aesthetic surface. It will always be used to replicate masonry claddings and wood detailing on those projects desiring a more traditional look. But can it have an aesthetic of its own? People have never quite been sure what it was supposed to be. It sometimes looked like concrete, sometimes stucco. (At the same time, designers seem to prefer stucco that looks like EIFS with the use of acrylic coatings instead of cementitious ones.) EIFS is a plastic material, which can be applied in larger joint-free areas than stucco. It has an almost infinite selection of colors and a thickness that adds depth to a wall. But we need some key to recognize it. Europe, where it is more likely to be used as a flat field, offers interesting examples that utilize a variety of colors to create depth and pattern. EIFS is a modern material and should be recognized as such. Large expanses, utilizing geometric shapes enhanced with color, could be a new aesthetic. Sto has a division in Germany called StoDesign that focuses exclusively on aesthetics. In studios throughout Germany, design experts develop color and material concepts for exteriors and interiors. In the U.S., Sto Studio offers similar services. Perhaps the key to EIFS is in thinking of it as just EIFS, rather than a product that replicates other materials, just as terra-cotta is no longer thought of as an imitative material.

9.3 AESTHETICS AND DURABILITY: CAN YOU HAVE BOTH WITH CARRARA MARBLE?

Two of the most notable cladding failures of the last few decades involved stone—that material we think of as being the most enduring of all. One might assume that if the budget allows for a stone cladding, durability and aesthetics are part of the package. But this is not always the case, as noted with the Standard Oil Building (later called the Amoco Building and now the Aon Center) in Chicago and Finlandia Hall in Helsinki, Finland. Both buildings were clad in Carrara Bianco marble, and both claddings failed spectacularly. There is still debate as to the exact failure mechanisms; but the problem was the thinness of the marble panels, fabricated with a new cutting technology. Research groups around the globe continue to investigate the problems with these thin marble panels, especially their permanent bowing and loss of strength.

9.3.1 CARRARA MARBLE

Carrara, Italy, has about 90 active quarries, with another 70 in the surrounding basins. The earliest dates from more than two thousand years ago. There are approximately 20 commercial varieties of marble quarried in Carrara and the surrounding areas, all defined by their aesthetic properties and not their physical-mechanical properties. The final decision to use a particular marble should be made only *after* an accurate evaluation of the overall characteristics. One of the more popular marbles is the Bianco (or White) Carrara; it is homogeneous in a color that ranges from white to off-white to light gray, in some cases interrupted by grayish veins. Bianco Statuario is the marble that was widely used by sculptors from Michelangelo to Henry Moore. It is a pure white stone, verging on ivory in color, with no veins or only very minuscule ones. It is easy to see why designers would select a Carrara marble. Edward Durell Stone, the architect of the Amoco Building, wanted a pure white stone exterior. Alvar Aalto wanted to introduce the Mediterranean culture into Finland.[26] But what about durability? Aalto thought marble would be a more durable finish than stucco in Finland's harsh environment, but in the end, well-designed stucco cladding may have lasted longer.

Marble is the final transformation of limestone. Because of this metamorphic transformation caused by pressure, heat, and time, marble is generally the least predictable of the stones.[27] Edward Ford pointed out the particular nature of marble in his observations on Finlandia Hall. He commented that "the slabs have warped like so much plywood, giving a sad confirmation of Aalto's analysis of the 'biological' nature of stone."[28] Thin (defined as 1 inch to 1½ inches, 25–38 mm, in thickness), crystalline marble slabs will "release their stress of geological origin" and permanently deform due to thermal expansion and moisture ingress.[29] The fine-grained, relatively pure marbles will slightly bow with each heating cycle. In addition to deforming, there is a corresponding loss of strength. This cumulative and irreversible process is called hysteresis. Hysteresis is less of a problem with thicker marble veneers, and it is not a problem with all marbles.

Freeze-thaw cycling becomes more problematic the more porous the stone, and marble is much more permeable than granite. At 50 psi per square foot per hour for ½ inch (13 mm) thickness, the permeability of granite is 0.11 cubic inch, whereas the permeability of marble ranges from 1.3 to 16.8.[30] The final assault on marbles comes in the form of acid rain.

9.3.2 FAILURES OF THE AMOCO BUILDING AND FINLANDIA HALL

The 80-story Amoco Building in Chicago (designed by Edward Durrell Stone) was the fourth tallest building in the world when it was completed in 1973, as well as the tallest building clad in marble—1¼-inch (32 mm) and 1½-inch (38 mm) panels of Alpha-Gray White Carrara. Two decades later it became the tallest building ever completely reclad,[31] and the tallest building clad in granite. By the 1980s there was considerable concern over whether or not the stone would stay on the building. The panels were showing permanent distress in the form of cracking and bowing. Amoco's manager of engineering said the bowing started soon after the building was completed.[32] Beginning in 1979 the engineering firm of Wiss, Janney, Elstner Associates (WJE) was hired to inspect periodically the exterior facade in accordance with the City of Chicago's new building facade inspection ordinance.[33] The first investigation revealed some distressed panels. Seven with outward bowing were replaced and others with cracks were repaired. These panels did not represent a significant problem, but by 1985 the cracking and bowing was "accelerating at a rapid rate."[34] In 1988 a retrofit of steel bands around each of the 44,406, 50 x 42 inch (1,270 x 1,070 mm) panels, painted the color of the marble, and canopies at the entries protected the occupants of the building until a solution could be found. Typical outward bowing of the panels was ½ inch (13 mm) with a maximum of 1⅛ inch (29 mm). The worst bowing was on the south and east faces of the building, which had no adjacent structures to block direct sun.[35] WJE was hired to fully investigate the problem and, ultimately, to design the solution. They estimated that the marble could lose up to 70 percent of its original flexural strength in another 10 years.[36] Ian Chin of WJE noted that the panels at the top of the building, where the exposure was the highest, had deteriorated to the extent that they had to be removed in pieces, not panels. This building, which had cost $125 million to construct in 1973, would cost between $70 and $80 million to reclad less than 20 years later.

A similar problem was developing in Helsinki on Finlandia Hall, designed by Alvar Aalto. Within a few years of its completion in 1972, the panels began to "warp severely."[37] The panels were bowing, or "dishing," forming a basket-weave pattern on this modernist icon. These panels had also taken advantage of new fabrication techniques, cutting the stone to a thickness of only 1⁵⁄₁₆ inches (34 mm). The temperature extremes and pollution added to the marble failure. During the investigation it was discovered that not only was the anchorage inadequate but each panel was also fastened to the adjacent panel, exacerbating the differential movement problems. After a marble panel fell off the building, tubular metal braces that resembled "giant paper clips" were installed to secure the marble to the building.[38]

FIGURE 9.20 Recladding of the Amoco Building started at the third floor and proceeded to the top. Custom designed aluminum scaffolding was suspended from outriggers attached to the window-washing track. Materials were moved by a monorail system that circled the building at five locations. Photo Tigerhill; © Tigerhill.

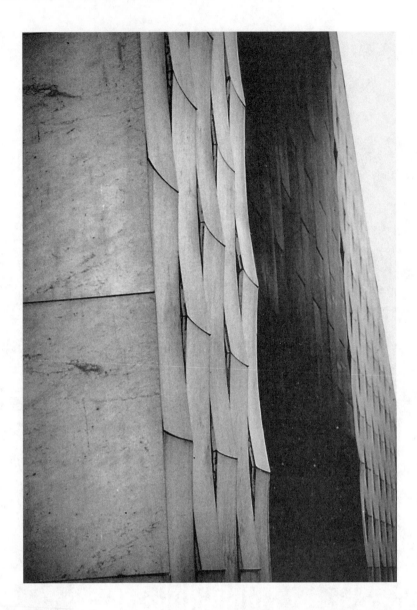

FIGURE 9.21 The Bianco Cararra marble of Finlandia Hall had bowed over 1½ inches (4 cm) before it was removed. Note that the black granite to the right shows no distress. Photo by Elmar Tschegg, TU Vienna, http://www.tuwien.ac.at.

The failure mechanisms were similar for both buildings. The problem was fabricating crystalline marble in thinner panels than had previously been used. Finlandia Hall's problems were made worse by poor anchorage, while Amoco's anchorage was found to be adequate. Helsinki's pollution is a problem, as are wind loads on an 80-story building in Chicago. The failures posed serious life-safety problems on both buildings, prompting expensive remedial construction to keep the marble on the building until it could be replaced. With both buildings, it was determined that the marble had to be removed. How could such catastrophic failures have happened with such important projects, seemingly without the budget constraints that less prominent buildings might have?

9.3.3 HOW DID THIS HAPPEN?

The answer to this question may be simply that the architects of the two buildings had a vision for the appearance of the exterior wall without fully understanding how cutting the marble thinner than in the past would affect the durability of the cladding. The image of the building overrode common sense. Little if any investigation was done on the long-term durability of thin marble. In the case of the Amoco Building, the limits were further pushed by the height of the building. Wind loads were modeled on part of the building, and there were attempts to develop tests of accelerated weathering on samples of marble. However, the marble that was actually used for construction was significantly weaker and less durable than the marble samples that were used to develop the design criteria. The use of marble on Finlandia Hall was more modest, but still long-term durability should have been questioned when using a stone in very thin panels from a Mediterranean climate. To be fair, such testing had not been fully developed at the time, and any testing done was not published worldwide.

But the decision to use marble was made many decades after problems with the stone had been noted. It had long been known that marble cut in thin slabs could deform permanently. A traveler in Cuba first noted the permanent bowing of marble exposed to the sun in the early 1900s.[39] Why did no one ask the question: Is this the proper stone for use in this climate, in a thickness not used before? This may have been posed by a Finnish chemistry professor who reportedly told Aalto that the marble would not withstand Helsinki's climate, but "nobody listened."[40] Unfortunately, when a heavy cladding fails, life-safety is at stake. Equally interesting are the decisions made in considering the recladding of the two buildings.

9.3.4 Mount Airy Granite for the Amoco Building

Various claddings were considered for the Amoco Building, including granite, marble, limestone, and aluminum panels. In the end, they decided on granite. Granite is initially stronger, maintains its strength better, and is less porous than marble and most other stones. The search was on for the whitest granite to match the white marble on the building. Mount Airy granite, from North Carolina, was selected as one of the whitest of the granites. This was a reasonable and pragmatic solution. Although granite does not have the translucent quality of marble, it is a very durable stone. A superior anchorage system utilizing extruded, stainless-steel shelf angles, with continuous lateral tab connections, was designed.[41] The continuous anchors provide uniform support for the new 2-inch (50 mm) thick granite panels. Because of the increased weight of the panels, some of the structural columns of the below-grade floors of the building were reinforced. With the new anchorage system and the extensive testing of the installation, this building should not need recladding for a century or more. The owners made the decision to put durability ahead of aesthetics, unlike the original designer. There was no mention of paying homage to the original architect—to the contrary, litigation was instigated against the original architect, engineer, and others involved with the construction.

The Amoco Building is meant to project a corporate image but, most importantly, not to threaten life-safety. The image of the white tower was maintained with the Mount Airy granite. The building's final appearance to the general public is not unlike the original. A white marble that is similar to the original exterior marble remains in the lobby, where it can be seen next to the granite, separated only by the glass curtain wall.

9.3.5 Carrara Marble for Finlandia Hall

Finlandia Hall, owned by the city of Helsinki, Finland, was another matter entirely. The discussion over the selection of the cladding material raged for a decade. Again the search was on for a durable white stone. Over one hundred samples were reviewed by a committee that included architect Elissa Aalto, Aalto's widow. They narrowed the selection to five stones, including Mount Airy granite. Samples of the granite were attached to the building and the debate began. The pro-granite side, which included the manager of Finlandia Hall, was looking for a cladding that would last 75 to 100 years. This camp pointed out that the black granite on the exterior of Finlandia Hall was showing no distress. The pro-marble side was led by Elissa Aalto and involved paying homage to the original designer and his intent. Elissa Aalto commented that "it's a very big difference if you make the building gray. I would like marble again, but Helsinki engineers are very much against it. So we're trying to find a light colored granite, but it doesn't exist!"[42] The local architectural community, with the support of international icons such as James Stirling, Herman Herzberger, and Sverre Fehn, protested the use of "grey granite."[43]

The people of Helsinki carried the debate to the newspapers, and most had an opinion one way or the other—granite or marble. The city left no stones unturned in finding a suitable replacement. During the process, a composite panel of concrete surfaced with marble was considered. The city rejected the panel because it had "not been adequately tested."[44] Some favored the use of a local stone, which would have, in the opinion of some, made the building more an icon of the people of Finland. The city also came close to approving a white granite from China in 1997.[45]

But in 1997, three years after the death of Elissa Aalto, the citizens of Helsinki approved the purchase of 7,000 square meters of Carrara Bianco from Italy. Finlandia Hall was a symbol of the country, the crowning achievement (although not the most critically acclaimed work) of Finland's best-known architect and possibly citizen. The opinion was that even if it has to be replaced in several decades, the building is too important to lose sight of the designer's original intent. Under the headline "Finlandia Saved," the *Architectural Review* noted that gray granite "would have destroyed the building's grace and delicacy."[46]

After only six months, bowing of the new marble panels on Finlandia Hall was noticeable.[47] (See Figures 9.22 and 9.23.) Some thought that the superior connections would give the marble a longer life, but it is not happening. It will be interesting to see where the debate heads with the next recladding. As stated by the director of Finlandia Hall in 1991, a proponent of using granite for the initial recladding, "I don't see how we can afford to replace marble every 25 years."[48]

9.3.6 Advancing the Envelope

What can be learned from these examples? Advancement of one technology, the thin slicing of stone, needs to be extensively field- and laboratory-tested—certainly before using it on a high-rise building. (Stone can now be sliced ⅜ inch [10 mm] thick. These thin panels of marble, granite, or limestone are bonded to a stabilizing panel. One system bonds the stone to lightweight aluminum honeycomb board.) All information on the material and the system should be carefully studied. Not all materials or systems are suitable for all situations or all climates. Greater care should be taken in the detailing of a new system, with safety factors considered.

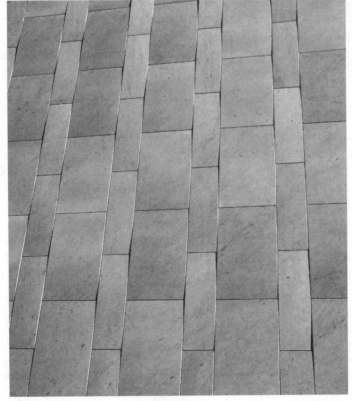

FIGURES 9.22 AND 9.23 The new marble cladding on Finlandia Hall is experiencing problems similar to those of the original cladding. Bowing of the panels was noticeable only six months after they were installed. Photos by Björn Schouenborg, http://www.sp.se/building/team.

TEAM (Testing and Assessment of Marble and Limestone)[49] is a consortium of nine European Union countries with 15 industry partners who are investigating the problems with facade bowing of marble and the expansion of marble and limestone with consequential loss of strength. The investigation, estimated to be completed in 2005, should benefit designers who are considering stone as a cladding material.

9.4 BUILD IT RIGHT THE FIRST TIME OR REPAIR IT QUICKLY: ANCHORED BRICK VENEER FAILURES*

Failures of anchored brick veneer caused by designs that did not incorporate the use of rectangular veneer panels separated by expansion joints are well understood and have been described in many publications.

Among the most commonly reported failures are spalling and buckling of veneer due to a lack of horizontal expansion joints under shelf angles and vertical cracking near corners, returns, and offsets that are not protected by vertical expansion joints. These failures are worsened and made considerably more dangerous if the veneer has poor lateral anchorage to its backup wall due to improperly spaced or poorly installed veneer anchors. Corrosion of veneer anchors can cause or exacerbate poor lateral anchorage.

In their work, the authors have noted that the restoration of anchored brick veneer failures is often delayed more than a decade for a variety of reasons, including the tendency of owners, with a need for more space, to defer repairs in favor of new construction. Part of the rationale behind these decisions to defer the repair or replacement of a failing facade may be the false sense of security that comes with the apparent stabilization of cracking shortly after it is first observed.

Two investigations by the authors indicate that the tendency of these failures to slow, or even completely stop, does not ensure that they will remain dormant during unusual weather conditions not yet experienced by the building envelope. ("Reducing Confusion," in Chapter 6, provides definitions for several terms used in this section.)

9.4.1 COLLEGE DORMITORY

Built in 1967, this seven-story dormitory is located about 50 miles from the mid-Atlantic coast of the United States. Apparently, due to a change made in the anchorage design during construction, its anchored brick veneer was poorly attached to a concrete masonry backup wall.

Its almost complete lack of vertical expansion joints caused vertical cracks at the first head joint to one side of many corners, as is typical of this failure (see Figures 4.1 and 6.8) and sometimes at the jambs of the nearest windows (Figure 9.24). The latter condition, in combination with the poor anchorage of the veneer, resulted in the further rotation of the corner veneer "panels" created by the cracks.

---

*This section is based on a paper by Russell Heliker and Linda Brock presented at the Sixth North American Masonry Conference; it was originally published in the conference proceedings under a different title. Its content has been modified, including the addition of four figures. Reprinted with permission of the Masonry Society. (Phil Green, P.E., helped the authors with the investigation and analysis of the failures described in these two case studies.)

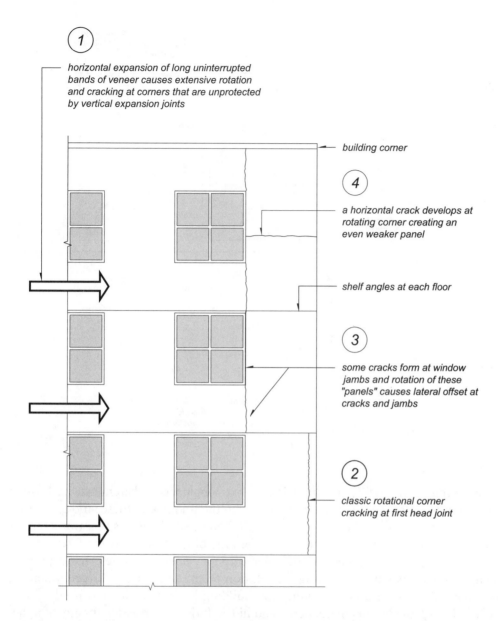

1 horizontal expansion of long uninterrupted bands of veneer causes extensive rotation and cracking at corners that are unprotected by vertical expansion joints

building corner

4 a horizontal crack develops at rotating corner creating an even weaker panel

shelf angles at each floor

3 some cracks form at window jambs and rotation of these "panels" causes lateral offset at cracks and jambs

2 classic rotational corner cracking at first head joint

FIGURE 9.24 Veneer failures caused by lack of vertical expansion joints at or near building corners.

This rotation could be seen along the window jambs, where the veneer had rotated slightly away from the building.

The total lack of horizontal expansion joints beneath shelf angles (located at each floor) allowed considerable vertical movement of the veneer. The cumulative vertical growth was completely unconstrained by the shelf angles due to their attachment to the concrete beams with wedge-pocket inserts (see Figure 6.13 for a detail of a wedge-pocket insert). Consequently, the upper-level veneer was lifted about one inch, resulting in damage to windowsills and parapet veneer and also causing the classic penthouse veneer failure shown in Figure 9.25.

The upward movement described above took place on all elevations and was essentially unchanging from season to season; therefore, much of it was caused by permanent moisture expansion, which can be surprisingly large. Shortening of the concrete columns probably added little to this differential movement, because building loads were also supported by the 10-inch (250 mm) deep concrete masonry backup walls, thereby minimizing load-induced creep of the concrete frame.

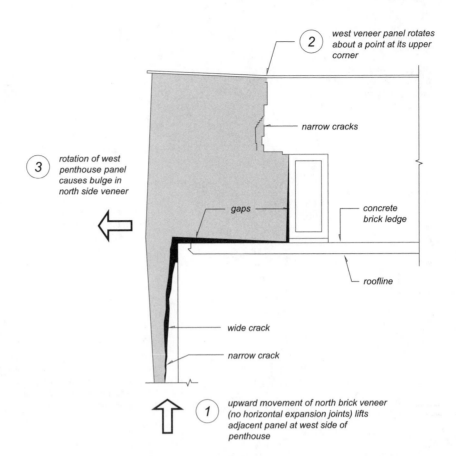

west veneer panel rotates about a point at its upper corner — ②

narrow cracks

③ *rotation of west penthouse panel causes bulge in north side veneer*

gaps

concrete brick ledge

roofline

wide crack

narrow crack

① *upward movement of north brick veneer (no horizontal expansion joints) lifts adjacent panel at west side of penthouse*

FIGURE 9.25 Penthouse veneer fai ure caused by lack of horizontal expansion joints under shelf angles West elevation of penthouse and of set below.

Between the mid-1970s and mid-1980s, local engineers and architects performed several mostly noninvasive studies. Comparing the findings of these studies to each other and to the authors' observations in 1988 and 1989 indicates that the extent of the veneer movements had stabilized by the time of the first study in 1976.

In 1987, possibly because of a change of policy concerning deferred repairs, a local architect was hired to design a solution to the problems. He recommended removing the veneer and recladding the building but due to limited funding was only able to provide "an emergency 'band-aid' solution," consisting mainly of adhesive anchors secured to the ungrouted cells of the concrete masonry backup walls by the screen-tube technique. But these anchors were confined to the locations where there had been the greatest movement. This construction was completed in 1988.

The investigation of 1989 included the use of a mobile construction lift and the opening of several exploratory holes, where few veneer anchors were found, except at concrete columns. This resulted in a recommendation of three options. Two involved the complete removal of the veneer and a third incorporated an extensive and complicated reattachment of the veneer. Also recommended was that design work begin immediately, because although the differential movements appeared to have abated, the veneer was not capable of withstanding significant lateral wind-loading. However, the design was delayed a year for various reasons, including a lengthy distraction concerning speculation that the asbestos fibers in the building felts that covered the cavity side of the concrete masonry backup walls had contaminated the interior side of the brickwork, thereby making its demolition too expensive.

The building was next visited about a year later in March 1990. Surprisingly, the veneer was discovered to be moving again, and a few of the previously mentioned corner panels had become quite unstable. Whereas they had previously only rotated slightly at the window jambs, now one had rotated away from the building enough to create a lateral offset of about 1 inch (25 mm) (Figure 9.26). Another had developed a horizontal crack (Figure 9.24) as it rotated. It was possible to easily "flex" this panel about this horizontal crack with a pry bar inserted in the gap between the window jamb and the brick veneer.

The event that caused this rapid increase in differential movement has not been positively identified. At first it was believed to be a single "thermal shock," a rapid rise in temperature that caused damage elsewhere on the campus in February 1990. But correspondence with the campus engineer indicates that there was also an unusually hot and dry period during the summer of 1989, with an extreme temperature of about 95°F (35°C), which caused damage to other campus facilities.

FIGURE 9.26 Lateral movement of veneer at a window jamb (note that the sealant has been destroyed, but the jamb is unharmed because the window frame was attached to the backup wall). Photo by G. Russell Heliker.

A review of National Oceanic and Atmospheric Administration's (NOAA) *Surface Weather Observations,* taken at a nearby airport, seems to confirm both these events. At the airport, the "thermal shock" was less than dramatic but did seem out of the ordinary. The NOAA data also points to a series of episodes during the spring and summer of 1989. Generally, these months were very hot, which conforms to the owner's description of the period. If this data is representative of what happened at the building site, it was probably both the duration and magnitude of these temperatures that caused the owner's problems, possibly including the newly destabilizing movements in the brick veneer.

Sunlight probably contributed to the new movements by raising the temperature of the veneer, as the greatest of the new differential movements were found on the southwest elevation of the building. However, sunlight is a common event during most summers and therefore it is not believed to be the proximate cause of the additional movements. Regardless of the cause, the accelerated movements meant that the entire building had to be fenced and expensive overhead structures installed at several entries to protect the occupants. The veneer was completely removed and replaced with a panelized EIFS cladding before the end of 1991.

9.4.2 CONCERT HALL

First occupied in the mid-1970s, this brick-clad structure is located in the rainy marine climate of the Pacific Northwest. Its almost complete lack of vertical expansion joints and entire lack of horizontal expansion joints resulted in vertical cracking at the first head joint to one side of many corners and offsets in addition to the interesting failure shown in Figure 9.27. The brick-clad inclines depicted here were decorative forms located high on the building, at the base of the parapets (Figure 9.28). The horizontal offsets at the toe of the inclines were caused by the vertical expansion of several stories of veneer below. The shelf angles in the veneer below the inclines were either poorly attached or, as is typical of even the most rigidly attached angles, could not completely constrain this movement. The offsets allowed substantial water into the drainage cavity, where it ran down the surface of the cast-in-place, concrete backup walls (Figure 9.29). Water also entered higher on the incline, because inclined veneer is very difficult to seal due to small cracks that inevitably appear over the years. The considerable amount of calcium carbonate evident in Figure 9.29 was picked up from the mortar in which the inclined brick was bedded (Figure 9.27). In addition, the lack of a gutter at the toe of these inclines allowed the remainder of the water shed by the inclines to run down the exterior of the brick veneer, where some of it was absorbed and some driven into delaminated mortar joints by wind. This two-pronged attack resulted in the rapid corrosion of many zinc-coated, dovetailed veneer anchors. (Delaminations are fine cracks caused by a poor brick-to-mortar bond. Bed-joint delaminations are made worse by a flexible backup wall, which was not a contributing cause in this instance.)

In early 1976, personnel of the owner, architect, and contractor participated in an investigation of cracking and water entry at the southwest building corner. Using stationary scaffolding, several square feet of veneer was removed from both sides of the corner, a few stories above grade. Among the problems observed were the absence of veneer anchors, corner cracking, and an area of thinner veneer made of bricks that had been cut to avoid a bulging concrete backup wall. The veneer

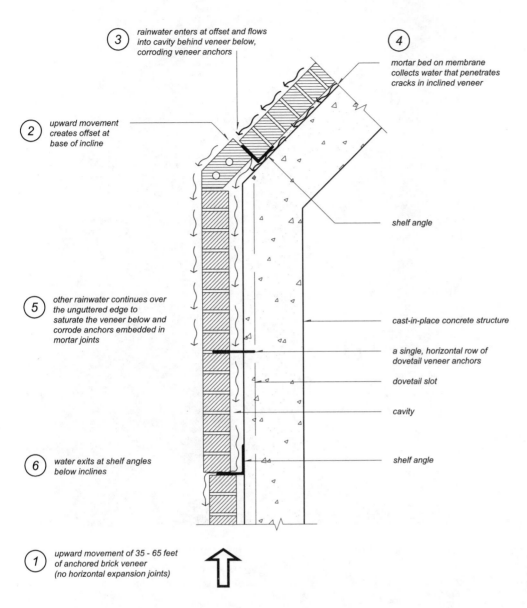

③ rainwater enters at offset and flows into cavity behind veneer below, corroding veneer anchors

④ mortar bed on membrane collects water that penetrates cracks in inclined veneer

② upward movement creates offset at base of incline

shelf angle

⑤ other rainwater continues over the unguttered edge to saturate the veneer below and corrode anchors embedded in mortar joints

cast-in-place concrete structure

a single, horizontal row of dovetail veneer anchors

dovetail slot

cavity

⑥ water exits at shelf angles below inclines

shelf angle

FIGURE 9.27 Failures caused by the use of veneer on an inclined surface and the lack of horizontal expansion joints under shelf angles supporting the vertical veneer below.

① upward movement of 35 - 65 feet of anchored brick veneer (no horizontal expansion joints)

was summarized as bearing little resemblance to that which had been detailed by the architect.

Other than the drilling of some weep holes, little repair or restoration was undertaken during the next ten years, probably because the cracking appeared to have stabilized by 1980 and the corrosion of the dovetail anchors had not yet been discovered. But due to the prolonged rains of this region, the inclines were a constant source of water, and by the mid-1980s considerable organic growth had accumulated on the walls below the inclines. This occurred either directly below the inclines or (as in Figure 9.28) below shelf angles lower on the facade, where water flowing down the drainage cavity was directed to the surface by shelf-angle flashing. This was an eyesore, and the cracking at corners was a reminder that all was not well with the veneer. In addition, the building envelope had other problems, including skylights that leaked and flat roofs in need of repair. Therefore, in 1987,

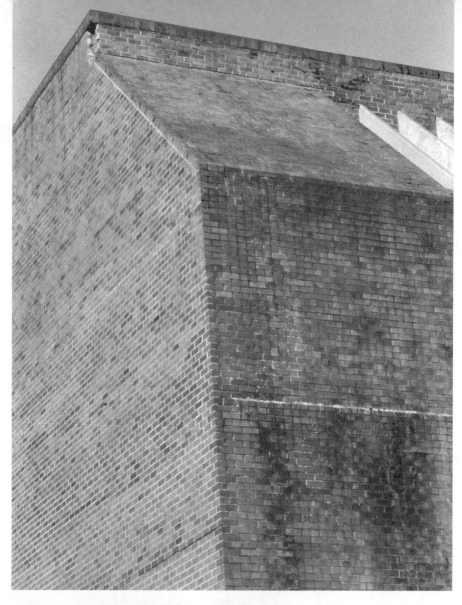

FIGURE 9.28 Brick-clad, inclined roof (note the organic growth below incline). Photo by G. Russell Heliker.

FIGURE 9.29 Exploratory hole showing evidence of water entry into drainage cavity behind veneer. Note the buildup of calcium carbonate on the face of the backup wall and the organic growth on the veneer in the lower left corner. Photo by G. Russell Heliker.

a local architect was hired to restore the building exterior; and in 1988, at the owner's request, the authors were hired by the local firm to perform a thorough investigation of the brick veneer.

This investigation, which included the use of a mobile construction lift and the opening of about ten exploratory holes, resulted in a number of observations. Many shelf angles were poorly attached and could not be relied upon to support the veneer if horizontal expansion joints were installed beneath them. The specified spacing of the veneer anchors (36 inches (914 mm), horizontally, by 18 inches (457 mm), vertically) was not conservative, and a surprising number of the specified veneer anchors were missing. This was especially worrisome, as there were areas of veneer that had been "trimmed" to miss bulges in the concrete backup walls and therefore could not be trusted to transfer lateral loads to the nearest anchor.

A number of dovetail veneer anchors were badly corroded, given their age, and some had completely rusted away, often because of the situation depicted in Figure 9.27. In addition, the polyvinyl chloride (PVC) shelf-angle flashing did not extend to the exterior face, and water entering the drainage cavity at the toe of the inclines was apparently able to travel downward within the veneer system more than one story. Two areas of vertical veneer, just below the inclines, had moved laterally away from the building (Figure 9.27).

This investigation resulted in a recommendation that the veneer and its shelf angles be replaced or reattached; expansion joints be installed; the brick-clad inclines be covered with some other material; and gutters be created at the base of the inclines.

The next four years brought a number of delays. Each taken on its own merits may have been justified, but the cumulative delay they caused was too long, especially since the questionable condition of the veneer had first been discovered in 1976 and confirmed by the investigation of 1988.

In the fall of 1992, the authors again had a chance to observe the building's exterior, and this second look—although of limited scope—also included the use of a mobile construction lift, which allowed observation of the upper level veneer. It was discovered that the veneer movements at some corners had increased and that the lateral movement of one section of veneer, just below an incline, had almost doubled. This veneer could easily be flexed by inserting a pry bar into the ½-inch (13 mm) wide, vertical crack of Figure 9.30. At another corner, a 12-foot (3.7 m) high section of veneer had begun to buckle, creating a bulge at its lower-third point.

These observations, together with the previously discovered poor anchorage, resulted in the conclusion that the owner should no longer tolerate the increasing risk to the occupants. Because the design of the restoration was progressing slowly, it was decided that measures should be taken to protect pedestrians at the base of the building by fencing off some areas and that the section of buckling veneer should be quickly removed.

Over four years had passed between the authors' two investigations, so the timing of the new movements was not clear. However, the movements may have been due to a long period of abnormally hot weather during the spring and summer of 1992. The number of days on which the ambient temperature rose above 90°F (32°C), a fairly rare occurrence in the area, was almost twice the 30-year average, and there were eleven record highs during the period. Although, according to

FIGURE 9.30 Crack at the end of the displaced vertical veneer described in Figure 9.27. Photo by G. Russell Heliker.

NOAA, the "percent of total possible sunshine" was higher than normal during this period, it is not believed that increased sunlight was the proximate cause of the new movements. It could certainly have been a contributing factor, which conforms to the observation that the increased movements were limited to the south and west elevations.

9.4.3 CONCLUSION

Although there is no conclusive evidence that abnormal weather conditions caused the destabilization described in the above two cases, there appears to be no other explanation. For example, the owners reported no occurrence of increased lateral loading, either from high winds or seismic activity. Of greater importance, of course, is not the cause but the fact that these failures did begin to worsen again, after years of being virtually dormant.

Poorly attached brick veneer is dangerous and should be replaced or reattached before it results in a critical situation. A go-slow policy not only defers the inevitable but, in the case of poorly anchored brick veneer, may add cost to the restoration and may also result in unnecessary risk to pedestrians at the base of exterior walls and those entering or exiting the building.

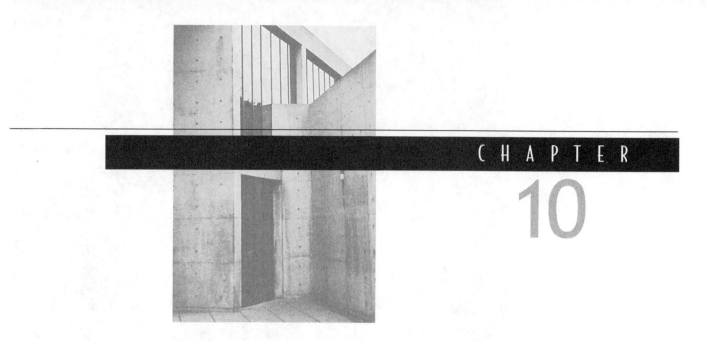

Architect's Design Kit: Form, Surface, Color, and Thick and Thin Walls

10.1 THE EXTERIOR WALL

The exterior wall is one of the most critical elements of the design aesthetic. The wall gained even greater prominence as the sloped roof of the past disappeared into a horizontal plane with the Modernist movement. With today's technologies, the wall can morph into the roof plane in a myriad of tortuous curves before we realize what has happened. Frank Gehry's recent buildings have defined the digital skin, tautly stretched over an amorphous armature. The Experience Music Project (EMP) in Seattle is a good example, with its 4,000 panels constructed of 21,000 red, blue, mirrored purple, silver, and gold shingles. The flat wall surface of the Westin New York at Times Square, New York City, by Arquitectonica is a flamboyant addition to Times Square. And while called "a building on the edge of a breakdown," in contrast with the EMP, it is straightforward in form.[1] The excitement and energy comes from the 8,000 glass lites of varying colors, reflectivity, and transparencies.

Environmental demands force new interpretations of the exterior wall. Mario Botta, revered for his heavy load-bearing masonry structures in Europe, was select-

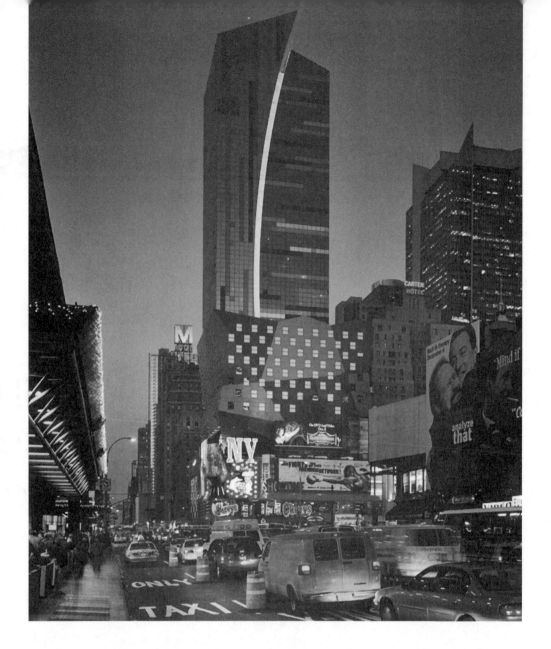

ed as the design architect for the San Francisco Museum of Modern Art, his first North American commission. Load-bearing masonry was not economically feasible, nor was conventional anchored brick veneer a viable option because of the complications associated with a building this size in an area of high seismic risk. The solution was a thin brick tile, cast in concrete, and fabricated in such a way that to the public the building appears to be a heavy load-bearing masonry wall.

Tadao Ando's signature is the concrete wall. His straightforward walls exhibit an honesty generated from their simplicity. They are concrete, nothing more. But what happens if codes require insulation in such walls? Can this aesthetic remain or does it need reinterpretation? This was the question for the Vitra Conference Pavilion in Germany, Ando's first European building.

If the exterior wall is vision glass, controlling heat transfer and light is possible only because of the sophisticated coatings, tinted glass, and insulating units available today. But if one wall of glass does a credible job of mediating the environment, what would happen with two? In Europe, especially Germany, the double-skin facade is gaining popularity. The cavity, and its two transparent leaves, allows for an elaborate configuration of passive and active environmental controls. Is this the best use of resources? Does it make sense to have two walls instead of one? Are there advantages in addition to energy savings? The Seattle Justice Center, designed by NBBJ Architects, addresses these questions in a North American context.

10.2 AESTHETIC KIT: FORM, SURFACE, AND COLOR

A wall begins as a plane—flat or articulated, thick or thin, sometimes curved, often perforated, and at times dense. It may be a distinct plane, contained at its edges, or it may wrap the form. Floors and roof may appear to be supported by the wall or pulled back from this face. The wall may be transparent, letting the interior play to the outside and vice versa, or opaque, giving little reading of the building's interior. This wall provides a canvas on which the designer can paint, boldly or subtly. Articulation forms patterns on the surface as the cladding reflects or absorbs light and colors or evokes the landscape. While it is the structure that creates the form, the exterior skin defines the visual reading of the form.

Color usually plays a small role in architectural facades, except for the subtle variation of natural materials such as stone or the metallic reflections of metal. The Westin New York at Times Square by Arquitectonica and the Experience Music Project by Gehry Partners, LLP are two exceptions. In all of its manifestations of hue, intensity, value, and reflectivity, color, along with form and surface texture, distinguishes these projects.

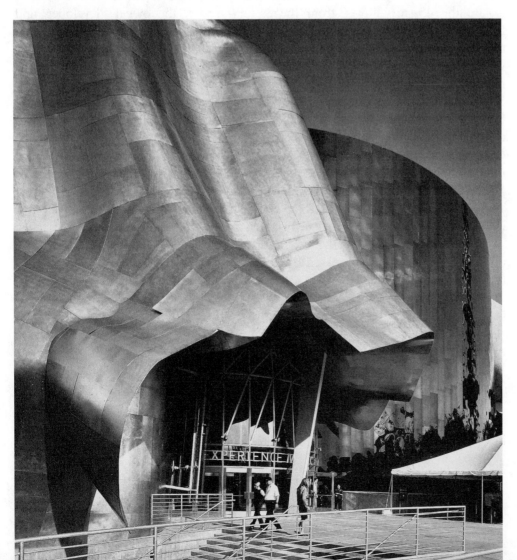

FIGURE 10.2 Experience Music Project, Seattle (Gehry Partners, 2000). Photo by Laura Swimmer; © 2000 Experience Music Project.

10.3 WESTIN NEW YORK AT TIMES SQUARE

The Westin New York at Times Square (2002) illustrates how two relatively straightforward curtain wall systems can enliven simple forms by playing with color and pattern. The first large hotel to be constructed in Manhattan in 20 years, the site produced unique challenges not the least of which was a busy urban site adjacent to the subway and an existing four-story building that was to be incorporated in the design. In addition, everyone had a different opinion of what was appropriate for Times Square. In the end, the conclusion may be that everything is appropriate for Times Square. Laurinda Spear, principal of Arquitectonica, commented: "It's a building that could only be in Times Square....Only in Times Square would you use colored glass. Only in Times Square would we have pulsating beams of light that define one facade of the building."[2]

The Westin New York adjoins the existing four-story entertainment, retail, and restaurant E Walk complex on Forty-second Street. The hotel has two parts: a 45-story, concrete frame, high-rise tower fronting Forty-third Street and an 8-story, concrete frame, low-rise portion (called the bustle) that extends over the E Walk complex. (See Figure 10.4.) The concrete structure of the bustle required a different column grid from that of the E Walk complex. Thirteen steel trusses, each 11 feet (3.35 m) deep, transfer the gravity loads of the bustle to the E Walk, but laterally the bustle is tied to the tower. While a simpler solution may have been to isolate the 45-story tower from the 8-story bustle, the owner, developer, and builder—an affiliate of Tishman Reality and Construction Company—looked ahead to the maintenance problems created by such a large isolation joint. They were also concerned with the potential for water leakage at the joint, a maintenance nightmare. As owner of the building, they were willing to increase the construction budget to alleviate problems in the future. To allow the two hotel segments to move together and independently of E Walk, 18 seismic isolators, used more typically to dampen seismic loading, were installed on top of each of the E Walk columns. Composed of up to 25 layers of ⅜-inch (10 mm) thick rubber and ⅛-inch (3 mm) thick round steel plates, the isolators allow up to 4 inches (100 mm) of lateral displacement between the bustle and the E Walk building.[3] Permasteelisa Cladding Technologies designed, fabricated, and erected the curtain walls on the tower with insulated glass units from Viracon. The bustle is clad with Alucabond ACM panels.

The building fits perfectly into the envelope created by zoning codes and urban design guidelines prepared by Robert A. M. Stern.[4] Anything "weird about the exterior, like the bulk, was due to zoning," commented Spear.[5] Zoning codes and the need to maximize square footage may have dictated the form of the building, but the desire for an architecturally significant building that met the construction budget defined the exterior articulation. What emerged is a sophisticated manipulation of a box and a tower to produce what the *New York Times* called a "Latin jolt to the skyline." The *Times* t described the bustle as an "abstract domino of punched-up masonry colors...a lop-sided crown is one of the larkiest on the skyline. Instead of one more Art Deco retread, it forgoes symmetry for syncopation." The tower was described as a "post-modern Mondrian: [a] Broadway Samba."[6]

FIGURE 10.3 A curved beam of light separates the two halves of the tower of the Westin New York at Times Square. The curtain wall frame and glass colors to the right of the curved light emphasize the horizontal, while the left side creates a vertical pattern. Reproduction courtesy of Tishman Construction Corporation. Photo by Norman McGrath.

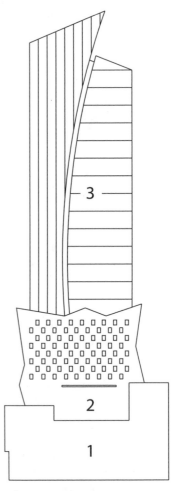

FIGURE 10.4 The lower "bustle" of the hotel, 2, bears on the E Walk complex, 1, but it is connected laterally to the 45-story tower, 3. Drawing courtesy of Permasteelisa Cladding Technologies.

This "syncopation" and "samba" were the result of a carefully detailed study and a long collaborative process between the architect, curtain wall and glazing manufacturers, and the owner and builder. While Tishman established the criteria for building efficiency, constructability, and the budget, Arquitectonica used models, sketches, and three-dimensional computer models to "push" this tightly defined envelope. As each floor plate of the tower needed to be maximized, the skin took on greater importance than the manipulations of form. The simple rectangular tower of the hotel is cut by a 40-story curved line of light. The design began with the curved beam of light representing the curved tail of a meteor slicing through the tower facing Forty-second Street. On one side of the curved light, the facade is a composition of horizontally patterned copper tones. On the other are blues and purples in a vertical pattern. The two contrasting patterns represent a meeting of earth and sky. A similar curve bisects the Forty-third Street side, effectively creating two halves of blue sky and copper earth, which form the tower. The easterly, earth-colored volume is anchored to the ground, while the westerly sky volume levitates above the entry at the corner of Forty-third Street and Eighth Avenue. Behind the curtain wall is a standard hotel layout, with rooms surrounding the elevator core, designed for efficiency of floor space. Yet little of this ordinary organization can be predicted from the facade.

10.3.1 CURTAIN-WALL DESIGN: A GLOBAL PROPOSITION

The project began to take form through a complicated process involving Tishman and Arquitectonica, which "painstakingly" developed models for each portion of the facade.[7] The next step was to find a curtain-wall manufacturer who could turn the ideas into a system. The story of the design of the aluminum and glass curtain wall for the Westin New York is one of global collaboration. Permasteelisa was awarded the design, fabrication, and construction contract through a competitive bidding process.

The extrusion dies for the frame were designed and fabricated exclusively for the project. The frame sections were extruded in 20- to 25-foot (6 to 7.6 m) sections in Permasteelisa's factory in Italy and then shipped to the Netherlands for specialty painting. A silver finish was used on the blue vertical, or sky-half, with a copper finish for the warmer horizontal, or earth-half. After painting, the frame sections were returned to Italy for cutting to length and machining for slots and holes. (Each panel frame has 13 to 15 aluminum extrusion pieces.) Only then were they bar-coded and shipped to Permasteelisa's plant in Connecticut for fabrication into the completed panels.

Viracon, based in Minnesota, was awarded the architectural glass contract because of its large color palette and reputation for versatility. More than 1,000 permutations of shapes, connection devices, and colors (of both frames and glass) constitute the 4,500 panels covering the 184,000 square feet of the tower. Because of the inordinate number of different pieces, each section of frame and each glass unit was bar-coded at the respective factory.

10.3.2 1,000 PERMUTATIONS OF GLASS

The glass gives the surface pattern and color. Bernardo Fort-Brescia, principal, of the design firm Arquitectonica, called the project " 'an arts and crafts solution with high-tech materials' and many colors made possible by a 'huge leap forward' in the

FIGURE 10.5 The curtain wall frames and the glass units were assembled in Connecticut. A robotized manipulator moves the glass unit as workers ready the frame. Photo courtesy of Tishman Construction Corporation.

FIGURE 10.6 The typical curtain-wall panel is 5 feet wide by 9 feet high with a vision glass unit and a spandrel glass unit. Photo courtesy of Tishman Construction Corporation.

glass sector."[8] Arquitectonica worked with Viracon over an eight-month period to determine the colors and combinations to be used. In the end, six coatings (low-E, copper, gold, antique silver, stainless steel, and gold eclipse); five Vanceva Interlayers (50 percent blue, red, 78 percent blue, black, and yellow); three colors of tinted glass (gold eclipse, bronze, and blue); and a medium gray frit were used on the project. The Vanceva layers, sandwiched in laminated glass, can create up to 1,000 color possibilities. The standard hotel room is three glass units wide. Most have one relatively clear glass unit and two with tints of blue and purple or bronzes, providing a dynamic vista, as the view is subtly shaded from one side of the room to the other.

Energy codes, heating, ventilating, and air-conditioning (HVAC) operating costs, and lateral loading influence curtain wall design. The frames on the Westin New York are designed as a pressure-equalized system with a thermal break. The insulating units have a ⅝-inch (16 mm) air space. (See Figures 10.7 and 10.8.) The inboard surface of the outer lite (#2) has a low-emissivity coating to reduce further thermal transmission on many of the units. (When the gold eclipse was on the outboard glass ply, then the low-E was applied on the #3 surface—this pertained to a typical insulating glass unit incorporating two glass plies and no inboard laminate.) The heat-absorbing, colored lites also help control heat transfer. Additional coatings were applied to the #2 surface. Ceramic frit was applied to the

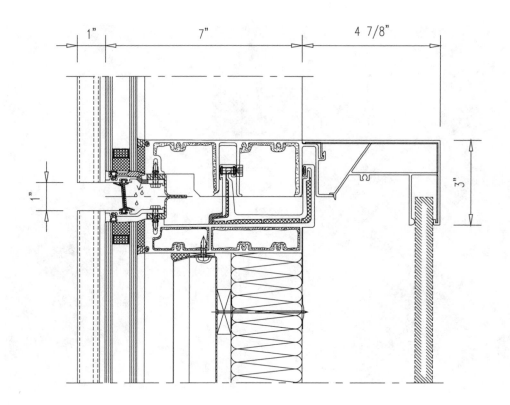

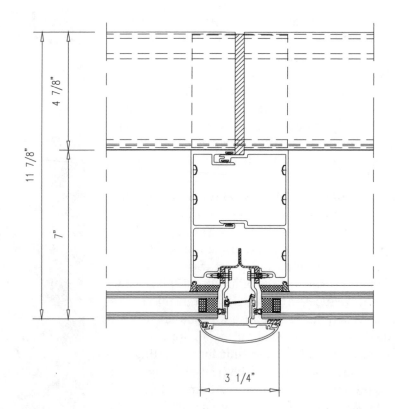

FIGURES 10.7 AND 10.8
The typical stack joint between the vision glass unit and the spandrel glass unit is seen in Figure 10.7. The typical vertical mullion between two vision panels in shown in Figure 10.8. Drawing courtesy of Permasteelisa Cladding Technologies.

#4 surface on some of the coated glass and also the laminated glass. Both lites in the glass units were heat-strengthened for thermal- and wind-load resistance. Most vision glass units are comprised of one ¼-inch (6 mm) colored ply or two ³⁄₁₆-inch (5 mm) laminated plies for the outside glass lite and a ¼-inch (6 mm) clear inside glass lite.

Thirty different glazing unit combinations were designed for the project before considering the different sizes and shapes. Most glass units were 55 x 55 inches (1400 x 1400 mm). Some colors were so similar that Viracon etched the product with the glass type to ensure Permasteelisa was glazing the right glazing unit in the right frame. The Vanceva product also has a directional run to it, so assemblers had to be sure of the base dimension of the trapezoidal shapes. When completed, the 8,000 insulated units were bar-coded and shipped to the Permasteelisa plant for panel fabrication in Connecticut, where the frames were assembled by hand from the pieces crafted in Europe. Moving down the assembly line, insulation and a metal back panel was added to the spandrel panels. A robotized manipulator handled the glass units. (See Figure 10.5.) After they were checked for quality and cleaned, the manipulator set the glass in the frame, and a structural silicon sealant was applied. The units snap together with a male and female connection designed to accommodate differential movement. The panels, most of which were 5 feet (1.5 m) by 9 feet (2.7 m) (some were double-story height of 18 feet, 5.5 meters), were fabricated within a ½-inch (0.80 mm) tolerance. All panels include operable windows and tieback receivers to secure a window-washing platform. The curtain wall is designed to weather a hundred-year storm, including hurricane-force winds.

10.3.3 Installation

Installation of the curtain wall occurred at a rate of two floors per week. Panels were initially omitted at the location of the hoist tower so that materials and personnel could be transported to the interior. These areas were filled in at the projects completion. Cladding began when the concrete structure was half completed. Connection to the structure occurred at Halphen metal channels cast into the floor slabs. Serrated anchor plates were bolted to the channels, allowing adjustment for construction tolerances of the concrete slab. The panels were then set onto clips attached to the anchor plates. According to David Horowitz, project director of Tishman Construction, the anchorage details easily accommodated construction tolerances and allowed for smooth installation of the panels.[9] The curtain wall of the bustle is an ACM panel system, Alucabond (fabricated by Sobotec, Ontario, Canada), with a steel-stud backup wall. The panels are a variety of bronze and golden colors in trapezoidal and rectangular shapes that create an origami pattern punched with a checkerboard of windows.

The lighted meteor, 355 feet in height and visible inside the eight-story atrium as well as the entire height of the tower outside, is lit with 466 miniature halogen lights having 10,000-hour lamps to minimize maintenance. All lights are accessible from the window-washing equipment. Seven 400-watt metal halide floodlights and a single xenon 4,000-watt fixture usually found at outdoor rock concerts pulse the light into the night. A hybrid architectural and theatrical lighting control system coordinates the meteor.[10]

FIGURES 10.9 AND 10.10
No two curtain-wall panels or metal "shingles" were the same on the EMP. Figure 10.9 courtesy of Gehry Partners, LLP. Figure 10.10 photo by John Stamets; © John Stamets.

10.4 EXPERIENCE MUSIC PROJECT, SEATTLE, GEHRY PARTNERS

Coming on the heels of the highly acclaimed Bilbao Guggenheim, Gehry's Experience Music Project (EMP) pushed the envelope even further. The Guggenheim was described by the EMP design and construction manager, Paul Zumwalt, who had visited the Guggenheim several times, as "bending on X and Y whereas the EMP bends on X, Y and Z." He noted that the EMP breaks all of the rules and is "much more complicated structurally than Bilbao."[11] The project has met with mixed public reaction, but people have reacted. As alternative rocker Isaac Brock of Modest Mouse, whose lyrics are critical of the modern landscape, says, "It's a pretty goofy-looking building. . . . But I kind of like it because . . . at least it's something to talk about, complain about, or whatever you decide to do with it."[12] The context of the EMP is worth noting. It is located at the base of the Space Needle, next to the Fun Forest amusement park, with the Monorail running through the project—all elements of the 1962 Seattle World's Fair, the Century 21 Exposition, which looked into the future.

The six sculptural forms are clad in five distinct colors of treated stainless steel and factory-painted aluminum panels. The mass has a footprint of 35,000 square feet enclosing 140,000 square feet of museum space. The A. Zahner Company designed, fabricated, and installed the 180,000-square-foot skin, comprised of 4,000 panels. The company has worked on projects with Frank Gehry for over 20 years. Roger A. Reed of A. Zahner Company commented that the EMP showed them "there were absolutely no limits, whatsoever" in terms of curtain-wall design.[13]

The seemingly random form is anything but random. As Leatherbarrow and Mostafavi comment in *Surface Architecture:* "The use of the term 'formless' to describe [buildings such as Gehry's] . . . is thus appropriate only if comparisons are made with buildings that exhibit traditional geometries, for the unity that results from these surfaces is nothing other than 'formal': form that intends to be original, nonreferential (to place or program), spectacular in its chromatic and luminous effects, and insistently coherent."[14]

10.4.1 THE SWOOPY FORM

Its beginnings, consisting of loose sketches, were also coherent. Gehry worked closely with Paul Allen, whose Microsoft fortune financed the project's construction, and Allen's sister, Jody Patton, EMP director, to develop ideas. Despite much talk about the forms coming from the idea of broken guitars, it was not that simple. Gehry did cut up a Stratocaster electric guitar, arranging the shapes as inspiration, just as he walked the grounds around the Space Needle and toured the Fun Forest. Three main models were constructed with one hundred others filling in between. The collaborative design process between Gehry, Allen, and Patton brought the Monorail into the project; originally it was to pass by the side of the EMP. Paul Allen popularized the word "swoopy" in describing the EMP.

Going from physical model to actual building is a complex process with a nonorthogonal building. First the final model was digitized. This information was then "rationalized," allowing the forms to be translated into pieces that could be unfolded and fabricated from flat sheets of metal.[15] The program that translated the information was CATIA, developed by the French company Dassault Systemes for designing fighter jets. Boeing and Chrysler now use it in their design programs.

FIGURE 10.11 The Monorail, designed for the 1962 Seattle World's Fair, passes through the EMP. Photo by John Stamets; © John Stamets.

A structural frame of steel ribs, covered with 5 inches (128 mm) of 5500 psi reinforced concrete, creates the basic form. Wire mesh was welded to the ribs to further define the form. On top of this was stapled a fine stainless steel mesh that acted as backing for the shotcrete. The steel ribs were tied to the shotcrete with Nelson studs and the steel reinforcing. Also welded to the steel ribs are the pedestals that hold the curtain wall to the structure. (See Figures 10.12 and 10.13.)

The water barrier was applied directly to the concrete shell. The hot-applied, Hydrotech waterproofing has a reinforcing mesh in the final coat. Preformed neoprene-flashing boots sealed each of the 3,000 curtain wall pedestals projecting through the waterproofing. Two inches (50 mm) of polyurethane foam were sprayed on top of the waterproofing, creating an inverted roof system. A UV protective coating was painted on the surface primarily for protection prior to the installation of the curtain wall.

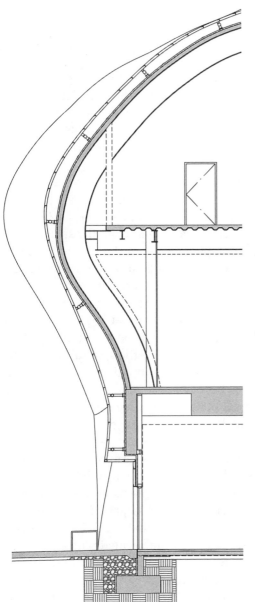

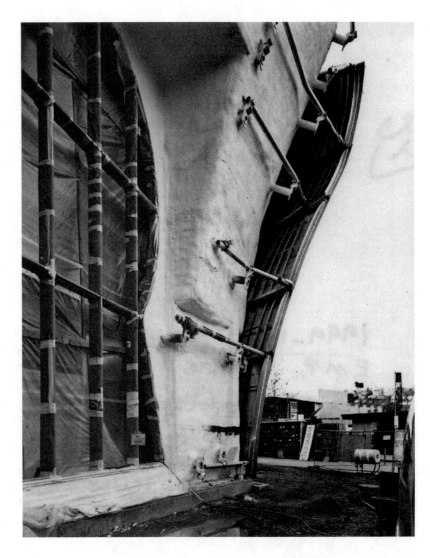

FIGURES 10.12–10.14 The structural frame of steel ribs was covered with wire mesh to define the form. Stainless steel mesh was used as a backing for the 5 inches of shot-crete seen in the center of Figure 10.13. Aluminum pipe girders were attached to pedestals secured to the structural steel frame. Figures 10.12 and 10.14 are courtesy of Gehry Partners, LLP. Figure 10.13 is a photo by John Stamets; © John Stamets.

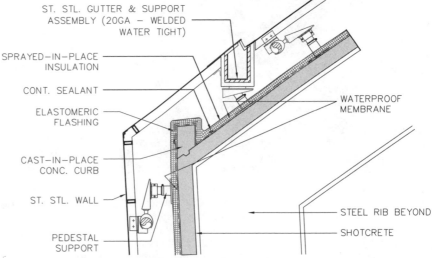

ST. STL. GUTTER & SUPPORT ASSEMBLY (20GA — WELDED WATER TIGHT)

SPRAYED–IN–PLACE INSULATION

CONT. SEALANT

ELASTOMERIC FLASHING

CAST–IN–PLACE CONC. CURB

ST. STL. WALL

PEDESTAL SUPPORT

WATERPROOF MEMBRANE

STEEL RIB BEYOND

SHOTCRETE

10.4.2 THE DIGITAL SKIN

The curtain wall serves two purposes. It provides the color, texture, and pattern of the skin. It also provides a water shedding surface intended to protect the waterproofing layers below. The metal shingles on the EMP shed most of the water to a drain at the perimeter of the building or to gutters fabricated as part of the system. Any water that might pass through the curtain wall—primarily due to pressure differences—will flow down the surface of the insulation. At the low spots, there are internal roof drains. Finally, the actual water barrier to stop moisture that makes it past the first two layers is below the insulation.

Aluminum pipe girders are attached to the steel pedestals to form a frame onto which the panels are attached. The minimum dimension required for the pedestal is 9 inches (230 mm); 5 inches (128 mm) for the concrete and 4 inches (100 mm) for the pedestal flashing. But some of the pedestals cantilever from the structure as much as 10 feet (3 m) to accommodate the complex curves of the facade. To compensate for construction tolerances, A. Zahner developed "a device that allowed the location of the pipe girts to be adjusted in any direction within a four-inch sphere."[16] Each pedestal had a CATIA datum aligned using GPS (Global Positioning System). CATIA and Pro/Engineer workstations at the construction site provided data during construction. Area take-offs could be accomplished in a matter of seconds. A former Boeing employee was hired by the general contractor to transmit the required information and facilitate smooth operations between the various subcontractors.

The curtain wall panels have an extruded aluminum head and sill that bolt to the pipe girders (see Figure 10.15). Computer numerical control—that is, CNC-fabricated aluminum ribs—gives form to the panel. The panels are designed to bear their own weight and lateral loads. Multiframe software was used to model wind loads, as testing each of the 4,800 panels was unrealistic. The panels in turn were clad with 21,000 metal "shingles." The shingles were fabricated with CNC software that guided the machine that cut the odd shaped pieces, no two of which were identical. The fabrication tolerance of the panels was 1/64 inch (0.40 mm). The panels were installed by a crane aided with lifts for manually positioning the panels. As with the shingles, no two panels were identical. The panels, called ZEPPS, for Zahner Engineered Profile Panel System, are typically about 8 feet (2.4 meters) wide by 12 to 15 feet (3.7 to 4.6 m) long. The shingles range from 6 inches (150 mm) square to 2'10" by 12'0" (0.9 by 3.7 m).

The colored stainless steel sheet was produced in the United Kingdom by the Rimex Group. The "interference coating" was applied to the raw metal—a process that regulates the thickness of the transparent chromium oxide film on the stainless steel surface.[17] This "interference" with the natural reflection of the light spectrum produced the mirrored purple and glass bead-blasted gold. The natural stainless steel surface has a propri-

FIGURE 10.15 Each panel has a subframe of CNC-fabricated ribs with an extruded aluminum head and sill. The shingles were screwed to this frame, which was then attached to the pipe girders. Some shingles were installed at the factory, others left for on-site installation. Photo by John Stamets; © John Stamets.

etary angel-hair finish applied by A. Zahner at its Kansas City, Missouri, plant. The aluminum surfaces have baked-on finishes (PPG Megaflon MC) of red and blue enamels. Gehry described his color decisions: "I liked the idea of red because it will fade like an old truck...The gold and silver are colors of rock 'n' roll...and the baby blue is from a baby-blue Stratocaster...The purple is from Jimi Hendrix's 'Purple Haze.'"[18] The gold bead finish, designed to change with rain and light, had never been used on an exterior before. The shingles were attached with counter-sunk, tamper-resistant screws, which were interference color-coated. The glass roof sculpture, also designed by Gehry Partners, was installed by Permasteelisa. It consists of 621 pieces of ¾-inch laminated glass, produced by Cricursa of Spain, anchored to three to four sets of support hardware, which in turn were attached to 4-inch (100 mm) diameter steel pipes and a frame system.

10.5 COMPARISONS: MONDRIAN PLANES AND SWOOPY FORMS

Cladding an irregular form is most easily accomplished with small pieces. Lapping the pieces shingle style allows for water to run off—the rationale behind the centuries of shingling both roofs and walls. Gehry commented that "all I've done is taken roofing materials and made a building out of it."[19] This simple concept is used to clad the amorphous shape of the EMP. And a screen for the rain is used as the way to manage water. By definition this is a drainage cavity system. The oddity is that the cavity, which should be called an attic in some locations, ranges from 4 inches (100 mm) to almost 10 feet (3 m).

The system is not pressure equalized, but the water barrier and the air barrier systems are very complete and are also repeated. The waterproofing functions as an air barrier, as does the urethane foam insulation. Vapor diffusion should not be a problem, as it is stopped from the inside by the water membrane and on the exterior by the insulation. There may, under certain circumstances, be condensation on the curtain-wall frame and the panels, but these are of stainless steel and aluminum. This layered approach is even more critical considering that the roof construction is indistinguishable from the wall construction.

In comparison, the aluminum and glass curtain wall on the Westin New York at Times Square is unforgiving of any moisture that might penetrate. For this reason the frame is a sophisticated pressure-equalized system. It is also helped by the fact that it is vertical in all locations. The ACM curtain wall is a standard drainage cavity wall with a metal stud back up wall. The building wrap, Tyvek CommercialWrap, provides both the water and the air barrier.

The EMP could not have been designed without 3-D modeling programs. The Westin New York curtain wall is similar to earlier aluminum and glass curtain walls, but assembling and installing the combination of different glass units and frames would have been nothing short of chaotic without computerized tracking of the pieces. Fabrication would have been difficult as well, compared to standard, uniform assembly.

Of the two buildings—the Westin New York and the Experience Music Project—the EMP was the most experimental. Everything was new and challenging and, for the most part, worked because of the extensive up-front design efforts. Everyone who worked on the construction of the EMP learned something. Some things did not work and were changed. Rigid polystyrene boards held down with aluminum straps were originally intended to provide the insulation. This was changed to sprayed-in-place urethane, making it more constructible, as well as offering better thermal, air, and vapor barriers.

In comparison, the construction of the Westin New York was very straightforward. Minor problems were easily dealt with as affiliates of the owner were also the construction manager and developer. This prompted decisions based on long-term functioning rather than decisions based only on initial cost or expedience, which is often the case. It also allowed for easy fast-tracking of the project. With the high level of organization, the $300 million plus project came in under budget, even though it was constructed during a period of labor shortage. The fast-tracked project was also helped by the cooperation of the all-union crews working together.[20]

The similarities of the two buildings lie in the commitment to a functioning exterior wall that mediates the environment as well as creates the particular aesthetic. Both of these projects are good examples of the collaboration necessary between designers, manufacturers, and installers with sophisticated curtain wall design. It also points out the invaluable role of the owner and the construction manager or general contractor. Without a team effort, it is doubtful that either of these projects would have been accomplished in the time frame and within the projected budget. Where these two pieces will find themselves in 25 years and in the annals of contemporary architectural history is yet to be known; but whatever the assessment, the walls should not be leaking.

10.6 FUNCTIONAL KIT: THICK AND THIN WALLS

There is nothing deceptive in the wrapping of the forms of the EMP or the Westin New York at Times Square—they are what they appear to be, thin skins of metal and glass. The EMP's cladding reads as a thin membrane, stretched over the amorphous structure. The shingles that cover the form, and their thinness, are clearly discernable. However, the thickness of the actual exterior wall and roof, which varies greatly, is not. The canvas of the Westin is composed of thin planes of glass and metal—an ordinary reading of a curtain wall. On the hotel tower, the thickness of the wall is the thickness of the insulated glass unit. Masonry and concrete walls are expected to have a certain thickness. The following sections discuss a concrete wall made even thicker by the demands of energy codes and a brick veneer made thinner to meet seismic restraints.

10.7 VITRA CONFERENCE PAVILION: THICKER WALLS IN GERMANY

The German furniture manufacturer Vitra turned to international architects to design their complex of buildings in Weil am Rhein. It is the site of Frank Gehry's first European buildings—the Vitra Design Museum and Factory Hall—which are a jumble of white rectangular and curved forms. In 1993, Tadao Ando designed his first building outside of Japan, separated from the design museum by a Claes Oldenburg sculpture.

Adding thermal insulation to a poured-in-place concrete wall is the challenge Tadao Ando faced when designing to European norms. Ando's trademark of exposed interior and exterior concrete is a finely articulated system predicated on the Japanese way of building. In Japan the formwork is spaced 10 inches (250 mm) apart and held together with closely spaced ties. There are no additional water barriers or insulation. Often glass seemingly disappears into the concrete in Ando's projects. At the time of construction of the Conference Pavilion, German codes required thermal insulation in the wall. The result is a double wall of 16 inches (400 mm) with a core of thermal insulation. Desiring the look of the closely spaced ties common in Japan but needing to minimize the number of thermal breaks created by the ties, a series of "fake" tie cones were cast into the concrete. The codes also required more thermally responsive windows. The glass does not disappear into the concrete; rather, insulated glass units bound by metal frames with thermal breaks were used by Ando. The frequently spaced vertical mullions give the facade "an industrial look," according to one critic.[21] The building, while imitating the fine texture of Japanese concrete practices, nonetheless has a heavier feel to it. Energy codes changed Ando's simple use of uninsulated concrete and single sheets of glass. And while the markings are reminiscent of the finely crafted Japanese concrete wall, with its traditional module of 6 x 3 feet (1.8 x 0.9 m) with six tie holes, the thickness comes from the need to insulate exterior walls.[22]

FIGURE 10.16 Vitra Conference Pavilion (Tadao Ando, 1993). Photo by Inge Roeker.

10.8 SAN FRANCISCO MUSEUM OF MODERN ART: THIN BRICK THAT WORKS

Through an international search based on past work and qualifications, the Swiss architect Mario Botta was selected as the architect, with HOK of San Francisco, to design the San Francisco Museum of Modern Art (SFMOMA). This was his first North American commission and his first in a highly active seismic zone. Botta's signature style of bold masonry forms was not lost on SFMOMA. His preliminary proposal was for a poured-in-place concrete frame with anchored brick veneer. The actual construction was a steel frame clad with precast concrete panels with cast-in-place thin brick.

FIGURE 10.17 San Francisco Museum of Modern Art (Mario Botta and HOK, 1994). Photo by Linda Brock.

10.8.1 THE BRICK RUSE

Brick, possibly the first building product and in production for over 10,000 years, also deserves the title of Great Impostor, along with terra-cotta and EIFS (see Chapter 9). The difference with fired-clay brick is that it imitates itself. (Other materials, such as EIFS, stucco, and precast concrete can be formed to replicate brick.) Masonry walls usually denote load-bearing walls, not lightweight panels. With market competition from lower-cost and more quickly erected cladding systems, there is increasing pressure for more economical fired-clay brick claddings, particularly in the residential market. While some question the durability of anchored brick veneer with a steel-stud backup wall (see Chapter 6), a number of attempts have been made to decrease even further the cost and weight of brick masonry cladding. Many "brick" buildings are clad with a thin-fired clay and shale tile, called thin brick.

One of the earliest attempts to produce a thin-fired clay product that, when installed, gave the appearance of load-bearing masonry occurred in eighteenth-century England. These so-called "mathematical tiles" of fired clay, a few centimeters in depth, were widely used as a way of circumventing brick tax laws. (See Figure 10.18.) Brick was a popular face material for houses, but it was also heavily taxed. The original law, which taxed all brick equally, was instigated to discourage undersizing of brick—the more brick on a house, the higher the tax. The result was the production of larger units, called "tax brick," because the fewer the bricks, the lower the tax. This lead to still more legislation, which set a maximum brick size for the unit tax; any brick larger than this maximum size was taxed twice.

The mathematical tiles were not taxable under the existing law. These tiles had been produced for some time as a fire-resistive and imitative brick covering for frame houses. However, they never became popular until the full-sized brick was taxed. The tiles were nailed, shingle style, on wood battens to give the impression

FIGURE 10.18 Reproductions of fired-clay mathematical tiles that imitate brick masonry from nineteenth-century England. Photo by G. Russell Heliker.

of a wall of brick. The lower half of the tile was molded to resemble a standard-sized brick while the upper half comprised a nailing lip over which the next tile would be positioned. After the tiles were nailed to the structure, the joints were mortared. Special corner pieces completed the ruse. All brick taxes were finally repealed in the 1850s, and the tiles again fell into disfavor.[23] Today the tiles are produced primarily for restoration purposes, although they recently were used in combination with fiber-cement siding on the winning entry of a national housing competition in the United Kingdom. The competition, whose theme was "innovation from tradition," explored "environmentally efficient and cost effective methods of construction."[24]

Today thin brick is generally applied in one of three ways:

- As part of a lightweight panel, which is often completely prefabricated
- Adhered directly to a masonry or cementitious substrate, descriptively called "lick 'em and stick 'em brick" by masons
- Cast into concrete panels

10.8.2 Reducing Construction Costs on the SFMOMA

The change from a concrete frame with anchored brick veneer to a steel frame with precast concrete panels on the SFMOMA was due to "vigilant value engineering." Without altering the look of the building, $17 million was slashed from the initial $62 million construction estimate, according to the project manager from Bechtel Group, Inc.[25] Costs were also reduced by close cooperation among all subcontractors, who met weekly for four months to catch problems in the drawings and specifications and to determine scheduling of the work. This was possible because the contracts were negotiated, allowing for early input from the general contractor and subcontractors. The basic program was reviewed and reduced in square footage and bay sizes and ceiling heights were regularized. Using a steel frame instead of a poured-in-place concrete frame was estimated to have saved up to nine months construction time. The use of black and white granite from Canada instead of Italian marble was a savings of nearly $200,000. The thin brick cast into the concrete panels was a savings in part because of the lower labor costs in this strong union city.[26] (At the precast plant, one worker can lay 33 thin bricks per minute.)

10.8.3 Thin Brick in Precast Concrete Panels

One of the major design problems the SFMOMA faced was accommodating seismic loading. Casting thin brick in precast concrete panels provided the solution. "Seismic restraints in San Francisco made conventional masonry construction unfeasible. The brick gasket system produced a unique masonry facade at a significant cost savings," according to Eric Foster of Swinerton & Walberg, the general contractors.[27] The average panel was 10 by 28½ feet (3 by 8.7 m) and contained 1,500 to 2,300 bricks, 1 inch (25 mm) in thickness.[28] The reinforced concrete was 9 inches (230 mm) thick with the first 3 inches (75 mm) comprised of a colored concrete with fine aggregate exposed at the formed, raked joints.[29] Not only was this system more economical than anchored brick veneer, the building was completed in record time, with the panels erected in 20 twenty days.

The Scott System of Denver, Colorado, manufactured the thin brick system used on the San Francisco Museum of Modern Art. The company designs and fabricates the elastomeric-urethane form liner, selects the thin brick, and prequalifies and trains the precaster if necessary. The system offers infinite design flexibility, as the gasket liner can accommodate any bonding pattern, ornate cornices, or radii. The most costly of the various form liners, the urethane liners are also the most flexible and can be reused—up to 100 times—so economy is based on repetition. Ridges in the liner position the thin brick and create the joint profile on the surface of the panel. These ridges also stop the majority of the cement paste from reaching the face of the thin brick during casting. Because the fit of the brick in the gasket liner is critical, the tolerances of the thin brick (+0 and −1⁄16 inch, 1.5 mm) and the liner (+ or −1⁄32 inch, 0.80 mm), are very tight. The tight size tolerance also makes installation easier for the concrete producer. SFMOMA had an unusual brick pattern with high relief. Besides the main liner, two additional liners were used, one to set back one row of bricks and the other to set rows of half-brick on a 45-degree angle in a sawtooth pattern.[30] (See Figures 10.19 and 10.20.)

The liner is attached to the precast form bed and a release agent is applied. A very light coating of a retardant is also sprayed on the face of the thin brick to aid in removing any cement paste that seeps around the liner. After the thin brick is inserted, face down in the liner, steel reinforcing is placed on chairs, and the concrete is poured in the same manner as any precast panel. Within 24 hours, the liner is removed, and the brick face is cleaned. No mortar is necessary, as the mortar joint, formed by the liner, is concrete. The bond of the concrete to the thin brick is dependent on a mechanical key provided by dovetailed slots in the thin brick as well as the balance between the initial rate of absorption of the brick and the cement-to-water ratio of the concrete. One test of brick-to-concrete bond indicated that "the apparent point of failure was in the brick itself, as the layer bonded to the epoxy [used to bond a steel cross-plate for the testing apparatus] pulled away from the rest of the brick."[31] The bond between thin brick cast integrally with concrete is generally stronger than the bond between brick and mortar in conventionally laid systems.[32] There have been few, if any, reported instances of a thin brick coming loose when integrally cast in concrete, an advantage over anchored brick veneer. Even if a thin brick delaminates from the panel, it is much less hazardous than a section of nominal four-inch veneer that has lost its anchorage. Also, if one or more of the brick faces fails, it does not affect the ability of the precast panel to stop water. The rich patterning of the projecting sawtooth brick on the SFMOMA would have been difficult to produce with anchored brick veneer. It also

FIGURE 10.19 The three different types of thin-brick bonds can be seen at the end of this precast unit for the San Francisco Museum of Modern Art. Photo courtesy of Scott System, Denver, Colorado.

FIGURES 10.20 AND 10.21 Special corner panels were cast. The vertical joint between the precast panels can be seen in Figure 10.21. Photo 10.20 courtesy of Scott System. Photo 10.21 by Ray Cole.

would have created ledges where water might enter, as would have the raked joints—a durability problem with anchored brick veneer.

Advantages of thin-brick faced precast panels include the ability for year-round fabrication in a controlled environment and elimination of skilled masons. The panels can be erected by crane, saving scaffolding costs, and on-site storage is minimized. Any innovations possible with precast concrete panels, such as the inclusion of rigid insulation in the panel, can be realized with the brick-faced panels. The only apparent disadvantages of precast brick cladding systems are the weight and thickness of the precast panel. The initial cost may be more than some other systems, but it may prove more economical in the long run. However, this is a system that must be designed by an engineer who understands both good design practices for precast concrete and the anomalies created with the thin brick. For example, bowing of precast concrete panels can be more pronounced when there is a thin-brick face.[33] Differential movement, resulting from thermal and moisture expansion of fired-clay products and concrete shrinkage, must be considered. The use of glazed clay products should be carefully reviewed. Problems from vapor diffusion or water ingress behind the glazed surface can result in freeze-thaw damage.

Just as with metal and glass curtain walls, this is a system that requires the collaboration of the architect, manufacturer of the thin-brick system, concrete precaster, owner, general contractor or construction manager, and structural engineer from the project's inception through its completion. The manufacturer of the thin-brick system (brick and liner) should participate in the selection of the precaster. The cladding on the SFMOMA is successful aesthetically and durable, in part because of the close working relationship of all parties, including architect Mario Botta. As well, the project met budget restrictions.

10.9 ARE TWO WALLS BETTER THAN ONE?

The Westin New York at Times Square is an example of the level of sophistication possible with coated and tinted glazing in insulated units. Even as energy codes are becoming more restrictive, the desire for vision glass is not likely to disappear. Are two glass walls better than one? In 1903 the Steiff factory in Giengen, Germany, incorporated a double glass exterior wall. The two glass walls, separated by 10 inches (250 mm), maximized daylighting while reducing heat loss due to low temperatures and high winds. Additions to the factory, in 1904 and 1908, used the same system, attesting to its success. The first modern double wall that integrated ventilation was in the United States. Cannon Design, in association with HOK, designed the Hooker Office Building in Niagara Falls, New York. The double-skin wall, constructed in 1983, had an outer wall of double-glazed insulating units and an interior wall of single-glazing, separated by 5 feet (1.5 mm). The blue-green, iron-oxide glass on the exterior maximizes light penetration while limiting solar gain.[34] Louvers in the space prevent direct radiation into the interior. For its time, Michael Wigginton called it "perhaps the largest passive solar collector in the world, and possibly the most energy efficient office building in its climatic zone."[35]

In spite of this early example, the double-skin facade is making a slower appearance in North America than Europe. Part of this lag has been attributed to higher energy costs in Europe, where the double-skin facade is gaining widespread popularity, particularly in Germany, where access to daylight and fresh air is mandated for office workers. Some think that adopting the newly revised ASHRAE 90.1 will discourage construction of glass buildings, but it may also lead to looking for more innovative ways of retaining the same effect.[36]

Energy savings is only one of the reasons to consider a double-skin wall. If this is the sole reason, the life-cycle analysis may not justify its use. Klaus Daniels, speaking of European examples, in *The Technology of Ecological Building*, states that "the use of double-leaf facades is currently in fashion and is normally justified by an apparent early return on the initial high cost investment. This is generally, in simple terms, a misconception."[37] (It should be noted that this is a 1997 publication, and the economies of the system are rapidly changing.) Initial costs include the construction of two walls and the cost of additional environmental systems' controls within the plenum. Ongoing costs include the loss of leasable space because of the increased thickness of the walls. Maintenance costs include cleaning four glass surfaces (and can be very high, depending on accessibility), maintaining sealant on two walls, and maintaining the system controls. It is safe to say that if an owner is looking to recoup fully the capital and maintenance costs through reduced energy bills, it probably is not going to happen in the short term nor, in North America, in the foreseeable future. Werner Lang and Thomas Herzog of the Technical University of Munich estimated in 2000 that twin-face facades cost about double that of conventional curtain walls in central Europe, and this jumps to four to fives times the cost in the U.S.[38] How quickly this might change remains to be seen. A double skin system at the University of Pennsylvania's School of Engineering and Applied Science has a 4 inch (100 mm) cavity separated by external double-glazing with single-glazing units on the interior. According to Robert Bicchiarelli of Permasteelisa Cladding Technologies, which manufactured and installed the system, the cost is about 20 percent higher than a "high-quality standard curtain wall system."[39]

Currently, double-skin facades are usually one of three types.[40] A *buffer wall* is essentially a grossly oversized insulated glass wall with 10 to 30 inches (250 to 760 mm) between the glass lites. Warm air may be exhausted at the top of this plenum. *Extract-air facades* link the plenum created by the two glass walls with the heating, ventilating, and air-conditioning (HVAC) system. The extract air is circulated through heat exchangers to save energy. Generally, the exterior wall is single-glazed and the interior double-glazed. These are most useful in areas with high winds, noise, or fumes that would hinder natural ventilation. The third manipulation of double walls, called *twin-face facades,* provides openings in both skins for natural ventilation. In buffer walls and twin-face facades, either or both walls can be insulating glass units to enhance energy savings. The dimension of the space between the two walls is largely dependent on the system used to maintain the plenum, including window washing. There are moves to use thinner walls, such as the 4-inch (100 mm) Permasteelisa example at the University of Pennsylvania previously noted.

The advantages of double-glazed walls go beyond energy savings. Some of these advantages are shared with single walls, for example provision of outside views, natural light, and a connection to the outdoors. Other advantages singular to the double wall include: natural ventilation in buildings with high wind loads; sound isolation; and a protected space for louvers and shades to control glare and heat gain, light shelves to direct daylight deeper into a floor plate, and prismatic components to control thermal transfer. The operation of mechanical systems integrated with this double envelope can enhance overall performance of the building. Studies in Germany have shown improvement of 5 to 30 decibels with double walls—although a downside can be the transmittal of noise from one floor to another if windows open on the plenum.[41] Finally, there are ecological and social values. Reducing dependence on limited natural resources and contributing to the health and well-being of the occupants are considerations.

10.10 SEATTLE JUSTICE CENTER

The City of Seattle, Washington, has a goal of promoting sustainable building practices with a mandate for the new Civic Center campus buildings to stand as models of this philosophy. In a charrette with the city and the designers, three goals were established that were later refined for the design of the Seattle Justice Center. First, it was to have a minimum LEED silver rating. Second, it was to emphasize sustainable features that were "legible to people using the building." Finally, ideas were to be pursued that may not influence the LEED rating but would have value as demonstration projects.[42] In addition, the city stipulated that the building should last 100 years (such durability criteria per se is presently not part of LEED 2.1).

FIGURE 10.22 Seattle Justice Center (NBBJ Architects, 2002). Photo by Christian Richters; © 2003 Christian Richters. Reproduced courtesy of NBBJ Architects.

FIGURE 10.23 The punched openings of the stone cladding on the police headquarters to the left sharply contrasts with the double-glazed wall of the municipal court. Photo courtesy of NBBJ Architects.

The two tenants of the Center—the Seattle Police Headquarters and the Seattle Municipal Court—needed separate identities. (See Figures 10.22 and 10.23.) The stone cladding with the punched openings of the police headquarters reflects the traditional integrity and strength associated with the police force. The city wanted something different for the court, something that would "symbolize the transparency and accessibility of justice."[43] The double-glazed wall provides this image while serving as a demonstration project easily understood by the general public. (The other component serving this purpose is a green roof.) The double-glazed wall consists of two glass walls separated by a 30-inch (760 mm) air space. (See Figure 10.24.) Natural ventilation of the plenum, controlled with louvers, reduces solar gain in the summer and reduces heat loss during the winter when the vents are closed. The system, by definition a buffer wall, is independent of the mechanical systems with the exception of buffer sensors. These are connected to the building management system so that louvers can be opened or closed, depending on the buffer temperature and whether the mechanical system is in heating or cooling mode. A light shelf, located 8 feet above each floor, shields direct daylight while

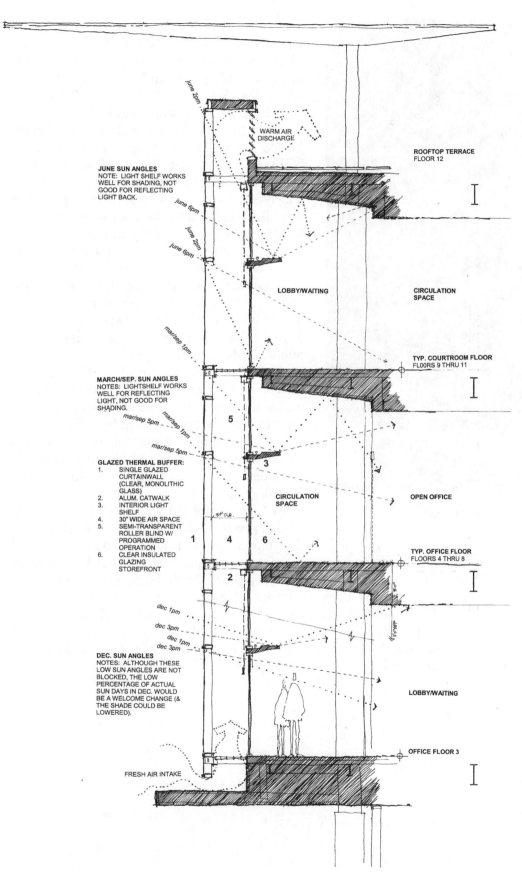

WARM AIR DISCHARGE

ROOFTOP TERRACE
FLOOR 12

JUNE SUN ANGLES
NOTE: LIGHT SHELF WORKS
WELL FOR SHADING, NOT
GOOD FOR REFLECTING
LIGHT BACK.

june 2pm
june 6pm
june 2pm
june 6pm

LOBBY/WAITING

**CIRCULATION
SPACE**

mar/sep 1pm

TYP. COURTROOM FLOOR
FLOORS 9 THRU 11

MARCH/SEP. SUN ANGLES
NOTES: LIGHTSHELF WORKS
WELL FOR REFLECTING
LIGHT, NOT GOOD FOR
SHADING.

mar/sep 5pm
mar/sep 1pm
mar/sep 5pm

5

3

GLAZED THERMAL BUFFER:
1. SINGLE GLAZED
   CURTAINWALL
   (CLEAR, MONOLITHIC
   GLASS)
2. ALUM. CATWALK
3. INTERIOR LIGHT
   SHELF
4. 30" WIDE AIR SPACE
5. SEMI-TRANSPARENT
   ROLLER BLIND W/
   PROGRAMMED
   OPERATION
6. CLEAR INSULATED
   GLAZING
   STOREFRONT

**CIRCULATION
SPACE**

OPEN OFFICE

1   **4**   **6**

TYP. OFFICE FLOOR
FLOORS 4 THRU 8

2

dec 1pm
dec 3pm
dec 1pm
dec 3pm

DEC. SUN ANGLES
NOTES: ALTHOUGH THESE
LOW SUN ANGLES ARE NOT
BLOCKED, THE LOW
PERCENTAGE OF ACTUAL
SUN DAYS IN DEC. WOULD
BE A WELCOME CHANGE (&
THE SHADE COULD BE
LOWERED).

LOBBY/WAITING

OFFICE FLOOR 3

FRESH AIR INTAKE

FIGURE 10.24 The ventilated buffer wall in combination with light shelves brings daylight into the building while controlling glare and heat before it enters the interior, conditioned space. Illustration and photo courtesy of NBBJ Architects.

FIGURE 10.25 Buffer wall under construction.

directing daylight deeper into the space. Operable shades reduce glare. The increased use of daylighting reduces the need for artificial light in the south bays, which have daylighting from two sides. Sensors adjust the artificial light, depending on the available daylight.

With the double-skin wall on the Seattle Justice Center, it was noted by the architect, NBBJ Architects, that "benign climates such as Seattle's and projects like the Justice Center with a high percentage of core floor area to perimeter zone floor area make the realization of overall building energy savings difficult to achieve." The double wall effected a 33 percent energy savings in the adjacent perimeter zone, but the preliminary estimates indicate that this translates to only a 2 percent overall building energy savings.[44] Innovative mechanical systems, not nearly as visible nor as interesting to the general public, reduced energy bills by 32 percent, according to Joe Llona of CDi Engineers (mechanical engineers for the project). It is estimated that the initial cost of these mechanical systems will be repaid within three to five years.[45] The additional cost of the double-skin facade was approximately $320,000 more than a traditional facade, on this $70 million project, according to NBBJ Architects.[46]

In Canada and the U.S. it is hard to justify doubling walls because of the costs. Reducing the amount of vision glass in the exterior wall and increasing the thermal insulation of the opaque areas will realize the same goal much more quickly. But energy expenditure should be considered as part of a larger package that includes our desire for light and views (the Justice Center faces Elliot Bay in Seattle); the quality of the space for people working or visiting the building; the monumental impact of a double-glazed wall; the decreased dependence on fossil fuels; and, finally, the message sent by a city, using a public building, about the importance of sustainability.

Wood-Frame Construction: Designing for the Climate and the Future

11.1 DURABILITY—THE LINCHPIN OF SUSTAINABILITY

The impact of buildings on the environment is of growing concern. Architects are interested in, and sometimes required by codes to design, more sustainable buildings. Using "green" components, reducing energy consumption, and developing off-grid systems are all sustainable practices. But the element of sustainability as concerns construction that could make a marked difference, in a short amount of time, is increasing the durability of exterior walls. Durable walls would not only last longer but perform better. This is especially true for residential construction—most of which is light-wood frame—as it represents such a large percentage of new construction. But increasing durability requires true innovation in the way exterior walls are designed as well as dogged diligence in executing and maintaining the design.

11.1.1 INNOVATION IN WOOD FRAMED WALLS

Light-wood, or western platform, framing may be North America's most significant contribution to innovative construction. While sophisticated glazing, high-tech materials, and space-age cladding systems are more likely to originate in Europe or Asia, when it comes to light-wood framing countries look to the U.S. and Canada. As more countries experience a housing shortage in light of dwindling resources, they are becoming more interested in our century-old method of constructing light-wood frames. (In addition to the English and French versions, Canada Housing and Mortgage Corporation, or CMHC, now publishes its *Canadian Wood-Frame House Construction* in German and Spanish.) But there have been serious failures with wood framed walls. Is this a system worth exporting, particularly as a sustainable construction method?

Innovation in wood framing has generally occurred outside of the architectural community. One such area is in the production of more and more economical housing to meet market demands—sometimes to the detriment of durability and aesthetics. The best example may be the proliferation of "manufactured" houses in the United States. Defined by having an integral steel chassis, manufactured or mobile housing—its predecessor was the mobile home—has been the fastest-growing segment of the housing market. The production cost of such factory-built homes is low due to the cost-effective manufacturing process and absence of regional building code restrictions. Since 1976, manufactured housing in the United States has been governed by a single federal building code (known as the HUD Code) administered by the Department of Housing and Urban Development. Because manufactured homes are moveable, they can be situated on leased or rented sites in many jurisdictions. This further reduces the initial cost of owning a home. It should be noted that manufactured housing has the potential, sometimes realized, of producing a superior product because of the quality control possible with factory construction.

There have also been new developments, some more successful than others, in materials and systems, particularly with engineered wood products, claddings, water and air barriers, vapor retarders, and windows. For example, window frames, once made almost exclusively of wood and later steel, have gone through several translations. The technology developed during and after World War II produced aluminum sliders. Today, good, functional windows may have frames of wood, extruded aluminum, steel, vinyl, or fiberglass. Further innovations are occurring within the design of the frame. Thermal breaks are common in aluminum windows. Exterior finishes last longer. Finally, some window frames are being designed to shed water that enters the frame and drain any interstitial water. There have also been tremendous innovations in glazing; double and even triple glazing, suspended films, low-E glass, and spectrally selective glazing are now common in residential windows in many climates. However, water entry still remains a major problem. While well-designed windows are available, they are not necessarily commonly used or required by codes. Future developments and code requirements will undoubtedly focus on more energy efficient and watertight windows.

11.1.2 ARCHITECTS AND THE WOOD-FRAMED WALL

Much of the experimentation in wood-framed walls by architects has focused more on design aesthetics than economics or durability. Architects from Frank Lloyd

Wright to Peter Eisenman have used wood framing to test their formal ideas, and (unfortunately) many have had their share of failures. The large overhangs on Wright's Meyer May House (1908) were originally constructed of wood. When Steelcase restored the house in 1987, the badly sagging overhangs had to be reconstructed in steel to maintain the thin profile at the roof's edge, which is so important to the design. Using the depth of wood necessary for the roof beams—which Wright did not do—would have substantially altered the appearance. Whether the fault of the designer or the contractor, Eisenman's House VI was noted for being "improperly flashed, under structured, uninsulated, and, certainly in its stucco work, poorly executed."[1]

Edward Ford, in "The Theory and Practice of Impermanence: The Illusion of Durability," talks about the necessity of layering walls whatever the design intent may be.[2] This is perhaps no more true than with wood-frame construction, which may also be the least well detailed of all the construction systems. An architect's involvement is often limited to floor plans and elevations, if an architect is even involved. The details are frequently left to the contractor. This is most obvious with projects where a "stamp" is not required, as is the case with single-family houses and small multifamily and commercial projects in many jurisdictions. This chapter looks at the failures of exterior walls on wood-framed condominium projects in Vancouver, British Columbia, and Seattle, Washington, and the success of two innovative walls, one on a house in Japan and the other on a house in Vancouver, to discover how architects might help create more durable and hence sustainable exterior walls in wood-framed construction.

11.1.3 LEAKY CONDOS

Rainy cities like Seattle and Vancouver serve as laboratories for water ingress problems in exterior walls. Because the volume of residential construction is so large, the problems can become monumental, particularly since they often go undetected for a number of years. Industry generally responds as soon as it is apparent that a new product that addresses the problem will be successful. But the new product may solve only part of the problem and, in some cases, introduce new ones. What is required for true innovation, as it concerns durability, is an examination of the entire wall system, which is where the designer comes in. Architects must fully understand the problems to evaluate new products in view of the whole wall. An example is the elastomeric coatings that are guaranteed to stop all water, which they most likely do. But what happens to water that inevitably enters at interfaces and penetrations?

Owners are also culpable in the proliferation of projects with poorly designed exterior walls. When purchasing a condominium, they are often looking for the largest unit with the most amenities for the lowest price. The first impression is generally what sells a unit; buyers do not thoroughly investigate the durability of the exterior wall. The push to build more quickly and more cheaply is often deemed responsible for failures of the exterior wall. While this may be true, it offers no excuse. The problems of water ingress are neither complicated nor have they changed over the years.

The failure of the exterior wall on a single-family house or even a larger wood-framed project may not be viewed as catastrophic in scope. The buildings are low-rise, and the failures are concentrated on water ingress that causes mold and mildew, certainly a health hazard and possibly devastating economically but usually only life threatening in rare cases. Often the problem with water entry is seen as a maintenance problem—something cured by that magic coat of elastomeric paint. The public, and sometimes designers, are not aware of the cases where deterioration of the wood framing is severe enough to create structural problems.

The catastrophic nature of these problems comes from their pervasiveness. Vancouver, British Columbia, and Seattle offer good examples. By 2003, the cost of repairing exterior walls of failed wood-framed condominium projects, constructed after 1985 in Vancouver, had reached $1.14 billion and was continuing to grow.[3] Similar problems were also occurring in Seattle condominiums, where the cost of water entry problems on 52 multifamily projects constructed between 1984 and 1998 approached $100 million.[4] It was estimated that the cost to repair all of the moisture damaged structures in the multifamily housing stock built in Seattle during this 14-year period could reach $1 billion.[5]

The two cities share a similar climate, although Vancouver receives slightly over 50 inches (1280 mm) of precipitation annually while Seattle receives around 36 inches (910 mm). Both have temperate climates, with the temperature rarely dipping below freezing in the winter and average high temperatures seldom rising above 80°F (27°C) in the summer. The majority of the precipitation is in the form of rain during the cool winter months. Both Seattle and Vancouver experienced housing booms during the periods when many of the buildings with failing exterior walls were constructed.

11.2 VANCOUVER, BRITISH COLUMBIA: "THE LOOK THAT DIDN'T LAST"

The newspapers in Vancouver told the story with such headlines as "The Look that Didn't Last: Trendy Stucco Design Comes Unstuck" and a series titled "Rotten to the Core."[6] Hard-luck stories of foreclosures, when owners were unable to pay the retrofit assessment, abounded. One owner, the president of the condominium association, was forced into foreclosure when she was unable to pay the retrofit assessment on her 680-square-foot apartment. She found herself left with not only the assessment bill but also a $52,500 shortfall between the mortgage and the selling price because of the devaluation of the project.[7] A banner recently stretched across the project, which is still undergoing repairs, proclaimed that $2.4 million had been spent in repairs on the seven-year-old building, at an average cost of $22,000 per unit. The only certainty was that water was getting into the walls in copious amounts. It was estimated that 75 percent of the condos built between 1988 and 1997 had leakage problems.[8] Everyone was looking for a single problem, an easy answer. Building wraps, oriented-strand board (OSB), several cladding systems, and other wall components all had their 15 minutes of fame. Building codes requiring "airtight" construction were blamed. Rumors spread that contractors were slashing the polyethylene, specified as a vapor retarder, prior to installing the gypsum board, thinking that this would solve the problem. A letter from the Architectural Institute of British Columbia listed "profit motivation, untested systems, unskilled workforces, poor detailing, poor quality components, insufficient inspection, inadequate building codes, inappropriate design, and uneven enforcement of standards" as possible causes of the water leakage.[9] Finding no single culprit and thus no panacea, a multidirectional approach was proposed.

The first task was to determine where the water was coming from. In 1996, Canada Mortgage and Housing Corporation (CMHC) sponsored the *Survey of Building Envelope Failures in the Coastal Climate of British Columbia* to "correlate building envelope performance problems which are currently being experienced in low-rise wood frame residential buildings...with sources of moisture, and design and construction features."[10] This study looked at a total of 46 three-to four-story condominium projects, each no more than eight years old. Thirty-seven were "problem" buildings, the rest were "control" buildings, defined as exhibiting no "outward signs of moisture problems" and a minimum of five years old. Cladding types were restricted to stucco, wood siding, and vinyl siding. (Exterior Insulation and Finishing Systems [EIFS] were excluded, as they were part of another study, and brick veneer was not commonly used on residential projects at the time of the study.) While not a statistically significant sampling, the results were not surprising. (It is estimated that between 1985 and 1991, six hundred such buildings were constructed in the greater Vancouver area.)

FIGURE 11.1 AND 11.2 Water entering from the outside, primarily at interface details, caused this wood-frame deterioration. Often the wood frame has rotted away, looking like charred remnants from a fire. Photos courtesy of RDH Building Engineering Ltd.

Below is a summary of the findings from the survey, by category:[11]

WATER ENTRY
- Water entering from the exterior caused "by far the majority" of the performance problems.
- Moisture trapped during construction, or water vapor from the interior, were not "found to be significant."
- 90 percent of the problems occurred at interface details or at penetrations and openings in the wall.
- Only 10 percent of the problems were caused by water entering through the field areas of the wall. (However, additional problems were caused if the cladding restricted either the drainage of water or the drying of the wall components.)
- Significant amounts of water entered at windows, decks, balconies, exterior walkways, and saddle flashings at intersecting walls.

CONSTRUCTION AND COMPONENTS
- Poor construction of details contributed to the problems, whether or not they were included in the drawings.
- The number of problems with stucco claddings was greater than those with wood or vinyl sidings. (This may relate to the fact that the application of stucco is skill related, and the "product" can be easily modified on site. For example, detergents were reputedly used as plasticizers during this time. Also vinyl and wood claddings were more likely to have overhangs because of the preference for a traditional style. They were also more likely to have a drainage plane.)
- There was "insufficient evidence" to determine differences in performance between OSB and plywood or between building wraps and building paper or felt.

DESIGN
- The absence of details (or, to a lesser extent, "poor details") was a "significant contributor to the poor performance of the as-constructed details."
- Buildings with roof overhangs performed "significantly better."
- Buildings with "simple details," or those that contained fewer of such problem details as exterior walkways and intersecting walls, performed better.

The City of Vancouver responded to the failures with a number of directives for multifamily residential construction. These included maximum moisture rates for enclosed framing lumber and sheathing of 19 percent and the inclusion of a ¾-inch (19 mm) drainage cavity. Also required was a "building envelope specialist," who would be responsible for the functional design of the exterior wall from design through construction. A joint committee of the engineering and architectural professions administered this new group of professionals called building envelope professionals. The requirements for becoming a building envelope professional included registration as an architect or engineer, experience in envelope design, and completion of a building envelope program. While acknowledging the efficacy of this idea, British Columbia later ruled that the professions could not grant the designation of a specialty. As of 2004, there was no official designation for building envelope professionals.

FIGURE 11.3 When the failed cladding was replaced on this building, an overhang at the roof was added. This should significantly help keep water off the wall. Rehabilitation design by Neale Staniszkis Doll Adams Architects. Photo courtesy of RDH Building Engineering Ltd.

The Vancouver failures produced a number of highly skilled professionals specializing in building envelope design. They continued their work with or without the official title. Unfortunately, the majority of these professionals were engineers, not architects. In abdicating this task of designing the envelope, architects once again relinquished part of their control over the greater design. Some thought that this reduced their liability, but others rightfully stated that the design of the building envelope should remain the architect's purview.

Developers in Vancouver responded to the public's fear of buying a "leaky condo" by advertising the fact that a building envelope professional was involved with their project. In their glossy prospectus—right next to the photos of future owners sipping coffee and admiring the view—were drawings of the wall construction or photos of the building envelope professional. Architects themselves were granted a higher profile than ever before. The buzzword was "rain screen." If you had a rain-screen wall, you were safe—if not, watch out.

11.2.1 POSITIVE CHANGES

The "leaky condo crisis" in Vancouver and the coastal zone of British Columbia brought about positive changes. Architects and engineers became better informed on good envelope design. Trades instituted training sessions and wrote manuals to educate their members, and research sponsored by governmental agencies, associations, and manufacturers looked at a number of specific problems. A provincial commission studied the problems and reported to the public, which led to the passage of the Homeowner Protection Act in 1998. Under this act, a Homeowners' Protection Office was formed that licenses residential builders and monitors the provision of third-party home warranty insurance for the entire province. They also function as a resource for research and promote education. CMHC published the Best Practice Guide for *Wood Frame Envelopes in the Coastal Climate of British Columbia,* which set a standard for construction.[12] CMHC also sponsored the Home 2000 with its rain-screen wall, discussed later in this chapter. Built for a popular Vancouver home show, a model of the wall showed visitors how a rain screen was constructed. In general, the public, particularly potential home buyers, became much better educated about the problems of water ingress.

The survey conducted by CMHC, and borne out through the numerous investigations of building envelope consultants, made several things clear:

- Water was coming from the exterior primarily at interfaces and around openings such as windows.
- No single component was the culprit, although poor quality construction was certainly a problem.
- The form of the building had much to do with the ability of the exterior wall to shed water.
- The lack of detailed drawings was a significant factor.[13]

Architects have control over all but the quality of construction, and even here they can exert some influence. As discussed in Chapter 1, architects should not take on projects where the budget does not allow for complete detailing and contract administration of the project. The construction budget and schedule should be adequate to assure quality construction. A building boom is no reason for architects to take on projects bound to fail. In fact, it is a time when greater caution should be exercised. Skilled workers are often in short supply and schedules even more rushed during building booms.

This also was a period of experimentation. For example, the self-ahesive membrane, peel-and-stick, was seen as a panacea to keep out water. Headers at window openings were wrapped with peel-and-stick only to be seen later to have essentially formed a bathtub from which water could not escape. Recommendations to wrap the entire window opening with peel-and-stick (or any other impermeable material) were revised.

Have all of the problems in Vancouver been solved? Certainly not. But at least the design community and the public are more aware of what the problems are and how they can be avoided.

11.2.2 NOT ONLY A WEST COAST PROBLEM

The problems in Vancouver, British Columbia, became very public. Articles originating on the East Coast of the United States referred to it as a "world-class" failure. It is not only a Vancouver problem. Moisture in wood-framed walls will create the same problems no matter where the wall is located—the damage might be slower to appear in dryer climates or may be of a different nature in hot-humid climates. A study by the building engineering firm of Morrison Hershfield looked at several "rotting wood framed apartments" in eastern Canada that required costly rehabilitation. As with the Vancouver failures, it was noted that the majority of the water came from the exterior, with interior moisture sources not contributing to "any significant degree." They also concluded that, in many cases, "very little attention has been paid at the detailing and design stage and often insufficient information is provided to the builder."[14]

11.3 SEATTLE: "WHEN IT RAINS, IT POURS IN"

During a similar time frame, Seattle experienced its own "leaky condo" crisis, with on headline reading "Condo Dwellers Lament: When It Rains, It Pours In."[15] Many attributed the failures to a building boom that created a shortage of skilled workers. Others blamed synthetic stucco or EIFS. Face-sealed barrier wall EIFS can be a problem if water gets into the wall, as it then has no path to get out. But EIFS was not the only cladding that was failing. In an informal survey of 74 multifamily buildings, conducted by the City of Seattle in 1998, 96 percent of the respondents reported that their building leaked.[16] Again, as in Vancouver, the only clear message was that water was getting into the walls.

The survey conducted by Seattle's Construction Codes Advisory Board noted that 100 percent of the 53 structures constructed after 1984 reported leaks.[17] The buildings were predominantly condominiums but also included apartments and townhouses. Over 70 percent of the structures were of wood framing, and 19 percent had concrete or steel frames. EIFS was the most widely used cladding (26 percent) with wood siding (23 percent) and stucco (20 percent) following close behind.[18] The source of the problems correlated with the findings of deficiencies noted in the 1996 *Survey of Building Envelope Failures in the Coastal Climate of British Columbia*. Nothing new here—the damage stemmed from "water intrusion through interface details, i.e., building envelope penetrations at decks, windows, and doors."[19]

While the problems in Seattle were not seen to be as pervasive as those in Vancouver, they nonetheless demanded attention. Some felt the problem was not as serious in Seattle because of one simple but important difference—overhangs were more prevalent in Seattle. Other differences focused on the fact that the building industry in Washington State was somewhat more regulated than in British Columbia.

In 1999 CMHC conducted a study comparing the Seattle and Vancouver failures.[20] It included an analysis of four stucco-clad, four-story condominium projects. Two were "problem" buildings and two were "control" buildings, one of each in Vancouver and Seattle. While minor differences were noted between the two cities, the problems were more similar than different.

The condos that did not leak were contrasted with the problem buildings. The nonleaking buildings had:

- Less wind exposure.
- "Significantly larger" roof overhangs with fewer parapet walls.
- Flashing on a greater number of openings and penetrations.
- Fewer "architectural features and details," with a greater percentage of the details flashed. The Seattle control building was noted as having "clean and simple" architectural forms, with decorative elements detailed to shed water, while the problem building had, for example, improper detailing of stucco at horizontal trim such that a bathtub was created at the bottom of the stucco panel.[21]

It is apparent that the designer may have influenced the success of the control buildings and contributed to the problem buildings' failures. It is also clear that the form of the building and quality of the construction are important. While the wind speed or direction cannot be changed, the approach to the design of the cladding on those elevations with higher exposure can be modified. The study noted that some details—such as saddle connections at the intersection of balcony and walkway and of low walls with the exterior wall, and penetrations and openings in the exterior wall—were problematic for all buildings in the survey. Furthermore, these details were not included in the building plans; typically, there was no indication as to how they were to be "made, flashed, and terminated."[22] This was left to the contractor to determine in the field.

The Northwest Wall and Ceiling Bureau (NWCB), a stucco trade association, which participated in the study, related the good performance of the control building in Seattle to properly detailed and installed stucco and "good" windows. All four buildings were stucco-clad with drainage planes. An architect, Keith Soltner of Soltner Group Architects, also part of the study, commented: "I have been designing and investigating stucco buildings for years in the Pacific Northwest. When water intrusion problems occur, it is almost always a failure in the details and not a problem with the stucco and certainly not the stucco as a system."[23]

11.3.1 TACKLING THE PROBLEMS IN SEATTLE

The energy crisis of the 1970s produced building and energy codes that changed how the exterior wall worked—vapor retarders were required, air infiltration was limited, insulation minimums were increased, and interior spaces were ventilated. The first requirement for a vapor barrier in Seattle appeared in the 1974 amendment to the Seattle Building Code, and by 1977 the Seattle Building Code included provisions for limiting air infiltration. Wall components also changed as new products, such as building wraps and rigid board insulation, became available.

To try and determine the scope of problems in Seattle and how they might be solved, the Seattle Department of Design, Construction, and Land Use (DCLU) partnered with Washington State University Cooperative Extension Energy Program and the Oak Ridge National Laboratories (ORNL). One outcome was a study conducted by the ORNL's Buildings Technology Center (BTC) to determine the effect of these code changes and new wall components. Among other things, they were looking at the following problems that related to energy use in buildings:

- The cause and effect between building airtightness and moisture intrusion. The study stated that airtightness, which "may account for 30–50 percent of the energy efficiency gains in buildings," is also responsible for "moisture induced damage." (Damage usually only occurs if the air barrier is also a vapor retarder.)
- The extent to which higher energy costs are related to degraded thermal insulation because of moisture intrusion. Thermal transfer through wet materials can be 5–150 percent higher than with dry materials.[24]

BTC's study used the computer model MOISTURE EXPERT 1.0 to analyze 33 wood-frame walls typical of multistory wood-frame construction after 1984 in Seattle. They also looked at several walls of construction types that were common before 1984. This "hygrothermal" program modeled heat, air, and moisture moving through a wall section based on the interior and exterior environment. The wall was subjected to hourly changes of temperature, relative humidity, solar radiation, wind-driven rain, wind speed, and wind direction from the exterior, and to hourly changes of temperature, relative humidity, and air pressures from the interior. "Leaks" were calculated for each rain event. The resulting moisture in the wall was then analyzed on a "mold growth index." Water that might enter a wall during construction or leakage from poorly functioning details such as unflashed windows were not part of the computer model. (Future phases of this study will include the construction of a full-scale testing facility to monitor the wall assemblages in real time and real weather.)[25]

Some observations of the computer modeling for the Seattle climate included:

- *Water barriers:* Two layers provide better drainage than one.
- *Water management system:* Drainage cavity walls with ventilation performed better than walls with an internal drainage plane.
- *Vapor retarders:* If the interior relative humidity (RH) is less than 60 percent, a semipermeable (1 to 10 perms) is preferable. Between 60 and 75 percent RH, the vapor retarder should be around 1 perm; above 75 percent, it should be less than 0.1 perm or what is considered vapor-tight. Mechanical ventilation does increase infiltration and exfiltration, but a semipermeable assembly was able to manage the additional moisture if the interior RH was below 60 percent.
- *Insulation:* Increasing the insulation has a "marginal" effect with a vapor-tight wall to "negligible" on a "vapor-open" assembly in which all components have a permeability of 10 perms or higher. (This refers only to the effect of insulation on moisture intrusion, not heat loss.)
- *Sheathing:* Plywood generally performed better than OSB, though the "difference in performance was not great." (The values used by the ORNL were from a specific set of samples previously tested in their laboratory and were not representative of all plywood or OSB.)
- *"Pre-1984" walls:* The walls typical of construction prior to the introduction of energy codes did dry better than post-1984 walls. This was attributed to the use of the more vapor permeable gypsum sheathing, lower R-value insulation, more vapor permeable stucco, and the use of wood-frame windows.[26]

This study started a debate in Seattle as to whether walls should be breathable, or vapor-open, that is, all the components should be highly permeable, with the idea that drying can occur to both the interior and exterior of the wall. This excludes using components such as polyethylene and peel-and-stick and encourages the use of more permeable gypsum sheathing over plywood or OSB. It also means that the air barrier system must be vapor permeable. While a vapor-open approach may make sense in temperate climates, such as Seattle and Vancouver, with minimal vapor drive, a building envelope specialist should carefully review the design—nothing is worse than a de facto vapor retarder in the wrong place.

11.4 WHAT CAN BE LEARNED FROM THE LEAKY CONDOS?

The Cities of Vancouver and Seattle (as well as the Province of British Columbia) contributed substantial resources to understanding their problems. The problems are very similar and are seen in other areas across the United States and Canada. In summary, the following can help solve the "leaky condo" as well as other building type problems:

- Wood frames are vulnerable to moisture, so keep the water out of the wall! In most climates this moisture is from rain and snowmelt and not water vapor from the interior. Select a water management system appropriate for the expected precipitation. Then make sure the water barrier is continuous from the wall to the glass on the window and back to the wall, with flashings and sealants. A continuous air barrier also helps keep water out of the wall.

- Single components or systems are generally not the root cause—it is how they are installed, detailed, placed in relation to other components, and how appropriate they are for the climate. (Windows might be the one exception—poorly performing windows guarantee problems.)
- The interior relative humidity should be kept at less than 60 percent and preferably less than 50 percent. But it must be assumed that mechanical ventilating equipment may fail; the owner may interfere with the humidity or ventilation controls at some point during the life of the building; or the interior RH may be considerably higher than the design anticipated. Another consideration is that the vapor permeability of the interior wall surface will change over the years as numerous coats of paint or wall coverings are added.
- Finally, architects can do much to stop the ingress of moisture in walls by carefully detailing all transitions; selecting the right components for the climate; and designing the building form and articulation of the facade to deflect water. Chapters 2 and 3 discuss how to select the right components, while Chapter 8 details wood framing.

If there is one common denominator with these failures it might be the lack of detailing at transitions, penetrations, and openings. Many construction companies, often using their own staff architects, are creating standard details that they know will work. Wood-frame construction is simple and complex at the same time. A firm that designs wood-frame construction projects should develop or adopt details and strategies that decrease the possibility of failures. These should include details for openings and transitions as well as formal guidelines—for example, overhangs will be used if a less durable cladding is selected, or there will be no decks over habitable spaces. If a client is determined to eliminate features that compromise durability, they should be made fully aware of the possible outcome, and the architect should understand that the liability on the project has increased.

Everyone understands that water does not belong in walls and that it can be kept out with proper design, construction, and maintenance. Furthermore, it must be understood that such design, construction, and maintenance may be more costly in the short term (but not in the long term) and may slow the construction schedule. As mentioned previously, endemic failures often follow boom times in construction. With an adequate budget and the necessary time allotted to both design and construction, failure does not need to be a by-product of economic booms. Architects can play an important role in preventing these systemic failures.

11.5 HOW TO DO IT RIGHT: TWO COUNTRIES, TWO CLIMATES, AND TWO SOLUTIONS[27]

Understanding the exterior wall of a simple house can lead to better understanding walls of more complex buildings. Two houses, the KST-Hokkaido House[28] in Hokkaido, Japan, and the Home 2000,[29] sponsored by CMHC and initially constructed for the 2000 British Columbia Home Show in Vancouver, exemplify good design in wood framing. The two houses respond to very different climates—one to a harsh, cold climate and the other to a temperate, rainy climate. The two case studies are offered for discussion on how form, construction methods, component selection and placement, and detailing determine functional design. Both were designed with function (durability being an inherent component) as the first priority and broad public acceptance the second priority. Neither house will likely be reviewed in the architectural design periodicals, but both houses should be around to usher in the twenty-second century. Intuitively understanding the functional design of these examples can help the architect who may want a different aesthetic or is designing for a different climate. Building for a hundred years provides a low life-cycle cost—the only obstacle is the first-time cost. With this exception, the conundrum of juggling economics, aesthetics, and durability has been solved with these two houses.

One might argue that a detached house is the antithesis of sustainability. This is not about the larger issues of sustainability—it is simply about designing durable buildings. That in itself is a huge move toward sustainable development. The average life of a house in Hokkaido (and Japan) is 26 years.[30] A house that

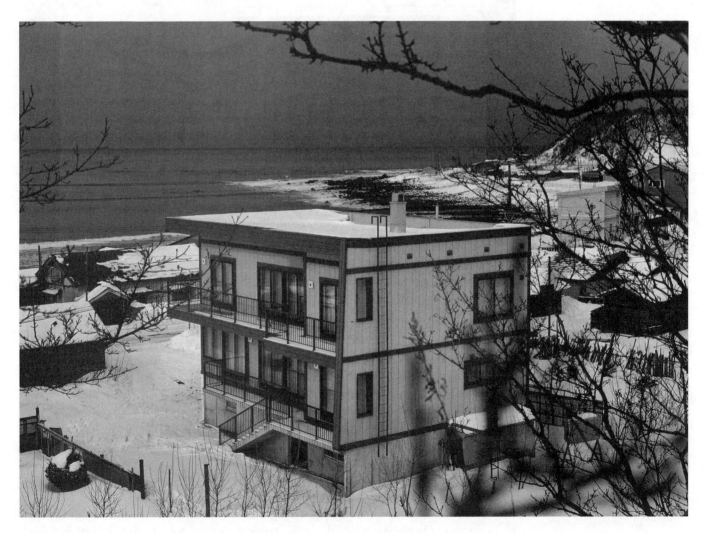

FIGURE 11.4 KST-Hokkaido House. Photo by KST/WRI.

FIGURE 11.5 Home 2000. Photo by Elizabeth Mackenzie.

lasts 100 years or more uses one-quarter the natural resources and contributes one-quarter the demolition materials to landfills as four houses built over the same time span. Cladding and shielding a detached house such that it can withstand decades of heavy rains is a more sustainable option than building a multifamily project that needs to be reclad and, in some cases, have its wood framing replaced after several years, as happened with the "leaky condos."

Designed to deal with problems created by the deep snows of Hokkaido, the KST-Hokkaido House is a site- and factory-built structure with walls that "breathe" and an inverted roof system. (KST stands for *kinoshiro taisetsu*—loosely translated as "wooden castle endures the snow"—which is the name of the company as well as the house.) The Home 2000, with its steeply pitched roof, features a wall section that is detailed to handle the winter rains of the northwest coastal climate. The Home 2000 and the KST-Hokkaido House are alike in many ways. They share a similar footprint. Both houses are three stories in height and larger than the typical affordable home; they are designed to be occupied by a multigenerational family, a family and a home business, or by a family and tenant in the case of the Home

2000. The Home 2000 has 2,000 square feet (186 sq m) while the KST-Hokkaido house is approximately 2,150 square feet (200 sq m). Both emphasize components that create a so-called healthy house and are partially or wholly prefabricated.

The exterior walls and forms of the houses, however, are strikingly different, as the design is predicated on the climate. Vancouver's annual precipitation is approximately 50 inches (1280 mm) and Hokkaido's 45 inches (1140 mm). But in Hokkaido the precipitation comes in the form of winter snows that begin in mid-October and last through early April. The heavy snows cause the deterioration of the exterior walls, affecting the longevity of the house as well as the health of the occupants. Among other concerns, people have died as a result of snow sliding off roofs or accidents involving the hazardous removal of snow from roofs. In Vancouver, the heavy winter rains occur when there is little chance for materials to dry, resulting in the dramatic deterioration of wall systems in wood-framed buildings, as discussed in previous sections on the "leaky condo" crisis.

11.6 HOME 2000 AND WINTER RAINS OF VANCOUVER, BRITISH COLUMBIA

The Home 2000 is described as an "affordable, durable, healthy, and environmentally conscious home that is designed to easily change as the lifestyle of its occupants change."[31] Sustainability is promoted by a floor plan that allows for flexibility of use as family patterns change; components and systems that assure healthy indoor air quality; low maintenance and energy requirements; and a durable building envelope.

The exterior wall, called a rain screen in the brochure, is designed to handle heavy winter rains.[32] The roof form keeps water away from the walls. The basic components of the two-by-four wood-frame wall are fiber-cement lap siding; two-by-two wood furring that creates a 1½-inch (38 mm) drainage cavity; nonperforated building wrap (Tyvek) that acts as an air and water barrier but allows for passage of water vapor; plywood sheathing; rock-wool batt-insulation used in the drainage cavity as well as the stud cavity; and gypsum board with vapor-retarding paint on the interior. Protected openings at the top and bottom of the drainage cavity at each floor promote ventilation as well as drainage and help to moderate the pressure across the wall. (One choice this author disagrees with is the use of rock-wool insulation in the drainage cavity. Although the insulation increases the thermal resistance of the wall and reportedly water will drain through the material, it could potentially slow down the drying process by decreasing ventilation and holding moisture against the building components.) The building wrap, with all joints lapped and taped, minimizes air leakage and consequently moisture movement through the wall as a result of air pressure differentials. The vapor-retarding paint limits vapor migration from diffusion. The fiber-cement siding will stand up to repeated saturation.

A single gable roof, steeply pitched, guarantees that water will run off. Overhangs on all four sides keep the walls dry with a carefully designed gutter system directing the water away from the house. There are no balconies over habitable spaces, and all balconies are covered by the roof. The overall form is as simple as possible. Projections and intersecting walls were kept to a minimum. For example, the balcony wall is attached to the intersecting exterior wall only at the top and bottom rail—there is no saddle connection.

FIGURE 11.6 The Home 2000 was prefabricated for quick erection at a home show in Vancouver, British Columbia. It also allowed for the air and water barrier systems and windows to be carefully installed in the factory. Photo by Roy Kim.

FIGURE 11.7 Home 2000 wall components. From Canada Mortgage and Housing Corporation (CMHC), *Home 2000: Building Your Home for Life* (Ottawa, Ont: 2000). All rights reserved. Reproduced with the consent of CMHC. All other uses and reproductions of this material are expressly prohibited.

1. Low-VOC, water-based paint over low-VOC vapour-retarding primer
2. 16mm gypsum wallboard
3. 38mm x 89mm (2 x 4) kiln-dried SPF stud wall
4. RSI2.47 rockwool batt insulation
5. 13mm plywood sheathing
6. Housewrap moisture and air barrier (air tightness of 1.5 ACH @ 50 Pa)
7. 38mm x 38mm (2 x 2) pressure-treated strapping
8. RSI0.95 rockwool draining insulation
9. Fibre-reinforced cement bevelled siding

Building Envelope

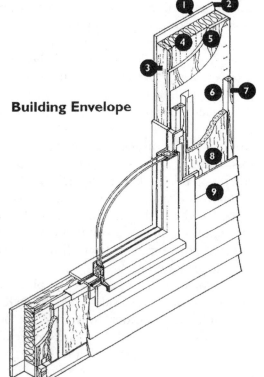

The traditional design appeals to a broad market of potential homeowners. The house was prefabricated as six modules solely for ease of erection at the home show. However, for the wall to be effective, all of the various barriers, but especially the building wrap acting as the air and water barrier, must be very carefully installed. Windows must be carefully flashed and sealed against water and air ingress As well, all components must be dry when the building is finally "closed in." This level of precision is much more easily accomplished, particularly during the wet winter months, when the construction occurs in a factory. The house was permanently installed at a local polytechnic institution. Among other innovations on the house is a photovoltaic roof, which is being monitored.

11.7 KST-HOKKAIDO HOUSE AND HEAVY SNOW LOADS OF NORTHERN JAPAN[33]

Hokkaido, the northernmost of the archipelago of islands that make up Japan, has almost a quarter of Japan's land mass but only five percent of its population. This lower density makes the production of larger, detached family houses more viable. The KST-Hokkaido House averages 200 square meters (2,150 sq ft) to accommodate more easily a multigenerational family in a single dwelling. A recent survey indicated that 21 percent more people lived in a KST house than in a convention-

FIGURE 11.8 The KST-Hokkaido house is designed for a multigenerational family. The open floor plan allows for a single kerosene fueled fireplace to heat the house. Drawing courtesy of KST/WRI.

FIGURE 11.9 KST-Hokkaido house under construction. A two-story, wood-framed structure of structural precuts and panelized walls sits on the poured-in-place concrete first floor. The water barrier and cladding are installed on site. Photo by Linda Brock.

FIGURE 11.10 Removable boards cover first story windows, on many buildings in Hokkaido during the winter, for protection from snow. Photo by G. Russell Heliker.

al house.[34] The building is a hybrid of structural precuts, panelized walls, and on-site construction. The interiors, exterior cladding, and roofing are installed on site. The style of the house, which satisfies its clients' desire for a comfortable and "modern" house, is very different from the traditional Japanese home.

If you went to Hokkaido, you would observe some initially puzzling features in residential construction. For example, first-story windows may be covered by wooden boards, fastened from the exterior, on one or more sides of the home. (See Figure

11.10.) On the coast of the Sea of Japan, high solid fences are built several meters in front of residential windows, blocking the view of one of the more spectacular coastlines in the world. Houses often have ladders affixed to the walls that provide access to their roof. Many roofs have odd little gables, or crickets, installed up-slope of vertical roof vent stacks. The reason for these oddities lies with the climate. If the boards did not protect the windows, they would collapse under the weight of the heavy snow that builds up at the ground floor of the house. The Sea of Japan boasts the world's third-largest waves; the fences protect the windows from the sea's brutal storms. The ladders are necessary because heavy snows would collapse many roofs if they were not shoveled periodically. And the little gable roofs protect the vents from snow that avalanches down the roof.

It is snow that threatens the durability of the exterior wall in Hokkaido. The KST-Hokkaido house has a wall that resists the snow as well as a roof that helps keep it away from the wall. In areas with heavy snow loads, roofs are traditionally sloped, and Hokkaido is no exception. But steeply pitched roofs create uneven loading patterns. In more populated areas, such as Sapporo, homeowners are required to keep all snow on their property, which further complicates matters. As a result, elaborate systems for snow retention on sloped roofs have been developed, and high steel fences ensure that snow does not fall on a neighboring lot or damage a neighboring house. (See Figures 11.11 and 11.12)

Good management of snow involves keeping it on the roof. To address this problem, KST developed, and patented in Japan, what they call the Snowslip-Free Roof System. (The patent has since expired.) In this system, the roof appears to be flat but actually slopes to a trench running lengthwise of the roof,

FIGURES 11.11 AND 11.12 Elaborate snow fences between buildings are necessary to keep snow that avalanches off roofs on the owner's property and not the neighbor's. Photos by G. Russell Heliker.

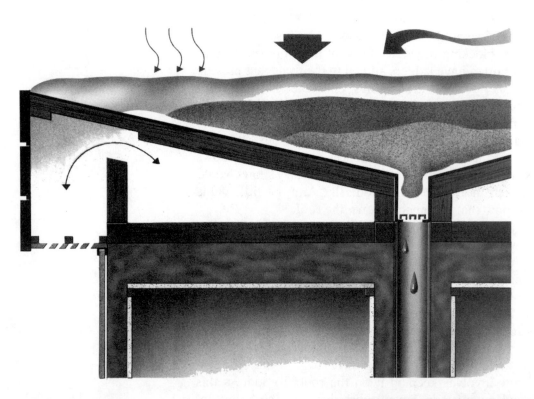

FIGURES 11.13 AND 11.14 The Snowslip-Free Roof System. The snow slowly melts under the insulating blanket of snow and drains to the large-diameter pipe duct (Figure 11.14). Figure 11.13, courtesy of KST/WRI. Figure 11.14, photo by Linda Brock.

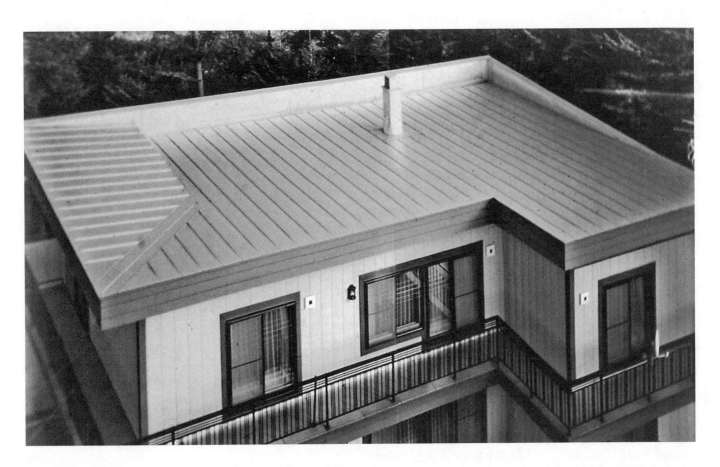

FIGURE 11.16 Roofs are rarely thought to be an item of interest to tourists, particularly if they appear to be flat and not visible to the passerby. However, in the popular guide *Japan Handbook,* 2nd ed., under the section on arts and crafts of Hokkaido, the first craft form mentioned is the "Kinoshiro home…with a flat roof that catches, and can support, enormous snow loads." The section describes the specially designed Snowslip-Free Roof System. Stating that survival is the main focus in this harshest of Japanese climates, with arts and crafts becoming secondary pursuits, the KST-Hokkaido House is used as an example of environmentally inspired craft. From J. D. Bisignani, *Japan Handbook,* 2nd ed. (Chico, Calif.: Moon Publications, 1993), 765. Illustration courtesy of KST/WRI.

which in turn is sloped toward a large diameter, unheated, interior drainpipe called a pipe duct.

The Snowslip-Free Roof System is designed to keep an insulating layer of snow on the standing-seam sheet metal roof while avoiding excessive buildup. The roof edge maintains a constant elevation, allowing snow above a certain height to be blown clear. Under a blanket of snow that averages from 2 to 5 feet (0.6 to 1.5 m), the roof surface is warmed by calculated heat loss from the house. (The roof is designed to support 10 feet (3 m) of snow, and over 6 feet (2 m) of snow has been observed during windless periods.) The snow slowly melts from the underside of the insulating blanket and flows to the pipe duct. The duct drains into a small holding tank at the foundation of the house and then to a dry well or a storm system. The large size (approximately 12 inches, 300 mm, in diameter) of the plastic pipe duct eliminates the possibility of ice damming and the need for heating tape on the duct or roof.

The roof also protects the walls with eaves. Most homes now have eaves on three sides, and the company is developing designs with eaves on all four sides that will offer even greater protection for the walls.

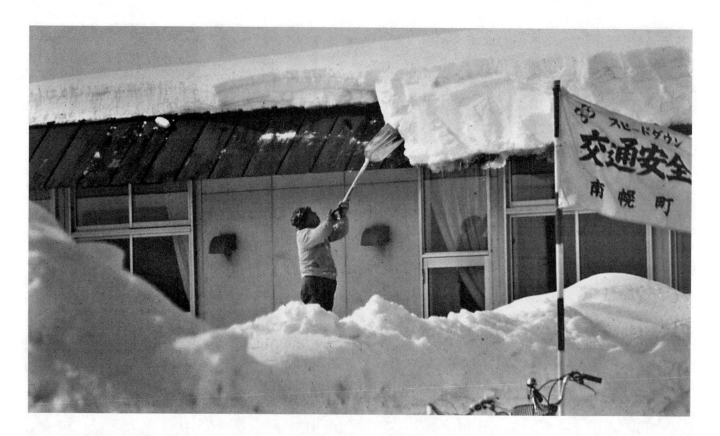

FIGURE 11.15 Keeping sloped roofs free of avalanching snow is a time-consuming and dangerous task. Each year several deaths in Hokkaido are attributed to removing snow from roofs. Photo by KST/WRI.

11.7.1 BREATHABLE WALLS

Even with this level of control, it is common for the snow to reach the second story. In the winter, from the interior, windows on the ground floor of houses in Hokkaido emit a soft blue light that is filtered through the wall of snow. It takes little imagination to understand what is happening to the window frame and exterior wall. KST solved the problem by constructing the first story as the foundation, an above ground, reinforced concrete box that offers protection from moisture problems created by the deep snows that often cover the ground floor wall. There really is no other way to design for snow that piles up against the wall, although there are numerous examples of failures when less durable assemblies, such as wood framing, are used. The garage and storage areas occupy this ground floor. Some homes have offices or retail outlets on this floor with storefront glazing to the street side. (KST also manufactures attached units with retail and offices on the ground floor as a way of increasing density and reducing heat loss.)

On top of the concrete box sits the two-story wooden section of the house proper, consisting of prefabricated panels that fit within a precut post-and-beam structure. This frame, which uses two to three times as much wood as a conventionally wood-framed house, offers improved durability through increased stiffness and redundancy of the structure. The stiffness means fewer cracks open in the wall, so less water and air-carrying vapor enter the wall, compromising the insulating value and causing deterioration of the wood frame.

The wood-framed walls are "breathable," and—unlike the Home 2000—there is no vapor diffusion retarder. Breathability refers to the ability of the wall to take on and then release water vapor rather than for air to move through the wall. The fiberglass-batt insulation is encased with perforated polyethylene. The interior sur-

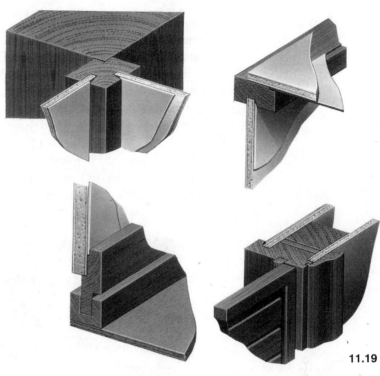

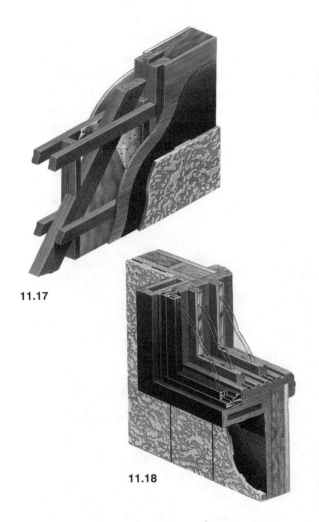

11.17

11.18

11.19

FIGURES 11.17–11.19 Exterior wall details include multilayered walls (Figure 11.17), five-lite windows (Figure 11.18), and slip joints to minimize air flow while accommodating movement at the interior trim (Figure 11.19). The walls are "breathable," meaning that the wood in the wall can take on a certain amount of moisture, tempering the interior relative humidity levels, but air movement is limited. Illustrations courtesy of KST/WRI.

faces are sheathed with gypsum board panels covered with permeable fabric (see Figure 11.17). To avoid excessive use of sealant, the interior wood trim pieces, at the edges of the panels, are shiplapped to allow for differential movement while still stopping the flow of air (see Figure 11.19). The increased wood in the house allows the wall to take on and slowly give off more moisture. Wood is also used extensively in the interiors, creating a kind of "vapor storage" in the same way that high-density materials create thermal storage.

The exterior plywood sheathing is covered with building paper and then a manufactured siding of prefinished aluminum bonded to 1 inch (25 mm) of isocyanate insulation. The locking mechanism between the vertical panels is effective in keeping water out of the wall. Should any water enter the wall, the building paper directs it to the exterior—this would be classified as an internal drainage plane wall.

The windows are a unique configuration of five panes of glass—two double-glazed units and a storm unit (see Figure 11.18). If ventilation is desired, small vents at the top of the wall can be opened from the interior. High levels of insulation allow for the house to be heated with one centrally located kerosene stove in a Russian-type fireplace called a *petchka*. Open stairwells and floor plans encourage natural circulation of the heat.

11.7.2 DESIGN ORIGINS OF THE KST-HOKKAIDO HOUSE

The design of this simple house is the culmination of over 40 years of experimentation by KST's founder and owner, Akira Yamaguchi, and more recently by the work of Fuyusoken, the Winter Research Institute. Although the KST-Hokkaido House has attracted the interest of researchers from around the globe, the house is not exported, even to the northern region of Honshu, which has a similar climate. It is designed specifically to meet the environmental and social needs of Hokkaido, where the company has sold approximately 16,000 houses.[35] An overview of the life of Yamaguchi helps in understanding the origins of the KST-Hokkaido House and is instructive in how problems of function and economy in a harsh climate can be solved with a long-term commitment to quality.

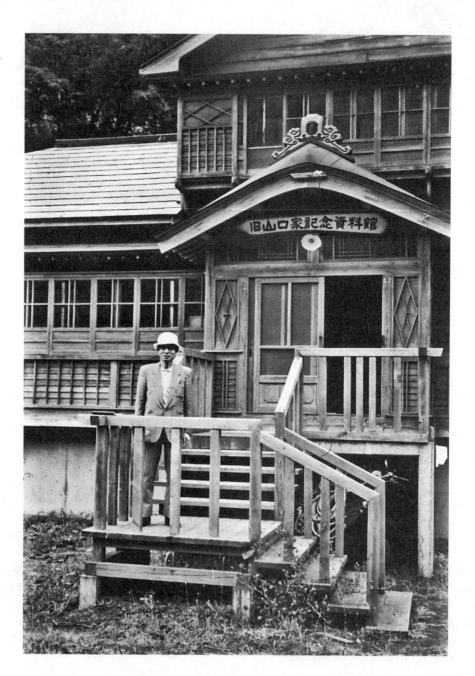

FIGURE 11.20 KST's founder and owner, Akira Yamaguchi, in front of the house he built for his mother in 1951. Photo by Linda Brock.

Yamaguchi started his construction career as an 18-year-old apprentice to a temple and shrine carpenter. He was especially "impressed with the spirit of shrine carpentry, which applied the minutest care to the part that was to be hidden when the building was completed."[36] Yamaguchi used this experience in 1953 when constructing a house for his mother in the isolated fishing village of Chiyoshibetsu. This project was also the beginning of his interest in design innovation, as he developed a three-layered window and shutter system to mediate the harsh winds off the Sea of Japan.

Several years of working as an apprentice and later operating his own construction firm led Yamaguchi to a number of concerns about housing in Hokkaido. The first was snow buildup on roofs. In 1961, with Hokkaido architect Toshio Maeda, he designed and constructed the first "snowslip-free roof" with a snow duct. The two men built full-size mock-ups to test their ideas. Today this system is frequently copied in Hokkaido, because it has solved many of the problems associated with deep, heavy snows. In an interview, a grandmother who had recently purchased a KST-Hokkaido House for herself and her son's family stated that she chose the house because of its "durability." She also added: "I am too old to shovel snow off the roof, and the younger generation isn't interested."[37]

As a result of the harsh winters, construction often stops for up to six months of the year in Hokkaido. Yamaguchi believed that the year-round construction of houses was important for the community. He also noted that the highly specialized temple carpenters could never meet the post–World War II housing demands. During this period he observed and experimented with "two-by-four" construction, as used by American companies in Hokkaido. The benefits of using small, modular pieces that could easily be assembled by unskilled workers were obvious. Poor-quality housing was also a major problem in Hokkaido, as in the rest of Japan. To keep costs down and still maintain quality, he started prefabricating as much of the KST-Hokkaido House as possible. In the factory, unskilled workers perform only a few tasks using precision equipment in an assembly-line fashion. The use of materials, particularly wood, is maximized; and the work can continue through the winter months. KST mills its own logs and fabricates engineered products, such as plywood, as well as controlling sales, on-site construction, and after-sales service. Their level of concern is illustrated in the saw blade–sharpening facility. KST has developed techniques and schedules for sharpening blades that minimize the amount of wood lost in the saw kerf.

Perhaps Yamaguchi's greatest concern is respecting the natural environment. As stated in one of its brochures, "KST-Hokkaido works with nature, not against it." The attempt to use only locally available renewable materials, coupled with an emphasis on durability, promotes sustainability. Sustainability, for the company, is measured not only in conserving resources but conserving the traditional multigenerational Japanese family and the social structure of the region. (The tradition of the house is clearly very important in Japan. Consider that the Japanese word for house also means family. To say that one has a house thus also means that one has a family.)[38] The KST-Hokkaido House is part of a "total system" designed as a sustainable model for living and working on the island of Hokkaido. This combination of modern industrial house-building techniques and traditional values makes the KST-Hokkaido House distinct. The house is intrinsically linked with the culture and region where it was developed, which is why Akira Yamaguchi has refused to export the KST-Hokkaido House.

11.8 WHAT CAN BE LEARNED FROM THE TWO HOUSES?

These two seemingly ordinary houses have addressed specific problems created by climatic conditions through design innovations that respond to their cultures. The Home 2000 is a model home that is similar to the typical suburban house; but it should perform noticeably better, for a longer period of time. The form of the house helps to mitigate water problems, with overhangs and roofs over balconies keeping water away from the wall. Adding a drainage cavity behind the cladding greatly enhances durability where rain or snowmelt is a problem. The detailing of the cavity wall is similar to that of Wall Type D (see Section 8.10) and to what has been required by the City of Vancouver for multifamily residences for some time. A housing market more comfortable with a "traditional look" favors its design.

The KST-Hokkaido House has met with market success while maintaining an ideal of sustainable development. While the house is not appropriate for most, if any, locations in the United States or Canada, the environmental concerns addressed through the design serve as a model for addressing other problems in different climates and cultures. It can be argued that the construction cost of each of these houses is higher than the average construction costs of the area, which is true. But the initial capital cost ensures a long-life exterior wall, which should be well worth the investment. Putting the emphasis on durability over first-time costs is both sustainable and economical.

11.8.1 QUALITY DESIGN AND CONSTRUCTION

Ultimately, a commitment to quality must be made, unwaveringly, to form the platform from which decisions are made. Such a commitment will present different solutions, depending on the design, the construction type, the climate, and the culture.

The prefabrication of both houses allows for a greater degree of quality control—especially important for the Home 2000, which does not have the redundancy of the increased wood framing of the KST-Hokkaido House. Today, modular wood-frame construction in the United States and Canada can produce highly engineered homes constructed in a climate-controlled environment. The efficient building process and material usage, coupled with consistent quality and speed of construction, make for durable, long-lasting homes that can meet the stylistic and functional demands of clients. However, site-built houses remain the preferred construction method and are often more affordable as well. In North America, the efficiencies of the factory do not seem to result in a product that is popular or competitively priced, with the exception of some manufactured housing. Reservations resulting from the marginal quality of manufactured mobile homes in the past, as well as the desire for a distinctive house designed for a specific site, have sustained the preference for site-built housing. This preference holds, even though few mass-produced site-built houses take advantage of their sites, and most are no more distinct than modular homes.

The prefabricated home in Japan has many advantages over a site-built house and is preferred by the public. It is erected more speedily, is generally of quality and long-lasting construction, and often includes the highest-tech gadgets as part of the package. The same advantages could be, and in some cases are, realized in North

America. Prefabricating parts of the wall, particularly those containing windows and doors that require careful detailing, could increase the quality of the detached home and also multifamily projects.

11.8.2 Advancing the Envelope

The iconic gable roof of the Home 2000, with its broad overhangs, and the inverted low-slope roof of the KST-Hokkaido house achieve the same results. They divert water and snow away from the exterior wall. One can say that the KST-Hokkaido roof is truly an innovative form, while the Home 2000 roof is the result of millennia of empirical design.

While not exactly newsbreaking, the multilayered walls show a commitment to innovation on both houses. The continual search for a solution, given a specific problem, is what drives innovation. KST's link with the past is crucial in defining its role as a builder of modern housing. The company uses examples of ancient wooden temples in Japan as a reference point for design. The connection of the post to the beam in the frame reflects traditional Japanese joinery, that is, complex wooden joints using few metal fasteners (see Figure 11.21). But these joints are not fashioned by a skilled carpenter using hand tools but rather by highly specialized machinery that requires few skills to operate.

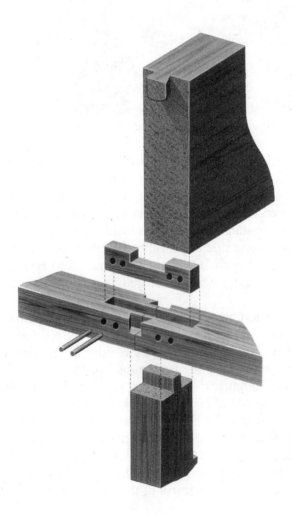

FIGURE 11.21 KST fabricates traditional Japanese joinery with highly specialized, digitally controlled machinery. Illustration courtesy of KST/WRI.

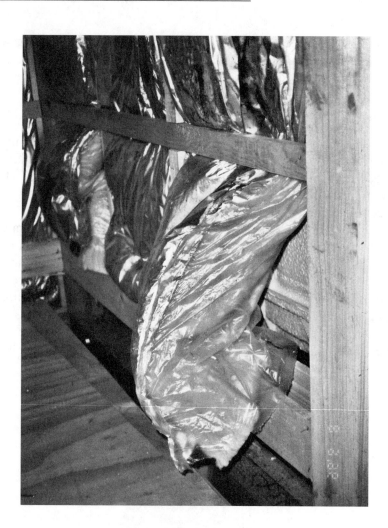

FIGURE 11.22 The fiberglass insulation is faced with perforated polyethylene on one side and reflective mylar on the other. Photo by Linda Brock.

Both houses use a variety of engineered wood products. Generally stronger than the equivalent sized lumber, these products can make use of smaller and faster growing trees. While wood siding is traditional in both Canada and Japan, the KST-Hokkaido House has metal cladding, and fiber-cement siding is used on the Home 2000. The KST house uses standard fiberglass insulation, but its casing—a perforated thin polyethylene on one side and a reflective mylar on the other—is another invention of KST's (see Figure 11.22). The Home 2000 reverted to an older insulation, rock wool, as it can be manufactured as a drainable insulation for use in drainage cavities.

Much of the information in this chapter is basic and perhaps redundant. However, the proliferation of failures says there is still a need for the basics. The means for preventing these pervasive failures is outlined in Part I and Part II. Understanding how a wall works is the beginning. Proper selection and placement of components, good and complete drawings and specifications, proper installation, and proper maintenance would alleviate the majority of problems with premature deterioration and compromised aesthetics of the exterior wall. All of this may be more costly in the first analysis, but it will prove more economical in the long term. If sustainability is a real concern to architects, then the place to start is to design a wall that is functional and long lasting. That wall can be beautiful as well, which is why we, as architects, need to be in control of the exterior wall.

Appendix A: Hygrothermal Maps

Comments within this book are referenced to heating, cooling, or mixed climates; precipitation and relative humidity are not addressed. (See map in Using This Book). Temperature, precipitation, and humidity combine as an indicator of climate in hygrothermal maps. The following information offers general guidelines that should be verified with local weather data. Microclimates may exhibit very different conditions in a small geographical area.

The Building Science Corporation (BSC) has further divided these regions, adding in a component for precipitation, as follows. (See Figure 1.) The division of climate zones comes from the BSC Web site (http://www.buildingscience.com) and is closely aligned with the Department of Energy's proposed climate codes. The Web site explains further the similarities between the DOE climate codes and the BSC zones. Also useful on this Web site are the annual rainfall map of North America and the material's property table. Note: 12,600 heating degree days (HDD) (65°F basis), converts, in Celsius, to approximately 7,000 HDD (18°C basis); 9,000 HDD (65°F basis) converts to 5,000 HDD (18°C basis); and 5,400 HDD (65°F basis) converts to 3,000 HDD (18°C basis).

SUBARCTIC/ARCTIC ZONE

Region with greater than 12,600 heating degree days (HDD) (65°F basis) or Celsius 7,000 HDD (18°C basis)

VERY COLD REGION

Region with between 9,000 (Celsius 5,000 HDD) and 12,600 HDD (65°F basis)

COLD REGION

Region with between 5,400 (Celsius 3,000 HDD) and 9,000 HDD (65°F basis)

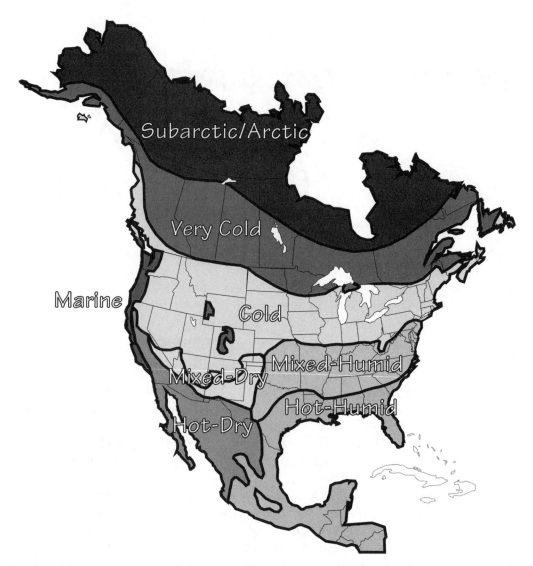

FIGURE 1 Hygrothermal map.
Courtesy of Joseph Lstiburek.

MARINE REGION

Region with a mean temperature of the coldest month between 27°F and 65°F (−3°C–18°C) and a warmest month mean of less than 72°F (22°C), with at least four months with mean temperatures over 50°F (10°C). The dry season is summer. The month with the heaviest precipitation in the cold season has at least three times as much precipitation as the month with the least precipitation.

MIXED-DRY REGION

Region with less than 5,400 HDD (65°F basis) and less than 20 inches (50 cm) of annual precipitation. The average monthly outdoor temperature drops below 45°F (7°C) during the winter months.

MIXED-HUMID REGION

Region with more than 20 inches (50 cm) of annual precipitation and 5,400 HDD (65°F basis) or less. The average monthly temperature drops below 45°F (7°C) during the winter months.

HOT-DRY REGION

Region with less than 20 inches (50 cm) of annual precipitation. The average monthly temperature remains above 45°F (7°C) throughout the year.

HOT-HUMID REGION

Region that receives more than 20 inches (50 cm) of precipitation and one or both of the following occur: a 67°F (19.5°C) or higher wet bulb temperature for 3,000 or more hours during the warmest six consecutive months or a 73°F (23°C) or higher wet bulb temperature for 1,500 or more hours during the warmest six consecutive months of the year. (This closely aligns with a region where the monthly temperature remains above 45°F (7°C).)[1]

The U.S. Department of Energy (DOE) recently developed a new climate map with eight climate zones.[2] It replaces the old climate maps that had 19 zones, and is included in the 2003 *International Energy Conservation Code.* Information on the status of the map and a copy is available on the DOE's Web site (http://energy-codes.gov). Zone 1, the hottest zone, occupies the southern tip of Florida and Hawaii, while zone 8 covers the northern half of Alaska. The zones are divided by temperature: 1 for very hot, 2 for hot, 3 for warm, 4 for mixed, 5 for cool, 6 for cold, 7 for very cold, and 8 for subarctic. Subdivisions define precipitation and relative humidity: A represents humid, B represents dry, and C represents marine. Representative cities are listed below.[3]

1A	Very hot-humid	Miami, Florida
1B[1]	Very hot-dry	
2A	Hot-humid	Houston, Texas
2B	Hot-dry	Phoenix, Arizona
3A	Warm-humid	Memphis, Tennessee
3B	Warm-dry	El Paso, Texas
3C	Warm-marine	San Francisco, California
4A	Mixed-humid	Baltimore, Maryland
4B	Mixed-dry	Albuquerque, New Mexico
4C	Mixed-marine	Salem, Oregon
5A	Cool-humid	Chicago, Illinois
5B	Cool-dry	Boise, Idaho
5C[2]	Cool-marine	
6A	Cold-humid	Burlington, Vermont
6B	Cold-dry	Helena, Montana
7	Very cold	Duluth, Minnesota
8	Subartic	Fairbanks

1. This climate does not exist within the United States. Locations would be in areas such as Saudi Arabia.

2. This climate does not exist within the United States. Areas of British Columbia are examples of this climate.

Climate information can be obtained from:
 U.S.: National Oceanic and Atmospheric Administration (NOAA), http://www.noaa.gov
 Canada: Environment Canada, http://www.ec.gc.ca

Note: See the sidebar in Chapter 1 on "Computer Models of Wall Performance" for more information on hygrothermal performance of a wall.

Appendix B:
Building Form

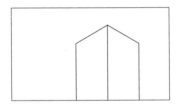

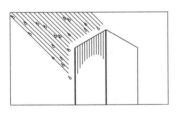

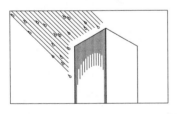

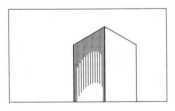

The form of the building, including overhangs and the height, affects the exposure from rain. Figure 2 shows the wetting patterns on a tall building. Note the accumulation of moisture at the corners and top of the building. The more porous the cladding—for example, brick masonry or precast concrete panels—the more water will be absorbed. Impervious surfaces such as metal and glass will direct the water to lower floors.

A study of building envelope failures on wood-framed multifamily buildings,[4] completed by Canada Mortgage and Housing Corporation (CMHC) in the Vancouver, British Columbia, area, noted that the wider the overhang at the top of the exterior wall, the fewer water leakage problems there were. The study included 37 wood-frame buildings of three to four stories—some were "control" buildings (i.e., they were not exhibiting problems), and others were "problem" buildings. Figure 3 shows the results of the study as it pertained to overhangs. Walls with 24-inch (600 mm) or greater overhangs had one-third the problems of walls with no overhangs. While the number of buildings surveyed was small, the results were not surprising.

The simple graph in Figure 4 is from CMHC's Best Practice Guide *Wood-Frame Envelopes in the Coastal Climate of British Columbia*. It relates the width of the overhang, as a percentage of the wall height, with the surrounding terrain to produce an exposure category. By drawing a straight line from the "overhang ratio" to the "terrain," the exposure is determined. While not necessarily applicable to other climates and designed for up to four-story, wood-frame buildings, it is a good indicator of how—in an area with wind-driven rains—the surrounding terrain and the overhang can affect the exposure.

FIGURE 2 Wetting pattern on a tall building. Source: Canada Mortgage and Housing Corporation (CMHC), *Rain Penetration Control: Applying Current Knowledge* (Ottawa, Ont.: CMHC, 1999). All rights reserved. Reproduced with the consent of CMHC. All other uses and reproductions of this material are expressly prohibited.

338

Percent of all walls that have problems				
100				
90				
80				
70				
60				
50				
40				
30				
20				
10				
0				
	0	1–300 mm 0 to 12 inches	301–600 mm 12 to 24 inches	over 600 mm over 24 inches
	width of overhang above wall			

FIGURE 3 Effect of overhangs on wall performance. (Source: Canada Mortgage and Housing Corporation (CMHC), *Survey of Building Envelope Failures in the Coastal Climate of BC,* 1996.) All rights reserved. Reproduced with the consent of CMHC. All other uses and reproductions of this material are expressly prohibited.

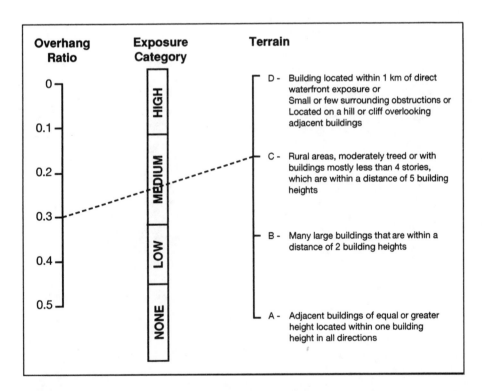

FIGURE 4 Exposure category based on overhang ratio and terrain. The overhang ratio is obtained by dividing the wall height, not including the foundation, by the overhang width. (Source: Canada Mortgage and Housing Corporation (CMHC), Best Practice Guide for *Wood-frame Envelopes in the Coastal Climate of BC,* 2001.) All rights reserved. Reproduced with the consent of CMHC. All other uses and reproductions of this material are expressly prohibited.)

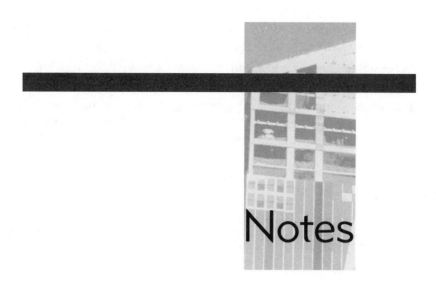

Notes

PREFACE

1. *2002 Ducker Report* (Bloomfield Hills, Mich.: Ducker Worldwide, 2002). Statistics used with permission of Ducker Worldwide, http://www.ducker.com

CHAPTER ONE

1. Edward Ford, "The Theory and Practice of Impermanence," *Harvard Design Magazine* (Fall 1997): 18.

2. Christine Beall, *Thermal and Moisture Protection Manual: For Architects, Engineers, and Contractors.* (New York: McGraw-Hill, 1998), 5.

3. *LEED Green Building Rating System for New Construction and Major Renovations, Version 2.1* (Washington, D.C.: U.S. Green Building Council, November 2002).

4. Chris W. Scheuer and Gregory A. Keoleian, "Evaluation of LEED Using Life Cycle Assessment Methods," NIST GCR 02-836 (Washington, D.C.: National Institute of Standards and Technology, U.S. Department of Commerce, 2002).

5. LEED Canada-NC Version 1.0 (Ottawa, Ont.: Canada Green Building Council, 2004), 56–57.

6. "50% of Masonry Failures Caused by Poor Design," *Magazine of Masonry Construction* (November 1988): 362–363.

7. Mohsen Mostafavi and David Leatherbarrow, *On Weathering: The Life of Buildings in Time* (Cambridge Mass.: MIT Press, 1993), 5.

8. Canada Mortgage and Housing Corporation, *Survey of Building Envelope Failures in the Coastal Climate of British Columbia* (Ottawa, Ont.: Canada Mortgage and Housing Corporation, 1996), 35.

CHAPTER TWO

1. Heinz R. Trechsel, ed., *Manual on Moisture Control in Buildings,* ASTM, MNL 18 (West Conshohocken, Pa.: ASTM, 1994), vii.

2. Richard Quirouette and Canada Mortgage and Housing Corporation, Laboratory Investigation and Field Monitoring of Pressure Equalized Rainscreen Walls. (Ottawa, Ont.: CMHC, 1996), 38.

3. PATH, ToolBase Services, http://www.toolbase.org

4. U.S. Census Bureau, American Housing Survey 2001, Table 2-2 Height and Condition of Building-Occupied Units (Washington, D.C.: updated August 2004).

5. Series of guides for different climates written by Joseph Lstiburek and published by the Building Science Corporation (BSC), http://www.buildingscience.com.

6. M. Z. Rousseau, G. F. Poirier and W. C. Brown, *Pressure Equalization in Rainscreen Wall Systems,* Construction Technology Update No. 17 (Ottawa, Ont.: IRC, NRCC, 1998).

7. Paul Fisette, "Housewrap vs. Felt," *Journal of Light Construction* (November 1998).

8. Sheet Metal and Air Conditioning Contractors' National Association, *Architectural Sheet Metal Manual,* 6th ed. (Chantilly, Va.: Sheet Metal and Air Conditioning Contractors' National Association, 2003).

9. Michael T. Kubal, *Construction Waterproofing Handbook* (New York: McGraw-Hill, 2000), 1.12–1.13.

CHAPTER THREE

1. Neil B. Hutcheon, "Forty Years of Vapor Barriers," *Water Vapor Transmission Through Building Materials and Systems: Mechanisms and Measurement,* ASTM STP 1039 (West Conshohocken, Pa.: ASTM, 1989), 5.

2. Joseph Lstiburek, Kim Pressnail, and John Timusk, "Air Pressure and Building Envelopes," *Journal of Thermal Envelope and Building Science* (July 2002): 91.

3. Mark Bomberg and Donald Onysko, "Heat, Air and Moisture Control in Walls of Canadian Houses: A Review of Historic Basis for Current Practices," *Journal of Thermal Envelope and Building Science* (July 2002): 7.

4. Canada Mortgage and Housing Corporation, "Structural Requirements for Air Barriers," Research and Development Factsheet, Technical series 91-201 (Ottawa, Ont.: CMHC, n.d.).

5. Canada Mortgage and Housing Corporation (CMHC) and American Architectural Manufacturers Association (AAMA), "Rain Penetration Control: Applying Current Knowledge" (Palatine, Ill.: AAMA, 2000), 21.

6. Richard L. Quirouette, Building Practice Note: "The Difference Between a Vapour Barrier and an Air Barrier," BPN 54 (Ottawa, Ont.: Division of Building Research, National Research Council of Canada, July 1985).

7. Paul H. Shipp, "What You Ought to Know About Air Barriers and Vapor Retarders." *Form and Function* 1 (1989).

8. DOE, "Airtight Drywall, and Simple Caulk and Seal for Air Movement Control," Consumer Energy Information: EREC Reference Briefs (March 2003).

9. Richard L. Quirouette, "The Air Barrier Defined: Building Science Insight" (Ottawa, Ont.: IRC-NRCC, n.d.).

10. Bomberg and Onysko, "Heat, Air and Moisture Control in Walls of Canadian Houses: A Review of Historic Basis for Current Practices."

11. Canada Mortgage and Housing Corporation (CMHC), *Wood Frame Envelopes,* Best Practice Guide: Building Technology (Ottawa, Ont.: CMHC, 1999), 5.2.

12. Ronald Brand, *Architectural Details for Insulated Buildings* (New York: Van Nostrand Reinhold, 1990), 169.

13. Bomberg and Onysko, "Heat, Air and Moisture Control in Walls of Canadian Houses: A Review of Historic Basis for Current Practices."

14. Paul Creighton, "Technical: Sheet Metal Air Barriers," *Canadian Architect* (July 1997): 27.

15. Kevin L. Chouinard and Mark D. Lawton, "Rotting Wood Framed Apartments—Not Just a Vancouver Problem," *Solutions to Moisture Problems in Building Enclosures.* Eighth Conference on Building Science and Technology (February 2001).

16. Ryan Dalgleish and Kevin Knight, "Air Barriers: Building Essentials," *Construction Canada* (November 1999): 10.

17. Heinz R. Tressel, ed., *Manual on Moisture Control in Buildings,* ASTM, MNL 18 (West Conshohocken, Pa.: ASTM, 1994), 353.

18. CMHC, *Wood Frame Envelopes,* 5.8.

19. "Summary of Wood-Framed Exterior Wall Performance Study," City of Seattle, Department of Design, Construction and Land Use, August 2002.

20. Joseph Lstiburek, "Moisture, Building Enclosure, and Mold," *HPAC Engineering: Heating/Piping/Air Conditioning* (December 2001).

21. Mark D. Lawton and William C. Brown, "Considering the Use of Polyethylene Vapour Barriers in Temperate Climates," Design and Construction of Durable Building Envelopes: Proceedings of the 9th Canadian Conference on Building Science and Technology (February 2003).

22. DOE, "Vapor Diffusion Retarders and Air Barriers," *Consumer Energy Information: EREC Reference Briefs* (November 2002).

23. Bomberg and Onysko, "Heat, Air and Moisture Control in Walls of Canadian Houses: A Review of Historic Basis for Current Practices."

24. "Health and Safety Facts for Fiber Glass: Insulation Facts #62," North American Insulation Manufacturers Association (n.d.).

25. Kathleen Posteraro, "Insulation Permeability," *Construction Specifier* (January 2002).

26. Mark T. Bomberg and Donald M. Onysko, "Control of Air Leakage with Polyurethane Foams," Eighth Conference on Building Science and Technology (February 2001).

27. Kathleen Posteraro, "Insulation Permeability," 45.

CHAPTER FOUR

1. Project of Brock Associates.

2. Thomas L. Smith, "Hurricane Andrew—10 Years Later," *Professional Roofing* (August 2002): 1.

3. Lester Hensley, correspondence with the author (August 2004).

4. Karen Warseck, "Why Sealant Joints Fail," *Architecture* (December 1986): 100–103.

5. Thomas F. O'Connor, "The One Percent of Cost That Can Become 90 Percent of Trouble," *ASTM Standardization News* (June 2003): 1.

6. Jerry Klosowski, "Questioning Silicone Weathersealing Myths," *Construction Canada* (May 1999): 28–31.

CHAPTER FIVE

1. Kenneth Frampton and Yukio Futagawa, *Modern Architecture 1851–1945* (New York: Rizzoli International Publications, 1983), 194.

2. Sara Hart, "Facade Engineering Emerges as a Highly Specialized Science and a Striking Art Form," *Architectural Record* (August 2002) 163.

3. *Curtain Wall Design Guide Manual,* AAMA Aluminum Curtain Wall Series, CW-DG-1 (Palatine, Ill.: AAMA, 1996), 3–5.

4. Steve Gusterson, "Curtain Wall Primer: An Energy-Efficient and Cost-Effective Way to Enclose a Structure," *Construction Canada* (May 2002): 19.

5. Ibid.

6. Michael Wigginton, *Glass in Architecture* (London: Phaidon Press, 2002; orig. 1996), 64.

7. Ibid., 51.

8. Ibid., 284.

9. Stephen H. Daniels, "Improving Glass Performance," *Architectural Record* (August 1998): 131.

10. *GANA Glazing Manual* (Topeka, Kans.: Glass Association of North America, 2004).

11. Ibid., 21.

12. Mark Brook, "The Evolution of the Curtain: Issues and Challenges," *Construction Canada* (May 2002): 12.

13. Thomas A. Schwartz, "A Pane in Your Pane?" *Building Renovation* (July–August 1993). Quote modified by Schwartz (May 2004).

14. Mark Brook, conversation with author, April 21, 2004.

15. Thomas A. Schwartz of Simpson, Gumpertz & Heger, Inc., consulting engineers (SGH), and an article titled "John Hancock Tower" on the SGH Web site, Building Technology Practice Area: http://www.sgh.com

16. C. C. Sullivan, "Designing with Aluminum Components," *Architecture* (June 1997): 174.

17. L. William Zahner, "The Selection, Specification, and Performance of Metals in Architecture," *Journal of Metals* (March 1996): 15.

18. L. William Zahner, *Architectural Metals* (New York: John Wiley & Sons, 1995), 79.

19. Zahner, "Selection, Specification," 14.

20. Bethlehem Data Sheet on Galvalume Sheet and Galvalume Plus Sheet

21. Zahner, *Architectural Metals,* 340.

22. Ibid., 348–349.

23. Ibid., 344–351.

24. Annette LeCuyer, *Steel and Beyond: New Strategies for Metals in Architecture* (Boston: Birkhauser-Publishers for Architecture, 2003), 120.

25. Zahner, *Architectural Metals,* 291.

26. Chris Santilli, "Metallic Luster: High-Tech Titanium and Zinc are Changing the Face of Architectural Cladding," *Architecture* (June 1999): 141.

27. Zahner, *Architectural Metals,* 280.

28. Nickel Institute, *Stainless Steel in Architecture, Building and Construction: Guidelines for Building Exteriors,* Series No. 11015 (London: Nickel Development Institute Reference Book, 1994).

29. Christine Beall, "The New Stone Age," *Magazine of Masonry Construction* (May 1990): 222.

30. Edward A. Gerns, "Lessons Learned from Thin-Stone Cladding," *Magazine of Masonry Construction* (February 2000): 36.

31. Christine Beall, "Selecting the Right Stone," *Magazine of Masonry Construction* (June 1989), 231.

32. Christine Beall, "The Makings of Good Stone," *Magazine of Masonry Construction* (December 1988): 39.

33. Michael D. Lewis, *Modern Stone Cladding: Design and Installation of Exterior Dimension Stone Systems* MNL 21 (Philadelphia: ASTM, 1995), 35.

34. Ibid., 59.

35. Carolyn Schierhorn, "Sandstone: Use Care When Specifying this Beautiful Material Because Its Quality Varies Widely," *Magazine of Masonry Construction* (November 1995): 530.

36. Lewis, *Modern Stone Cladding,* 59.

37. *Curtain Wall Design Guide Manual,* AAMA Aluminum Curtain Wall Series, CW-DG-1 (Palatine, Ill.: AAMA, 1996), 12.

38. Mark Brook, "The Evolution of the Curtain Wall: Issues and Challenges," *Construction Canada* (May 2002), 10. Modified in telephone conversation with author, March 12, 2004.

39. Notes from seminar by Simpson Gumpertz & Heger, Inc., consulting engineers, "Elements of the Building Envelope," © 2003, and correspondence with SGH.

40. Canada Mortgage and Housing Corporation, *Architectural Precast Concrete Walls,* Best Practice Guide (Ottawa, Ont.: CMHC, 2002), 53, 75, 87.

41. *GFRC: Recommended Practice for Glass Fiber Reinforced Concrete Panels,* 4th ed. (Chicago: Precast/Prestressed Concrete Institute, 2001), 8.

42. Ibid.

43. Sara Hart, "Facade Engineering Emerges as a Highly Specialized Science and a Striking Art Form," *Architectural Record* (August 2002): 166.

44. Nadine M. Post, "More than an Academic Exercise," *Engineering News-Record* (January 27, 2003): 35.

45. Joann Gonchar, "Glass Facades Go Beyond Skin Deep," *Engineering News-Record* (February 10, 2003).

46. D. A. Rutila, "Investigation and Repair of Leakage Problems in Recently Constructed Curtain Walls," in *Water Leakage Through Building Facades,* ed. R. J. Kudder and J. L. Erdly, ASTM STP 1314 (West Conshohocken, Pa.: American Society for Testing and Materials, 1998), 185.

CHAPTER SIX

1. Leon Battista Alberti, *Ten Books on Architecture* (London: A. Tiranti, 1955).

2. 2002 Ducker Report (Bloomfield Hills, Mich.: Ducker Worldwide, 2002). Statistics used with permission of Ducker Worldwide, an industrial market research firm with more than 40 years of experience studying the building materials industry. http://www.ducker.com

3. Clayford T. Grimm, "What is Wrong with Brick Masonry Veneer over Steel Studs?" *The Masonry Society Journal* 10, no. 2 (1992): 10.

4. Brick Industry Association, *Technical Notes 28B: Brick Veneer / Steel Stud Walls* (Reston, Va.: Brick Industry Association, Nov. 1999), 7.

5. J. Patrick Rand, *The Masonry Wall as an Enclosure System; Findings and Recommendations.* Proceedings, Ninth North American Masonry Conference, Clemson, SC, June 2003. Proceedings available from The Masonry Society, Boulder, Colorado.

6. KPFF Consulting Engineers, *Design Guide for Anchored Brick Veneer over Steel Studs* (Los Angeles: Western States Clay Products Association, 1995, repro., 2000), 20.

7. Robert G. Drysdale, Ahmad A, Hamid, and Lawrie R. Baker, *Masonry Structures:* Behavior and Design (Englewood Cliffs, N.J.: Prentice Hall, 1994), 525.

8 KPFF Consulting Engineers, *Design Guide for Anchored Brick Veneer over Steel Studs,* 14.

9. Brick Industry Association, *Technical Notes 28B: Brick Veneer / Steel Stud Walls,* 3.

10. James B. Posey, *Brick Veneer/Steel Stud, Best Practice Guide Building Technology* (Ottawa, Ont.: Canada Mortgage and Housing Corporation, 2001 edition), A-3.

11. Keller Engineering Associates, *Performance Monitoring of a Brick Veneer/Steel Stud Wall System—Phase 4 Results, Revision* (Ottawa, Ont.: Canada Mortgage and Housing Corporation,1999) 9–10.

12. Brick Industry Association, *Technical Notes 18A: Design and Detailing of Movement Joints, Part 2* (Reston, Va.: Brick Industry Association, 1991; repr., 2001), 3.

13. LePatner and Johnson, *Structural and Foundation Failures,* 25–33.

14. KPFF Consulting Engineers, *Design Guide for Anchored Brick Veneer over Steel Studs,* 29.

15. Brick Industry Association, *Technical Notes 6A: Colorless Coatings for Brick Masonry* (Reston, Va.: Brick Industry Association, reissued 2002), 2.

16. Brick Industry Association, *Technical Notes 6A: Colorless Coatings for Brick Masonry,* 8.

17. Masonry Standards Joint Committee, *Building Code Requirements for Masonry Structures,* ACI 530-02 (Boulder, Colo.: The Masonry Society, 2002), C-47.

18. A370-94 *Connectors for Masonry* (Mississauga, Ont.: Canadian Standards Association, 1994), 7.

19. Posey, *Brick Veneer/Steel Stud,* 6–8.

20. See, for example, the Internet web sites for Ferro Corporation, a Canadian Company, and Helfen, a German company.

21. Brick Industry Association, *Technical Notes 7: (Revised) Water Resistance of Brick Masonry—Design and Detailing, Part I of III* (Reston, Va.: Brick Industry Association, 1985; repr. 2001), 8.

22. For a details on a variety of seams, see: Sheet Metal and Air Conditioning Contractors National Association (SMACNA), *Architectural Sheet Metal Manual,* 6th ed. (SMACNA, 2003) 3.6–3.7.

23. Posey, *Brick Veneer Steel Stud,* A-4.

24. Larry Nelson (project manager, University of Washington), conversation with author, March 22, 1996.

25. Brick Industry Association, *Technical Notes 17: Reinforced Brick Masonry— Introduction* (Reston, Va.: Brick Industry Association, reissued 1996), 1.

26. Brick Industry Association, *Technical Notes 28C: Thin Brick Veneer—Introduction* (Reston, Va.: Brick Industry Association, 1986; reissued 2001), 4.

CHAPTER SEVEN

1. Thomas C. Jester, ed., and National Park Service, *Twentieth-Century Building Materials: History and Conservation* (New York: McGraw-Hill, 1995), 80.

2. *Sears, Roebuck Homebuilder's Catalog: The Complete Illustrated 1910 Edition* (New York: Dover Publications, Inc., repr. 1990), 152.

3. Pamela H. Simpson, *Cheap, Quick, and Easy: Imitative Architectural Materials, 1870–1930* (Knoxville, Tenn.: University of Tennessee Press, 1999), 21.

4. Renee Young, "Lightweight Contender," *Building Design and Construction* (August 1998).

5. National Concrete Masonry Association (NCMA), *TEK 19-1: Water Repellents for Concrete Masonry Walls* (Herndon, Va.: NCMA, 2002).

6. V. Tamburrini, "The History and Development of EIFS—From the Original Concept to Present Day Activities," *Development, Use, and Performance of Exterior Insulation and Finish Systems (EIFS),* ed. Mark F. Williams and Richard G. Lampo, ASTM STP 1187 (Philadelphia, Pa.: ASTM,1995), 3–8.

7. Tamburrini, "The History and Development of EIFS," 8.

8. *2002 Ducker Report* (Bloomfield Hills, Mich.: Ducker Worldwide, 2002). Statistics used with permission of Ducker Worldwide, an industrial market research firm with more than 40 years of experience studying the building materials industry. http://www.ducker.com

9. Kevin C. Day, "Exterior Insulation Finish Systems," *Construction Canada* (March 2002).

10. K. M. Konopka, J. L. McKelvey, J. W. Rimmer, and M. J. O'Brien, "Selected Performance Characteristics of a Dual Purpose 100% Acrylic Polymer-Based Coating That Performs as Both a Weather Resistive Component for Exterior Insulation Finish Systems (EIFS) and as an Adhesive for Attachment of the Insulation Board," *Performance of Exterior Building Walls,* ASTM STP 1422, ed. Paul G. Johnson, (West Conshohocken, Pa.: ASTM, 2003), 268.

11. Kevin Day, "Rainscreen EIFS," *Canadian Architect* (November 1994): 34.

12. Warren R. French, "Design and Renovation of a High-Rise Retrofit EIFS Cladding: A Case Study," in *Water Problems in Building Exterior Walls: Evaluation, Prevention and Repair,* ed. Jon M. Boyd and Michael J. Scheffler, ASTM STP 1352 (Philadelphia, Pa.: 1999), 63. Also, Richard Piper and Russell Kenney, "EIFS Performance Review," *Journal of Light Construction* (June 1992).

13. Peter Cuyler, correspondence with author, August 2004.

14. Russell J. Kenney and Richard S. Piper, "Proposed Material and Application Standards for More Durable Exterior Insulation and Finish Systems," *Development, Use, and Performance of Exterior Insulation and Finish Systems,* 72.

15. Stephen S. Ruggiero (engineer and principal, Simpson Gumpertz & Heger), correspondence with author, May 2004.

16. EIFS Industry Members Association (EIMA), *Guide to Exterior Insulation and Finish Systems Construction* (Morrow, Ga.: EIMA, 2000), 4. Also: http://www.eima.com/Guide_to_EIFS.pdf

17. Warren R. French, "Design and Renovation of a High-Rise Retrofit EIFS Cladding: A Case Study," 64.

18. Richard R. Reese, "Lessons Learned from the Investigation and Repair of a High-Rise, EIFS-Clad Residential Building," *Water Problems in Building Exterior Walls,* 84.

19. J. B. Posey and Jacques Rousseau, "Avoiding Problems with EIFS," *Canadian Architect* (February 1996): 32.

20. Kevin C. Day, "Exterior Insulation Finish Systems: Designing for a Predictable Service Life," *Construction Canada* (March 2002): 13.

21. Posey and Rousseau, "Avoiding Problems with EIFS," 32.

22. Day, "Exterior Insulation Finish Systems: Designing for a Predictable Service Life," 13.

23. EIFS Industry Members Association (EIMA), *White Paper on the Use of EIFS in Commerical Construction* (Morrow, Ga.: EIMA, n.d.), http://www.eima.com/commerical/performance.htm (accessed October 5, 2004).

24. National Association of Home Builders (NAHB), *Moisture Protection of Wood Sheathing: An Installer's Guide* (Upper Marlboro, Md.: NAHB, n.d.), http://www.nahbrc.org/Docs/MainNav/MoistureandLeaks/792_Moisture.pdf (accessed October 5, 2004).

25. Elena Marcheso Moreno, "Detailing That Weathers Better," *Architectural Record* (November 1996): 42.

26. Moreno, "Detailing That Weathers Better," 42.

27. The word *rainscreen* is registered by Sto Corp.

CHAPTER EIGHT

1. Cecil D. Elliott, *Technics and Architecture: The Development of Materials and Systems for Buildings* (MIT Press, Cambridge, Mass., 1992).

2. *2002 Ducker Report* (Bloomfield Hills, Mich.: Ducker Worldwide, 2002). Statistics used with permission by Ducker Worldwide, an industrial market research firm with more than 40 years of experience studying the building materials industry. http://www.ducker.com

3. Ibid.

4. Norman Davey, *A History of Building Materials* (London: Phoenix House, 1961), 113.

5. Mark D. Lawton, William C. Brown and Andy M. Lang, "Stucco-Clad Wall Drying Experiment," Proceedings for Performance of Exterior Envelopes of

Whole Buildings VIII: Integration of Building Envelopes, December 2–7, Clearwater Beach, Florida, 2001.

6. Dennis McCoy, "A Close Look at Stucco," *Journal of Light Construction* (September 2003).

7. Northwest Wall and Ceiling Bureau (NWCB), *Stucco Resource Guide* (Seattle, Wash.: NWCB, 1997), 63.

8. Building Science Corporation, "Drainage Planes and Air Spaces," http://www.buildingscience.com

9. Canada Mortgage and Housing Corporation, *Drying of Stucco-Clad Walls,* Technical Series 99–107 (Ottawa, Ont.: CMHC, February 2003).

10. Achilles Karagiozis, "Building Enclosure Hydrothermal Performance Study, Phase 1," ORNL/TM-2002/89 (Oak Ridge, Tenn.: Oak Ridge National Laboratory, April 2002).

11. *Stucco Resource Guide,* 51.

12. McCoy, "A Close Look at Stucco," *Journal of Light Construction.*

13. A. J. Downing, *The Architecture of Country Houses* (New York: Da Capo Press, 1968; original ed. 1850).

14. Francesco J. Spagna and Stephen S. Ruggiero, "Stucco Cladding—Lessons Learned form Problematic Facades," *Performance of Exterior Building Walls,* ed. Paul G. Johnson, ASTM STP 1422 (West Conshohocken, Pa.: ASTM, 2003.)

15. John M. Melander, James A. Farny, and Albert W. Isberner, Jr., *Portland Cement Plaster/Stucco Manual,* 5th ed. (Skokie, Ill.: Portland Cement Association, 2003), 28.

16. Ibid., 27.

17. *Stucco Resource Guide,* 32.

18. Ibid., 142.

19. Ron Weber, "Top Quality Three-Coat Stucco," *Journal of Light Construction* (September 2000).

20. Spagna and Ruggiero, "Stucco Cladding—Lessons Learned from Problematic Facades."

21. Ibid.

22. Warren R. French, "Design and Renovation of a High-Rise Retrofit EIFS Cladding: A Case Study," *Water Problems in Building Exterior Walls: Evaluation, Prevention and Repair,* ASTM STP 1352, ed. John M. Boyd and Michael J. Scheffler (West Conshohocken, Pa.: ASTM, 1998), 64.

23. CMHC, "Static and Dynamic Earthquake Testing of Rainscreen Stucco Systems for B.C. Residential Wood-Frame Construction," CMHC Research Highlights, Technical Series 03-127 (December 2003).

24. NWCA, *Stucco Resource Guide,* 26.

25. Steve Thomas, "Extreme Stucco," *Journal of Light Construction* (February 1997).

26. *National Building Code of Canada* (1995), Part 9, 290.

27. M. J. Dell and S. B. Liaw, "Performance of Stucco-Clad Wood-Frame Buildings in a Temperate Rain Forest," *Water Leakage Through Building Facades*, ed. Robert J. Kudder and Jeffrey L. Erdly, ASTM STP 1314 (West Conshohocken, Pa.: ASTM, 1998), 157.

28. Melander, Farny, and Isberner, *Portland Cement Plaster/Stucco Manual*, 5th ed., 19.

29. *2002 Ducker Report*, http://www.ducker.com

30. See http://www.jameshardie.com/corporatehistory.htm

31. Jon Carter, "Fiber Cement Siding," *Southface Journal of Sustainable Building* (February 1998).

32. Paul Fisette, "Alternatives to Solid Wood Exterior Trim," *Building Materials and Wood Technology* (University of Massachusetts, Amherst, 1997).

33. Sheri Olson, *Miller/Hull: Architects of the Pacific* (New York: Princeton Architectural Press, 2001), 89.

34. *HDO/MDO Plywood: Product Guide* (Tacoma, Wash.: APA, Engineered Wood Association, 2002).

CHAPTER NINE

1. A. Plumridge, W. Meulenkamp, *Brickwork* (New York: Harry N. Abrams, 1993), 14.

2. Cecil D. Elliott, *Technics and Architecture* (Cambridge, Mass.: MIT Press, 1992), 24.

3. Brock, Linda. "The Future of Brick Veneer in North America," in *Ceramics in Architecture: Monographs in Materials and Society,* Proceedings of the International Symposium on Ceramics in Architecture of the Eighth CIMTEC-World Ceramics Congress and Forum on New Materials held in Florence, Italy June 28–July 1, 1994, ed. P. Vincenzini (Florence: Techna, 1994), 41–48.

4. John Ruskin, *The Seven Lamps of Architecture* (New York: Noonday Press, 1977), 39.

5. Michael Benedikt, *For an Architecture of Reality* (New York: Lumen Books, 1987), 46.

6. Ibid., 44.

7. Ruskin, *The Seven Lamps of Architecture,* 53.

8. Benedikt, *For an Architecture of Reality,* 48.

9. Susan Tunick, *Terra-Cotta Skyline* (New York: Princeton Architectural Press, 1997), 22.

10. Donald Friedman, *Historical Building Construction: Design, Materials, and Technology* (New York: W. W. Norton & Co., 1995), 62.

11. Ibid., 115.

12. Gary F. Kurutz, *Architectural Terra-Cotta of Gladding, McBean* (Sausalito, Calif.: Windgate Press, 1989), 8. See also *Economist* 11 (August 1894): 206.

13. Friends of Terra-Cotta, "The Reliance Building," *Restoration Survey,* no. R-32.

14. Virginia Guest Ferriday, *Last of the Handmade Buildings: Glazed Terra-Cotta in Downtown Portland* (Portland Ore.: Mark Publishing Company, 1984), 25.

15. Ibid., 120.

16. Ibid., 126

17. Margaret F. Gaskie, "The Woolworth Tower: A Technology Revisited, A Material Understood, A Landmark Restored," *Architectural Record* (August 1981).

18. Ibid.

19. Kimball Beasley (Wiss, Janey, Elstner Associates), correspondence with author, May 2004.

20. Russell J. Kenney and Richard S. Piper, "Proposed Material and Application Standards for More Durable Exterior Insulation and Finish Systems," *Development, Use, and Performance of Exterior Insulation and Finish Systems (EIFS),* ASTM STP 1187, ed. Mark F. Williams and Richard G. Lampo (West Conshohocken, Pa.: ASTM, 1998), 59.

21. Richard Quirouette, "Review of the NRCC and USG Study of the EIFS Barrier Walls for Wood Framed Houses in Wilmington, North Carolina," *Thermal Insulation and Building Envelope,* 20 (April 1997): 350–351.

22. Ian R. Chin, Timothy S. Thompson, and Bryan K. Rouse, "Exterior Insulation and Finish Systems (EIFS) Water Resistance/Leakage," *Water Problems in Building Exterior Walls: Evaluation, Prevention and Repair,* ASTM STP 1352, ed. Jon M. Boyd and Michael J. Scheffler (West Conshohocken, Pa.: ASTM, 1998), 3.

23. J. B. Posey and Jacques Rouseau, "Avoiding Problems with EIFS," *Canadian Architect* (February 1996): 32–34.

24. Kenney and Piper, "Proposed Material and Application Standards for More Durable Exterior Insulation and Finish Systems," 64.

25. Richard S. Piper and Russell J. Kenney, "EIFS Performance Review," *Journal of Light Construction* (June 1992).

26. Maria Stieglitz, "Restoring Aalto Landmark Leaves Few Stones Unturned," *Historic Preservation News* (March/April 1992): 20.

27. Michael D. Lewis, *Modern Stone Cladding: Design and Installation of Exterior Dimension Stone Systems MNL 21* (Philadelphia, Pa.: ASTM, 1995), 35.

28. Edward R. Ford, *The Details of Modern Architecture, Volume 2: 1928–1988* (Cambridge, Mass.: MIT Press, 1992), 149.

29. Alex S. Gere, "Design Considerations for Using Stone Veneer on High-Rise Buildings," *New Stone Technology, Design, and Construction for Exterior Wall Systems,* ed. Barry Donaldson, ASTM STP 996 (Philadelphia, Pa.: ASTM, 1988), 39.

30. Ian R. Chin, J. P. Stecich, and B. Erlin, "Design of Thin Stone Veneers on Buildings," *Proceedings of the Third North American Masonry Conference* (Boulder, Colo.: The Masonry Society, 1985), 10.8.

31. Gail Hook, "Look Out Below: The Amoco Building's Cladding Failure," *Progressive Architecture* (February 1994): 59.

32. Jeffrey Trewhill, "Amoco May Replace Marble on Chicago Headquarters," *Engineering News-Record* (March 24, 1988): 11.

33. Ian R. Chin, "Invesigation of Original Marble Panels on Building," Seminar on Recladding of the Amoco Building in Chicago, Illinois," *Proceedings: Report No. 15,* ed. Ian R. Chin (Chicago, Ill.: Chicago Committee on High Rise Buildings, 1995), 3.1.

34. Ibid., 3.4.

35. Ibid., 3.3.

36. Ibid., 3.3.

37. Eric Adams, "Wintry Discontent," *Architecture* (October 1998): 167.

38. Stieglitz, "Restoring Aalto Landmark Leaves Few Stones Unturned," 20.

39. D. W. Kessler, "Physical and Chemical Tests of the Commercial Marbles of the United States," National Bureau of Standards Technical Paper 123 (1919).

40. Stieglitz, "Restoring Aalto Landmark Leaves Few Stones Unturned," 20.

41. Jack Stecich, "Design and Testing of Granite Panels and of Stainless Steel–Shelf Angles," Seminar on Recladding of the Amoco Building in Chicago, Illinois. 12.4.

42. Stieglitz, "Restoring Aalto Landmark Leaves Few Stones Unturned," 20.

43. "Finlandia Saved," *Architectural Review* (May 1993).

44. Eric Adams, "Wintry Discontent," *Architecture* (October 1998): 171.

45. Ibid., 171.

46. Stieglitz, "Restoring Aalto Landmark Leaves Few Stones Unturned," 20.

47. Björn Schouenborg (TEAM coordinator, SP Swedish National Testing and Research Institute), correspondence with author, April 2004.

48. Stieglitz, "Restoring Aalto Landmark Leaves Few Stones Unturned," 21.

49. The TEAM Web site: http://www.sp.se/building/team.

CHAPTER TEN

1. Herbert Muschamp, "Latin Jolt to the Skyline," *New York Times,* October 20, 2002.

2. Carlo Wolf, "Cutting Through the Clutter," *Lodging Hospitality* (January 2003).

3. Nadine M. Post, "Coating of Many Colors," *Engineering News-Record* (December 30/January 6, 2003): 15.

4. Information provided by Arquitectonica, "Westin New York at Times Square and E Walk."

5. Wolf, "Cutting Through the Clutter."

6. Muschamp, "Latin Jolt to the Skyline."

7. Information provided by Tishman Reality and Construction, "Builder, Architect, and Curtain Wall Specialist Orchestrate the Sophisticated Design, Fabrication and Installation of Imaginative Facade for The Westin New York at Times Square."

8. Post, "Coating of Many Colors."

9. David Horowitz (project director, Tishman Construction), conversation with author, April 2003.

10. "Tower of Light," *Construction Industry Times International* 4 (winter 2003): 53. Lighting designers were Brandston Partnership Inc., Arquitectonica, and Tishman.

11. Robin Updike, "Vision of the Future," *Seattle Times,* April 2, 2000.

12. Richard A. Martin, "e.m.p. (What Is It?)," *Seattle Weekly,* June 15–21, 2000.

13. Roger A. Reed (A. Zahner Company), interview with author, February 17, 2004.

14. David Leatherbarrow and Mohsen Mostafavi, *Surface Architecture* (Cambridge, Mass.: MIT Press, 2002), 198.

15. Charles Linn, "Creating Sleek Metal Skins for Buildings," *Architectural Record* (October 2000): 173–178.

16. Ibid.

17. L. William Zahner, *Architectural Metals: A Guide to Selection, Specification, and Performance* (New York: John Wiley and Sons, 1995), 233.

18. Updike, "Vision of the Future."

19. Ibid.

20. David S. Chartock, "Westin New York Team Key to Project Solutions," *New York Construction News* (November 2001).

21. François Chaslin, "Centre de Conferences Vitra," *Architecture d'Aujourd'hui* (September 1993).

22. "Conference Pavilion in Weil am Rhein," *Detail* (June–July 1995).

23. N. Lloyd, *A History of English Brickwork* (New York: William Helburn, Inc., 1925), 11, 25.

24. Sergison Bates, "Semi-Detached House," *Housing and Flexibility a+t* 13 (1999).

25. David B. Rosenbaum, "Square Peg Fit into Seismic Hole," *Engineering News-Record* (October 25, 1993): 22–24.

26. Ibid.

27. Scott System, "Brick Gasket Liner and the San Francisco Museum of Modern Art," news release, August 1993.

28. Sidney Freedman, "Clay Product–Faced Precast Concrete Panels," *PCI Journal* (January/February 1994): 20–36. This is a very good primer.

29. Elizabeth Keating, "Ten Top Masonry Projects," *Magazine of Masonry Construction* (April 1998): 235.

30. Desiree Ward, "A Landmark in the Making," *Concrete Journal* (March 1994).

31. Tests Run on Endicott Brick at Valley Forge Laboratories, Devon, Pennsylvania, on October 8, 1992. Information supplied by Scott System, Inc.

32. Sidney Freedman, "Clay Product–Faced Precast Concrete Panels," 27.

33. Ibid.

34. Michael Wigginton, *Glass in Architecture* (London: Phaidon Press Ltd., 1996; repr. 2002), 03.156.

35. Ibid.

36. Joann Gonchar, "Glass Facades Go Beyond Skin Deep," *Engineering News-Record* (February 10, 2003).

37. Klaus Daniels, *The Technology of Ecological Building: Basic Principles and Measures, Examples and Ideas,* trans. Elizabeth Schwaiger (Basel: Birkhauser Verlag, 1997), 153.

38. Werner Lang and Thomas Herzog, "Using Multiple Glass Skins to Clad Buildings," *Architectural Record* (July 2000): 173. This is a good primer on double glass walls.

39. Gonchar, "Glass Facades Go Beyond Skin Deep."

40. Lang and Herzog, "Using Multiple Glass Skins to Clad Buildings," 171–182.

41. Ibid., 173.

42. Case Study by the Cascadia Region Green Building Council, "Seattle Justice Center" (n.d.).

43. City of Seattle Department of Design, Construction & Land Use, "Case Study: Sustainable Building, City of Seattle Justice Center," *dcluINFO* (February 2003).

44. NBBJ. "Naturally Vented, Double-Skin Facade — Thermal Flue Facade," documentation on the Seattle Justice Center (n.d.).

45. Joe Llona, "Justice Center Takes the LEED," *Seattle Daily Journal of Commerce,* April 23, 2004.

46. Gonchar, "Glass Facades Go Beyond Skin Deep."

CHAPTER ELEVEN

1. Edward Ford, "The Theory and Practice of Impermanence," *Harvard Design Magazine* (Fall 1997): 12.

2. Ibid., 12.

3. Information provided by the BC Home Protection Office (2003).

4. "Summary of Wood-Framed Exterior Wall Performance Study," City of Seattle, August 2002, Attachment 1.

5. Oak Ridge National Laboratories, "BCT Helps Solve Mystery of Crumbling Buildings in Seattle" (Oak Ridge, Tenn.: Oak Ridge National Laboratories Publication, n.d.).

6. "The Look That Didn't Last," *Vancouver Sun,* December 5, 1992. Also, "Rotten to the Core," a series of articles in February 1993.

7. Condo owner, interview by author, January 2004.

8. Canada Mortgage and Housing Corporation (CMHC), "Comparative Analysis of Residential Construction in Seattle, WA and Vancouver, BC" (January 27, 1999), 1.

9. Building Envelope Task Force, "Building Envelope Failures," letter to AIBC members from the Building Envelope Task Force, May 4, 1998.

10. Canada Mortgage and Housing Corporation (CMHC), *Survey of Building Envelope Failures in the Coastal Climate of British Columbia,* executive summary (Ottawa, Ont.: CMHC, November 22, 1996).

11. Ibid., 35–36.

12. Canada Mortgage and Housing Corporation (CMHC), *Woodframe Envelopes in the Coastal Climate of British Columbia* (Ottawa, Ont.: CMHC, 2001).

13. Canada Mortgage and Housing Corporation (CMHC), *Survey of Building Envelope Failures in the Coastal Climate of British Columbia,* 35–36.

14. Kevin L. Chouinard and Mark D. Lawton, "Rotting Wood Framed Apartments—Not Just a Vancouver Problem."

15. "Condo Dwellers Lament: When It rains It Pours In," *Seattle Times,* September 6, 1998.

16. Oak Ridge National Laboratories, "BCT Helps Solve Mystery of Crumbling Buildings in Seattle."

17. Seventy-four structures were surveyed, of which 53 were constructed after 1984. It was estimated that 938 buildings were built during this period.

18. Handout from Seattle Moisture Intrusion Discussion Forum, conducted by the City of Seattle Department of Design, Construction, and Land Use, Construction Codes Advisory Board, Moisture Damage Subcommittee, June 23, 1999.

19. "Summary of Wood-Framed Exterior Wall Performance Study," City of Seattle (August 2002), Attachment 1.

20. Canada Mortgage and Housing Corporation, "Comparative Analysis of Residential Construction in Seattle, WA and Vancouver, BC," 17.

21. Ibid., 17.

22. Ibid., 17.

23. Northwest Wall and Ceiling Bureau, "NWCB Comments on the Comparative Analysis of Residential Construction in Seattle, WA and Vancouver, BC," letter from Mark Fowler (NWCB), December 1, 2000.

24. Oak Ridge National Laboratories, "BCT Helps Solve Mystery of Crumbling Buildings in Seattle."

25. Information about the study can be found on the City of Seatle Department of Design, Construction, and Land Uses Web site, http://www.cityofseattle.net/dclu.

26. "Summary of Wood-Framed Exterior Wall Performance Study," City of Seattle (August 2002), 4.

27. Some of the information for this section comes from Linda Brock, "Wooden Houses in Northern Tier Countries—Two Design Solutions for Building Envelope Problems," *Proceedings of the International Association for Bridge*

and Structural Engineering Conference, held at Lahti, Finland, August 2001, reprinted with permission of IABSE, Zurich, Switzerland.

28. KST-Hokkaido House was developed by Akira Yamaguchi, founder and president of Kinoshiro Taisetsu (KST) Corporation of Hokkaido, Japan.

29. Home 2000 is the result of a team effort by Canada Mortgage and Housing Corporation, University of British Columbia School of Architecture, British Columbia Institute of Technology, Greater Vancouver Home Builders' Association, and a host of other product and service providers. It was prefabricated by Britco Structures Ltd.

30. Raymond J. Cole and Richard Lorch, eds., *Buildings, Culture and Environment: Informing Local and Global Practices* (Oxford: Blackwell Publishing, 2003), 318.

31. CMHC, *Home 2000: Building Your Home for Life,* 2.

32. Ibid., 2.

33. Much of the information on the KST-Hokkaido House was gathered by the authro during a series of trips to Hokkaido that included visits to the KST factory, KST houses, and conventional houses.

34. Cole and Lorch, *Buildings, Culture and Environment: Informing Local and Global Practices,* 322.

35. Ibid., 307.

36. Akira Yamaguchi, *Mottaninai: Waste Not, Want Not* (Sapporo, Japan: International Ecodevelopment Institute, 1995), 45.

37. KST homeowner of Sapporo, interview by author, February 1999.

38. Kiyosi Seike, "What We Mean by 'A Home,'" *Japan Architect* 108 (1965): 12.

APPENDICES

1. Building Science Corporation (BSC), http://www.buildingscience.com/housesthatwork/hygro-thermal.htm

2. Information from: Robert S. Briggs, Robert G. Lucas, and Z. Todd Taylor, *Climate Classification for Building Energy Codes and Standards,* Table 2B—Climate Zone Definitions for New Classification (Part B), technical paper, final review draft. (Pacific Northwest National Laboratory, March 26, 2002).

3. Ibid., 22.

4. Canada Mortgage and Housing Corporation (CMHC), *Survey of Building Envelope Failures in the Coastal Climate of British Columbia* (Ottawa, Ont.: CMHC, 1996).

Bibliography and Resources

BIBLIOGRAPHY

The following books clearly and concisely set forth the basics of building science and the methods of construction. This book assumes the reader has a familiarity with the contents of both.

Allen, Edward. 1995. *How Buildings Work,* 2nd ed. New York: Oxford University Press.

Allen, Edward, and Joseph Iano. 2004. *Fundamentals of Building Construction: Materials and Methods,* 4th ed. Hoboken, N.J.: John Wiley & Sons, Inc.

The following publications are specifically for wood-frame construction, but the building science is applicable to any construction type:

Lstiburek, Joseph, and John Carmody. 1994. *Moisture Control Handbook: Principles and Practices for Residential and Small Commercial Buildings.* New York: John Wiley & Sons, Inc. Lstiburek's Web site for the Building Sciences Corporation has an update (in pdf form) of this book.
http://www.buildingscience.com

Lstiburek, Joseph. 2000–2002. *Builder's Guides for Different Climates.* Westford, Mass.: Building Science Corporation. Climates included are: Cold Climate (revised January 2001); Mixed-Humid Climate (revised March 2001); Hot-Dry and Mixed-Dry Climate (revised September 2000); and Hot-Humid Climate (revised January 2002). They are available from
http://www.buildingscience.com

The Canada Mortgage and Housing Corporation (CMHC), http://www.cmhc.gc.ca, and the Institute for Research in Construction of the National Research Council of Canada (IRC/NRC), http://www.irc.nrc.gc.ca, publish a wealth of information. Two important series are:

CMHC's Best Practice Guides offer user-friendly, detailed information based on sound research and practical experience. Each is a binder, usually with a CAD-compatible CD-ROM. Wall details, explanations, and specifications are included. An example of the detail is included in Section 5.6, "Precast Concrete Panels." Guides are available for *Architectural Precast Concrete Walls, Brick Veneer Steel Stud, Brick Veneer Concrete Masonry Unit Backing, Flashings, Wood Frame Envelopes, Wood-Frame Envelopes in the Coastal Climate of British Columbia, Fire and Sound Control in Wood Frame, Multifamily Buildings, Glass and Metal Curtain Walls,* and *Exterior Insulation and Finish Systems.* They can be ordered from CMHC's Web site, http://www.cmhc.ca

IRC/NRC's Construction Technology Updates are practical four- to six-page publications on building science principles and research results. They can be downloaded from IRC Web site. The *Canadian Building Digests (CBD)* are also available on the Web site, http://www.nrc.ca

The National Institute of Building Sciences publishes the *Building Science Newsletter.* Their Web site is a source of information (http://www.nibs.org). The Building Environment and Thermal Envelope Council (BETEC) is a NIBS council that focuses on the performance and interaction of building envelope components and systems and their effect on the environment. In the spring of 2004, NIBS and the American Institute of Architects (AIA) signed an agreement to establish regional building enclosure councils across the U.S.

More in-depth coverage of building science is found in:

Hutcheon, Neil B., and Gustav O. P. Handegord. 1983; repr. 1995. *Building Science for a Cold Climate.* Ottawa, Ont.: National Research Council of Canada. The basics of building science as covered are good for any climate, not just cold climates.

Tressel, Heinz R., ed. 1994. *Manual on Moisture Control in Buildings,* ASTM, MNL 18. West Conshohocken, Pa.: ASTM.

Tressel, Heinz R., ed. 2001. *Moisture Analysis and Condensation Control in Building Envelopes* ASTM, MNL 40. West Conshohocken, Pa.: ASTM, book and CD-ROM.

RESOURCES

TRADE AND INDUSTRY ASSOCIATIONS

Glass and metal curtain walls and windows and doors
- American Architectural Manufacturers Association (AAMA), http://www.aamanet.org
- Laminated Glass Information Council, http://www.igcc.org
- Insulating Glass Manufacturers Alliance, http://www.igmaonline.org
- Window and Door Manufacturers Association (WDMA), http://www.wdma.com

Masonry general
- Masonry Institute of America (MIA), http://www.masonryinstitute.org
- International Masonry Institute (IMI), http://www.imiweb.org

- The Masonry Society (TMS), http://www.masonrysociety.org
- National Concrete Masonry Association (NCMA), http://www.ncma.org

Stone and terra-cotta
- Marble Institute of America, http://www.marble-institute.com
- National Building Granite Quarries Association, http://www.nbgqa.com
- Indiana Limestone Institute of America, http://www.iliai.com
- Canadian Stone Association, http://www.stone.ca

Concrete block
- National Concrete Masonry Association (NCMA), http://www.ncma.org
- Canadian Concrete Masonry Producers Association (CCMPA), telephone (905) 948-9718

Fired-clay brick veneer
- Brick Industry Association (BIA), http://www.bia.org
- Masonry Canada, http://www.masonrycanada.ca

Precast concrete and glass-fiber reinforced concrete (GFRC) panels
- Precast/Prestressed Concrete Institute (PCI), http://www.pci.org
- Architectural Precast Association, http://www.archprecast.org
- Canadian Precast/Prestressed Concrete Institute (CPCI), http://www.cpci.ca

EIFS (Exterior Insulation and Finishing Systems)
- EIFS Alliance, http://www.eifsalliance.com

Stucco
- Northwest Wall and Ceiling Bureau (NWCB), http://www.nwcb.org
- Association of the Wall and Ceiling Industries International (AWCI), http://www.awci.org

Sidings, pressed wood, wood, vinyl, typically for light frame construction
- American Architectural Manufacturers Association (AAMA), http://www.aamanet.org
- Engineered Wood Products (APA), http://www.apawood.org
- Canadian Wood Council (CWC), http://www.cwc.ca
- Vinyl Siding Institute (VSI), http://www.vinylsiding.org
- Western Red Cedar Lumber Association (WRCLA), http://www.wrcla.org
- California Redwood Association, http://www.calredwood.org

Insulation
- Reflective Insulation Manufacturers Association (RIMA), http://www.rima.net
- North American Insulation Manufacturers Association (NAIMA), http://www.naima.org
- Alliance for the Polyurethanes Industry, http://www.polyurethane.org
- EPS Molders Association, http://www.epsmolders.org

Flashing
- Sheet Metal and Air Conditioning Contractors National Association (SMACNA), http://www.smacna.org

Roofing
- National Roofing Contractors' Association (NRCA), http://www.nrca.net
- Canadian Roofing Contractors' Association (CRCA), http://www.roofingcanada.com

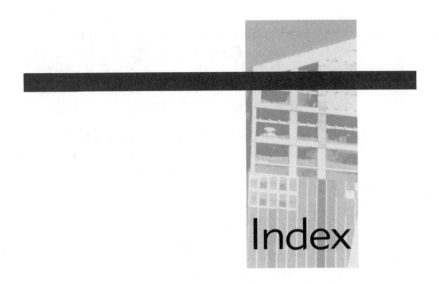

Index